Coding for Medical Necessity in the Physician's Office

An In-Depth Approach to Record Abstracting

D0218350

Coding for Medical Necessity in the Physician's Office

An In-Depth Approach to Record Abstracting

Deborah Kelly-Farwell, CCS-P, CPC, CPC-GENSG

Cecile Favreau, MBA, BS, AS, CPC

DELMAR
CENGAGE Learning

Australia • Brazil • Japan • Korea • Mexico • Singapore • Spain • United Kingdom • United States

Coding for Medical Necessity in the Physician's Office: An In-Depth Approach to Record Abstracting

Deborah Kelly Farwell and Cecile Favreau

Vice President, Career and Professional Editorial: Dave Garza

Director of Learning Solutions: Matthew Kane

Senior Acquisitions Editor: Rhonda Dearborn

Managing Editor: Marah Bellegarde

Product Manager: Jadin Babin-Kavanaugh

Vice President, Career and Professional Marketing: Jennifer McAvey

Marketing Director: Wendy Mapstone

Senior Marketing Manager: Lynn Henn

Marketing Manager: Michele McTighe

Marketing Coordinator: Chelsey Iaquinta

Production Director: Carolyn Miller

Production Manager: Andrew Crouth

Senior Content Project Manager: Stacey Lamodi

Senior Art Director: Jack Pendleton

Technology Project Manager: Ben Knapp

Production Technology Analyst: Thomas Stover

Library of Congress Control Number: 2007940325

ISBN-13: 978-14180-5021-4

ISBN-10: 1-4180-5021-0

Delmar
5 Maxwell Drive
Clifton Park, NY 12065-2919
USA

Cengage Learning products are represented in Canada by Nelson Education, Ltd.

For your lifelong learning solutions, visit **delmar.cengage.com**
Visit our corporate website at **cengage.com.**

Notice to the Reader
Publisher does not warrant or guarantee any of the products described herein or perform any independent analysis in connection with any of the product information contained herein. Publisher does not assume, and expressly disclaims, any obligation to obtain and include information other than that provided to it by the manufacturer. The reader is expressly warned to consider and adopt all safety precautions that might be indicated by the activities described herein and to avoid all potential hazards. By following the instructions contained herein, the reader willingly assumes all risks in connection with such instructions. The publisher makes no representations or warranties of any kind, including but not limited to, the warranties of fitness for particular purpose or merchantability, nor are any such representations implied with respect to the material set forth herein, and the publisher takes no responsibility with respect to such material. The publisher shall not be liable for any special, consequential, or exemplary damages resulting, in whole or part, from the readers' use of, or reliance upon, this material.

Printed in the United States of America
1 2 3 4 5 XX 10 09 08

Contents

Preface

Coding for Medical Necessity in the Physician's Office was written to fill a need among medical coding students for more exposure and experience in abstracting from medical records. While teaching in a medical billing and coding program that utilizes standard textbooks, students often expressed concern regarding their ability to read medical records and identify the appropriate information needed to code accurately. With the increasing number of third-party payer audits, students need to learn to abstract accurately.

This text is meant to be a working text for students who have already learned the basics of procedural and diagnostic coding. Students can utilize this single text to review the subject matter briefly and then complete the abstracting exercises. The book is unique in that, unlike many products currently on the market, it provides significant practice in abstracting. Most texts currently available focus more on the coding of procedural and diagnostic statements.

ORGANIZATION OF THE TEXT

The first three chapters of the text review the manuals and tools utilized by a medical coder: ICD-9-CM, CPT, and HCPCS. These chapters discuss the use of these manuals; particular coding conventions and the related symbols are identified and defined. Chapter 4 discusses modifiers and CCI edits and the importance of their correct use. In Chapter 5, the importance of establishing medical necessity through the linking of diagnosis and procedure is reviewed in detail. The remaining chapters expose the student to detailed coding related to the individual chapters in the *CPT* manual, and the final chapter is meant to be utilized as a self-test for students to assess their knowledge once they have studied the entire text.

Each chapter contains the following learning tools:

- **Key Terms** related to the information in the chapter. These terms are found either in the content of the chapter or in supplemental resources, such as the *ICD-9-CM*, *CPT*, and *HCPCS* manuals.
- **Learning Objectives** are defined in each chapter to help the student understand what they can expect to learn when they complete the chapter.
- **Find the Code** is a feature available in Chapters 1, 2, 4, and 8 that allows the student to practice abstracting prior to completing the scenarios for the chapter and to receive immediate feedback with rationales for the correct answers.
- **Scenarios** are used to give the student extensive practice in abstracting from medical reports.
- **Chapter Review** tests the student's knowledge of coding concepts, guidelines, and definitions based on information in the chapter or the appropriate manuals. This review is presented in the format of ten questions at the end of each chapter.

SUPPLEMENTS

The following supplements are available to enhance the usefulness of *Coding for Medical Necessity in the Physician's Office*:

StudyWARE at the Online Companion

The StudyWare to accompany *Coding for Medical Necessity* was developed to further reinforce the student's knowledge of the basic concepts and principles. It features chapter quizzes with wrong answer feedback as well as crossword puzzles to help reinforce learning. Instant feedback tells you whether you're right or wrong, and explains why an answer is correct or incorrect.

StudyWare also features unique coding cases paired with real forms to simulate coding from actual medical documentation. StudyWare can be found at the Online Companion site at *www.delmarlearning.com/companions*. Search for it by author name or ISBN.

Case 11

SURGICAL PROCEDURE

PATIENT: George Jenkins

DOS: 01/15/20xx

PREOPERATIVE DIAGNOSIS: Bilateral lower senile (involutional) ectropion.

POSTOPERATIVE DIAGNOSIS: Bilateral lower senile (involutional) ectropion.

PROCEDURE: Bilateral lower lid ectropion repair, lateral tarsal strip.

ANESTHESIA: IV sedation.

COMPLICATIONS: None.

INDICATIONS: This 72-year-old patient has bilateral lower lid ectropion with lacrimation. Consent was obtained to proceed with surgery. He was aware of and accepted the risks, including but not limited to the anesthetic, bruising, swelling, scar, wound infection, wound dehiscence, possible need for further management.

PROCEDURE: The patient was taken to the operating room where he was positioned in the supine position. A drop of tetracaine was applied to each eye, and he was prepped and draped in the usual fashion. Throughout the procedure, a total of 3 mL of 2% Lidocaine with 1:100,000 epinephrine was used to infiltrate the lateral canthal areas. Attention was first drawn to the left side. A lateral canthotomy and cantholysis were performed. Bipolar cautery was used for hemostasis throughout the procedure. A lateral tarsal strip was created in the usual fashion. This involved excising the superior aspect of the eyelid margin, excising skin and orbicularis from tarsus, and then incising inferior to tarsus. The excess tarsus was excised. Blunt dissection was carried out to the posterior aspect of the lateral orbital rim. Two interrupted 4-0 chromic sutures were used to reattach tarsus and orbicularis to the posterior aspect of the lateral orbital rim. The metallic corneal shields were removed, and each of these was then tied and cut. The skin was resutured using 6-0 fast-absorbing gut. Attention was then drawn to the right side and the same procedure performed. Erthromycin ointment but no patches were applied. He tolerated the procedure well and left the operating room in good condition.

Dictated and signed by,

Ju Jong Sun, M.D.

Encoder Pro 30-Day Free Trial CD-ROM

The Encoder Pro software included in the back of this textbook is a 30-day free trial of Ingenix's powerful medical coding solution that allows you to look up ICD-9-CM, CPT, and HCPCS Level II codes quickly and accurately. This software can be used in conjunction with coding manuals to assign codes to any of the exercises in the textbook.

Features and Benefits of Encoder Pro

Encoder Pro is the essential code lookup software for CPT, ICD-9-CM, and HCPCS code sets. It gives users fast searching capabilities across all code sets. Encoder Pro can greatly reduce the time it takes to build or review a claim and helps improve overall coding accuracy. Should you decide to subscribe to the full version of Encoder Pro, the following tools will be available to you:

- **Powerful Ingenix CodeLogic search engine.** Improve productivity by eliminating time-consuming code lookup in outdated codebooks. Search all three code sets simultaneously using lay terms, acronyms, abbreviations, and even misspelled words.

- **Lay descriptions for thousands of CPT codes.** Enhance your understanding of procedures with easy-to-understand descriptions.

- **Color-coded edits.** Understand whether a code carries an age or sex edit, is covered by Medicare, or contains bundled procedures.

- **Quarterly update service.** Rest assured you are always using accurate codes. You can code confidently throughout the year with free code updates.

- **Great value.** Get the content from over 20 code and reference books in one powerful solution.

For more information about Encoder Pro software, click on the Help menu from inside the free trial version and select Features by Product, or go to *www.ingenixonline.com*.

Instructor's Manual *at the Online Companion*

The *Instructor's Manual* for this text is located on the Online Companion to accompany this book, which is found at *www.delmarlearning.com/companions*. The *Instructor's Manual* provides the answers to all text exercises, plus additional instructor support materials as follows:

- Sample lesson plans: a five-week plan and a ten-week plan

- Medical Documentation Auditing Tool that can be copied and given to the students to use when they are reviewing Evaluation and Management notes

- Tool that maps book content to exam topics for the CCS, CMRS, CPC-P, CPC-H, and CPC exams

Acknowledgments

This, my first textbook project, was quite an eye-opener. I had no idea of the amount of work and the number of people involved in the process. There are a few people I would like to personally thank for their support, advice, and guidance:

- Rhonda Dearborn, senior acquisitions editor, for entertaining this idea and giving us the support to bring this to fruition.
- Jadin Babin-Kavanaugh, product manager, without whose support, encouragement, and sincere belief, this project would never have become a reality. Jadin, you were an awesome manager. Thank you for your support, patience, and understanding during this whole process.
- Julie Russo, coworker and friend who coauthored the StudyWare with me. Your expertise and your dedication to detail and accuracy made this part of the project relatively effortless and enjoyable.

Thanks must be given to the reviewers of the text and StudyWare for the long and hard work that was necessary to ensure the accuracy of the information.

Lastly, to my wonderful husband for the tremendous amount of support and understanding you provided to me during all the hours I spent working on this project. Your faith in me and my abilities gives me the strength and fortitude to keep plugging along.

Cecile Favreau

About the Authors

Deborah Farwell, CCS-P, CPC, has worked in the coding industry for multiple specialties for 20 years and has taught medical coding for 14 years. She is employed as a senior coder/trainer at a large multispecialty medical practice in Worcester, Massachusetts. She was awarded the Joel Miller Award for Outstanding Teacher in 1996.

Cecile Favreau, MBA, BS, AS, CPC, has worked in health care for over 25 years with a large concentration of that time spent in the health insurance industry working for two large insurers. Currently employed as a professional relations specialist for a very large multispecialty group practice of a teaching hospital, Cecile is responsible for training providers regarding accurate billing as well as for the creation and revision of encounter forms (superbills) and researching payment issues. She also teaches in the Allied Health curriculum of a postsecondary school. Cecile is very committed to the concept of providing an environment of quality learning and enjoys celebrating the successes of her students.

Reviewers

The authors and the publisher would like to thank the following professionals for their valuable expertise and insights:

Barbara Desch, CPC, AHI
Division Manager, Allied Health
San Joaquin Valley College, Inc.
Visalia, California

Susanna M. Hancock, AAS, RMA, CMA, RPT, COLT
Medical Program Consultant
Former Medical Assistant Director-Instructor
American Institute of Health Technology
Boise, Idaho

Cathy Kelley-Arney, BSHS, CMA, MLTC
Institutional Director of Health Care Education
National College of Business & Technology
Bluefield, Virginia

Pat King, MA, RHIA
Adjunct Faculty
Baker College of Cass City
Cass City, Michigan

Karen D. Lockyer, BS, RHIT, CPC
Health Information Consultant
Takoma Park, Maryland

Tonia Seay-Josephina, CPAR, RMC, CPC
Program Director
Lincoln Educational Services
Norcross, Georgia

Margaret A. Stackhouse, CPC, RHIA
Adjunct Instructor
Pittsburgh Technical Institute
Oakdale, Pennsylvania

Lori A. Warren, MA, RN, CPC, CCP, CLNC
Medical Department Co-Director
Medical Coding/Healthcare Reimbursement Program Director & Instructor
AAPC Approved PMCC Instructor
Spencerian College
Louisville, Kentucky

TECHNICAL REVIEWER

Deborah J. Grider, CPC-EMS, CPC-H, CPC-P, CCS-P
Medical Professionals, Inc.
Indianapolis, Indiana

Chapter 1
Diagnostic Coding

KEY TERMS

abstracting	Index to Diseases	see also
assessment and plan	mandatory multiple coding	see condition
bullet	modifying terms	slanted brackets
chief complaint (CC)	nonessential modifiers	square brackets
colon	not elsewhere classified (NEC)	Tabular List
excludes	not otherwise specified (NOS)	triangle
impression	parentheses	
includes	see	

LEARNING OBJECTIVES

Upon completion of this chapter, the student will be able to:

1. Abstract diagnoses from medical notes
2. Understand the ICD-9 conventions terminology, symbols, and punctuation
3. Utilize the tools of the ICD-9 coding manual to advance his or her coding abilities

TOOLS OF ICD-9 CODING MANUAL

The ICD-9 for the physician's office consists of two volumes:

- Volume I: Tabular List
- Volume II: Alphabetical List

Volume I: Tabular List

The organization of the ICD-9 **Tabular List** is as follows:

1. Infectious and Parasitic Diseases	001–139
2. Neoplasms	140–239
3. Endocrine, Nutritional and Metabolic Disease, and Immunity Disorders	240–279
4. Diseases of the Blood and Blood-Forming Organs	280–289
5. Mental Disorders	290–319

Continued

Volume I has four appendices. (Appendix B was removed in 1995.)

1. Appendix A: Morphology of Neoplasms: These are M codes, used in the classification of neoplasms by the histological type and only in reporting to cancer registries. These codes are *never* used for insurance purposes.
2. Appendix C: Classification of Drugs by American Hospital Formulary Service List Number and Their ICD-9-CM Equivalents
3. Appendix D: Classification of Industrial Accidents According to Agency
4. Appendix E: List of Three-Digit Categories

And new for 2008 are eight additional tables within Volume 1:

1. Valid Three Digit Code Table: Codes that have no fourth or fifth digit.
2. Abortion Table
3. Complication Table
4. Diabetes Table
5. Hernia Table
6. Normal Pregnancy Table
7. Antepartum Pregnancy Table
8. Postpartum Pregnancy Table

Tables 2 through 8 provide a more concise presentation of codes that would otherwise be very complex to locate in the Index to Diseases. Any codes found using these tables should always be cross-referenced by looking them up in the Tabular List.

Volume II: Alphabetical List

Volume II is the Alphabetic Index of Diseases. This volume contains two indexes:

1. The Index of Diseases
2. The Index to External Causes (E Codes)

This volume also includes three tables:

1. Neoplasm Table
2. Hypertension Table
3. Table of Drugs and Chemicals

Coding Conventions and Guidelines

The ICD-9 coding manual has coding conventions and guidelines to help you locate the correct code. You do not have to memorize the rules or conventions, but you must be capable of finding the rules and be knowledgeable in applying them to obtain the correct diagnostic code.

The conventions are located at the beginning of the book to save room in the manual. Even though several publishing companies have their own versions of the manual, they all have the same standard coding conventions and symbols.

Abbreviations in the Manual

The following abbreviations are often found in the diagnostic descriptions, and you must understand their meaning to be sure the correct code is selected.

Not Otherwise Specified (NOS)

This notation indicates that the diagnosis should be used when there is no other more specific code to be found for the patient's condition.

> **EXAMPLE**
>
> With a diagnostic statement of acute sinusitis and no additional information regarding the location, assign 461.9. In the Tabular List, the description reads, "Acute sinusitis, unspecified / *Acute sinusitis NOS.*"

Not Elsewhere Classified (NEC)

Not Elsewhere Classified (NEC) designates a code that has no further clarification. Use this when you have no further information available in assigning a more specific code.

EXAMPLE

Use 176.8 Kaposi's sarcoma oral cavity NEC either when you do not know where in the oral cavity the sarcoma exists or when there is no other code.

Tip *The goal is always to use a code that accurately describes the condition to the highest level of specificity.*

Punctuation

The use of punctuation in the coding manual is very important. Each symbol is used to help you identify whether the code you are looking at is appropriate for the condition you are coding.

Parentheses ( )

Parentheses are also found in the Alphabetic Index. They are used to enclose supplementary words called **nonessential modifiers**.

EXAMPLE

Abscess (acute) (chronic) (infectional) (lymphangitic) (metastatic) (multiple) (pyogenic) (septic) (with lymphangitic) (*see also* Cellulitis) 682.9

The words in the parentheses do not change the code. They are possible terms the coder may see written in the record. In the example, an acute abscess would have the same code as a metastatic abscess: 682.9. Therefore "acute" and "metastatic" are both nonessential modifiers in this description because they are not required to be in the diagnostic statement but they may be included. Nonessential modifiers provide the coder with information when selecting a code.

Square Brackets [ ]

Square brackets [] are used to enclose synonyms, alternative wording, or explanatory phrases.

EXAMPLE

Erythema infectiosum [Fifth disease]

The brackets are also used to indicate which fifth digit can be used for some codes.

EXAMPLE

Code 651.0 Twin pregnancy [0, 1, 3]

Only the three fifth digits shown (0, 1, or 3) can be used for that code.

Slanted Brackets [ ]

Slanted brackets *[ ]* are found in the Alphabetic Index, and they indicate **mandatory multiple coding**.

> ## EXAMPLE
>
> Diabetic neuropathy 250.6 *[357.2]*

The bracketed code is always the second code reported and must be reported. It should be noted that when you see any slanted brackets, they are always in italics.

Colon :

The **colon (:)** is used after an incomplete phrase or term that requires one or more other terms for a complete and accurate description.

> ## EXAMPLE
>
> 721.0 Cervical spondylosis without myelopathy
>   Cervical or cervicodorsal:
>
> arthritis
> osteoarthritis
> spondylarthritis

Symbols

The use of symbols in the manual provides a quick indication that something is new or different about the entry. Special attention should be given to these symbols so that you do not use an inappropriate code or miss using a new code that provides more specificity for the condition you are reporting.

Bullet ●

A bullet ● indicates a new code for the current year.

> ## EXAMPLE
>
> Some new codes for 2007 were:
>
> - V85.5 Body Mass Index, pediatric
> - V85.51 Body Mass Index, pediatric, less than or equal to 5th percentile
> - V85.52 Body Mass Index, pediatric greater than 5th percentile, but less than or equal to 85th percentile
> - V85.53 Body Mass Index, pediatric greater than 85th percentile, but less than or equal to 95th percentile
> - V85.54 Body Mass Index, pediatric greater than 95th percentile

Triangle ▲

A triangle ▲ preceding a code indicates that the title of an existing code has been revised.

EXAMPLE

In 2006: 389.11 Sensory hearing loss

In 2007: ▲ 389.11 Sensory hearing loss, bilateral

The symbols for the fourth and fifth digits are different depending on the publisher of the manual.

EXAMPLE

The *PMIC* ICD-9 manual has the symbol of ④⑤.
   Ingenix uses ✓4th and ✓5th.

One version of the manual has the symbol of a stop sign ● with the "4th" and "5th" inside it. No matter what symbol is used, the meaning remains the same: The medical coder *must* find and report the code with a fourth or fifth digit. This is known as *coding to the highest level of specificity.*

EXAMPLE

✓4th 250 Diabetes mellitus

   0 type II or unspecified type, not stated as uncontrolled

   1 type I [juvenile type] or unspecified type uncontrolled

   3 type II or unspecified type, uncontrolled

   4 type I [juvenile type] uncontrolled

✓5th 250.0 Diabetes mellitus without mention of complication

When you see a symbol that indicates a fourth or fifth digit is needed, you can find this digit either at the beginning of the three-digit category for the code or directly under the code.

Tip *If a symbol is used anywhere on a page in the Tabular List (Volume I), the symbol will be footnoted on the bottom of the page with its meaning. So you do not have to memorize each symbol and its meaning.*

Instructional Notations

ICD-9 also has instructional notations. Instructional notations are found only in the Tabular List. These aid the medical coder in finding other terms or other code possibilities that could be used.

Includes

The note **includes** identifies additional diagnostic statements that are applicable to the code. It can also explain more about the key term and where to find more information.

> **EXAMPLE**
>
> 402 Hypertensive heart disease
>
> > *includes* hypertensive
> > > cardiomegaly
> > >
> > > cardiopathy
> > >
> > > cardiovascular disease
> > >
> > > heart (disease) (failure)
> > >
> > > any condition classifiable to 429.0–429.3, 429.8, 429.9 due to hypertension
>
> If any of these statements is used in the record, this code is the correct code to use.

Excludes

The term **excludes** indicates which diagnoses are not to be coded using that particular code. After each term listed as excluded, the code to be used for that statement is listed.

Take a look at the hypertensive heart disease code in the previous example. If the provider gave a diagnosis of pulmonary hypertension, you soon discover, upon looking at code 403, that there is an excludes notation.

> **EXAMPLE**
>
> 403 Hypertensive chronic kidney disease
> > *includes* arteriolar nephritis . . .
> > > arteriosclerosis of:
> > > > kidney
> > > >
> > > > renal arterioles
> > >
> > > arteriosclerotic nephritis (chronic) (interstitial)
> > >
> > > hypertensive:
> > > > nephropathy
> > > >
> > > > renal failure
> > > >
> > > > uremia (chronic)
> > >
> > > nephrosclerosis
> > >
> > > renal sclerosis with hypertension
> > >
> > > any condition classifiable to 585, 586, or 587
> > > > with any condition classifiable to 401
> >
> > *excludes acute renal failure (584.5–584.9)*
> > > *renal disease stated as not due to hypertension*
> > >
> > > *renovascular hypertension (405.–405.9 with fifth-digit 1)*

Note
Excludes *notations are always in* italics.

The ICD-9 manual directs you to the acute renal failure codes (584.5–584.9). This is where you find the correct code.

Notes

The notes are found throughout the ICD-9 manual contained in boxes:

- To define terms
- To clarify entries
- To list choices for fifth-digit subclassifications

EXAMPLE

Take a look at the notes for 250: ✓4ᵗʰ 250 Diabetes mellitus

✓5ᵗʰ 250.0 Diabetes mellitus without mention of complication

See

The term **see** indicates that you should reference another term in the index to find the correct code.

EXAMPLE

Look up ganglioneuroblastoma in the index. ICD-9 instructs you to *see* Neoplasm, connective tissue, malignant. This provides you with the information needed to find the correct code.

See Also

The **see also** notation gives the medical coder another term or another place to find the correct code that may be more suitable based on what the provider has written.

EXAMPLE

If you look up gangrene, gallbladder, or duct, ICD-9 instructs you to *see also* cholecystitis, acute.

See Condition

The **see condition** instruction always stumps new medical coders. When they see this instruction, they always try to find the code under the main term of "Condition." Looking under Condition, they find only a few conditions under this heading, not the code they seek. The see condition notation means that the medical coder must look up the actual condition.

EXAMPLE

For a diagnosis of breast lump, the medical coder looks up "breast" in the Index to Diseases in Volume I. The description reads, "see condition." This notation directs you to look for the code under "lump." The lump is the *condition* of the breast, and you find this condition listed as 611.72.

Code First the Underlying Disease

This instructional note indicates that the code cannot be a principal diagnosis or that it should not be sequenced before the underlying disease. This notation is found only in the Tabular List.

EXAMPLE

Look up the following code in the Tabular List.

583.81   Nephritis and nephropathy, not specified as acute or chronic, in disease classified elsewhere

The note instructs you to "Code first underlying disease" as:

amyloidosis (277.30–277.39)

diabetes mellitus (250.4)

gonococcal infection (098.19)

Goodpasture's syndrome (466.21)

systemic lupus erythematous (710.0)

tuberculosis (016.0)

This indicates that 583.81 should not be listed as a primary diagnosis. One of the codes listed should be the primary diagnosis, and 583.81 should be a secondary code.

Use Additional Code

This instructs the medical coder to use an additional diagnosis code to provide further information. The notation is located only in the Tabular List (Volume I).

EXAMPLE

Look up the following code in the Tabular List.

337.3 Autonomic Dysreflexia

Use additional codes to identify the cause, such as:

decubitus ulcer (707.00–707.09)

fecal impaction (560.39)

urinary tract infection (599.0)

Typeface and Color

Boldface type is used:

- For all of the codes and titles in the Tabular List (Volume I)
- For page headers and to designate individual terms in the Alphabetical List (Other possibilities are listed below in regular type.)

Italics are used for:

- All exclusion notes
- Codes that should not be used for primary diagnoses

Color coding and other symbols vary in their use, depending on the publisher of the manual. Each publisher uses different colors in different ways, and some use symbols that are not in the normal conventions. The one thing that all of the publishers have in common is that they all use footnotes to identify the use of the colors at the bottom of each page of the Tabular List. The symbols are sometimes footnoted, whereas others are placed to the right of the text only.

Familiarize yourself with the color coding and symbols used in the particular manual you are using. If, in any given year, you use a manual published by a different company, take extra care in using it and become familiar with the format.

ICD-9 CODING GUIDELINES

The ICD-9 coding manual has coding guidelines that are used to further describe the proper usage of codes. Depending on the publisher of the manual, the guidelines can be either very detailed or more generalized.

The 10 Steps for Accurate Diagnostic Coding

1. *Locate the main term in the diagnostic statement:* This can be found in the chief complaint section, in the impression, or sometimes in the personal or family history. You can also find it in the body of the notes along with any comorbidities.

2. *Locate the main term in the Alphabetic Index (Volume II):* The primary arrangements for the main terms are in alphabetic order by lay terms, such as nerve pain, as well as the medical terms, such as neuralgia.

Tip	*Remember that this index has key main terms that can make it easier to look up a code.*

Some of these key main terms are as follows:

Abnormal	Failure	Obstetrical trauma
Abnormality	False	Patient, Pathologic
Admission	Follow-up	Positive
Complex	Foreign body	Post
Complications	Health, Heat	Premature
Condition	(effects)	Reaction
Contraception	Impaired	Replacement
Damage	Injury	Resistance
Deficiency	Insufficiency	Retention
Deformity	Lack of	Screening (for)
Degenerative	Large	Short
Effusion	Late effects	Stasis
Elevation	Maternal condition	Surgery
Encounter for	Narrowing	Therapy
Examination	Newborn	Tight
Excess	Observation	Vaccination

Note

Use the following fifth-digit subclassification with category 250:

0   type II or unspecified type, not stated as uncontrolled
1   type I [juvenile type] or unspecified type uncontrolled
2   type II or unspecified type, uncontrolled
3   type I [juvenile type] uncontrolled

3. *Refer to all of the notes under the main term, as well as to any instructional notes:*

> **EXAMPLE**
>
> Diabetes diabetic (brittle) (congenital) (familial) (mellitus) (poorly controlled) (severe) (slight) (without complications) 250.0

4. *Check any **modifying terms** that appear in the parentheses next to the main term:* This is to determine whether any of these are the same as any used in the diagnostic statement.

> **EXAMPLE**
>
> Diabetes diabetic (brittle), (congenital), (familial), (mellitus), (poorly controlled), (severe), (slight), (without complications) 250.0

5. *Take note of the subterms that are indented under the main term:* These terms provide a heightened level of specificity.

Tip *Always code to the highest level of specificity.*

Note

Use the following fifth-digit subclassification with category 250:

0   type II or unspecified type, not stated as uncontrolled
1   type I [juvenile type] or unspecified type uncontrolled
2   type II or unspecified type, uncontrolled
3   type I [juvenile type] uncontrolled

> **EXAMPLE**
>
> Diabetes diabetic (brittle) (congenital) (familial) (mellitus) (poorly controlled) (severe) (slight) (without complications) 250.0
> With coma (with Ketoacidosis) 250.3

6. *Follow any cross-reference instructions, such as see or see also:* These instructions must be followed to find the correct code.

> **EXAMPLE**
>
> Developmental
> imperfect, congenital–see also Anomaly

7. *Confirm the code selection in the Tabular List (Volume I):* This is where you make sure that you have selected the correct and appropriate classification as stated in the diagnosis statement.

> **EXAMPLE**
>
> √4th   250   Diabetes mellitus
>
> √5th   250.0   Diabetes mellitus without mention of complication
>   Diabetes mellitus without mention of complication or manifestation classifiable to 250.1–250.9

continued

> ✓5th   250.3   Diabetes with other coma
>   Diabetic coma (with Ketoacidosis)
>   Diabetic acidosis hypoglycemic coma
>   Insulin coma NOS

This is where many medical coders go wrong. They code from the Alphabetic Index only, and they do not check to see if this is the right code in the Tabular List. If this step is not done, the medical coder cannot be sure of having selected the correct code. If the code is not correct, the claim will be submitted—and rejected. If this mistake is made consistently, it will result in an increased rejection rate for the medical practice.

8. *Follow the instructional terms, exclusion terms, notes, and fifth-digit instructions that apply to the code to verify it is correct to use:* Review the selected code to be certain no notes or instructions have been overlooked.

9. *Assign the code number determined to be correct.*

10. *Code the encounter form, surgery slip, or other document in the patient record.*

ABSTRACTING FROM MEDICAL NOTES

When abstracting the "why" of the visit—the diagnosis—you must understand the methods of reporting medical information in a medical record. In the record, the physician reports old diagnoses, signs and symptoms, what to rule out, what is probable, impressions, findings, and the reason the patient is there at the office. If the physician does not state a definitive diagnosis in the note, the coder must look for signs and symptoms that are indications of the disease to report. As the coder knows, qualified diagnoses are never reported on a professional claim.

◼ *Find the Code 1-1*

HISTORY AND PHYSICAL

CC: Patient is here today complaining of lower backache for the last 3 weeks.

PFSH: Started a new job working on her feet all day stacking items in a store. Patient has very well-controlled hypertension, and a Hx of neck and upper back pain from an old work-related injury.

HPI: Patient has had a lower backache for the past three weeks. Patient has been taking aspirin for the pain, but it has not relieved the pain. Denies any added neck or upper back pain.

EXAM: On exam, the patient's neck is soft and supple. The upper back is without muscle strain and has healed reasonably well. The lower back is stiff. Patient reacted to pain when touched and when the patient bends at the waist.

IMPRESSION: The lower back pain is probably due to the patient's new job, being on her feet for 8 hours and having to bend.

PLAN: Rx for 500 mg Naprosyn t.i.d. as needed. Patient will call if the back pain gets any worse.

From the scenario, what diagnosis would you abstract for the primary diagnosis? _____

How many diagnoses would you code? _____
List them: _____

In what section of the medical record did you find this information?

_____

There would only be one diagnosis of lower back pain: (724.2). You would not code neck or upper back pain as they did not play a part in the lower back pain. Lower back pain could be a sign or symptom, but in this case it's why the patient was seen in the office that day and the physician did not have any other findings. You would find this information under the section Chief Complaint or under the Impression in this case.

■ *Find the Code 1-2*

Use the same scenario and change the HPI, examination, and impression, as follows:

HISTORY AND PHYSICAL

HPI: Patient has had lower back pain for the past three weeks. Patient has been taking aspirin for the pain but has had no relief. Patient also has neck and upper back pain. Patient states that the neck and upper back pain is a little worse than the last visit. The pain level is up from a 6 to an 8.

EXAM: On exam, the patient's neck and upper back is stiff. The lower back is with muscle strain probably due to the way the patient has been moving to control the neck and upper back. This put a strain on the lower back.

IMPRESSION: The neck pain is the cause of the lower back pain.

PLAN: MRI to r/o cervical radiculitis, arthritis, or bone spurs of the cervical spine. Will try to control the neck and upper back pain better with PT and medication therapy.

From the previous scenario, what diagnosis would you abstract for the primary diagnosis for this visit? _____

How many diagnoses would you code? _____
List them: _____

In what section of the medical record did you find this information?

_____

The primary diagnosis is still lower back pain (724.2), with the neck pain (723.1) as the secondary diagnosis. Code only the primary and secondary diagnoses in entry 1. You would not code the rule-out statements described in the plan. The information would be found in the HPI and in the impression.

CHAPTER EXERCISES

Scenario 1-1

HISTORY AND PHYSICAL

Patient is here for follow-up of right knee pain. The patient states that he went to the Pain Clinic for his back and received an epidural steroid injection. He feels that there was no significant difference after the epidural steroid. He has a follow-up appointment in 2 weeks to get another shot. He questions whether he should take this second shot or go to a chiropractor to see whether some manipulation might help him with his symptoms. He also notes that since the Pain Clinic put him on Trilisate 1,000 mg twice a day, he has noticed some improvement in his back symptoms. There is a remarkable improvement in his knee symptoms. He had complained of pain in his right knee especially when squatting. X-rays were done and showed mild osteoarthritic changes. The patient states that he has been stretching regularly, trying to exercise and strengthen his quadriceps daily, and has taken the Trilisate regularly. He states that his knee feels quite good. He is still taking the OsteoBioflex and feels it has made a lot of difference in relieving his knee pain; he was told that he could continue the same. He also informs me that he has seen Dr. Hajjar for his varicosities. Dr. Hajjar has recommended against surgery for the varix and suggests the use of compression stockings. He feels the compression stockings have worked very well for him, but he would like a prescription to get black colored stockings because he goes dancing over the weekends. He states that he has been able to dance over the last couple of weekends, because his knee feels significantly better.

PHYSICAL EXAMINATION:

General: This is a pleasant white male who appears to be in no distress.

Vital Signs: Weight is 235 lb, pulse is 60, and blood pressure is 112/72.

HEENT: No pallor or icterus.

Back: Does not reveal any vertebral tenderness to palpation today. There is no increased paraspinal muscle tone.

Extremities: Straight leg raising test is bilaterally negative today with intact strength in his lower extremities and intact reflexes. Plantars are down going. He has mild decreased pinprick in his lower extremities, which has been noted in the past, suggestive of peripheral neuropathy. Examination of his knee does not reveal any erythema or effusion. There is slight tenderness to palpation over the patella, but no tenderness to palpation over the medial and lateral joint lines. Anterior and posterior drawer signs are negative. Gait appears to be normal.

ASSESSMENT AND PLAN:

1. Back pain due to spinal stenosis. He has received one epidural steroid injection and did not derive significant benefit. I recommended he try the second time before considering referral to a chiropractor because he may derive some benefits with the second shot. The patient is agreeable to that. He will continue the Trilisate 1,000 mg b.i.d. in the meantime.

2. Right knee pain is improved since he has been on the Trilisate. He was told he could continue the OsteoBioflex. He will continue to do regular strengthening exercises for his quadriceps and gentle stretching.

3. Varicose veins with a large varix, right leg. He was given a prescription for black TED stockings per his request.

4. Events of peripheral neuropathy. He needs to have some baseline blood work done, which was recommended by Dr. Fine. He has not had the tests so far and will be scheduled for them today. He will follow up with me in 3 months for a comprehensive physical or sooner if needed.

How many diagnoses would you code? _____

List them: _____

In what section of the medical record did you find this information? _____

Scenario 1-2

HISTORY AND PHYSICAL

This is a follow-up for this 52-year-old woman with metastatic malignant melanoma.

HPI: Melanoma was found in January 2005; removed a 2.2-mm lesion from distal left leg. Sentinel node was negative. Stage IIA disease. She did not receive adjuvant therapy. Earlier this year, routine screening CT scan showed liver lesions. Biopsy confirmed presence of metastatic malignant melanoma. She has been receiving DTIC as a single agent. Past history of diffuse large cell lymphoma, Stage IIIA. Presently being treated with CHOP with Rituxan. In this regard, she remains in complete remission. She has tolerated her chemotherapy fairly well. Her next scheduled dose is in about 2 weeks. Routine medications include Lipitor, Fosamax, and alprazolam.

REVIEW OF SYSTEMS:

CNS: No headaches or lateralizing motor or sensory problems.

ENT: No sinus or epistaxis.

Metabolic: Benign.

Derm: No rash or zoster.

Heme: No bleeding or easy bruising. Cardiac and pulmonary are both okay. No chest pain, palpitation, or dyspnea.

GI: No nausea, no diarrhea.

GU: Negative.

Musculoskeletal: Nonfocal.

Constitutional: Good appetite. She has actually done quite well with her chemotherapy, no weight loss.

PHYSICAL EXAM: On exam she looks well. Weight is 127 lb. Blood pressure is 162/78. No cervical or supraclavicular adenopathy in the head or neck area. Heart and lungs are okay. Abdomen is benign. Liver and spleen are not palpable. No cervical, axillary, or inguinal adenopathy in the lymph nodes.

She recently underwent CT scan of the chest, abdomen, and pelvis. This revealed three well-defined lesions in the liver. The radiologist felt these to have increased

continued

slightly in size. In addition, they thought there might be a new hypodensity, but it was very difficult for them to ascertain this and so no conclusion was made. A small pericardial effusion was identified. A possible bit of pleural thickening on the right side could also be seen. A CT scan of the lower extremities showed no mass. No evidence of local recurrence.

Her white count is 4,100, hematocrit 39, platelets 266,000. ANC was 1,700. CHEM-7 normal. Creatinine 0.8, liver function tests normal. LDH 206.

IMPRESSION: Malignant melanoma, metastatic to the liver, status post 3 cycles DTIC. CT scan shows that there has really been no improvement. If anything, a slight degree of worsening may have occurred. I discussed the findings with her. We could consider any of several clinical approaches. One would be to increase the dose of the DTIC to make it more aggressive. Another would be to switch the therapy, employing a combination program, perhaps Temodar and taxol. A third approach would be to go to chemoimmunotherapy with an IL-based regimen. We have discussed facets of different treatment plans. I favor preserving the DTIC-like activity with Temodar in this situation, which might give us better results. Also, in view of the evident growth, it might be reasonable, at this point, to place her on a combination. The combination of temozolomide plus a dose of taxol seems to be effective. Temozolomide at a dose of 150 mg/m^2 days 1 to 5, every 4 weeks, along with Taxotere 80 mg/m^2 q.4 weeks seems to be a program that achieves responses in a larger fraction of patients. She is willing to try this, and we will get her started on this switch in therapy.

How many diagnoses would you code? _____

List them: _____

In what section of the medical record did you find this information? _____

Scenario 1-3

HISTORY AND PHYSICAL

CHIEF COMPLAINT: CHF, chronic atrial fibrillation, dementia, and type 2 diabetes.

HISTORY OF PRESENT ILLNESS: Florence is here with her husband, doing well, having celebrated her 65th birthday earlier in the year.

MEDICATIONS: Glipizide 10 mg b.i.d. and atenolol 50 mg once a day. She has been off warfarin now for the last 4 months. In a well-documented note related to the risk-benefit ratio of persisting with her anticoagulation along with her chronic atrial fibrillation in which she had had very difficult to control protimes. She is on aspirin 325 mg a day, Lasix 80 mg b.i.d. She has been off the Zestril (lisinopril) since last visit.

She apparently had been in Status 1 in the CHF program, but this has been unknown to the patient, and she and her husband do not believe that they are actually in any case management. At any rate, she is doing well. She is using her cane. She denies any problems with activities of daily living and is quite happy and content. They are not checking home glucoses. She denies any symptoms of hyperglycemia.

REVIEW OF SYSTEMS:

ENT: Negative. Annual eye examinations are up-to-date.

Cardiopulmonary: She denies any recent dyspnea, orthopnea, or PND. She does have peripheral edema. She does her daily weights, which she states have been stable. She is 135 lb here today and was 124 lb four months ago.

GI: Otherwise negative.

GU: Otherwise negative.

MS: Otherwise negative.

PHYSICAL EXAMINATION:

General: She is pleasant, alert, and oriented. Husband is helping her with some issues.

HEENT: Sclerae are clear.

Chest: Clear to auscultation.

Heart: Heart sounds are distant but irregular with an apical rate of about 80.

Extemities: Show 1+ edema bilaterally. Skin is warm. Peripheral pulses are absent. There are no neurovascular changes.

IMPRESSION AND PLAN:

1. CHF. She has had a 9- or 10-lb weight gain over the last 4 months. I am presuming at least some of this is fluid related to her peripheral edema, although she has no symptoms of any CHF otherwise. We will reintroduce lisinopril 2.5 mg once a day, given her blood pressure being 160/80. We will recheck her CHEM-7 and watch for any worsening of her azotemia.

2. Chronic atrial fibrillation. She is on a regular aspirin regimen. Off anticoagulation, as noted, with risk of stroke.

3. OBS/dementia, stable and early. Considered Aricept or other, but not introduced at this juncture. She is doing well with her husband at home.

4. Type 2 diabetes, not monitored, but asymptomatic. Her glycohemoglobin was 7.6 3 months ago. We will recheck today. She will have a CHEM-7, lipids, CBC, TSH, and glycohemoglobin today.

How many diagnoses would you code? _____

List them: _____

In what section of the medical record did you find this information? _____

Scenario 1-4

HISTORY AND PHYSICAL

The patient states that her shoulder pain is much better and range of motion has improved. She has one more physical therapy visit scheduled. She has been doing a home exercise program and she is scheduled to see Dr. Grossman again this summer. Her cough has increased recently, and she is coughing up green sputum. No fever, sweats, or chills. No chest pain.

continued

MEDICATIONS: Lisinopril 10 mg, Flovent twice a day, albuterol inhaler 2 times a day, furosemide 40 mg, ibuprofen 600 mg, and nortriptyline but she is not sure of the dose. It might be 25 mg.

ALLERGIES: Codeine and sulfa.

HISTORY: She has not smoked in 15 years.

PHYSICAL EXAMINATION:

Weight: 238 lb. She is trying to lose weight and she is down 6 lb from September.

Blood pressure: 136/74.

Pulse: 92.

She is a well developed and well nourished overweight white female in no acute distress. She coughs occasionally during the visit. Throat is normal. Neck is supple with no adenopathy or masses and no jugular venous distention. Chest is clear. Cardiovascular is regular. Extremities with zero to trace edema. No erythema or tenderness. On the skin there are some scratch marks from her dog.

ASSESSMENT:

1. Overweight, improved.

2. Chronic obstructive pulmonary disease with mild exacerbation.

PLAN:

1. She will have a tetanus/diphtheria booster since she is due and since she has scratches from her dog.

2. She was given a course of doxycycline because of the productive cough.

3. Follow-up office visit in 6 months. She is encouraged to continue the diet.

How many diagnoses would you code? _____

List them: _____

In what section of the medical record did you find this information? _____

Scenario 1-5

PROGRESS NOTE

Discussion with Beverly in regard to most recent cholesterol test, which is quite good but not quite low enough, given the LDL being 110 and her history of vascular disease, hyperlipidemia, and hypertension.

We will increase her Lescol to 40 mg daily (she currently is only on 20), and we will plan to recheck fasting lipid profile, AST, ALT in 2 months.

Patient is aware and agreeable.

How many diagnoses would you code? _____

List them: _____

In what section of the medical record did you find this information? _____

Scenario 1-6

PROGRESS NOTE

This 40-year-old's status is post very low anterior resection for synchronous 2 rectal carcinomas. One carcinoma was identified in the rectosigmoid area. It was removed, but then when I proceeded to perform a reanastomosis of the colon to the rectum, a second low-lying malignancy was detected and I proceeded with a very low rectal resection with end colostomy and a short Hartman stump. I did not think the patient would tolerate an abdominoperineal resection because he has cardiac problems and was recently admitted for a stent placement. He has done well after the surgery.

He returns today for a postoperative visit. He is able to take care of his colostomy adequately. The incision itself has healed well. Staples are removed. Skin is well approximated.

The visiting nurse is taking care of the colostomy appliance at the present, and the patient and his wife are learning to do it. I discussed the pathology with the patient and his wife. The rectosigmoid lesion is T3, N2, Mx, and the rectal lesion is T2, N0, Mx; 7/25 nodes were positive in the first specimen, and 2 negative nodes in the second specimen, which is a limited rectal resection. The distal margins are negative on both specimens. On the low rectal specimen, there is a 2 cm clear margin.

I will, however, proceed with the medical oncology appointment for possibility of chemotherapy and also a radiation oncology appointment to evaluate him and proceed from there. He will need routine surveillance colonoscopy in about a year.

How many diagnoses would you code? _____

List them: _____

In what section of the medical record did you find this information? _____

Scenario 1-7

HISTORY AND PHYSICAL

The patient is seen today for renal insufficiency chronic V, status post aortic valve replacement; chronic atrial fibrillation and history of melanoma 2 including a recently excised lentigo maligna (carcinoma in situ melanoma) of the left helix. He has not had any recurrent nosebleeds.

ALLERGIES: He has no allergies.

SOCIAL HISTORY: He lives at home with his wife. He is doing well. He is retired and stays active with yard work. Does not smoke or drink. No cough, chest pain, or shortness of breath. Has a chronic right pleural effusion, status post thoracoscopy and pleurodesis, probably related to his congestive heart failure. He has had recurrent epistaxis, which is no longer a problem since he is off Coumadin. He has had his aortic valve replaced with a tissue valve. Mild memory disturbance and hypertension. No orthopnea, PND, or dyspnea on exertion. No hemoptysis. No other masses. No nausea and no vomiting.

continued

REVIEW OF SYSTEMS: No diarrhea, constipation, or rectal bleeding.

PHYSICAL EXAMINATION:

HEENT: Extraocular muscle movements intact. Pharynx normal. Healing wound in the left ear lobe. Small sebaceous cyst in the right submandibular area about 1 cm in diameter with a punctum.

Neck: Supple.

Heart: Heart sounds are irregular. There is a 2/6 systolic murmur. No diastolic murmur.

Lungs: Lung fields are clear with diminished breath sounds at the right base.

Abdomen: Soft, flat, and nontender.

Skin: Small, irregular, melanotic lesion in the right chest. I am referring him to see Dermatology regarding this lesion.

ASSESSMENT AND PLAN:

Labs were reviewed. Schedule complete physical in three months. Continue current medication with the exception of decrease Lasix to half of a 40-mg tablet daily instead of 40 mg every other day.

Continue atenolol 100 mg a day, lisinopril 20 mg a day, Lasix 20 mg a day, potassium 10 mg every other day, aspirin 81 mg a day, and multiple vitamins. Monitor systolic blood pressure; attempt to get this down below 130–140.

Recheck in 3 months.

How many diagnoses would you code? _____

List them: _____

In what section of the medical record did you find this information? _____

Scenario 1-8

HISTORY AND PHYSICAL

Helen returns today for a blood pressure follow-up. She has been doing well. Her left foot drop has improved, and she continues on physical therapy. Her ambulation is improving, and she uses a cane at home and a walker outside the apartment. She remains very mobile. She denies any problem with her current medications. There has been no problem with shortness of breath, chest pain, or headache.

PAST MEDICAL HISTORY: Significant for hypertension.

REVIEW OF SYSTEMS: The patient notes no problem with peripheral edema.

PHYSICAL EXAMINATION:

Vital Signs: Blood pressure is 160/90 on my examination.

HEENT: Shows very poor dental hygiene.

Neck: No nodes.

Lungs: Clear.

Heart: S1 and S2 well heard. No murmurs or gallops noted.

Abdomen: Obese.

Extremities: No edema. The left foot drop has improved.

ASSESSMENT:

1. Foot drop question radiculopathy versus lacunar stroke.

2. Hypertension.

PLAN:

1. Continue current medications.

2. Add lisinopril 10 mg daily.

3. Encouraged continued participation in physical therapy.

4. Follow up here in 2 months for repeat evaluation, at which point we will do a CHEM-7.

How many diagnoses would you code? _____

List them: _____

In what section of the medical record did you find this information? _____

Scenario 1-9

HISTORY AND PHYSICAL

Yearly surveillance for a patient who has had basal cell skin cancer in the past, remotely from the left lateral fifth toe and also on the face, right upper lip. She has also had actinic keratosis treated in the past. She has one lesion on the right upper lip she wishes to have evaluated. It has been present for 1 to 1½ weeks. It has not been tender, bleeding, or scaling. It is just pink.

On review of systems, she says she generally feels well. She has been staying very active.

Chart review shows past history of hypertension, hyperlipidemia, and ulcerative colitis. Also had a history of a kidney stone.

Current medication list includes lisinopril, Lipitor, Fosamax, vitamin C and calcium replacement, aspirin, omega, and multivitamins.

EXAM: On exam, she is in no acute distress. Exam included face, neck, chest, back, abdomen, buttocks, upper and lower extremities, hands, and feet. She has no lesions today that are suspicious for cutaneous malignancy. She has scattered, verrucous papules, very few in number on the chest and arms consistent with seborrheic keratosis. She has no lesions suspicious for actinic keratosis. On the right upper lip toward the center adjacent to the scar where a basal cell carcinoma had been removed, there is a 3-mm, pink, very thin area of telangiectasia. It is very slightly raised.

IMPRESSION AND PLAN: History of actinic keratosis and basal cell carcinoma. She has one new 1- to 2-week-old, pink, telangiectatic, very thin area noted on the

continued

right upper lip. This will be monitored. She will return in 4 months for reevaluation of this or sooner if she notices the area increasing in size or bleeding. We will also establish a yearly surveillance for her as well.

How many diagnoses would you code? _____

List them: _____

In what section of the medical record did you find this information? _____

Scenario 1-10

HISTORY AND PHYSICAL

CHIEF COMPLAINT: Stage II colon CA.

INTERIM HISTORY: Ms. Mason now presents for follow-up of Stage II colon CA. She received her first cycle of adjuvant Xeloda. Unfortunately, she developed diarrhea from this after 14 days at 2,000 mg a day orally. She is feeling much better now. She still has a slight residual mouth ulcer. Her follow-up CEA is elevated at 16. We do not have a pretreatment CEA. Unfortunately, this was not drawn at the time of diagnosis or during her last visit. She denies any abdominal pain. She has some residual mouth ulcers; otherwise doing well.

PAST MEDICAL HISTORY: Stage II colon CA status post excision. The lesion was T3 N1, with three nodes involved.

MEDICATIONS: Ranitidine, potassium, Isordil, triamterene and hydrochlorothiazide, Fosamax, Norvasc, and stool softener.

REVIEW OF SYSTEMS: Resolving mucositis. Diarrhea.

PHYSICAL EXAMINATION:

Vital Signs: Stable.

Neck: Supple. No nodes.

Lungs: Clear to auscultation and percussion.

Abdomen: Soft and nontender. The incision is well healed.

LABORATORY DATA: CBC stable. CEA 16, LFTs normal.

ASSESSMENT: Stage II colon CA. Ms. Mason had a fair amount of side effects with the Xeloda. We kept the doses low. She will be dose-reduced by 25% to 1,500 mg. She will continue this for 14 days starting the first of the year. She will follow up here in 4–6 weeks and initiate Cycle 2 if she tolerates the reduced dosing. I am concerned about her elevated CEA. We will check this at the time of the next visit and monitor it serially. We will get a follow-up CT of the abdomen and pelvis after 4–6 cycles have been completed with oral therapy. It is possible it is a non-specific elevation or residual elevation from surgery, but I would have expected this to normalize at this point postop and this is somewhat ominous with possible chance of progression in the future.

PLAN: Cycle 2 oral Xeloda, decrease to 1,500 mg daily total dose.

Follow up in 4–6 weeks. Repeat CT after 2–3 months.

How many diagnoses would you code? _____

List them: _____

In what section of the medical record did you find this information? _____

Scenario 1-11

HISTORY AND PHYSICAL

The patient is 71-year-old male, here today for a routine follow-up.

PAST MEDICAL HISTORY:

1. History of hypertension.

2. History of type 2 diabetes mellitus.

3. History of nodular prostate per Dr. Kumar's note of 09/09/2003 with a normal PSA.

4. Question of a Parkinsonian tremor and cogwheeling. Seen by neurologist, Dr. Young; the exam proved consistent with a mild case of Parkinson's. Not on medications at this point.

5. Left lacunar infarct. Sees Dr. Young periodically.

6. Obesity, with patient continuing with his weight loss program, currently having lost 20 lb through Weight Watchers.

7. B12 deficiency. Continues with shots. Last flu shot given 12/15/2003. The patient refuses colon cancer screening. Pneumococcal vaccine 06/10/2003.

MEDICATIONS: Include one aspirin per day, hydrochlorothiazide 60 mg one per day, verapamil 240 mg b.i.d., lisinopril 20 mg per day, glipizide 10 mg b.i.d., metformin 1,000 mg p.o. b.i.d., and vitamin B12 at 1,000 mg strength IM q. months.

The patient states he is feeling quite well. His glucoses are running in the 134 range by his history with intermittent checks only, but the patient denies any hypoglycemic spells. The patient states he gets only a rare glucose above 150 if he is not good on his diabetic program. He says he has been watching his calories and diet much more carefully since starting Weight Watchers. The patient's recent hemoglobin A1c was 7.7 up from 6.9 with a mean blood glucose of 172, but the patient declines any adjustment in his oral agents today. He states he wants to leave his meds alone and continue on his weight loss plan to see if he can handle this with his diet. Secondly, the patient had a repeat PSA of 0.5 for today. He declines a rectal exam today but agrees to a six-month follow-up when he is due in the fall for repeat prostate assessment at that point. The patient's UA is negative for any protein. His creatinine count is 1.2 with a BUN of 28 and a normal Panel-7. Today's glucose was 134.

PHYSICAL EXAMINATION:

General: The patient was in no acute distress.

Vital Signs: Physical exam today showed a blood pressure of 138/80.

HEENT: No oral lesions. He has some erythema over his face consistent with rosacea.

Neck: Supple neck. No bruits or JVD. No palpable thyroid nodules.

continued

Lungs: Clear.

Heart: Normal heart sounds.

Abdomen: Soft and nontender. No audible bruits. No masses. No rebound. No guarding.

Extremities: No foot lesions. His foot care for onychotic nails is done by Dr. Cannon. The patient has right upper extremity tremor as monitored by Dr. Dowing with Parkinson's concerns and slight cogwheeling and some cogwheeling noted in his upper extremities. The patient's gait is slightly wide-based but steady. The patient agrees to continue his current medical regimen and follow up in 6-month intervals.

ASSESSMENT: No change in the above mentioned medical issues. Medications remain the same.

How many diagnoses would you code? _____

List them: _____

In what section of the medical record did you find this information? _____

Scenario 1-12

HISTORY AND PHYSICAL

This is a 78-year-old gentleman who is in for a follow-up on his diabetes. He also carries a history of COPD and a history of glaucoma and chronic atrial fibrillation.

The patient, in general, feels well. He did get his flu shot last week when he came in for his blood work. The cholesterol is a little bit more generous than I would like.

The patient prefers not to consider any further medication. He says he had been eating a lot of ice cream and he wants to just try diet alone, and so we will certainly have him give a shot at it. His glycohemoglobin was good at 6.2. His mean blood glucose over 60 days also was very good at 143. That particular day he came in, his blood sugar was a little high at 154. Creatinine is slightly high also at 1.6, but he has no evidence of microalbuminaturia.

The patient's hemoglobin was 18.7, hematocrit 54.6. I think it is consistent with his COPD.

PRESENT MEDICATIONS: At present, he remains on atenolol 50 mg q.d., lorazepam 1 mg b.i.d. for chronic anxiety, and Trusopt solution for his glaucoma. He is also taking multivitamins. The patient is also on aspirin as a protective against his atrial fibrillation.

PAST MEDICAL HISTORY: There is nothing new.

PERSONAL HISTORY: There is nothing new.

FAMILY HISTORY: There is nothing new.

REVIEW OF SYSTEMS:

General: The patient denies any significant weight change, chronic malaise, fever, or chills.

Eyes: Denies vision change.

ENT: Denies hearing change or persistent hoarseness.

Lungs: Denies chronic cough, sputum production, or dyspnea.

Cardiac: Denies chest pain, palpitations, or edema.

GI: Denies chronic dysphagia, chronic heartburn, change in bowel habits, nausea, vomiting, and rectal bleeding.

GU: Denies dysuria, urgency, or hematuria.

Musculoskeletal: Denies severe muscle or joint pain.

Neurologic: Denies chronic headaches, weakness, or numbness.

Skin: Denies changing moles or rashes.

PHYSICAL EXAMINATION:

General: The patient looks good and does not look in any acute distress.

Vital Signs: His blood pressure today is 130/82, apical rate is 84, peripheral rate is 60, temperature is 97.4°, and weight is 190 lb.

HEENT: Normocephalic.

Lungs: Breath sounds are distant.

Heart: There is an irregularly regular beat.

Abdomen: Soft.

Extremities: There is no evidence of any joint swelling or ankle edema.

IMPRESSION: Hyperlipidemia could be better if the patient ensures diet control. Diabetes mellitus, well-controlled. History of chronic atrial fibrillation; patient elected to stay with the atenolol and aspirin. COPD seems to be relatively stable. He did get his flu shot, so I feel more comfortable with that. For glaucoma he is followed carefully by Dr. Bleakley.

PLAN: To get him back around springtime. We will recheck and see his parameters for his diabetes at that time as well as his cholesterol. He will call if there are problems before then.

How many diagnoses would you code? _____

List them: _____

In what section of the medical record did you find this information? _____

Scenario 1-13

HISTORY AND PHYSICAL

Patient presents today for add-on office visit. He is a 73-year-old obese white male, patient of Dr. Camps, who has a past medical history of hypertension, osteoarthritis, and atrial fibrillation. He comes in today complaining of pain to the right buttock, radiating down the posterior right thigh. He has had this intermittently since the end of January when he had slipped on ice, held himself with a railing, and then felt a pulling in that area. He states he has never had it prior to this. He has increased

continued

discomfort with sitting, but walking and lying down seem to help. He has been taking Extra Strength Tylenol, which helps slightly. He also takes Celebrex for his knees; it does not seem to be helping this. He denies any paresthesias, numbness, or weakness to extremities. No incontinence. He states he has no known drug allergies, but ibuprofen causes GI upset.

MEDS: He is on the lisinopril, Celebrex, and Tylenol. Patient denies any abdominal pain. Denies any fever or nausea.

EXAM: On exam today he is an alert, cooperative, obese male. He weighs 231 lb, temperature 96.7° Fahrenheit, blood pressure 134/80, pulse 80 and regular.

Back: He had no tenderness to palpation to the lumbosacral area but some tenderness over the sciatic notch and just distal to that. There is no swelling, no spasm. Straight leg raising was negative, lower extremities, DTRs 2+ patella, 1+ Achilles. Toes were down going. Strength 5/5. Sensation intact to sharp, dull.

IMPRESSION:

1. Right-sided sciatica. Recommended physical therapy, which he agreed to. I gave him a small prescription for Tylenol 3, 1 to 2 every 5 to 6 hours p.r.n. He was warned of sedation, addiction, nausea, and constipation with that. Patient will call if his symptoms worsen or persist.

How many diagnoses would you code? _____

List them: _____

In what section of the medical record did you find this information? _____

Scenario 1-14

HISTORY AND PHYSICAL

The patient is a pleasant 69-year-old type 2 diabetic female who presents to us today for toenail care secondary to peripheral vascular disease. She has no complaints other than elongated thickened toenails.

LOWER EXTREMITY EXAM: Vascular: Dorsalis pedis and posterior tibial artery pulses are absent. Capillary refill, color, temperature decreased. No digital hair noted. Dermatological exam reveals thick discolored toenails, subungual debris, and onycholysis of the nail plates ×10.

IMPRESSION:

1. Dystrophic onychomycotic toenails ×10.

2. Type 2 diabetes mellitus.

3. Peripheral vascular disease due to the diabetes.

PLAN: Debridement of these toenails manually and mechanically to the patient's tolerance today. She will follow up with us in 12 weeks.

How many diagnoses would you code? _____

List them: _____

In what section of the medical record did you find this information? _____

Scenario 1-15

OPERATIVE REPORT

DATE OF OPERATION: 08/14/2006.

PROCEDURE: Colonoscopy and polypectomy ×3.

INDICATIONS FOR PROCEDURE: The patient is being evaluated for chronic diarrhea and weight loss. The patient had a barium enema on 12/22/2003. The colonoscopy questionedpersistent obstruction with a 1.5 cm circumscribed filling defect in the ascending colon near the hepatic flexure. This appears to probably represent a polypold lesion, although fecal material was difficult to exclude. Further evaluation was recommended with colonoscopy. There was some lucency in the region of the superior segment and adjacent ascending colon. This was thought probably due to formation of feces and a prominent ileocecal valve. Other lesion is difficult to exclude. Again, colonoscopy was recommended. Diverticulosis coli in the sigmoid was seen. The patient now comes in for colonoscopy. The patient apparently had a colonoscopy in 2002 in Florida. A polyp was removed. Histopathology of that polyp is not known.

MEDICATIONS: Versed 3 mg IV, fentanyl 100 mg IV, Robinul .2 mg IV before the procedure.

DESCRIPTION OF PROCEDURE: With the patient in the left lateral position, rectal exam was performed. It is normal except for hemorrhoids. The Olympus PCF I 60AL colonoscope was then introduced into the anal sphincter and advanced into the colon up to the cecum and then into the ileocecal valve and the terminal ileum. The scope was withdrawn and the colon reexamined. Just superior to the ileocecal valve, there was an approximately 1 cm sessile polyp. This was resected utilizing snare electrocautery and retrieved through the scope. There was good hemostasis. The scope was further withdrawn. The hepatic flexure and distal ascending colon area was thoroughly examined. 1.5 cm lesion was not seen. However, a 0.5 to 0.7 cm small sessile polyp was seen. This was resected utilizing snare electrocautery and retrieved through the scope. There was good hemostasis. Scope was then further withdrawn. In the proximal descending colon, a 5 mm polyp was seen. This was resected utilizing snare electrocautery and retrieved through the scope. This, however, had gone through the trap into the suction bottle. We will make attempts to obtain this polyp by straining the suction bottle. If polyp retrieval is successful, it will be sent for pathology. Retroflex exam in the rectum was performed.

ENDOSCOPIC FINDINGS: Visualized terminal ileum was normal. Polyps near the ileocecal valve, the hepatic flexure, and proximal descending colon as described.

IMPRESSION: Diverticulosis coli and hemorrhoids.

FINAL IMPRESSION: Cecal polyp, hepatic flexure polyp, and proximal descending colon polyp. The patient has hemorrhoids. The patient also has diverticulosis coli.

Histopathology will be assessed. The patient will refrain from Plavix and aspirin for an additional 10 days. The patient may start her Coumadin after 3 days.

How many diagnoses would you code? _____

List them: _____

In what section of the medical record did you find this information? _____

Scenario 1-16

OPERATIVE REPORT

PREOPERATIVE DIAGNOSIS: Right wrist ganglion.

POSTOPERATIVE DIAGNOSIS: Right wrist ganglion.

PROCEDURE: Excision of right wrist ganglion.

ANESTHESIA: Bier block.

INDICATIONS FOR SURGERY: This patient presented with a mass over the radial aspect of the right wrist, which she wished to have excised. She was brought to the operating room at this time with her informed consent for operative excision of this mass.

PROCEDURE: The patient is placed in a supine position. After adequate anesthesia had been obtained by mean of a Bier block with a well padded antebrachial tourniquet, she is prepared and draped in the usual sterile fashion. The procedure is carried out under 3.8× loupe magnification.

Hemostasis is maintained with bipolar cautery.

The proposed transversely oriented incision line is marked over the radial volar aspect of the wrist overlying the mass. Excision is made and carried sharply through the skin and into subcutaneous tissue. Once dissection is to the subcutaneous tissue, then down on the surface of the mass, the ganglion cyst is inspected. It is densely adherent to the radial artery and the vena comitantes. It is dissected free of the vessels and isolated on a stalk, which emanates from the volar aspect of the wrist deep to the flexor carpi radialis tendon. It is incised there with some wrist capsule and passed off the field for histopathologic review. Hemostasis is obtained. The wound is closed with interrupted 4-0 nylon sutures.

The skin margins and subcutaneous tissues are infiltrated with 0.5% Marcaine. A sterile bulky nonadherent dressing is placed over the wound and secured in place.

The tourniquet is released with the immediate return of blood flow to the fingertips. The hand is held elevated with compression over the wound after release of the tourniquet and maintained elevated thereafter.

Counts are correct. Blood loss is negligible. The patient tolerated the procedure well and leaves the operating room in stable condition.

How many diagnoses would you code? _____

List them: _____

In what section of the medical record did you find this information? _____

Scenario 1-17

OPERATIVE REPORT

DATE OF OPERATION: 03/06/2006.

INDICATIONS FOR PROCEDURE: Artery stenosis, chest pain.

PROCEDURE: Cardiac catheterization.

PRELIMINARY NOTE: Peak gradient 30 mm Hg with aortic valve area of 0.9 cm^2. Cardiac output 4.8. Ejection fraction of 60%. Angiography of the coronaries 60% to 70% stenosis in the midanterior descending artery. Ostial stenosis of the right coronary artery approximately 60%. Left main, no stenosis. Circumflex, no stenosis.

PLAN: Echocardiography to confirm the stenosis of the aortic valve. Consultation by Dr. Harrington for possible aortic valve replacement and bypass surgery.

Patient informed. The patient did well without any complications.

How many diagnoses would you code? _____

List them: _____

In what section of the medical record did you find this information? _____

Scenario 1-18

OPERATIVE REPORT

PREOPERATIVE DIAGNOSIS: Right middle finger mucus cyst.

POSTOPERATIVE DIAGNOSIS: Right middle finger mucus cyst.

PROCEDURE: Right middle finger mucus cyst excision.

ANESTHESIA: Sedation plus local.

DESCRIPTION OF PROCEDURE: After adequate sedation had been obtained, the patient was prepped and draped. One cc of 0.5% bupivacaine was infiltrated into the eponychial area of the right middle finger. The right upper extremity was exsanguinated and a tourniquet raised to 250 mm Hg.

An elliptical incision over the cyst was made. The cyst was excised in its entirety and traced back to its origin at the DIP joint. The DIP joint was rongeured. The incision line was closed using 4-0 nylon suture. A dry sterile dressing was applied. The patient tolerated the procedure well.

How many diagnoses would you code? _____

List them: _____

In what section of the medical record did you find this information? _____

Scenario 1-19

OPERATIVE REPORT

PREOPERATIVE DIAGNOSIS: Macromastia.

POSTOPERATIVE DIAGNOSIS: Macromastia, right breast mass.

NAME OF PROCEDURE: Bilateral reduction mammoplasty, right breast biopsy.

ANESTHESIA: General.

continued

DESCRIPTION OF PROCEDURE: After adequate anesthesia had been obtained, the patient was prepped and draped. Forty-two-millimeter-diameter nipple sizers were used to mark the nipple areolar complex locations. Ten-centimeter-wide inferiorly based pedicles were de-epithelialized. Two-centimeter-thick superiorly based flaps were created. Breast tissue was removed. The same procedure was performed on both sides. The incision lines were temporarily closed using 2-0 nylon and staples. The patient was placed in the upright sitting position. Good symmetry was noted. The new nipple areolar complex locations were marked. The patient was placed back in the supine position. The skin overlying the nipple areolar complex locations was excised. Prior to final closure, a fullness on the medial caudal aspect of the right breast flap near the junction of the inverted T was noted. The mass was biopsied and sent off as a permanent specimen. All incision lines were closed using 3-0 Vicryl and 3-0 Monocryl. Steri-Strips, a dry sterile dressing, and an Ace wrap were applied. A total of 224 grams were removed from the left, and 114 grams were removed from the right.

How many diagnoses would you code? _____

List them: _____

In what section of the medical record did you find this information? _____

Scenario 1-20

OPERATIVE REPORT

PREOPERATIVE DIAGNOSIS: Right buttock lesion.

POSTOPERATIVE DIAGNOSIS: Right buttock lesion.

OPERATION: Excision of right buttock lesion, 3-cm incision. The patient was taken to the OR, prepped and draped in the usual manner after IV sedation was given. The area around the right buttock was infiltrated with a 1% lidocaine solution with 0.25% Marcaine, 1:1 ratio. An elliptical incision was made around this lesion. It was then excised with Bovie electrocautery. Hemostasis was assured with cautery. We closed the deep dermis with 2-0 and 3-0 Vicryl. The skin was closed with a running 4-0 white Vicryl, benzoin, and Steri-Strips. The patient tolerated the procedure well. Sponge count was correct. Blood loss was minimal. The patient was sent to the recovery room in stable condition.

How many diagnoses would you code? _____

List them: _____

In what section of the medical record did you find this information? _____

CHAPTER REVIEW

Using the ICD-9 coding manual:

Define the following:

1. NOS _____
2. NEC _____

   3. Coding conventions _____

   4. Includes _____

   5. Signs and symptoms _____

Find the following ICD-9 codes and explain what coding convention or coding rule is used.

   6. Diabetic neuropathy

   Code: _____

   _____

   7. Pneumonia due to coccidioidomycosis

   Code: _____

   _____

   8. Admission for chemotherapy for metastatic carcinoma of the lung

   Code: _____

   _____

   9. Type I diabetes, uncontrolled

   Code: _____

   _____

   10. Peripheral arteriosclerosis

   Code: _____

   _____

Chapter 2
Procedural Coding

category

encounter form, charge slip, or superbill

evaluation and management (E&M)

level II modifiers

main terms

modifiers

place of service (POS)

physical status modifiers

section guidelines

symbols

third-party payers (TPP)

type of service (TOS)

LEARNING OBJECTIVES

Upon completion of this chapter, the student will be able to:

1. Understand the Current Procedural Terminology (CPT) manual rules, terminology, symbols, and punctuation
2. Utilize the tools of the Current Procedural Terminology (CPT) manual to advance his or her coding abilities

QUICK REVIEW OF CPT

The *Current Procedural Terminology* (CPT) manual is very different from the ICD-9 coding manual. When looking up diagnosis codes in the ICD-9 manual, the search for the correct code is comparatively direct. The coder first reviews the Alphabetical Index (Volume II) and then verifies the code in the Tabular List (Volume I).

In the CPT manual, codes can be found in the index listed as:

- One code
- Several codes separated by a comma
- A range of codes

EXAMPLE

Excision

Bladder

    Neck 51520

    Partial 51550–51565 (3 codes in this range)

    Total   51570, 51580, 51590–51597 (6 codes in this range)

It is up to the coder to refer to and read *all* of the code descriptions that are listed in the index to find the most appropriate code based on the description given in the clinical notes. All code descriptions *must* be checked. Even if only one code is given, the coder must still verify that the description accurately describes the procedure performed.

| Tip | *Never code directly from the index!* |

EXAMPLE

Let's use an example to demonstrate the incorrect way to code from the index: Removal and repair of a cheek scar. When repairing this scar, a split skin graft of 10 sq cm is needed. Let's find the code for the grafting.

The coder's first instinct is to look under Graft. Find Graft in the index. In the Graft section, find the code for Fascia Cheek: 15840. Now find the code and read the description. The description reads, ''Graft for facial nerve paralysis; free fascia graft (including obtaining fascia).'' If the coder coded just from the index, the code would be incorrect.

Now let's use the same example to demonstrate how to arrive at the right code. Determining the type of graft is the key. The coder is really looking for the skin graft of the cheek.

- Look in the index under Skin Graft and Flap.
- Find ''skin'' and then ''split graft.'' There are two ranges of codes: 15100–15101, 15120–15121.
- Go to these codes in the CPT book and read all of the descriptions. Within these ranges you will find the right code.

What code would you use?

The code would be 15120 ''Split thickness autograft face, scalp, eyelids, mouth, neck, ears, orbits, genitalia, hands, feet, and or multiple digits; first 100 sq. cm or less, or 1% of body area of infants and children (except 15050).''

The rule of never coding from the index is a vital and very important one. This rule must never be broken, because ignoring it is a primary reason for mistakes in coding.

The following example illustrates another reason for never coding from the index.

EXAMPLE

Hernia repair incisional abdominal incarcerated

Find Hernia Repair. The first code is 49590. Is this code right? It is not. When you look up this code, it describes the repair of an incisional or ventral hernia.

The next code is 49560. Is this code correct? Again the answer is no. When you look at this code description, it reads, ''Repair initial incisional or ventral hernia; reducible.'' The description is missing the term ''incarcerated.'' Keep reading from the index, and you will find ''incisional'' and below this the word ''incarcerated,'' with the code 49561.

Is this the correct code? Yes, it is.

If the coder took the first code without looking through the codes and reading the full descriptions, or without even looking further in the index for the correct code, then the code would be incorrect.

Main Terms

The index is set up using the following **main terms**:

- Body area
- Procedure
- Disease, or conditions
- Approach

Main terms help you find your code. This means that you can sometimes find the code you need in more than one way.

EXAMPLE

Excision of a breast lesion

- Look under Excision (procedure), breast, and then lesion. This leads you to a range of 19120–19126.
- Now look under Breast (body area), excision, and then lesion. This leads you to 19120–19126.
- Now look under Lesion (disease), breast, and then excision. This also leads you to the same range 19120–19126.

Find the Code 2-1

Find the code or range of codes for Ablation of polyp of the sigmoid colon, using a sigmoidoscopy.

Answer the following and find the code or range of codes.

What was done? _____

Disease? _____

Body area? _____

Approach? _____

Code or range of codes? _____

What was done? Ablation of polyp. Disease? Polyp. Body area? Sigmoid colon. Approach? Using a sigmoidoscopy. Code or range of codes? 45339

The key to understanding the CPT index is to know that sometimes the index does nothing more than lead you to the area where the code can be found. If the code from the index does not match the documentation, you have to review the descriptions of all of the codes the index has listed.

Find the Code 2-2

Give the code range for the following:

Excision of a lesion on the foot: _____

Excision of humerus: _____

I&D of a hip abscess: _____

Prenatal monitoring home service: _____

Total hysterectomy: _____

Dr. Smith's patient came into the hospital for a diagnostic sigmoidoscopy. The physician found two polyps. He removed one by snare technique and took a biopsy of the other. What code(s) would you use? _____

Excision of a lesion on the foot: 28080, 28090. Excision of humerus: 23184, 23220–23222, 24134, 24140, 24150–24151. I&D of a hip abscess: 26990. Prenatal monitoring home service: 99500. Total hysterectomy: 58150, 58200, 58956. Dr. Smith's patient came into the hospital for a diagnostic sigmoidoscopy. The physician found two polyps. He removed one by snare technique and took a biopsy of the other. What code(s) would you use? 45331 biopsy and 45338.

TOOLS TO UNDERSTANDING CPT CODING

The CPT coding book, written and copyrighted by the American Medical Association, has tools that can be used to help any medical coder code correctly. For example, the inside cover contains the symbols and brief descriptions of how they are used in the book. Also listed on the inside cover are the modifiers, with a brief definition for each one. (The complete definition can be found in Appendix A of the CPT book.)

This simple outline is just one tool that the AMA has placed in the coding book to help aid the medical coder in picking the most appropriate code to describe the procedure performed.

Symbols

The CPT manual makes use of symbols to indicate information about some codes. These symbols, with their descriptions, appear at the bottom of every page as a footnote for quick reference.

Three of the **symbols** used in the CPT book indicate change:

- The upward arrow (▲)
- The circle (●)
- The sideways arrows (▶ ◀)

The Upward Arrow (▲)

The upward arrow is very significant and important. If the medical coder does not pay attention to this symbol, the wrong code could be used. The upward arrow (▲) indicates a revised code description from the previous year. The changes can be to:

- Enhance and explain
- Add or remove terminology
- Indicate technology changes
- Completely change the description
- Change the meaning of the code

> ## EXAMPLE
> ### Enhancing the Meaning of the Code:
>
> *In 2006:* 26170 Excision of tendon, palm flexor, single (separate procedure), each
>
> *In 2007:* ▲ 26170 Excision of tendon, palm, flexor or extensor, single, each tendon
>
> The change removes the "separate procedure" indicator and makes the description specify that this code will be used for each tendon that is excised.

> ## EXAMPLE
> ### Adding Terminology and Technology:
>
> *In 2006:* 54150 Circumcision, using clamp or other device; newborn
>
> *In 2007:* ▲ 54150 Circumcision, using clamp or other device with regional dorsal penile or ring block
>
> This change removes the word "newborn" and adds the method used for anesthesia.

> ## EXAMPLE
> ### Changing the Description of a Code:
>
> *In 2006:* 99251–99255 Initial Inpatient Consultations
>
> *In 2007:* ▲ 99251–99255 Inpatient Consultations
>
> In 2006, the follow-up and confirmatory consultation code ranges were removed, so there is no need to identify the remaining consultation codes as initial.

> ## EXAMPLE
> ### Changing the Meaning of the Code:
>
> *In 2006:* 17000 Destruction (e.g. laser surgery, electrosurgery, cryosurgery, chemosurgery, surgical curettement), all benign or premalignant lesions (e.g. actinic keratoses) other than skin tags or cutaneous vascular proliferative lesions; first lesion
>
> *In 2007:* ▲ 17000 Destruction (e.g. laser surgery, electrosurgery, cryosurgery, chemosurgery, surgical curettement), premalignant lesions (e.g. actinic keratoses); first lesion
>
> This changes the meaning of the code to apply only to premalignant lesions. Benign lesion removal now requires a different code.

The Circle (●)

The circle symbol (●) indicates new codes. This symbol, placed in front of the code, is also a very important symbol: It indicates that a new code has been added because of a new procedure or technology that merits a code. The circle also represents an expansion of one code into two or more codes. The importance of this symbol when updating any printed encounter forms or when you are coding from medical records should not be overlooked.

EXAMPLE

In 2007: 25606 Percutaneous skeletal fixation of distal radial fracture or epiphyseal separation

---

The Sideways Arrows (▶ ◀)

The two sideways arrows (▶ ◀) indicate that the text between those arrows is either new or revised and relates to instructions for using the code.

EXAMPLE

30130–Excision *inferior* turbinate, partial or complete, any method
In 2006: ▶ (For excision of superior or middle turbinate, use 30999) ◀

This new instructional text helps direct the medical coder to the right code.

EXAMPLE

In 2006: 49080 Peritoneocentesis, abdominal paracentesis, or peritoneal lavage (diagnostic or therapeutic); initial

In 2007: ▶ (If imaging guidance is performed, see 76942, 77012). (49085 has been deleted. To report, see 49402)◀

This directs the medical coder to an additional code for imaging and to an alternative code for a deleted code.

Other symbols in the CPT manual have other meanings.

The Plus Symbol (+)

The plus symbol (+) indicates that the code is an add-on code. An add-on code designates a code that must be reported with another code. It is a supporting code.

EXAMPLE

11000 Debridement of eczematous or infected skin; up to 10% of body surface
+ 11001 each additional 10% of the body surface

The guidelines indicate that the medical coder should use this add-on code in addition to a code for the primary procedure, and to use 11001 in conjunction with 11000. There is a list of add-on codes in Appendix D.

The Symbol ⊘

This symbol ⊘ indicates a code that do not need to have modifier -51 appended. These codes should be reported in conjunction with other related procedures without -51.

> **EXAMPLE**
>
> ⊘ 20974   Electrical stimulation to aid bone healing; noninvasive (nonoperative)
>
> This code is reported in conjunction with another procedure. There is no need to use modifier -51 to indicate multiple procedures. There is a list of Exempt from Modifier -51 in Appendix E.

The Bull's-Eye (◎)

The bull's-eye symbol (◎) in front of a code indicates that moderate conscious sedation is included in the procedure description.

> **EXAMPLE**
>
> ◎ 35473 Transluminal balloon angioplasty, percutaneous; iliac
> This code is assumed to include moderate conscious sedation as part of the procedure.
> There is a list of codes that include moderate conscious sedation in Appendix G.

The Lightning Bolt (⚡)

New for the year 2006 is the lightning bolt symbol (⚡), which indicates that a vaccine is pending approval from the FDA.

> **EXAMPLE**
>
> ⚡ 90698 Diphtheria, tetanus toxoids, acellular pertussis vaccine, haemophilus influenza Type B, and polio vaccine, inactivated (DTaP-Hib-IPV), for intramuscular (IM) use

Tip *Some of the codes that were pending FDA approval at the time of printing may have been approved. So check all these codes on the AMA Web site at www.ama-assn.org to see if they were approved subsequent to publication of the CPT manual.*

Modifiers

Modifiers are used to modify a code for the circumstances surrounding the surgery, procedure, or service. The modifier completes the description of the procedure for the third-party payer (insurance company, worker's compensation, etc.). Using the correct modifiers can expedite payment from insurance companies.

On the inside front cover of the manual there is a quick reference with short descriptions of the modifiers. Use this reference with caution; the full descriptions of the CPT modifiers are found in Appendix A.

Remember that modifiers are used to "modify" the code that is being used for the circumstances surrounding the surgery, procedure, or service. The modifier completes the description of the procedure for the third-party payer (insurance company, worker's compensation, etc.).

Three types of modifiers are reported on the inside front cover:

1. CPT modifiers (all listed in Appendix A with full descriptions)

> **EXAMPLE**
>
> 21, 51, 62, etc.

2. Physical status anesthesia modifiers (also found in the Anesthesia Guidelines)

> **EXAMPLE**
>
> P1, P2, etc.

3. Level II (HCPCS) that are listed in the HCPCS coding book

> **EXAMPLE**
>
> LT, RT, T1, T2, etc.

HCPCS modifiers can also be used with CPT codes.

Using the correct modifiers could enhance payment from insurance companies.

Use the inside cover reference with caution, relying more on the full descriptions of the CPT modifiers in Appendix A.

> **EXAMPLE**
>
> **Brief Description on the Inside Cover:**
>
> Modifier 25 "Significant, Separately Identifiable Evaluation and Management Services by the Same Physician on the Same Day of the Procedure or Other Service."

> **EXAMPLE**
>
> **Full Description from Appendix A:**
>
> ▶ Significant, Separately Identifiable Evaluation and Management Service by the Same Physician on the Same Day of the Procedure or Other Service; It may be necessary to indicate that on the day a procedure or service identified by a CPT code was performed, the patient's condition required a significant,

separately identifiable E&M service above and beyond the other service provided or beyond the usual preoperative and postoperative care associated with the procedure that was performed. A significant, separately E&M service is defined or substantiated by documentation that satisfies the relevant criteria for the respective E&M service to be reported (see **Evaluation and Management Services Guidelines** for instructions on determining level of E&M service). The E&M service may be prompted by the symptom or condition for which the procedure and/or service was provided. As such, different diagnoses are not required for reporting of the E&M services on the same date. This circumstance may be reported by adding modifier 25 to the appropriate level of E&M service. **Note:** This modifier is not to be used to report an E&M service that resulted in a decision to perform surgery. See modifier 57 for significant, separately identifiable non-E&M services, see modifier 59. ◄

The full description explains that the coder can code for an E&M with another E&M or an E&M with a procedure as long as the documentation supports both services. Documentation for both services must be independent. The diagnosis can be the same for both services. When the documentation does support both services, then the coder can append a modifier 25.

Find the Code 2-3

HISTORY AND PHYSICAL

CC: Lesion on face.

HPI: This new patient states that this mole has been there most of his life, but it has been getting larger in the last 6 months. The mole also bleeds occasionally and has turned a darker color.

EXAM: On exam, this mole is asymmetrical; the edges are ragged and irregular. Color is brown to black with some red. The size is about 2 cm by 1.5 cm with the mole being elevated off the skin about 0.5 cm.

IMPRESSION: Melanoma.

PLAN: To biopsy this mole for removal at another date if necessary.

PROCEDURE: The face was prepped. A local anesthesia was given all around the mole. A small incision was made and a piece of the mole was taken. The piece of the mole was placed in fixation and marked as sample one. Another piece of the mole was excised and placed into fixation and marked as sample two. The wound was then dressed with a bandage and the patient went home with instructions on how to clean the wound. I asked the patient to return in two days for the results of the biopsy and possible complete removal of the mole.

From the scenario, does the documentation support both an E&M and a procedure?
_____

What procedure(s) would you code for? _____

Code them: _____

Would you use a modifier 25? _____

From the scenario, does the documentation support both an E&M and a procedure? Yes. What procedure(s) would you code? An E&M and the biopsy. Code them: 99201–99205, 11100. Would you use a modifier 25? Yes.

▬ *Find the Code 2-4*

HISTORY AND PHYSICAL

CC: The patient is back for the results of his biopsy on the mole on his face. The report indicates that it is indeed a melanoma.

HPI: Patient was here two days ago with a chief complaint of a growing and darkening mole on his face. Two biopsies were preformed and sent to the lab in two separate containers, marked with the patient's name and either "sample 1" or "sample 2." With the results showing that the mole is a melanoma, the removal of the mole was done today.

PROCEDURE: The patient was prepped and local anesthesia was given all around the mole for the surgery. A 1 cm margin around the mole and the complete mole was excised. The mole with the margin was 3 cm across, 3.5 cm in length, and 3 cm in depth. The wound was then closed with a layered closure.

From the scenario, does the documentation support both an E&M and a procedure?
_____

What procedure(s) would you code for? _____

Code them: _____

Would you use a modifier 25? _____

Why? _____

From the scenario, does the documentation support both an E/M and a procedure? No. What procedure(s) would you code? The removal of the mole and the layered closure. Code them: 11644, 12052. Would you use a modifier 25? No. Why? No E/M was performed on this day, only the procedure.

Place of Service Code

The place of service chart on page 2 of the CPT manual helps the coder find the right **place of service (POS)** code that is needed on the CMS-1500 form, Block 24B. The place of service must be appropriate for the procedure. Insurance companies use coding edits that reject a claim if the POS code and procedure are incompatible.

EXAMPLE			
CPT		*POS*	
99222	Inpatient hospital care	21	Inpatient Hospital
99304	Initial nursing facility care	31	Skilled Nursing Facility
99213	Established patient office/outpatient visit	11	Office

CPT INTRODUCTION

The Introduction offers a great explanation of how to use the book.

The first part of the Introduction has a table indicating section numbers and the numeric sequence.

Evaluation and Management	99201–99499
Anesthesiology	00100–01999, 99100–99140
Surgery	10021–69990
Radiology (Including, Nuclear Medicine and Diagnostic Ultrasound)	70010–79999
Pathology and Laboratory	80048–89356
Medicine	90281–99199, 99500–99602

By looking at this table, you know the following types of service (TOS) by looking at the first digits of the codes as follows:

- All E&Ms start with "99."
- Anesthesia starts with a zero (except for four add-on codes, 99100, 99116, 99135, and 99140).
- Surgery starts with numbers 1 through 6.
- The radiology number is 7.
- The pathology and laboratory number is 8.
- The medicine number is 9.

The next part of the Introduction presents a quick instruction on the use of the CPT book. The format of terminology explains how the procedure description is abbreviated.

EXAMPLE

Bronchoscopy   31622–31656

The description for 31622 is as follows: "Bronchoscopy, rigid or flexible, with or without fluoroscopic guidance; diagnostic, with or without cell washing (separate procedure)."

Now look at the next code, 31623.

with brushing or protected brushings

Here is where CPT applies the indented text. The next code utilizes part of the description of the code in the previous example. But where does the code description end? The description before the semicolon (;) remains the same, and the description after it indicates the different description.

EXAMPLE

44140	Colectomy, partial; with anastomosis
44141	with skin level cecostomy or colostomy

Another indication that the text has been abbreviated is the indentation of the text with the subsequent code(s). This format is utilized throughout the book.

Section Guidelines

The CPT Introduction also explains the uses of the CPT guidelines, which are located at the beginning of each section of CPT. The sections are:

- Evaluation and Management (E&M) Services
- Anesthesia
- Surgery
- Radiology (including Nuclear Medicine and Diagnostic Ultrasound)
- Pathology and Laboratory
- Medicine

Each guideline contains information specific to each section. The Surgery, Radiology, Pathology and Laboratory, and Medicine sections all have Subsection Information. This information helps you find the codes with important note locators that lead you to special instructions for coding for that particular section.

CPT has fully detailed instructions throughout the book to help coders find the precise code. Utilizing these instructions can save many hours of looking for the code, as well as many hours of correcting incorrect codes.

Unlisted Procedures

The guidelines also give the coder a list of all the unlisted codes in the following categories:

- E&M
- Surgery
- Radiology
- Pathology and Laboratory
- Medicine

These codes are important because sometimes no code in the manual properly represents the work performed by the provider. Many of the new technologies and procedures have not yet been assigned a code. In these situations, the coder must find the most appropriate unlisted code to report the service. CPT also indicates that the usage of these codes will require a Special Report to be submitted to the payer.

Special Report

CPT also indicates that the use of unlisted procedure codes requires the submitting of a Special Report to the payer. The Special Report section in the CPT manual indicates what information should be included in the report that accompanies a claim with an unlisted code. The report helps the third-party payer determine the appropriate reimbursement for the procedure. Most third-party payers do not pay for unlisted services without some kind of operative report or clinic notes.

The AMA assigns new codes every year. For example, in 2006, seven new codes were assigned for endovascular repair and descending thoracic aorta, as well as five new codes for gastric restrictive procedures. In 2007, the Pathology and Laboratory section had eleven new codes, and the Medicine section had eighteen new codes. All of these services were unlisted procedures at one time. As the procedures become more used and are no longer considered experimental, CPT codes are assigned to them.

Evaluation and Management

The E&M guidelines explain what an E&M is and how to level the code. Most of these codes are provided by the physician with an **encounter form**, a **charge slip**, or a **superbill** (the form used to prepare claims for reimbursement). However, the coder *must* understand the system of leveling the code. The guidelines are very detailed on how to level an E&M visit.

Categories and Subcategories of Service

This table lists all of the E&M codes and the range of codes for each category and subcategory. The table also helps the coder understand that the E&M codes are not just for the office or hospital, but also for noncorporate hospital observation, both inpatient and outpatient consults, nursing home and preventive services.

Anesthesia Guidelines

Anesthesia coding is very different from any other coding. You need to know:

- Whether the anesthesia is local or general
- How much time the patient was under the anesthesia
- Any special circumstances of the patient's condition
- The procedure performed

The guidelines explain what can and cannot be reported with the anesthesia. These guidelines do not explain how to calculate the price of the service; price calculation is explained in the anesthesia chapter of this book.

Physical Status Modifiers

There are six **physical status modifiers**, all of which start with the letter "P." These modifiers are reported to the **third-party payer** (usually the insurance company) to help explain the patient's physical status and the reason for the extra care provided as it relates to the health of the patient.

- P1 is a normal healthy patient.
- P2 is a patient with mild systemic disease.
- P3 is a patient with severe systemic disease.
- P4 is a patient with severe systemic disease that is a constant threat to life.

- P5 is a moribund patient who is not expected to survive without the operation.
- P6 is a declared brain-dead patient whose organs are being removed for donor purposes.

Qualifying Circumstances

Qualifying circumstances are add-on codes explaining the circumstances that affect the anesthesia service.

- +99100 Anesthesia of a patient of extreme age (under 1 year and over 70 years)
- +99116 Anesthesia complicated by utilization of total body hypothermia
- +99135 Anesthesia complicated by utilization of controlled hypotension
- +99140 Anesthesia complicated by emergency conditions

The guideline also explains when to report moderate (conscious) sedation and directs the coder to these codes in the Medicine section.

Surgery Guidelines

Surgery guidelines outline the fact that, besides the surgical code, the provider could also report an E&M service in addition to the surgery services when applicable and when it is appropriate to report any other services. The CPT surgical package definition is given, as well as a description of follow-up care for both diagnostic and therapeutic surgical procedures. A list of the modifiers for surgical procedures and their use is also provided.

Separate Procedure

Some procedure codes include the phrase "Separate Procedure." This means that the procedure can be reported only when:

- No other service that incorporates it is being reported.
- Or it is carried out independently or considered to be unrelated or distinct from other procedures or services provided at that time.

> **EXAMPLE**
>
> 31505 Laryngoscopy, indirect; diagnostic (Separate Procedure)
>   This code can be reported alone, but, if a biopsy is performed, the coder reports 31510 Laryngoscopy indirect; with biopsy.

However, both codes can be reported if each procedure is carried out independently or if they are unrelated.

> **EXAMPLE**
>
> It is acceptable to bill a Laryngoscopy 31505 and a Tracheostomy 31600 if the procedures were unrelated to one another.

▬ *Find the Code 2-5*

OPERATIVE NOTE

PREOPERATIVE DIAGNOSIS: Coughing up blood, x-ray showing a large spot in the left lower lung. Right is clear.

POSTOPERATIVE DIAGNOSIS: Vocal cord tumor, left lower lung tumor.

PROCEDURE: The patient was brought into the operative suite and was draped and prepared for the procedure. The scope was advanced to the true vocal cords, and there was a large 3-cm tumor. A biopsy was taken and the scope was removed. The bronchoscopy was advanced through the vocal cords, being extra careful going past the vocal tumor, and advanced down to the lower left lung. A transbronchial lung biopsy was taken and the scope was taken out. The patient went to the recovery room in good condition.

How would you code this? _____

How would you code this? 31510 Laryngoscopy, indirect, w/biopsy. 31628 Bronchoscopy, rigid or flexible, with or without fluoroscopic guidance, with transbronchial lung biopsy(s), single lobe.

Radiology Guidelines

The radiology guidelines contain two sections that are not in the other guidelines:

1. Supervision and Interpretation
2. Administration of Contrast Material(s)

Supervision and Interpretation

This section provides instructions on appropriate billing for a procedure performed in addition to the radiological procedure.

Administration of Contrast Material(s)

These are instructions on how to properly code services that include or do not include the introduction of a contrast material as part of the radiological study.

CPT APPENDICES

The appendices offer additional tools for the medical coder.

• Appendix A—Modifiers: A full description of the modifiers
• Appendix B—Summary of Additions, Deletions, and Revisions: A listing of all changes for the current year by code
• Appendix C—Clinical Examples: Clinical examples to assist the provider in selecting the appropriate E&M code

- Appendix D—Summary of CPT Add-On Codes: A list of all of add-on codes
- Appendix E—Summary of CPT Codes Exempt from Modifier 51: A list of all of CPT codes that do not need modifier 51 when two or more procedures are performed
- Appendix F—Summary of CPT Codes Exempt from Modifier 63: A list of all CPT codes that do not need the modifier 63, because these code descriptions already indicate that these procedures are performed on infants
- Appendix G—Summary of CPT Codes That Include Moderate (Conscious) Sedation: List of all procedures that include moderate (conscious) sedation and that cannot be reported with moderate (conscious) sedation codes
- Appendix H—Alphabetic Index of Performance Measures by Clinical Condition or Topic: This is a crosswalk for the use of CPT Category II codes, providing an overview of the measures and the Category II codes to be used in reporting
- Appendix I—Genetic Testing Code Modifiers: Modifiers intended for reporting with molecular laboratory procedures related to genetic testing
- Appendix J—Electrodiagnostic Medicine Listing of Sensory, Motor, and Mixed Nerves: Assigns each sensory, motor, and mixed nerve with its appropriate nerve conduction study code to enhance accurate reporting of codes 95900, 95903, and 95904
- Appendix K—Product Pending FDA Approval: List of vaccines that are currently awaiting FDA approval
- Appendix L—Vascular Families: The vascular families branches and outline of the first, second, third, and beyond orders (Assumption is that catheterization began at aorta)
- Appendix M—Crosswalk to Deleted CPT Codes: Summary of codes deleted from the previous year and the current year codes that can be used in their place.

CHAPTER EXERCISES

Scenario 2-1

OFFICE NOTE

This patient returns to the clinic for evaluation of the plantar verruca to the right heel. Upon evaluation, there is hyperkeratotic tissue; however, upon partial thickness debridement ×5, the lesions are completely resolved.

ASSESSMENT: Plantar verruca, right heel ×5 with complete resolution.

PLAN: Partial thickness debridement ×5 was performed. The patient is instructed to continue with his regular activities and return to clinic as needed for podiatric care.

Code(s): _____

Scenario 2-2

OPERATIVE NOTE

PREOPERATIVE DIAGNOSIS: Melanoma in situ, right cheek.

PROCEDURE:

1. Wide local excision, melanoma in situ; 1.5 cm diameter.

2. Intermediate closure, less than 2.5 cm.

PROCEDURE: After receiving adequate preoperative consent and discussion of risk, the patient was placed in the supine position, at which time the lesion was identified under loop magnification, and a 0.5 cm diameter was marked for a lenticular excision. One percent lidocaine with epinephrine was sterilely infused. The patient's face was prepped and draped in the usual sterile fashion and a #15 blade scalpel was used to excise make the lenticular excision. Soft tissue was elevated with the #15 blade scalpel both anteromedially and superolaterally. Bleeding was controlled with bipolar electrocautery. Interrupted 4-0 Monocryl, followed by 5-0 Monocryl, followed by running 6-0 nylon was used to close the skin. He tolerated this well with no complications. Specimen was sent to Pathology. He will follow up in 7 days for suture removal. A sterile Steri-Strip was applied.

Code(s): _____

Scenario 2-3

OFFICE NOTE

PROCEDURE: Visit for Boniva injection for senile osteoporosis.

Vital signs prior to Boniva: 100/58, pulse 66, weight 148.

MEDICATIONS: Calcium with vitamin D 500 t.i.d., Centrum silver, Lasix, Prilosec, OxyContin, Percocet.

ALLERGIES: NKDA.

PROCEDURE: After sterile skin prep, a right antecubital vein was cannulated with a 23-gauge butterfly needle. The area was flushed well with normal saline; then 3 mg of Boniva was injected over 2 minutes and flushed with 4 cc of normal saline. The patient tolerated the procedure well without complications. Postinfusion vital signs: 110/58, pulse 60.

Boniva lot #NH68493-01, expiration 11/2007. She will return in 3 weeks.

Code(s): _____

Scenario 2-4

OPERATIVE REPORT

DATE OF OPERATION: 07/18/2006.

PREOPERATIVE DIAGNOSIS: Infertility, endometrial polyp.

POSTOPERATIVE DIAGNOSIS: Infertility, endometrial polyp.

PROCEDURE: Hysteroscopy, polypectomy.

OPERATIVE PROCEDURE: Under general anesthesia, the patient was placed in the lithotomy position, prepped and draped in the usual fashion. EUA revealed a small uterus. Both adnexa were clear. A diagnostic hysteroscope was inserted through the cervical opening after grasping the cervix with the tenaculum. Three polypoid lesions were identified. The cavity otherwise appeared normal. The deepest lesion was grasped with a polyp forceps and removed. The other lesions were then gently grasped and removed. There was an oozing from the surface of the cavity and good visualization was not obtained. Subsequent to this, gentle exploration with a sharp curette revealed a smooth surface. Minimal bleeding intraoperatively, and the patient was taken to the recovery room in good condition. The tissue was submitted for histologic study.

Code(s): _____

Scenario 2-5

OPERATIVE NOTE

PREOPERATIVE DIAGNOSIS: Right groin abscess and muscle weakness.

POSTOPERATIVE DIAGNOSIS: Right groin abscess and muscle weakness.

OPERATION: Incision and drainage of deep right groin abscesses, biopsy of muscle.

ANESTHESIA: Local with sedation.

INDICATIONS FOR SURGERY: The patient is a 16-year-old male who presents with recurrent fevers that failed to respond to IV antibiotics. The patient was found to have abnormalities in his right groin as well as in the left hamstring area. Given these two findings, a concern about polymyositis was raised versus a subcutaneous abscess. The patient presents for exploration of the right groin.

PROCEDURE: Using 1% Xylocaine under sterile conditions, a 5 cm skin incision was made. Dissection was carried down through the subcutaneous tissues using sharp dissection. Upon entering the pocket, there was some cloudy fluid, and this was aspirated and sent for culture. The abscess was followed deeply into the muscle compartments with drainage of again more cloudy fluid. After this was performed, a standard muscle biopsy was performed of the quadriceps muscle. This was performed by placing the muscle clip and removing a segment of muscle. An additional segment of muscle was removed. The wound was packed open. The patient tolerated the procedure well.

Code(s): _____

Scenario 2-6

OPERATIVE NOTE

PROCEDURE: Upper endoscopy with control of bleeding.

PREOPERATIVE DIAGNOSIS: The patient is an 83-year-old woman with a history of duodenal ulcer who has recurrent GI bleeding. Early this morning, the patient had GI bleeding and developed hypotension. Upper endoscopy is being performed to treat the visible vessel in a duodenal ulcer.

POSTOPERATIVE DIAGNOSIS:

1. Duodenal ulcer

2. GI bleeding

3. Epinephrine injection around the ulcer and clip deployed over visible vessel

4. Bleeding after endoscopic therapy

MEDICATION: Versed 2 mg IV, fentanyl 50 mcg IV.

DESCRIPTION OF PROCEDURE: After risks, benefits, and alternatives of the procedure were thoroughly explained, informed consent was obtained. The endoscope was introduced into the mouth and past the cervical esophagus under direct visualization. The endoscope was advanced down the esophagus to the gastroesophageal junction. The esophageal mucosa and the gastroesophageal junction appeared normal. The endoscope was advanced into the gastric cardia, fundus, body, and antrum, and retroflexion was performed in the stomach. The stomach mucosa appeared normal. The endoscope was then advanced to the pylorus into the duodenal bulb. There was a large duodenal ulcer with visible vessel in the duodenal bulb. Epinephrine 6 cc was injected around the ulcer and visible vessel with blanching of the mucosa. Subsequently one clip was deployed over the visible vessel. After the clip was deployed, there was a large amount of bleeding, which prevented visualization of the visible vessel. The endoscope was then withdrawn from the patient. The patient tolerated the procedure well.

RECOMMENDATIONS: The patient is actively bleeding after epinephrine injection and clipping of a visible vessel in a duodenal ulcer. The surgery service has been contacted and the patient will require surgery to control the bleeding.

Code(s): _____

Scenario 2-7

OPERATIVE NOTE

PREOPERATIVE DIAGNOSIS: Pilonidal cyst.

POSTOPERATIVE DIAGNOSIS: Pilonidal cyst.

PROCEDURE: Wide excision of pilonidal cyst. The patient was taken to the OR, prepped, and draped in the usual manner. After being placed in the prone jackknife position and being placed under general anesthesia, he had evidence of

continued

granulomatous tissue toward the left superior aspect of the pilonidal cyst disease. This was included in the excision. A wide elliptical incision was made around the pilonidal cyst area. Incision was made with a #15 blade. We then used cautery for hemostasis through subcutaneous tissue. Dissection was carried down, excising the entire area down to the sacral fascia. The specimen was excised. Hemostasis was assured with Bovie electrocautery. We then injected with large amounts of 0.25% lidocaine and 0.25% Marcaine, a total of 30 cc. We assured hemostasis and packed the wound. We had discussed, with the patient and others, the risks of the procedure preoperatively including risks of bleeding, infection, and possible deformity. The patient agreed to proceed.

Code(s): _____

Scenario 2-8

PROCEDURAL NOTE

PROCEDURE: Amniocentesis for fetal lung maturity. Under ultrasound guidance, a pocket of fluid was located around twin A. The skin was prepared with Betadine. The ultrasound guide was placed on the probe, and a long spinal needle was placed into the abdomen and 10 cc of clear fluid was withdrawn and sent to the laboratory for evaluation. The obturator was replaced and the needle was removed without difficulty. There was no bleeding. Good fetal heart tone was noted following the procedure. An attempt was made to find a pocket of fluid surrounding twin B; however, the only pocket was quite small and against the baby's face, and we decided not to run the risk of injuring the fetal eye. The likelihood that both twins are equally mature is quite good.

Code(s): _____

CHAPTER REVIEW

Using the Current Procedural Terminology (CPT) manual, complete the following exercises:

Define the following:

1. Main terms _____
2. Encounter form _____
3. Place of Service (POS) _____
4. CPT section guidelines _____
5. Code range _____

Find the following CPT codes and explain what coding rule or symbol the medical coder would use.

6. Insertion of intraperitoneal cannula or catheter for drainage or dialysis; permanent: _____

7. Excision of 4-cm benign lesion on hand: _____

8. Patient came into the ER with the following lacerations: head 1.5 cm simple, hand 2.1 layered closure, leg 4.5 layered closure. _____

9. Cervicectomy: _____

10. Two complete nail plate avulsions: _____

Chapter 3
Coding Using the Healthcare Common Procedure Coding System (HCPCS)

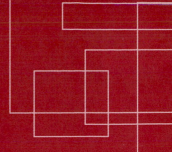

LEARNING OBJECTIVES

Upon completion of this chapter the student will be able to:

1. Understand the Healthcare Common Procedure Coding System (HCPCS) manual rules, terminology, symbols, and punctuation

2. Utilize the tools in the Healthcare Common Procedure Coding System (HCPCS) manual to advance coding skills

OVERVIEW OF HCPCS TOOLS

In the professional office setting, the medical coder does not use the Healthcare Common Procedure Coding System (HCPCS) as much as ICD-9 (International Classification of Diseases, 9th edition) and CPT (Current Procedural Terminology). Nevertheless, the HCPCS book is a very important tool to have available. This coding system has all of the medication codes that might be used in the office setting as well as supply codes. Within HCPCS, some procedure codes are the same or similar to CPT and are used as a replacement for CPT for some payers, especially Medicare.

HCPCS codes consist of a letter followed by four numbers. The coding system is very different from both CPT and ICD-9. HCPCS is used for:

- Procedures
- Supply codes

- Medicine codes
- Orthotic supplies
- Transportation codes

Table 3-1 presents the HCPCS codes by section.

TABLE 3-1 **HCPCS Codes by Category**

A
A0000–A0999	Transportation Service Including Ambulance
A4000–A8999	Medical and Surgical Supplies
A9000–A9999	Administrative, Miscellaneous, and Investigational

B
B4000–B9999	Enteral and Parenteral Therapy

C
C1000–C9999	Outpatient PPS

D
D0000–D9999	Dental Procedures

E
E0100–E9999	Durable Medical Equipment

G
G0000–G9999	Procedure/Professional Service (Temporary)

H
H0001–H2037	Alcohol and Drug Abuse Treatment Service

J
J0000–J9999	Drugs Administered Other Than Oral Method

K
K0000–K9999	Temporary Codes

K codes are assigned to DME regional carriers (DMERC).

L
L0000–L4999	Orthotic Procedures and Devices
L5000–L9999	Prosthetic Procedures

M
M0000–M0301	Medical Services

P
P0000–P9999	Pathology and Laboratory Service

Q
Q0000–Q9999	Temporary Codes

R
R0000–R5999	Diagnostic Radiology Service

S
S0000–S9999	Temporary National Codes (Non-Medicare)

TABLE 3-1   **HCPCS Codes by Category** (Continued)

T	
T1000–T9999	National T Codes Established for State Medicaid Agencies

V	
V0000–V2999	Vision Services

HCPCS modifiers can be and are often used with CPT codes. There are many more **HCPCS modifiers** than CPT modifiers, and the HCPCS modifiers are not always grouped with modifiers of similar types. This mismatch sometimes makes it very difficult to find the modifier needed. The front and back covers of the HCPCS manual list the modifiers that can be used with both CPT and HCPCS codes, and you can find a list of the modifiers, along with more detailed descriptions, in Appendix 2 of the HCPCS book. Take a look inside the front cover of HCPCS. Read down from modifier AA, Anesthesia Performed by an Anesthesiologist, to AS, Assistant at Surgery Services. These are all provider modifiers. Scattered throughout the rest of the modifiers are additional modifiers for other provider types, such as SA for Nurse Practitioner or TD for RN. As you might gather, there is no easy way to find a needed modifier.

> **Tip**   *Remember that LT (left) and RT (right) are often used with any procedure that can be performed on either side of the body. These codes can also be found in the inside front cover of the CPT modifiers.*

Among the tools for the medical coder in the HCPCS manual is an introduction, very much like that in the CPT manual, that explains the rules and how to use the book correctly. Understanding these rules helps the medical coder find the correct code.

The introduction explains that the codes are updated and placed in the **Federal Register** every November and updated throughout the year, unlike CPT, which is updated only yearly. Because the major changes are effective January 1 of each year, medical coders must check the code updates and then adjust their encounter and other charge forms, as well as their computer system, just as they would for ICD-9 and CPT changes.

HCPCS How-To's

In the HCPCS introduction is a section that provides details on how to use the manual. This section explains the color-coded blocks surrounding codes throughout the book. The color boxes indicate what Medicare pays for:

- Blue boxes indicate Special Coverage.
- Dark pink or red boxes indicate Non-Covered by Medicare.
- Yellow or gold boxes indicate Carrier Discretion.

The color of the box may determine which code the medical coder will use. (The color coding is footnoted at the bottom of each page.)

EXAMPLE

Look at code A4286. It is in a pink box, indicating that this code is not paid by Medicare.

Code A4290 is in a yellow box, which indicates that this code is paid depending on carrier discretion. In other words, the payer determines whether or not reimbursement will be made for the code and not all payers may recognize the code.

HCPCS Symbols

HCPCS also uses some of the same symbols as does CPT. They are as follows:

- ● New Code
- ▲ Revised Terminology

New symbols not seen in CPT are as follows:

- **O** Code has been reinstated.
- ☑ Quantity Alert: The coder must pay attention to the quantity limitations of the code.

EXAMPLE

Code J0515 Injection, Benztropine mesylate, per 1 mg. If the patient is given more than 1 mg, the coder must add the actual number of units to report the amount administered to the patient for correct pricing and reimbursement.

- ♀ Female symbol: Whenever the medical coder encounters a code with this symbol, the code can be used only for a female patient.
- ♂ Male symbol: Whenever the medical coder encounters a code with this symbol, the code can be used only for a male patient.
- Ⓐ This symbol indicates that the code is age related and restricted to a patient who is of the stated age. The services are the same; the only difference is the age of the patient for whom the service is being performed.

EXAMPLE

Code G0308 is for ESRD-related services for a patient under 2 years of age.

For the same service for someone 2–11, the code is G0311.

For a person 12–19, the code is G0314.

For a person 20 years and over, the code is G0319.

The services are the same; the only difference is the age of the patient.

- Ⓜ This symbol indicates that the code should be used for only maternity patients, generally between the ages of 12 and 55.

1–9 ASC (**ambulatory surgery center**) Groupings: ASC Groupings allow the provider or provider group to be compensated for the ASC facility charge along with the professional procedural charges. The medical coder codes for both the professional and the facility charges. When one of these numbers (1–9) appears in a box to the right of the description of the code, Medicare pays the code based on the number assigned. When these codes are used, and the service is performed in an ASC, Medicare will pay one price to the facility. You would be coding for the professional and facility charges. Payment is made based on the grouping for the CPT code (see Table 3-2).

EXAMPLE

The HCPCS code G0105 has a 2 next to the description; the Medicare reimbursement is $455 per procedure for the facility. See Table 3-2 for the pricing of the procedure.

Some of the services and supplies that the medical coder can report are for the sale, lease, or rental of **durable medical equipment** (**DME**) to ASC patients for their homes as well as leg, arm, back, or neck braces. It is very important that the medical coder understands what can be coded for reimbursement and what cannot. See Table 3-3.

TABLE 3-2   An Illustrative Payment Chart for ASC Groupings

Group 1	$ 340
Group 2	$ 455
Group 3	$ 520
Group 4	$ 643
Group 5	$ 731
Group 6	$ 840
Group 7	$1,015
Group 8	$ 989
Group 9	$1,366

TABLE 3-3   ASC Table of Inclusive and Non-Inclusive Charges

Included

Implanted DME and related accessories and supplies not on pass-through status under Subpart G of Part 419 of 42 CFR

Radiology services for which separate payment is not allowed under OPPS, and other diagnostic tests or interpretive services that are integral to a surgical procedure

Supervision of the services of an anesthetist by the operating surgeon

Simple preoperative laboratory test (e.g., urinalysis, blood hemoglobin, or hematocrit)

Patient use of the ASC operating and recovery rooms and prep areas

Administrative, record-keeping, and housekeeping items and services

Continued

TABLE 3-3 **ASC Table of Inclusive and Non-Inclusive Charges** (Continued)

Included

Worked performed by nurses, orderlies, technical staff, and others involved in patient care associated with the procedure
Anesthetic and any materials, disposable or reuseable, needed to administer anesthesia
Drugs and biologicals for which separate payment is not allowed under the OPPS, surgical dressings, supplies, splints, cast, appliances, and equipment
Implanted prosthetic devices, including intraocular lenses and related accessories and supplies not on pass-through status under Subpart G of Part 419 of 42 CFR

Not Included

Implantable DME and accessories
Non-implantable prosthetic devices
Implantable prosthetic devices except intraocular lenses and accessories
Procedures NOT on the ASC list
Physician's service, including anesthesia
The sales, lease, or rental of DME (durable medical equipment) to ASC patients for their homes
All prosthetic devices except for intraocular lens
Leg, arm, back, and neck braces
Artificial legs, arms, and eyes
Services furnished by an independent laboratory
Ambulance service

ASC reimbursement rates vary by locality, just like other Medicare services.

⅃ DMEPOS symbol: This symbol, which appears on the right side of a description, indicates that the coder must consult the CMS DMEPOS for payment of the durable medical item. The state in which the medical practice is located and possibly where the patient lives determine whether the carrier will pay for the DME supply. See code L8000.

⊘ In HCPCS, this symbol identifies certain items and services that can be billed directly to Medicare by the provider when the patient is in a **skilled nursing facility** (**SNF**). This symbol has a different meaning in HCPCS than it does in CPT. In CPT, it indicates that the CPT code is a modifier 51 exempt code.

All of these symbols are footnoted at the bottom of each page of the manual.

Color-Coded Footnotes

HCPCS also uses text footnotes (in blue) under the code descriptions. Some of this text is just a reminder for the medical coder to seek other documentation for additional information on how to submit the code. Other text states when the code can be used. The AMA, CMS, and AHA are some of the organizations that require this information from the medical coder.

> **EXAMPLE**
>
> Take a look at J0583, Injection, bivalirudin, 1 mg. Under the description are instructions in blue for the medical coder to "Use this code for Angiomax" (the brand name for bivalirudin).
>
> Now take a look at the code J0945, Injection, brompheniramine maleate per 10 mg. The note under this code is "Use this code for Histaject, Cophene-B, Dehist, Nasahist B, ND Stat, Oraminic II, Sinusol-B." In this case, all of the drugs noted in blue are other names under which this drug is marketed.

The AMA also provides explanations in blue under the codes. These footnotes not only help the medical coder understand how to use and bill the code, but also direct attention to another code that might be more appropriate.

> **EXAMPLE**
>
> Look at C9234 Injection, alglucosidase alfa, 10 mg. The footnote under the codes states "Use this code for Myozyme." An additional note refers the coder to "See also code: S0147." Upon reviewing S0147 it should be noted that the code is for the same drug but the dosage is 20 mg instead of 10 mg.

There are two other footnotes: the MED and AHA footnotes.

The *MED notation* precedes an instruction pertaining to the code. These instructions can be found in Appendix 4.

> **EXAMPLE**
>
> See code A4382 Ostomy pouch, urinary, for use on faceplate, heavy plastic, each MED: 100-2, 15, 120. Go to Appendix 4 and find CMS Publication 100, Chapter 15, Section 120. This information explains how to submit this service to the federal government or its contractors.

The *AHA footnotes* are from the American Hospital Association Coding Clinic for HCPCS citations and help the medical coder in very much the same way as do the MED footnotes. This information is used for Hospital Based Coding. The scope of this book does not include this footnote information.

APC Status Indicators Table

The codes in this table are used to indicate how a code is going to be paid or not paid under the **OPPS** (**Outpatient Prospective Payment System**), and they are used only in hospital setting coding.

> [A]–[Y] These APC Status Indicator symbols, found to the left of the code, indicate how to use the code. They help the medical coder to use the correct code and to code only for the most appropriate procedures and or supplies.

> **EXAMPLE**
>
> G0309 has an [A] to its left. This indicates that the services are paid under some other method, such as the DMEPOS fee schedule or the physician fee schedule.

HOW TO USE HCPCS LEVEL II

To use the HCPCS Level II, identify the service or procedure documented in the medical notes and look up the appropriate term in the index.

> ### EXAMPLE
>
> For a prostate PSA, find the appropriate term in the index (screening prostate), then find the code (G0103). Try to find the code by looking up prostate.

Unlike CPT, which offers more than one way to find a code and a more comprehensive index, the HCPCS codes can be found in the index in only one place. HCPCS is therefore not as user-friendly as either the CPT or the ICD-9 coding system.

In addition, when the medical coder finds the code in the index, there might be multiple codes (just like CPT). Upon finding multiple codes in the index, the medical coder must look up each and every code to determine the code that most closely matches what was documented in the medical notes.

Within the HCPCS manual there is a tip that instructs medical coders to look in the table of contents (TOC) for the type of procedure or service to narrow the code choices if they cannot locate the procedure or service. But there is no TOC! Instead, Table 3-1 at the beginning of this chapter is comparable to a TOC. The table outlines the service areas the medical coder might need, such as Dental service, Ambulance, Drugs, and DME.

Coding Standards for Level Use

The professional medical coder uses two coding systems for medical services, CPT and HCPCS. What happens when both systems have the same procedure with virtually the same description? HCPCS states that, when that happens, the CPT code should be reported instead of the HCPCS code. (See Appendix 5 in the HCPCS manual.)

However, when a CPT code description is not the same as HCPCS's, such as the code 99070 for supplies, then the medical coder should look for a more descriptive code in the HCPCS manual to describe which supply was used or given to the patient.

> *Tip*   *When using any supply codes from HCPCS, the medical coder must be aware that some of these supplies might be included with the service and should not be billed separately.*

Appendix 1: Table of Drugs

This appendix presents the instructions on how to use the table of drugs. This table is user-friendly. It is in alphabetical order, making the lookup very easy. It has the units and the routes of administration for the medications given to patients. The last column is the HCPCS code that should be used. The medical coder can find the medication by either the brand name or the generic name. This table is the best and the easiest way to find any of the medication codes, although the medical coder can also find the medication in the index at the beginning of the manual.

Appendix 2: Modifiers

The modifiers are found on each inside cover of the manual, but the complete modifier descriptions are found in Appendix 2.

> **EXAMPLE**
>
> The modifier FB on the cover states, "Item Provided without Cost," but in the appendix it states, "Item provided without cost to provider, supplier or practitioner, or credit received for replaced device (examples, but not limited to: covered under warranty, replaced due to defect, free samples)."

Appendix 3: Abbreviations and Acronyms

This appendix is a list of the abbreviations and acronyms used throughout the HCPCS manual.

Appendix 4: Pub100/NCD (National Coverage Determination) References

The Pub100/NCD References is the lookup section for the MED notation, which precedes an instruction pertaining to a code. These references are determinations by Medicare regarding rules and laws. Upon finding a footnote indicating that there is information or rules regarding this code, the medical coder should look in this index.

> **EXAMPLE**
>
> End Stage Renal Disease (ESRD) codes G0308–G0327. All of these have the footnote, "MED: 100-2, 11, 130.1." The footnote explains that the patient who has emergency inpatient dialysis services provided by a nonparticipating U.S. hospital is covered if requirement 130 is met. In this case, the professional medical coder need not be concerned about the footnote.
>
> However, code J1815, Injection insulin per 5 units, has the footnote, "MED: 100-2, 15, 50.5," which states that Medicare Part B does not pay for any self-administered drugs and biologicals. So, if the provider administers insulin to the patient in the medical office, Medicare Part B will not pay for the medication. It may pay for administration of the injection, but not for the medication itself.

Appendix 5: New, Changed, Deleted, and Reinstated Codes

As in the other two coding manuals, CPT and ICD-9, this appendix indicates which HCPCS codes are new, changed, or deleted. The reinstated codes are found only in HCPCS. Again, this appendix is not very user-friendly. It lists only the codes in their respective categories (i.e., new, changed, deleted, and reinstated) but does not give code descriptions.

Medical coders need to look up the codes to see if the codes affect their practice. In the table of new codes, the coder needs to look at each and every code every year to see if the HCPCS code might be used in their practice. The deleted codes must also be checked. Deleted codes found in the body of the manual indicate the replacement code to be used.

> ### EXAMPLE
> Code C9221 directs the medical coder to J7344.

Appendix 6: Place of Service and Type of Service Codes

This appendix has a list of both **place of service (POS)** and the **type of service (TOS)** codes with a full description for each. The medical coder must understand that many claims are rejected if the wrong POS or TOS codes are used.

With respect to POS and TOS coding, the medical coder must also understand how to use the HCPCS, the CPT, *and* the ICD-9 manuals. Without this knowledge, the medical coder can miss codes, and a very expensive medication may not be billed or reimbursed, resulting in a significant loss to the practice.

Appendix 7: National Average Payment

This appendix is a representation of the commercial and Medicare national average payment (NAP) for services, supplies, drugs, and nonphysician procedures reported using HCPCS **Level II Codes**. These averages are not meant to be used as actual reimbursement amounts. This data should be used only for benchmarking purposes.

CHAPTER EXERCISES

Scenario 3-1

OFFICE NOTE
A juvenile patient comes into the office today because he got his cast wet, and it has loosened around his leg. He is here today to get a new cast applied. **HX:** The patient fell off his skateboard two weeks ago and went to the ER where they applied the original short cast. Two days ago, he went to the park with his friends and he fell into the pool. He was afraid to tell his mom. She noticed today that the cast was still damp and looking loose. X-rays were taken in the office today, and the Fx is still not healed enough for a walking cast. **IMPRESSION AND PLAN:** Remove the old cast and reapply the short cast. **PROCEDURE:** Remove the old cast and reapply a short leg cast. **PLAN:** He is to return in three weeks for x-rays. The patient was advised how to take care of his cast.

HCPCS Code _____

Scenario 3-2

OFFICE NOTE
A 56-year-old woman is seen in consultation at the request of Dr. Smith. The patient has several complaints. First is that her right fourth and left third fingers have been

locking on her. I had seen her over a year ago for injection of the right fourth finger with excellent results. These have been bothering her for months. Her second complaint is that her right shoulder bothers her.

EXAMINATION: Vital signs per nursing note include BP 154/80. She is alert, in no distress. Skin shows no nodules or tophi. Cervical spine, left shoulder negative. Right shoulder has only about 60 degrees of motion in all directions with some tenderness over the subacromial bursa and some crepitus. Elbows, wrists, MCPs, PIPs, DIPs negative. The right fourth and left third flexor tendons are tender with some locking more on the left than tenderness, and some tenderness more than locking on the right. SCJs, costochondral junctions, thoracic spine, LS spine nontender. Some dorsal kyphosis. Hips, knees, ankles, and feet are okay. X-rays of the right shoulder were obtained today. There is evidence of the old fracture and some osteoarthritis of the glenohumeral joint.

ASSESSMENT:

1. Right shoulder pain. Probably both rotator cuff tendonitis and underlying osteoarthritis of the glenohumeral joint. After discussion, it was opted to treat her with local injections to see if that will give her some benefit. If not, we should not do this again.

2. Right fourth trigger finger.

3. Left third trigger finger. We will treat these with local injections.

PLAN: Right subacromial bursa and right shoulder anteriorly each injected with 0.75 ml of 1-percent lidocaine and 30 mg methylprednisolone acetate, and the right fourth and left third flexor tendon sheaths each with about 0.5 ml of 1-percent lidocaine and 20 mg methylprednisolone acetate, all after a sterile prep. The patient tolerated the procedures well.

HCPCS Code _____

Scenario 3-3

OFFICE NOTE

CC: Rheumatoid arthritis.

HX: A 35-year-old woman is here for a follow-up of her rheumatoid arthritis. Patient states that the pain is still bad enough to keep her up at night. She states that the medication has not worked at all. She is on Rituxan 100 mg infusion treatment. She is here for her second treatment.

HCPCS Code _____

Scenario 3-4

OFFICE NOTE

Vital signs prior to Boniva: 100/58, pulse 66, weight 148.

MEDICATIONS: Synthroid, MVI, calcium with vitamin D 500, Prilosec, OxyContin, Percocet.

continued

ALLERGIES: NKDA.

After sterile skin prep, a right antecubital vein was cannulated with a 23-gauge butterfly needle. The area flushed well with normal saline, then 3 mg of Boniva was injected over 2 minutes, then flushed with 4 cc of normal saline. The patient tolerated the procedure well without complications. Postinfusion vital signs: 110/58, pulse 60. Boniva lot #NH68493-01, expiration 11/2007. She will return in three weeks.

HCPCS Code _____

Scenario 3-5

OFFICE NOTE

CC: Pain when urinating.

HX: A 65-year-old woman, Medicare patient, has burning pain and urgency when she urinates. She also has itching and a white discharge in the vagina. She has been also running a 101°F temp for two days. She also states that she has been very worn out for the past week.

EXAM: A GYN exam was done, and a sample was taken and placed on a microscope slide. The vaginal walls were very red with a white to yellow discharge.

LABS: The urine dip showed blood and nitrates in the urine.

The slide shows classic Candida yeast.

ASSESSMENT: UTI and yeast infection.

PLAN: A single-dose treatment of vaginal suppositories and instruction were given to the patient and an antibiotic that should not affect the yeast infection.

HCPCS Code _____

Scenario 3-6

OFFICE NOTE

Nurse Visit

The only reason the patient is here today is for her flu shot. The patient was verbally told of the side effects and was told that if there was any temperature he should take an aspirin.

HCPCS Code _____

Scenario 3-7

OFFICE NOTE

Patient came into the office today after slamming her hand in the car door.

EXAMINATION: The hand is swollen and black and blue. No numbness or pins-and-needles. She was able to move all fingers with some pain, but not very much.

ASSESSMENT: X-ray showed no broken hand; therefore it is a very bad sprain.

PLAN: A hand splint will be applied.

HCPCS Code _____

Scenario 3-8

OFFICE NOTE

HISTORY: An 80-year-old female in good general health. She has a history of hypertension, coronary artery disease with occasional angina, adult-onset diabetes (diet controlled). Also has some irritable bowel syndrome with episodic diarrhea. She had a recent episode, which was sudden, where she turned around quickly, had sudden vertigo, fell to the floor, and hit her head, but did not lose consciousness.

Past medical history, allergies, social history, family history, and review of systems are reviewed with the patient and noted in the chart.

Current medications include atenolol 50, aspirin once per day, and nitroglycerin p.r.n.

EXAMINATION: Patient is alert, comfortable, no acute distress. Blood pressure 160/70. Pulse is 56. Skin is warm and dry. Pupils equal and reactive. Extraocular movements are full.

Neck is supple with no masses. Chest is clear. Heart has a regular rhythm with no murmur.

Breasts show no mass. Abdomen is soft and nontender. Extremities show no edema. Pelvic exam normal.

ASSESSMENT: Hypertension, history of angina and diabetes mellitus, and episodic vertigo.

PLAN: Will obtain CBC, CP7, glycohemoglobin, cholesterol, and electrocardiogram, and then follow up in six months. Patient will call sooner if vertigo returns.

HCPCS Code _____

Scenario 3-9

OPERATIVE REPORT

PREOPERATIVE DIAGNOSIS: Screening.

POSTOPERATIVE DIAGNOSIS: Negative screening colonoscopy.

INDICATIONS: This is a 66-year-old female scheduled for screening colonoscopy. The risk of bleeding, perforation, missing malignant lesions, any of which could necessitate surgery, were discussed. She understands the risks.

PROCEDURE: The patient was placed on the endoscopy table in the decubitus position. Digital exam was performed. The colonoscope was introduced under direct vision to the level of the cecum. The cecum was identified by anatomic

continued

landmarks and the presence of a light transilluminating low in the right groin. The scope was carefully withdrawn under direct vision. There is some liquid stool in the colon. However, the examination is fairly complete and reveals no evidence of tumors, polyps, or ulceration. She has a few scattered diverticula in the left colon.

IMPRESSION: Negative colonoscopy.

HCPCS Code _____

Scenario 3-10

OFFICE NOTE
Fred returns to the Plastic Surgery Clinic now approximately 6 weeks status post–Kenalog injection to his chest. He states that he was very happy with the result, because the firm, irritated nature of his keloid has subsided. It is now soft and less bothersome to him. He had no adverse reactions to the Kenalog. **PHYSICAL EXAMINATION:** His keloid is less irritated in appearance. It is moderately softer, but it is still very firm. No new areas have been identified. There is slight regression of the large keloid over the superior aspect. There is no hypopigmentation noted. **ASSESSMENT:** Doing well. Reinjection today sterilely with 1 cc of Kenalog. We will see him back in 6 to 8 weeks for results. He tolerated this today without incident.

HCPCS Code _____

CHAPTER REVIEW

Using the Healthcare Common Procedure Coding System (HCPCS) manual, complete the following exercises.

Define the following:

1. HCPCS modifiers _____
2. Federal Register _____
3. Skilled nursing facility (SNF) _____
4. Ambulatory surgical center (ASC) Groupings _____
5. **Advanced life support (ALS)** _____

Find the following HCPCS Level II codes and explain what coding rule or symbol would apply in selecting the code(s):

6. Patient, age 18, comes in for his third hemodialysis visit this month.
_____

7. Patient has a skin graft of dermal substitute tissue of human origin, 4 sq. cm.
_____

8. Patient, 6 years old, comes into the office for a replacement of a fiberglass long arm cast.

_____

9. A Medicare patient comes in for a hearing screening.

_____

10. A female Medicare patient comes into the office for a PE and Pap.

_____

Chapter 4
Coding with Modifiers and CCI Edits

KEY TERMS

bundled services
Centers of Medicare and Medicaid Services (CMS)
Correct Code Initiative edits (CCI edits)

CPT modifiers
global period
HCPCS modifiers

Office of Inspector General (OIG)
physical exam (PE)
third-party payer (TPP)

LEARNING OBJECTIVES

Upon completion of this chapter, the student will be able to:

1. Understand how and when to use modifiers
2. Utilize the CCI edits for correct coding

WHY USE MODIFIERS?

Modifiers are used for two primary reasons:

- To clarify the code that is submitted to the **third-party payers (TPPs)**. Modifiers give the TPP more information about the provider's encounter with the patient.
- To legally circumvent Medicare and other TPP **Correct Code Initiative edits (CCI edits)**. Modifiers are actually part of correct coding. Without modifiers, edits would stop the claim from being paid or result in incorrect reimbursement.

For the purpose of this book, we will use the most common modifiers in the manner in which CPT and HCPCS require their use.

CCI EDITS

Correct Code Initiative (CCI) edits were created by the **Centers for Medicare and Medicaid Services (CMS)** to enhance correct coding and correct payment. CCI edits are used not only by Medicare, but also by many TPPs to ensure correct coding. The edits are in place to prevent payment for any procedures that could be "bundled" into another procedure. They prevent overpayments for procedures that are already being paid within the reimbursement for another procedure done at the same time (**bundled services**).

Note
For more information on the National Correct Coding Initiative Edits, see http://www.cms.hhs.gov/ NationalCorrectCodInitEd/.

EXAMPLE

Bundled Service

69400 Eustachian tube catheterization, transtympanic

With this service the provider needs to do a myringotomy, including aspiration. So the medical coder would not also report 69420 (myringotomy including aspiration). In Table 4-1, locate the two codes: 69400 and 69420. Check to see if a modifier can be used: 0 = Modifier can never be used; 1 = A modifier can be used. The codes have a 1, which indicates that a modifier can be used. If the services were performed on different ears, the medical coder

TABLE 4-1   **CCI Edit Table 69420**

		Column1/Column 2 Edits			
Column 1	**Column 2**	**** = In Existence Prior to 1996***	**Effective Date**	**Deletion Date** **** = no data***	**Modifier** **0 = not allowed** **1 = allowed** **9 = not applicable**
69420	36000		20021001	*	1
69420	36410		20021001	*	1
69420	37202		20021001	*	1
69420	62318		20021001	*	1
69420	62319		20021001	*	1
69420	64415		20021001	*	1
69420	64416		20030101	*	1
69420	64417		20021001	*	1
69420	64450		20021001	*	1
69420	64470		20021001	*	1
69420	64475		20021001	*	1
69420	69210		20020701	*	1
69420	69400		19960101	*	1
69420	69401		19960101	*	1
69420	69405		19960101	*	1
69420	69424		20030101	*	0

TABLE 4-1   CCI Edit Table 69420 (Continued)

Column1/Column 2 Edits

Column 1	Column 2	*= In Existence Prior to 1996	Effective Date	Deletion Date *= no data	Modifier 0 = not allowed 1 = allowed 9 = not applicable
69420	69540		19960101	*	1
69420	69990		20000605	*	0
69420	90760		20060101	*	1
69420	90765		20060101	*	1
69420	90772		20060101	*	1
69420	90774		20060101	*	1
69420	90775		20060101	*	1
69420	90780		20021001	20041231	1
69420	C8950		20060101	*	1
69420	C8952		20060101	*	1
69420	G0268		20030101	*	0
69420	G0345		20050101	20051231	1

Important Note: The National Correct Coding Initiative Version 12.1 (effective April 1, 2006-June 30, 2006) originally posted on April 1, 2006 was replaced with a corrected version on April 20, 2006. The original version did not include all applicable edits for physicians and hospitals. At a minimum, we noted that some Category III (T codes) were not included. These T codes are now included in the corrected version. CMS apologizes for this error, and any inconvenience this may have caused. If you obtain your NCCI edits from the National Technical Information Service (NTIS), the original Version 12.1 distributed for April 1, 2006 is CORRECT. This web page is aimed at providing information to providers on Medicare's National CCI edits, but will not address specific CCI edits. If you have concerns regarding specific CCI edits, please submit your comments in writing to:

National Correct Coding Initiative
Correct Coding Solutions LLC
P.O. Box 907
Carmel, IN 46082-0907

would indicate this by using a modifier, in this case the modifiers LT and RT: 69400-RT and 69420-LT.

Modifiers thus help coders explain why they used both codes and why the claim for both services should be paid. Modifiers allow medical coders to give more information to explain why the service should be paid without a written description, just by adding digits, letters, or a digit-letter combination.

There are modifiers in both CPT and HCPCS. **CPT modifiers** are two numbers, and HCPCS consists of two letters or one letter and one number. The coder may use both the CPT and HCPCS systems when modifying a procedure code.

Code Ranges for CCI Edits

The code ranges for CCI edits are as follows:

Category III Codes	0001T–9999T
Surgery: Integumentary System	10000–19999
Surgery: Musculoskeletal System	20000–29999
Surgery: Respiratory, Cardiovascular, Hemic and Lymphatic Systems	30000–39999
Surgery: Digestive System	40000–49999
Surgery: Urinary, Male Genital, Female Genital, Maternity Care and Delivery Systems	50000–59999
Surgery: Endocrine, Nervous, Eye and Ocular Adnexa, Auditory Systems	60000–69999
Radiology Services	70000–79999
Pathology and Laboratory Services	80000–89999
Medicine Evaluation and Management Services	90000–99999
Supplemental Services	A0000–V9999

The most commonly used modifiers are found on the inside cover of the *CPT* manual. Table 4-2 is a table of modifiers indicating where they should or should not be used. Keep in mind that payer rules should always be followed when using modifiers. The use of modifiers is not consistent from one payer to another.

TABLE 4-2 Modifiers and Their Uses

Modifier	E&M Service	Medicine	Surgery	Radiology	Pathology and Laboratory
21 Prolonged E/M	Yes	No	No	No	No
22 Unusual Service	No	Yes	Yes	Yes	Yes
24 Unrelated E&M during the Global period	Yes	No	No	No	No
25 Separate and Identifiable E&M on the Same Day of a Procedure or Another Service	Yes	No	No	No	No
26 Professional Component	No	Yes	No	Yes	Yes
32 Mandated Service	Yes	Yes	Yes	Yes	Yes
47 Anesthesia by Surgeon	No	No	Yes	No	No
50 Bilateral Procedure	No	Yes	Yes	Yes	No

TABLE 4-2   Modifiers and Their Uses (Continued)

Modifier	E&M Service	Medicine	Surgery	Radiology	Pathology and Laboratory
51 Multiple Procedure	No	Yes	Yes	Yes	No
52 Reduced Service	Yes[1]	Yes	Yes	Yes	Yes
53 Discontinued Service	No	Yes	Yes	Yes	Yes
54 Surgical Care Only	No	No	Yes	No	No
55 Post-Operative Care Only	No	Yes	Yes	No	No
56 Pre-Operative Care Only	No	Yes[2]	Yes	No	No
57 Decision for Surgery	Yes	Yes[3]	No	No	No
58 Staged Procedure	No	Yes	Yes	Yes	No
59 Distinct Procedural Service	No	Yes	Yes	Yes	Yes
62 Two Surgeons	No	No	Yes	No	No
63 Procedure Performed on Infants Less than 4 kg	No	No	Yes	No	No
66 Surgical Team	No	No	Yes	No	No
76 Repeat Procedure by the same Physician	No	Yes	Yes	Yes	No
77 Repeat Procedure by another Physician	No	Yes	Yes	Yes	No
78 Return to the Operating Room for a related Procedure during the Po-Op Period	No	Yes	Yes	No	No
79 Unrelated Service by the Same Physician during the Po-Op Period	No	Yes	Yes	No	No
80 Assistant Surgeon	No	No	Yes	No	No
81 Minimum Assistant	No	No	Yes	No	No
82 Assistant Surgeon when Qualified Resident Surgeon is not Available	No	No	Yes	No	No

[1] Except Medicare.
[2] Rarely used and only with procedures that have global periods.
[3] Only on ophthalmologic services in this section.

Modifiers 25 and 57

Modifiers 25 and 57 are two common modifiers used with E&M codes. What is the difference between them? How are they used?

- *Modifier 25 Significant Evaluation and Management Service by the Same Physician on the Same Date of a Procedure:* CPT modifier 25 is used when a procedure or another service is performed on the same day as a visit and when each service is significantly and separately identifiable from the others. This is used only when the patient has come in for a scheduled visit and the provider then decides to perform a procedure while the patient is there rather than on a later date.

- *Modifier 57 Decision for Surgery:* This modifier is used for an evaluation and management service on the day of or on the day before a procedure with a global surgical period. CPT modifier 57 indicates that the service resulted in the decision to perform the procedure. Per Medicare, CPT modifier 57 may not be used on the day of or the day before a procedure with a 0- or 10-day global surgical period.

Why would the medical coder use these modifiers? These modifiers provide information to the payer for consideration of payment not only for the visit, but also for the procedure performed.

Both modifiers are being reviewed for correct use by the Office of the Inspector General. With regard to modifier 25, office notes are being checked to see if, in fact, the provider documented both the E&M service and the procedure and that the documentation for both services supports each separately. In addition, Medicare is auditing the use of modifier 57 to see if the service was performed within 24 hours before surgery. If it was performed 36 to 48 hours prior to the surgery, then the E&M service is considered part of the global service. What Medicare wants to see is that the decision for surgery was an immediate one and that the visit was not related to a planned surgery.

Find the Code 4-1

HISTORY AND PHYSICAL

An established patient of 45 comes into the office for a PE and states that he also has a sore throat. The provider will do the routine PE and also take a history, perform an exam, and make a medical decision on the sore throat.

CC: PE Exam.

HPI: This 45-year-old is here today for his yearly PE.

ROS: For his PE: As noted on the patient questionnaire, the patient does not have any health issues. He works out at the gym 4 times a week and he runs the other 3 days. His weight is great for his height.

The patient states that the sore throat started a couple of days ago and he has had a low fever of 101°F for the last 3 days. He also states it has been hard eating anything other than hot soups.

EXAM:

General: The patient looks well nourished and healthy, other than the sore throat.

Vital Signs: BP 120/80, temp 101°F.

HEENT: See below.

Neck: Swollen glands.

Chest: Clear.

Heart: Normal, no murmurs.

Abdomen: Soft without any masses.

Extremities: Normal pulses, color, and muscle tone.

Neurologic: Normal and within limits.

ASSESSMENT: Healthy 45-year-old except for the sore throat.

CC: Sore throat.

HEENT: Eyes and ears are clear. Throat is red with white spots.

Neck: Swollen glands. Ears are clear with no pain. A strep test was taken and came back positive.

ASSESSMENT: Strep throat.

An Rx for an antibiotic and instructions were given to the patient. If the sore throat persists for more than 5 days, he is to call me.

How would you explain the two significant, separately identifiable examinations on this patient? _____

Would you use two E&M codes for this? _____

From which E&M section would you choose the code(s)? _____

Why? _____

What diagnosis code(s) would be reported? _____

In this case, the medical coder would use modifier 25, which indicates that the provider did a PE and a sick visit and should be paid for both services. All of the office notes must support the use of this modifier, as stated by Medicare. The sections of CPT for the two significant, separately identifiable exams come from the established patient office or other outpatient service (range 99211–99215) for the sore throat and the preventive medicine service (99396, 40–64 years) for the **physical exam**. Given modifier 25, the TPP knows that two services were performed on the same day and that therefore both services should be paid.

The only diagnosis would be 034.0.

▬ *Find the Code 4-2*

Consult performed by a surgeon on a 10-year-old who presented to the Emergency Department (ED) complaining of pain in the right lower abdomen. Appendicitis is diagnosed and the surgeon immediately performs an appendectomy.

How would you indicate this was not a planned surgery? _____

What are the two services? _____

In what section would you find these services? _____

Would another modifier be used? _____

What is the diagnosis code? _____

In this case, modifier 57 (Decision for Surgery) would be used to indicate that the decision for surgery was made within a 24-hour period prior to its performance. This was not a consultation regarding a planned surgery and should not be considered part of the **global period**.

Find the Code 4-3

HISTORY AND PHYSICAL

First Visit

CC: Patient is complaining of a few "funny-looking" moles on his face, neck, and arm.

HPI: Patient states that he has had the moles most of his life but they have been growing and turning darker, and some bleed. The one on his face frequently bleeds. He states that he does use tanning booths and has gotten sunburned on a few occasions.

EXAM: On exam, I found that the patient has 3 irregularly shaped moles: one on his neck, one on his arm, and one on his face. The one on his face is about 2 cm in length, with irregular shape, and turning black with red at the edges. The one on his neck is also 2 cm and does not have the red on the edges but is also irregular in shape. The one on his arm is the largest, being 4 cm, with irregular shape.

IMPRESSION: These all appear to be melanoma.

PLAN: Due to the size of lesions, I will have the patient come back next week for removal and biopsy.

Second Visit One Week Later

CC: Patient comes back to the office to have 3 moles removed and biopsied.

HPI: Lesions of irregular shape and some are bleeding; appear to be melanoma.

PROCEDURE: The patient was prepped for the procedure to remove 3 lesions. The one on his face and the other on his neck both about 2 cm in length plus a 2 cm margin were removed, and both placed in fixation for Bx in separate containers labeled for face and neck. The one on his arm, being 4 cm plus a 3 cm margin, was removed and placed in fixation and labeled. The patient was told how to care for the wounds and will be returning to the office for the results of the Bx in about a week.

Would the medical coder use either modifier 25 or 57? _____
Why? _____

Would the medical coder use either the modifier 25 or 57? No. Why? Because the evaluation of the lesions was done on different days and one week apart, so neither modifier would be appropriate.

Modifier 50, 51, and 59

These modifiers are often confused and misused by medical coders and providers.

Modifier 50: Bilateral Procedure

Modifier 50 indicates that a procedure was performed bilaterally, that is, the same procedure was performed twice during the same operative session (i.e., both breasts, ears, arms). The payment is 100% of the allowable for the first procedure and 50% for the second, or 150% for both.

Some payers require coding for the bilateral procedure on two lines, with modifier 50 reported on the second line. Medicare and other payers require the procedure to be listed on only one line, with modifier 50 to indicate it was performed bilaterally. Exercise caution when using this modifier because it cannot be appended to a procedure when the description indicates that the procedure is a bilateral procedure.

> ## EXAMPLE
> Look at CPT code 58600 Ligation or transection of fallopian tube(s), abdominal or vaginal approach, unilateral or bilateral. Modifier 50 could not be used with this code because the description indicates it could be done either unilaterally or bilaterally.

Modifier 51: Multiple Procedures

The Centers for Medicare and Medicaid Services designates which procedure codes are valid for use with modifier 51. Use this modifier when multiple procedures other than E&M services are performed on the same day or during the same session by the same provider. When billing multiple surgeries, the primary procedure (the procedure with the highest relative unit value) should be the first code listed on the claim.

Tip *Do not apply modifier 51 to add-on codes.*

The first eligible procedure is reimbursed at 100% of the allowable, and the remaining procedures are reimbursed at 50%. Up to five procedures can be billed using this modifier.

> ## EXAMPLE
> Patient has a Bx of the liver (47100) and a choledochotomy with removal of calculus (47420).
> You need to check the CCI edits: If there are no edits on these two codes, then you can use a modifier 51. In this case, there are no CCI edits for these two codes. The modifier 51 indicates to the TPP that two procedures were performed.

Note
Medicare and some other payers do not require this modifier. Because of the CCI edits, it's not really necessary to use it any more. Some payers still require modifier 51; so adding it will not prevent payment from Medicare.

The TPP will pay 100% of the allowable of the higher of the two procedures or the first procedure listed (depending on the TPP policy), and it will pay the second at 50%. The 50% reduction is based on the TPP assumption that, when the second procedure is performed, the preparations for the second procedure were the same as the first; therefore the TPP will not pay for a second preparation.

The medical coder must also check to see if one of the two codes is:

• Either an add-on (a code that has a **+** before it in the CPT manual)
• Or a modifier 51 exemption code (which has a **Ø** symbol before the code).

Another place to find the add-on codes and modifier 51 exemption codes is Appendices D and E, respectively.

Modifier 59: Distinct Procedural Service

This modifier is used to clearly designate when distinct, independent, and separate multiple procedures are provided. The procedure must not be a component of another procedure.

EXAMPLE

Use Modifier 59 for:

Different procedures or surgeries

Surgery on different sites or organ systems

Separate incisions or excisions

Separate lesions

Treatment to separate injuries

Documentation may be required to support the use of modifier 59.

How does a medical coder know which modifier to use, 51 or 59? Both can be used for multiple services. New medical coders, as well as some seasoned ones, have problems with these two modifiers. Here are a couple of rules of thumb:

- Never use modifier 59 if another qualifying modifier can be used.
- You may use modifier 51 if there are no CCI edits. If there are, then you must first find another modifier.

EXAMPLE

Patient goes to a podiatrist for debridement of an ulcer on the great toe of the left foot and an incision and drainage (I&D) of an abscess of the right heel.

   Usually, when an I&D is performed, the provider cleans the wound (debridement). So the question is, how does the medical coder distinguish between the two separate procedures? The mistake most providers, as well as coders, make is to add modifier 59. In this case, the great toe procedure is coded as 11004-TA, and the right heel procedure is 10060-RT.

Modifier 59 is also under close scrutiny by Medicare for its correct use; so medical coders must be very careful when using it. What constitutes incorrect use of this modifier?

EXAMPLE

A patient comes into the ENT office, where the provider cleans out the patient's right ear (69210 Removal of cerumen) and then makes an incision into the tympanic membrane of the same ear (69420 Incision into the tympanic membrane).

This is a bundled service if these two procedures are done on the same ear. You cannot make an incision in the tympanic membrane if the ear canal is not clear; therefore, the removal of cerumen is part of the incision in the tympanic membrane. So using modifier 59 on either of these codes is incorrect coding.

Would you use the modifier 59 if the removal of cerumen (69210) was done on the right ear and the incision into the tympanic membrane (69420) was performed on the left ear? The answer is no; the correct coding would be 69420-LT, 69210-RT. Remember: If any other modifier can be used, modifier 59 should not be used.

What is the correct way to use this modifier?

EXAMPLE

The patient has two lesions on the same hand. One of the lesions was a biopsy only (11100), and the other lesion was removed. In this instance, the medical coder can append modifier 59 to the code.

▬ *Find the Code 4-4*

HISTORY AND PHYSICAL

Look again at the second visit for the removal of the three lesions in Find the Code 4-3.

CC: Patient comes back to the office to have 3 moles removed and biopsied.

HPI: Lesion of irregular shape and some are bleeding; melanoma lesion.

Procedure: The patient was prepped for the procedure to remove 3 lesions. The one on his face and on his neck are both about 2 cm in length plus a 2 cm margin were removed and both placed in fixation for Bx in separate containers labeled for face and neck. The one on his arm, being 4 cm plus a 3 cm margin, was removed and placed in fixation and labeled. The patient was told how to care for the wounds and will be retuning to the office for the results of the Bx in about a week.

Code these lesions. _____

Would you use a modifier? _____

Which one(s)? _____

Code these lesions. 11606, 12032 for the arm, 11644, 12052 for the face, and for the neck 11624, 12042. Would you use a modifier? Yes. Which one(s)? 59. Separate lesions should be paid at 100% of the allowable. If the medical coder uses 51, then the TPP will pay for removal of the second and third lesions at 50%. Modifier 59 is the appropriate modifier in this circumstance.

Postoperative Modifiers 24, 54, 55, 58, 78, and 79

Modifier 24

Modifier 24 reports an unrelated evaluation and management service by the same physician during a postoperative period. Services submitted with modifier 24 must be sufficiently documented to establish that the visit was unrelated to the surgery.

Modifier 24 is used for any E&M service that is provided to a patient during a postop global period. This modifier tells the TPP that the service is not part of the surgery that was performed during the 10- or 90-day global period.

Modifier 54

Modifier 54 is used by the surgeon who provides surgical care only, and it should be billed with the following information:

- Date of the surgical procedure
- Surgical procedure code
- Modifier 54

Modifier 55

Modifier 55 indicates that the services are for postoperative management only. Typically, this modifier is used to indicate that a transfer of postoperative care has occurred. The provider receiving the patient for postoperative care should include the following information on the claim:

- Date of the surgical procedure
- Surgical procedure code (same as surgeon)
- Modifier 55
- If only a portion of postoperative care is provided, you must indicate in Item 19 of the CMS-1500 claim form, or its electronic media equivalent, the date on which postoperative care was assumed in a MM/DD/YYYY format.

> **EXAMPLE**
>
> Assumed—10212006

Here are some things to remember about this modifier:

- Modifier 55 cannot be used unless the provider who performs the surgery uses modifier 54 and notes a formal transfer of care in the medical records.
- Many providers and medical coders use this modifier incorrectly with an E&M code.
- If the physician performing the surgery reports the procedure without any modifiers, the full reimbursement is made to that provider. Coordination between the physicians is necessary in order for them to be paid appropriately based on the part of the service they performed. Both providers must bill the same procedure code and append the modifier that describes the component of the service they provided.

Modifier 58

Modifier 58 can be used when a second surgery is performed in the postoperative period of prior surgery and when the second procedure is:

- Planned or "staged" at the time of the original procedure
- More extensive than the original procedure
- For therapy following a diagnostic surgical procedure
- Or for the reapplication of a cast within the 90-day global period

How is modifier 58 correctly used?

> **EXAMPLE**
>
> A patient had the removal of a breast lesion (CPT 19120) on one date, and the biopsy determines the lesion was positive for carcinoma of the breast. If the breast is removed within the 90-day global period, CPT 19303 is reported with modifier 58 appended. Another postoperative period begins when the second procedure is performed.

Modifier 78

Modifier 78 is used for a return trip to the operating room for a related surgical procedure during the postoperative period of a previous major surgery. The reimbursement is reduced because preoperative and postoperative care is included in the allowance for the prior surgical procedure.

CPT indicates that the term "operating room" is defined as a place of service specifically equipped and staffed for the sole purpose of performing surgical procedures. Therefore, a cardiac catheterization suite, a laser suite, and an endoscopy suite are all "operating rooms." The patient's room, a minor treatment room, a recovery room, or an intensive care unit do not qualify unless the patient's condition is so critical there is insufficient time for transportation to an operating room.

Modifier 79

This modifier is used for unrelated procedures by the same provider or by a provider of the same specialty in the same surgical group during the post-operative period. Unrelated procedures are usually reported using a different CPT code and a different ICD-9-CM diagnosis code.

Another postoperative period begins when the second procedure is billed.

Repeat Procedure Modifiers 76 and 77

Modifier 76

At times a provider needs to repeat a diagnostic exam or procedure for one reason or another. In these instances, modifier 76 can be used to indicate that the procedure or service was repeated after the original was performed.

Modifier 77

This modifier is used when a different physician performs the same procedure or service previously performed by another provider.

Modifier 22

This modifier is used when, due to unusual circumstance related to the patient's condition, the procedure takes longer or more services are provided than is usual for the procedure. Use of this modifier requires a special report explaining the circumstances.

The rules for modifier 22 differ from payer to payer. Most payers require documentation before they pay the claim. Most payers want to see why the procedure was longer than or different from what is normal.

HCPCS MODIFIERS

Medical coders need to know the proper use of **HCPCS modifiers** in their area of the country because their use differs from payer to payer. You have to follow rules and documentation guidelines to use these modifiers appropriately.

To access the CCI edits:

• Go to http://www.cms.hhs.gov.
• Select Browse by Provider Type.
• Scroll down to Billing/Payment links, National Correct Coding Initiative.
• At this screen select NCCI Edits—Physician.

CHAPTER EXERCISES

Scenario 4-1

OPERATIVE REPORT

PREOPERATIVE DIAGNOSIS: Right groin abscess and muscle weakness.

POSTOPERATIVE DIAGNOSIS: Right groin abscess and muscle weakness.

OPERATION: Incision and drainage of deep right groin abscesses, biopsy of muscle.

ANESTHESIA: Local with sedation.

INDICATIONS FOR SURGERY: The patient is a 16-year-old male who presents with recurrent fevers, which failed to respond to IV antibiotics. The patient was found to have abnormalities in his right groin as well as in the left hamstring area. Given these two findings, a concern about polymyositis was raised versus a subcutaneous abscess. The patient presents for exploration of the right groin.

PROCEDURE: Using 1% Xylocaine under sterile conditions, a 5-cm skin incision was made. Dissection was carried down through the subcutaneous tissues using sharp dissection. Upon entering the pocket, there was some cloudy fluid, and this was aspirated and sent for culture. The abscess was followed deeply into the muscle compartments with drainage of again more cloudy fluid. After this was performed, a standard muscle biopsy was performed of the quadriceps muscle. This was performed by placing the muscle clip and removing a segment of muscle. An additional segment of muscle was removed. The wound was packed open. The patient tolerated the procedure well.

Code(s): _____

Modifier: _____

Diagnosis Code(s): _____

Scenario 4-2

OPERATIVE REPORT

DESCRIPTION OF PROCEDURE: Interrogation of the pacemaker, which was done emergently 1 month ago in operating room #8. She has a Guidant device. Apparently, the pacemaker was not pacing. We went to the operating room with the pacemaker team to interrogate the pacemaker. She had a threshold of 5 V at 1.1 ms, but as a result, we increased the voltage to 7 V and kept her at 1 ms. Etiology of this quick rise in the threshold is not clear. Many potential possibilities such as myocardial infarction could do it. Electrolyte abnormality, medications, anesthetics, cautery are also potential causes.

The patient was reprogrammed and doing well in VVI mode. She is actually in DDDR mode, but it is the switch mode, which converts up to VVI because of the mode switch. She has underlying atrial fibrillation. So the DDDR can switch itself to VVI mode when atrial fibrillation occurs. The battery status is good. Estimated life span of the battery is probably less than 6 months. I would suggest at some point checking a chest x-ray, electrolytes, CPK, and the troponin levels. Pacemaker is functioning well at this time with a high output. I spoke with the daughter. In the next few months, she will have to have this reinterrogated and possibly have the ventricular lead and pacemaker generator replaced, if needed, that is, if the threshold continues to be high, because the life span of the battery will be shortened by high output.

Code(s): _____

Modifier: _____

Diagnosis Code(s): _____

Scenario 4-3

OPERATIVE NOTE

PREOPERATIVE DIAGNOSIS: Adenoid hypertrophy and bilateral middle ear effusions.

POSTOPERATIVE DIAGNOSIS: Adenoid hypertrophy, no middle ear fluid found.

PROCEDURE PERFORMED: Adenoidectomy and bilateral myringotomy without ventilation tube placement.

ANESTHESIA: General.

COMPLICATIONS: None.

ESTIMATED BLOOD LOSS: Less than 10 cc.

PROCEDURE: The 10-year-old patient was brought to the operating room and placed uneventfully under general endotracheal anesthesia. The operating microscope was brought into the field and attention was directed to the right ear. A speculum was placed in the ear canal and cerumen was cleaned with a curette. A radial myringotomy was made in the anterior-inferior quadrant with the myringotomy knife. No middle ear effusion was found. There was mild erythema of the middle ear membranes, and no tube placement was deemed necessary.

continued

Attention was then directed to the left ear. A speculum was placed and cerumen was cleaned. Radial myringotomy was made in the anterior-inferior quadrant of the tympanic membrane. No middle ear fluid accumulation was found. Mild inflammation of the middle ear membrane was noted. No tube placement was deemed necessary.

The bed was then turned 90° from the anesthetist in preparation for adenoidectomy. The Davis mouth gag was introduced into the oral cavity and was suspended over towel rolls. Palpation and inspection of the palate revealed no evidence of a submucous cleft. The soft palate was retracted with a Robinson catheter. Tonsils were 2+ hypertrophic. Adenoids were also hypertrophic. Adenoid curette was used to perform adenoidectomy, and then hemostatic packs were placed. The suction electrocautery was used to complete the hemostasis in the nasopharynx. The wounds were irrigated with saline and reinspected to assure that hemostasis was complete.

After removal of the instrumentation, the patient was awakened, extubated, and transported in satisfactory condition to the recovery area.

Code(s): _____

Modifier: _____

Diagnosis Code(s): _____

Scenario 4-4

OPERATIVE REPORT

PREOPERATIVE DIAGNOSIS: Left leg varicose veins.

POSTOPERATIVE DIAGNOSIS: Left leg varicose veins with left saphenous vein phlebitis and inflammation.

PROCEDURE: Left leg saphenous vein phlebitic femoral vein excision and open excision of varicose veins and TriVex transilluminator pulse phlebectomies and excision of varicose veins: 13 incisions total.

ANESTHESIA: General anesthesia.

BLOOD LOSS: Minimal.

REPLACEMENT: Crystalloid.

SPONGE COUNT: Checked and verified.

COMPLICATIONS: None.

BRIEF HISTORY: This is a 60-year-old patient with severe painful left leg varicose veins. The plan was left varicose vein excision. The patient understands the risks and benefits of the procedure, including risk of bleeding, infection, hematoma formation, possible compartment syndrome, possible DVT, possible phlebitis, possible thromboembolism, possible respiratory complications, and he consented to the operation.

DESCRIPTION OF PROCEDURE: The patient was wheeled into the operating room and placed in the supine position. After adequate general anesthesia was achieved by the anesthesiologist, the left lower extremity was prepped and draped in the usual sterile fashion. The veins had been previously marked while the patient was standing. Multiple incisions were made, a total of 13, along the course of the saphenous vein, which was relatively severely sclerotic and thrombosed. These incisions were made in a transverse technique and transected. The whole saphenous vein, from the saphenofemoral junction all the way down to the level of the ankle, was removed. All the sclerotic veins were removed, and the saphenous vein and saphenofemoral junction was oversewn with silk tie. Then incisions were made overlying the varicosities, and the varicosities were taken down between clamps, transected, and removed and ligated. Then using a transillumination device, we proceeded to perform primary tumescence of the varicosities in the anterior and lateral leg area and the medial leg area. Then using the large resector, we proceeded to resect all those varicosities and performed serial vein tumescence and placed an Ace bandage for hemostasis. After getting good hemostasis, we performed some more tumescence and made sure we did not have any further bleeding. Closure was subcutaneous with Vicryl sutures. The skin was closed with Vicryl sutures, and we placed some nylon sutures in the distal ankle for hemostasis. Then Ace bandages were applied.

The patient tolerated the procedure well and left the operating room in stable condition.

Code(s): _____

Modifier: _____

Diagnosis Code(s): _____

Scenario 4-5

OPERATIVE REPORT

PREOPERATIVE DIAGNOSIS: Basal cell carcinoma, left neck.

POSTOPERATIVE DIAGNOSIS: Basal cell carcinoma, left neck.

PROCEDURE: Excision of basal cell carcinoma, left neck with layered closure.

ANESTHESIA: Local.

FINDINGS: Basal cell carcinoma of left neck with negative margins.

COMPLICATIONS: None.

DISPOSITION: Stable to home.

TECHNIQUE: The patient was brought to the operating room and placed supine on the operating room table. A time-out was performed. The patient had marked the lesion preoperatively. The nose was inspected. I could not find the site from where a biopsy had been done. There was no definite lesion. I explained to her that I would continue to watch this area and we would excise it if something showed up; however, I was not certain where exactly to excise.

Subsequently, the left neck was infiltrated with 1% lidocaine with 1:100,000 epinephrine. The area was prepped and draped in the usual fashion. A fusiform excision was designed along relaxed skin tension lines. The lesion was sharply excised using a scalpel and tenotomy scissors through the full thickness of the skin into the subcutaneous tissue. This was marked at 12 o'clock and sent for frozen section. The frozen section measuring 1.6 cm showed basal cell

continued

carcinoma with negative margins. Wound edges were undermined. Hemostasis was obtained with a bipolar electrocautery. Layered closure of tissue was performed, and wound edges were approximated first with an interrupted 4-0 Vicryl in an inverted fashion. The skin was closed with a running 5-0 fast absorbing gut. The patient tolerated the procedure without any difficulty. She will follow up next week with my nurse for a wound check. I will see her back in 3 months.

At that time, I will reexamine the nasal area as well.

Code(s): _____

Modifier: _____

Diagnosis Code(s): _____

Scenario 4-6

OPERATIVE REPORT

PROCEDURE: Upper endoscopy with biopsy.

PREOPERATIVE DIAGNOSIS: The patient is an 18-year-old woman here for an upper endoscopy for evaluation of nausea and vomiting.

POSTOPERATIVE DIAGNOSIS:

1. Nausea and vomiting.

2. Nonerosive gastritis.

3. Antral biopsy obtained to rule out *Helicobacter pylori* infection.

MEDICATIONS: Versed 2 mg IV, fentanyl 50 mg IV.

PROCEDURE: After the risks, benefits, and alternatives of the procedure were fully explained, informed consent was obtained. The endoscope was introduced into the mouth and past the cervical esophagus under direct visualization. The endoscope was advanced down the esophagus to the gastroesophageal junction. The esophageal mucosa and the gastroesophageal junction appeared normal. The endoscope was advanced into the gastric cardia, fundus, body, and antrum, and retroflexion was performed in the stomach. There is nonerosive gastritis in the gastric antrum. Biopsy was obtained from the antrum and sent to pathology to rule out *Helicobacter pylori* infection. The endoscope was then advanced through the pylorus into the duodenal bulb and descending duodenum, both of which appeared normal. The endoscope was then withdrawn from the patient. The patient tolerated the procedure well, and there were no complications.

RECOMMENDATIONS: If the patient has evidence of *Helicobacter pylori* infection, she may benefit from antibiotic treatment to eradicate the infection since she has chronic nausea and vomiting. If the patient's nausea and vomiting persist despite treatment with PPI medications, a small bowel follow-through series or a gastric emptying study may be considered.

Code(s): _____

Modifier: _____

Diagnosis Code(s): _____

Scenario 4-7

OPERATIVE REPORT

PREOPERATIVE DIAGNOSIS: Right carpal tunnel syndrome.

POSTOPERATIVE DIAGNOSIS: Right carpal tunnel syndrome.

NAME OF PROCEDURE: Right carpal tunnel release.

ANESTHESIA: Bier block.

INDICATIONS: This patient presented with signs and symptoms of right carpal tunnel syndrome, which had been inadequately relieved by nonoperative measures. He is brought to the operating room at this time with his informed consent for right carpal tunnel release.

DESCRIPTION OF PROCEDURE: The patient is placed in a supine position, and after adequate anesthesia had been obtained by means of a Bier block with a well padded antebrachial tourniquet, he is prepared and draped in the usual sterile fashion. The procedure is carried out under 3.8× loupe magnification. Hemostasis is maintained with bipolar cautery. A proposed incision line is marked in the proximal palm in the axis of a ring finger ray over a 2-cm distance. The incision is now made and carried sharply through the skin and into the subcutaneous tissues. The patient complained of pain, and the area was supplemented with 0.5% Marcaine. This, of course, obscured visualization, and the incision is extended proximally in an oblique and ulnarly directed fashion up to the distal wrist crease. Dissection is now taken bluntly through the subcutaneous tissue, past the palmar fascia, and down onto the transverse carpal ligament. The transverse carpal ligament is now incised in its entirety under direct vision along its ulnar border. Its proximal and distal margins are incised with the assistance of retractors for visualization. There is now easy admission of the surgeon's small fingertip proximal and distal to the carpal tunnel. No other abnormalities are noted within the carpal tunnel. The skin is now closed with interrupted 4-0 nylon sutures. The skin margins and subcutaneous tissue are infiltrated with 0.5% Marcaine. A sterile, bulky, nonadherent dressing is placed over the wound and secured in place. The tourniquet is released with immediate return of blood flow to the fingertips. The hand is held elevated with gentle compression over the wound after the release of the tourniquet and maintained elevated thereafter. Counts are correct. The blood loss is negligible. The patient tolerated the procedure well and left the operating room in stable condition.

Code(s): _____

Modifier: _____

Diagnosis Code(s): _____

CHAPTER REVIEW

Using the Current Procedural Terminology (CPT) and Healthcare Common Procedure Coding System (HCPCS) manuals and this text book, complete the following exercises:

Define the following:

1. CCI edits _____

2. Global period _____

3. Office of Inspector General _____

4. Bundled services _____

5. HCPCS modifiers _____

For the remaining exercises, indicate the modifier to be used, if any, and the reason for your choice.

6. Application of a short leg cast for a right ankle Fx: _____

7. RT mastectomy two days after a lumpectomy: _____

8. Patient comes into the office and a level 4 office visit is performed. During this visit, a decision for surgery is made to perform a surgery the next day within the 90-day global period. _____

9. A patient comes into the office for removal of a wart. A quick evaluation was done just prior to the procedure to assess if any changes to the wart have occurred. _____

10. The provider performs two procedures. How does the medical coder determine whether the procedures are bundled? _____

Chapter 5
Abstracting from Medical Documentation

abstracting
assessment and plan
chief complaint (CC)
head, eyes, ear, neck, and throat
   (HEENT)

history of present illness (HPI)
medical necessity
operative notes (Op Notes)
personal, family, and social history
   (PFSH)

range of motion (ROM)
review of systems (ROS)
signs and symptoms

LEARNING OBJECTIVES

Upon completion of this chapter, the student will be able to:

1. Abstract the right diagnoses and procedures from medical notes

2. Correctly code and link diagnoses to procedures

3. Utilize all coding manuals properly

HOW TO ABSTRACT THE RIGHT DIAGNOSES AND PROCEDURES

When **abstracting** medical information from a medical record, you must always remember three things:

1. *Why* the patient was seen
2. *What* was done to the patient
3. *Where* the patient was seen

You handle each of these items differently.

1. The *why* is coded with ICD-9 CM codes.
2. The *what* is coded with CPT or HCPCS codes.
3. The *where* determines the part of the *CPT* manual that will be used to find the proper code.

On every claim there must be a diagnosis (why) and a procedure (what). The diagnosis establishes the **medical necessity** of the procedures reported. If either the diagnosis or a procedure is not correctly reported to the insurance company, the claim will not be paid.

The proper linking of the diagnosis and procedure should also be clear on the claim form. The diagnosis justifies the medical necessity of the visit to the doctor. If the diagnosis code does not match the service, the claim will not be paid.

The diagnosis (why the patient was seen) is abstracted from the medical record, and it is identified by the corresponding ICD-9 code.

When abstracting the diagnosis, you must be aware of the type of medical information in the medical record. The physician places in the record:

- Old diagnoses
- **Signs and symptoms**
- Conditions to be ruled out
- Probable conditions
- Impressions
- Findings
- The reason the patient is being seen (the **chief complaint**)

Also, if the diagnosis is not stated in the medical notes, you should never code it. Without documentation, do not code a diagnosis even if the condition is implied. If the diagnosis is not stated, the medical coder cannot code it. Remember that the diagnosis establishes the medical necessity for the services provided to the patient, but do not let this necessity lead you to code a diagnosis that is not there. Instead, code the signs and symptoms that lead the patient to seek care from the provider.

Further, the level of service provided must match the diagnosis. If you find yourself trying to code for a level of service that the diagnosis does not support, consult with the provider to determine a more appropriate level or have the provider add an addendum to the medical notes.

> **Tip** *All medical records are legal documents, and the medical coder must treat them as such.*

CHAPTER EXERCISES

Note

For the purpose of these scenarios, due to the complexity of assigning E&M codes, only the section the coder will find the code in can be reported at this time. (Leveling the E&M services is addressed in Chapter 6.)

Scenario 5-1

OFFICE NOTE

CC: Patient is here today complaining of headaches for the last 3 weeks.

PFSH: Patient started a new job working on computers for 8 hours a day. Patient has very well controlled hypertension, and a history of neck and upper back pain from an old work-related injury.

HPI: Patient has had a headache for the past 3 weeks. Has been taking aspirin for the pain, but this has not relieved the pain. Patient denies any additional neck or upper back pain. Patient states that the neck and back pain is a little better than at the last visit. This pain level is down from an 8 to a 5.

EXAM: Patient's neck is soft and supple. The back is without muscle strain and has healed reasonably well. BP is 120/80. Eyes are clear.

IMPRESSION: The headaches are probably due to the patient's new job, looking at the computer screen for 8 hours.

PLAN: Rx for 500 mg Naproxen t.i.d. Patient will call if the headaches get any worse.

From the scenario, what diagnosis would you select as primary for this visit?
_____

How many diagnoses would you code? _____

Why? _____

In what section of the medical record did you find this information? _____

Scenario 5-2

Use all the information from Scenario 5-1, but let's change the HPI, Exam, and Impression.

OFFICE NOTE

HPI: Patient has had a headache for the past 3 weeks and has been taking aspirin for the pain, without any relief. Patient has added neck and back pain. The patient states that the neck and upper back pain is a little worse than the last visit. The pain level is up from a 6 to an 8.

EXAM: The patient's neck is stiff with a ROM of 50%. There is unhealed muscle strain in the back. BP is 120/80.

IMPRESSION: The neck pain is the cause of the headaches.

PLAN: MRI to r/o stenosis, arthritis, or bone spurs of the cervical spine.

From the scenario, what diagnosis would you abstract as the primary Dx for this visit? _____

How many diagnoses would you code? _____

Why? _____

In what section of the medical record did you find this information? _____

Scenario 5-3

OFFICE NOTE

CC: The patient is here today for abdominal pains with nausea.

PFSH: Patient has just started a new school where she is a freshman in high school. Patient is sexually active.

HPI: Patient has been waking up every night with abdominal pains and some nausea. Patient denies any vomiting. She states that she has a hard time getting up in the morning.

EXAM: The patient's abdomen is soft and supple without any masses. Patient stated that the pain was at her belly when it was palpated. Patient does not seem to be in much distress at this time. A pregnancy test was negative.

PLAN: Ultrasound of the abdomen and pelvic area to rule out gallbladder disease and ovarian cyst that could not be felt on exam.

Why was the patient seen? _____

What code(s) would you use? _____

Would you assign a code for the gallbladder disease or ovarian cyst? Why or why not? _____

Scenario 5-4

OFFICE NOTE

CC: Patient is here today for abdominal pains with nausea. She has also missed her monthly menstruation.

PFSH: Patient has just started a new school, where she is a freshman in high school. Patient is sexually active.

HPI: Patient has been waking up every night with abdominal pains and some nausea. Patient denies any vomiting. She states that she has a hard time getting up in the morning. She has also been very tired.

EXAM: Patient's pelvic region was soft but very tender over the region of her right ovary. Patient seems to be in moderate distress at this time. A pregnancy test was positive. An ultrasound of the abdomen and pelvic region was done to rule out ectopic pregnancy because of the pain. It showed that she indeed has an ectopic pregnancy in her right fallopian tube.

DIAGNOSIS: Right fallopian tube pregnancy.

PLAN: Admit the patient today for surgery to remove the right fallopian tube.

What is the Dx for this scenario? _____

With respect to the diagnosis, what is the difference between this scenario and the previous one? _____

Would you report any of the signs and symptoms? Why or why not?

_____

Scenario 5-5

OFFICE NOTE

CC: Patient comes in today with extreme exhaustion.

PFSH: Patient states that there is nothing new in his life. He has had the same job for about 10 years and no problems at work. His home life is fine also. He has, however, started to diet within the last 3 months. He is taking some over-the-counter diet pills offered at the local health store. He is not exercising and he has decreased his food intake. He has lost about 60 lb.

HPI: Patient states that he has been feeling exhausted for about 2 months. He does not feel it's due to the diet. He denies any swollen glands but felt a hard spot on his neck. Patient denies any high temperatures or any other symptoms or illnesses.

EXAM: BP 150/98; heart rate: 130.

The patient is visibly worn out. He has lost a lot of weight, but too much, too soon. His muscle tone in his legs and arms is decreased. There are no swollen glands but there is a palpable solid mass on his neck, near or on his thyroid gland. His lungs are clear without any rhonchi, wheezes, or rales. There are good bowel sounds. No other masses are found.

IMPRESSION: Thyroid mass. The exhaustion and extreme weight loss could be due to this mass.

PLAN: Complex thyroid workup, with scan, and lab test. Also a thyroid biopsy.

What will the Dx be? _____

Why? _____

What are the signs and symptoms? _____

Would you code any of them? _____

If yes, which one(s)? _____

Remember, when pulling out information for diagnostic coding, the coder must always find the diagnosis that explains *why* the service was performed. The *what* represents the services provided to the patient, and they are coded using the CPT and HCPCS codes. The services could simply be an evaluation and management (E&M) code (see the range of codes in the guidelines of the *CPT*), or they may consist of surgery, laboratory services, x-rays, and the like.

Scenario 5-6

OPERATIVE REPORT

PROCEDURE: Salpingectomy.

PREOPERATIVE DX: Right fallopian ectopic pregnancy.

POSTOPERATIVE DX: Right fallopian ectopic pregnancy.

The patient was brought into the OR and prepared for the salpingectomy. A low midline incision was made and the peritoneal cavity was entered. Self-retaining retractor is put in place. The intestines are protected and the right fallopian tube was located and isolated from surrounding organs. The infundibulopelvic ligament is ligated and divided as is the broad ligament attachment of the tube and the ovary. The tube is then removed using electrocautery to arrest bleeding. The wound is closed in layers. The patient tolerated the procedure well and left the operating room in stable condition.

Tip *Pay attention to this scenario. The procedure noted on the top of the op note is not exactly the procedure that was performed.*

What was the procedure? _____

Where can you find this in the notes? _____

Can you be certain that the only procedure that is coded is the one indicated at the top of the notes? _____

Code the procedure: _____

Is this a bilateral procedure? Would you use a modifier? _____

Scenario 5-7

OPERATIVE REPORT

PROCEDURE: Myringotomy and insertion of eustachian tubes of both ears.

PREOP DX: Chronic tubotympanic suppurative otitis media.

POSTOP DX: Same as above.

The 6-year-old patient walked into the operating room with his mother and was placed onto the table. He was prepped for surgery and placed under general anesthesia. Once the patient was under anesthesia, he was placed with his head position at the edge of the table and with his right ear up. Using the operative microscope, some earwax was removed and an incision was made into the tympanic membrane and the tube was inserted. The other ear was also exposed and using the operative microscope, an incision was made in the tympanic membrane. About 1 cc of fluid or pus was suctioned out of the mastoid cavity behind the tympanic membrane. The tube was then placed into the left ear. The patient tolerated the procedure well and left the operating room in stable condition.

What was the procedure? _____

Where can you find name of the procedure in the notes? _____

Is it clear from the operative notes that the procedures stated at the beginning of the notes can be coded? _____

Code the procedure(s): _____

Is this a single procedure or bilateral procedure, and would you use a modifier? _____

There are other procedures in the notes for this scenario.

- The provider removed earwax from the right ear and suctioned out fluid and pus from the left.
- An operative microscope was used on both ears.

There are codes for these procedures. Look up the operative microscope in the *CPT* coding book. What do you find? Code 69990 is an add-on code. Can you code this? You cannot. According to NCCI, 69990 cannot be reported with the tympanostomy procedure. The other two procedures are clearly a part of the primary procedure, a key part of the surgery. The provider cannot put the tube into the ear without cleaning out the ear canal, nor can an ear tube be placed into the eardrum without clearing out any fluid or pus behind it. You would not code these procedures because they are a part of—bundled into—the major procedure.

How can you know what is considered bundled into a major procedure? Medicare has a list of codes that cannot be billed together (discussed in Chapter 4).

CPT © 2007 American Medical Association. All rights reserved.

Note

For coding purposes, it is very important to read all of the operative notes because the body of the text might indicate additional procedures that were not stated at the top of the notes. Another reason is that a procedure might be checked off on an encounter form, but nothing is stated in the medical records. One very important rule all medical coders must always remember is, "If it is not written down, it was not done." This rule is very important. If an insurance company audits your office's claims and medical records, the procedures reported to the insurance company for reimbursement must be indicated in the medical records. If they are not, there is no way the office can prove that the procedure was actually done.

Scenario 5-8

OPERATIVE REPORT

PROCEDURE: Excision of popliteal cyst and repair of a torn meniscus.

DX: Baker's cyst LT knee.

Torn meniscus LT knee.

This 50-year-old patient was wheeled into the operating room and spinal anesthesia was administered. The patient was then prepped for the procedure. She was placed on her right side, safety straps were applied to stabilize her on the table, and the popliteal area of the knee was exposed. An oblique incision was made over the mass and the deep fascia was incised, exposing the sac (Baker's cyst). The sac was then dissected free. The wound was closed and a splint was applied. The knee joint was then distended with saline. The scope was then placed into the intra-articular structure to directly visualize the torn meniscus for repair. The tear was located and was repaired using the power shaver. Following the procedure, the saline was aspirated and the scope was withdrawn from the knee joint. The wounds were closed and a compression bandage was applied. The patient tolerated the procedure well and was brought into the recovery room.

What procedure(s) was (were) performed? _____

Where can you find this information? _____

Is it clear from the operative notes that the procedure(s) stated at the beginning of the notes was (were) performed? _____

Code the procedure(s): _____

What modifier(s) would you use, if any? _____

Look again at the section that describes how the surgery was performed. The approach is stated here but not at the beginning of the notes. Determine the codes again, this time for both the procedure and the diagnosis.

Scenario 5-9

OPERATIVE REPORT

PROCEDURE: Cesarean section.

DX: Cephalopelvic disproportion and fetal distress.

This patient was transferred to my care after 36 hours of attempted vaginal delivery. The fetus came into distress, and it was felt that a cesarean section should be performed. The patient was wheeled into the operative room. The patient was given spinal anesthesia, draped, and prepped for surgery. A low transverse incision was made into the rectus muscles, and they were separated. The peritoneum was incised, exposing the uterus, and a transverse incision was also done to the uterus. The amniotic sac was entered and fluid aspirated. The fetal head was delivered using suction. The newborn's airway was aspirated gently and the delivery was completed. The umbilical cord was clamped and cut. The infant was then transferred to the neonatal team. Hemostasis was secured and the placenta was

continued

> delivered. The uterus was cleaned with saline and was then closed using a double-layer closure. The peritoneum and outer wound were also closed in layers.

What procedure(s) was (were) performed? _____

Code the procedure(s): _____

Code the Dx(s): _____

Scenario 5-10

OFFICE NOTE

CC: This established patient came into the office today because he fell off a ladder, hit his head while falling, and landed on his ankle. He complains of pain in the ankle and a headache.

HPI: Patient states that he fell off the ladder while he was painting his house last night and hit his head coming down on an overhang of the door. He also injured his right ankle. He does not think the ankle is broken, but this morning he could not move the ankle. He also complains of a bad headache. Patient denies any blackouts after the fall but he did vomit throughout the night. His pain level is 7 out of 10.

EXAM: On examination, the left pupil was slightly dilated and the right was normal. The neck and back show stiffness on movement with 40% ROM. His RT ankle is very swollen with a lot of bruising. When moving the ankle, the patient was in pain, but there do not seem to be any broken bones. A three-view x-ray was taken of the ankle and there was no fracture.

IMPRESSION: The ankle is very badly sprained. The headache and the vomiting are a concern to me. There may be a small bleed into the brain or a concussion.

PLAN: Strapped the ankle. Instructed the patient to put the foot up, put ice on the ankle for the next 24 hours, then put heat on it. I advised the patient to take Tylenol for pain, but no NSAIDs until the brain scan. I also instructed patient to stay off the ankle for a few days. Ordered a CT scan of the head for today to r/o a small bleed to the brain or concussion.

What diagnosis(es) should be coded? _____

What procedure(s) was (were) performed? _____

Match the procedure and diagnosis(es) and code them. _____

Would you use a modifier? _____

If yes, which one? _____

Scenario 5-11

OFFICE NOTE

CC: This new patient is here today at the request of his primary care provider. The patient is complaining of bouts of diarrhea for a few days, then having constipation for a few days.

PFSH: Patient denies drinking or smoking and does not take any medication except for an occasional pain medication. The patient states that his brother has colitis and his mother has IBS.

HPI: The patient has had these symptoms for the past 4 months. The patient denies any other illness in the past months. The patient denies any vomiting. The patient has had no fever and no other symptoms. The patient does, however, state that some foods cause cramps, sometimes very severe to the point that the patient has to "sit it out" until the cramps go away.

EXAM: The patient is not in distress, there are good bowel sounds, and a soft abdomen. A colonoscopy was performed. The patient was given moderate sedation. No masses or bowel obstructions were noted. Three biopsies were taken of the colon at the descending colon, at the transverse colon, and at the ascending colon near the cecum.

IMPRESSION: IBS.

PLAN: Gave patient a prescription of hyoscyamine 2 mg t.i.d. to inhibit smooth muscle contractions when needed. The patient will go on a well-balanced diet with added fiber. I will see patient in three months or sooner if the symptoms persist. Patient will be notified of biopsy results.

What is the diagnosis? _____

What procedure(s) was (were) performed? _____

Match the procedure(s) and diagnosis(es) and code them. _____

Would you code for the moderate sedation? _____

Why or why not? _____

Would you use a modifier? _____

If yes, which one? _____

Tip *Outpatient consultations are coded from the range 99241–99245 for both new and established patients.*

Scenario 5-12

VISIT NOTE

CC: The patient was brought into the ER by her parents with a temperature of 40°C (105°F) and a lacy rash all over her body.

HPI: This 1-year-old child has had a fever of 101°F for the last two days, with symptoms of a cold. She was given infant's Tylenol every 4 hours for the fever and broke out with a rash sometime this morning. It was about this time the temperature went up to 105°F w/o any relief from the Tylenol. The baby's mother called her primary care provider and was told to bring the child to the ER.

EXAM: The baby's eyes were bloodshot, and her nose and sinuses were congested. Her ears were clear without infection and the lungs were clear. The baby was dehydrated. Her throat was red, with white pustules on it, and her tongue had a

continued

white coating. A throat culture was taken and came back positive for streptococcus infection. The rash looks like a sunburn and feels like sandpaper all over the baby's body, including the palms of the hands and feet. The rash is redder under the arms and in the groin area.

IMPRESSION: Scarlet fever, strep throat.

PLAN: Hydrate the baby while she is here in the ER, start her on amoxicillin oral suspension 150 mg/ml, and give the parents a prescription of amoxicillin oral suspension 150 mg/ml 4 times a day until completed.

What diagnosis(es) should be coded? _____

What procedure(s) should be coded? _____

Match the procedure and diagnosis(es) and code them. _____

Would you code for the lab? _____

Would you code for the hydration? _____

Would you use a modifier? _____

If yes, which one? _____

Scenario 5-13

OFFICE NOTE

CC: This established patient is present for her follow-up diabetic check. She has been doing quite well. She has had two recent falls where she has fractured her left wrist and a finger on the right hand. These are healing nicely. She notes she feels off balance because of the size of her incisional hernia. She is using the walker and cane more often. She denies any other symptoms, such as syncope or vertigo. She notes blood sugars at home have been very well controlled by diet only. She is seeing a podiatrist for calluses on the bottom of both feet.

PAST MEDICAL HISTORY: Significant for hypertension, diabetes mellitus (DM) type 2, and unstable bladder.

ROS: The patient notes no problems with numbness of the feet. She notes that the Ditropan is only minimally effective to reduce her urinary frequency.

PHYSICAL EXAM:

General: She appears well.

Vital Signs: Her weight is 168 pounds, BP 130/70, and P is 74 and irregular.

HEENT: Exam is benign. TMs are normal. Pupils are equal, round, and reactive. No pharyngeal erythema.

Neck: Supple, no swollen lymph nodes, no carotid bruits.

Chest: Clear.

Heart: Heart sounds are normal.

Abdomen: Incisional hernia noted.

Extremities: No pedal edema.

Neurologic: Negative.

ASSESSMENT:

1. DM type 2.

2. Incisional hernia.

3. Recent fractures.

PLAN:

1. The patient has had a bone density study, and it shows low density. In light of the several minor Fx, I am recommending she start Fosamax 70 mg weekly. The patient was given detailed information on side effects.

2. Continue Ditropan as needed for urinary frequency.

3. Refer to a surgeon for the hernia.

4. Follow up in six months.

5. Flu shot given.

What is the diagnosis? _____

What procedure(s) was (were) performed? _____

Match the procedure(s) and diagnosis(es) and code them. _____

_____

Would you use a modifier? _____

If yes, which one? _____

If no, why not? _____

Tip	*This scenario has a procedure that is not found in the usual place.*

Scenario 5-14

OFFICE NOTE

CC: This patient comes in today with a request by Dr. Gray to see if this patient's dialysis AV fistula should be removed and, if so, for removal.

HPI: In the past 2 months, patient has had a few infections in the AV fistula that have caused problems with his health. He has been on antibiotics to clear up the current infection.

EXAM:

General: Doing well.

Vital Signs: Patient weight is 170, BP 130/90, and P is 80.

HEENT: Negative.

Neck: Supple, no swollen lymph nodes, no carotid bruits.

Chest: Clear.

continued

Heart: Heart sounds are normal.

Abdomen: Negative.

Extremities: The AV fistula is slightly pink but the infection appears to be clearing up.

ASSESSMENT: The AV fistula should come out. I will do this today. A replacement will need to go back in, but not today.

PROCEDURE: After informed consent, the left-side PermCath dialysis catheter was removed. Using a local anesthesia, 1% lidocaine, and Betadine for sterilization, incision was made at the site of entry, then I sharply dissected the tissues around. I was able to carefully dissect all the way up to the puncture site, then proceeded to remove the catheter. The wound was closed and a pressure dressing was then applied to the wound. Patient was instructed to go to the ER if there is any bleeding. The patient tolerated the procedure well. A note was sent to Dr. Gray.

What is the diagnosis? _____

What procedure(s) was (were) performed? _____

Match the procedure(s) and diagnoses and code them. _____

Would you use a modifier? _____

If yes, which one? _____

If no, why not? _____

Scenario 5-15

OFFICE NOTE

CC: Metastatic colon CA.

SUBJECTIVE: The patient now presents for a follow-up. She has been on single-agent oxaliplatin. She has done fairly well until now. Her carcinoembryonic antigen (CEA) is rising mildly. This has been accurately predictive of a relapse in the past. It has been as high as 9, more recently 4. It has now increased to a 5.6. She is having a little more hip pain. Appetite is stable. Mild neuropathy on the oxaliplatin.

PAST MEDICAL HISTORY: Metastatic colon CA, Hx of breast CA.

MEDICATIONS: Unchanged.

ROS: Worsening right hip pain.

PHYSICAL EXAMINATION:

Vital Signs: Stable.

Neck: Supple, no nodes.

Lungs: Clear to auscultation and percussion.

Cardiac: Regular rate and rhythm, no murmurs.

LABORATORY DATA: CBC is stable and the CEA increased to 5.6.

ASSESSMENT AND PLAN: Metastatic colon CA: The patient is showing signs of worsening metastatic disease. We will give her a final dose of oxaliplatin today. Obtain approval to switch her to Avastin, the monoclonal antivascular endothelial growth factor antibody. This is generally given in combination with 5-FU/leucovorin. The Avastin will be given at 2-week intervals with 5-FU/leucovorin also at 2-week intervals. Our plan is a total of 8 doses, i.e., 4 cycles, and reassess her response. Risk and benefits of treatment discussed with the patient. Avastin 5 mg/kg every 2 weeks with 5-FU 500 mg/m^2 and leucovorin 100 mg/m^2 every 2 weeks.

Patient had her treatment today of single agent oxaliplatin intra-arterial push in the infusion room.

What is the diagnosis? _____

What procedure(s) was (were) performed? _____

Match the procedure(s) and diagnoses and code them. _____

Would you use a modifier? _____

If yes, which one? _____

If no, why not? _____

Future chapters will explore more scenarios of different types of medical records. The key to coding the correct information is understanding the rules of medical coding—along with a lot of practical experience.

CHAPTER REVIEW

Using the *CPT*, the *HCPCS*, and the *ICD-9* manuals and this textbook, complete the following exercises.

Define the following:

1. PFSH _____
2. HEENT _____
3. Abstracting _____
4. Signs and symptoms _____
5. Medical necessity _____

Find the following:

6. In what three places can a medical coder find a diagnosis in the medical notes?

_____
_____
_____

7. In abstracting from medical records the *what* is _____ and the *why* is _____.

8. Every claim must be reported with a(n) _____ and _____, and the codes should be linked for _____.

9. Why would the medical coder read the whole operative note when the procedure is stated at the beginning of the notes? _____
_____

10. Does the medical coder use diagnoses from past medical history? _____
Why or why not? _____

Chapter 6
Evaluation and Management (E&M) Coding

KEY TERMS

body areas
chief complaint (CC)
established patient
evaluation and management
(E&M)

family history (FH)
history of present illness (HPI)
inpatient (Inpt)
level of service
medical decision making

new patient
organ systems
outpatient (Outpt)
review of systems (ROS)

LEARNING OBJECTIVES

Upon completion of this chapter, the student will be able to:

1. Understand how to audit evaluation and management (E&M) coding from medical documentation
2. Select a visit level that is supported by the documentation in a patient record

VERIFYING E&M CODES FOR COMPLIANCE PURPOSES

Evaluation and management (E&M) coding is the responsibility of the physician or other medical provider who has seen the patient. The medical coder needs to know how to level the E&M services for two major reasons:

1. Training the new physicians and other medical providers
2. Auditing the patient files for compliance purposes

To perform these two functions, the medical coder must understand how to level the service through reading medical documentation (the patient's medical records and notes). This section covers only the auditing and compliance requirements, not training.

When auditing a medical record, coders need to understand the purpose of an audit. A major reason for auditing charges is that Medicare requires self-auditing in a medical practice. The medical coder needs to use guidelines that Medicare created to help providers and medical coders correctly code an E&M service. Two sets of guidelines are currently valid for documenting in medical records:

1. 1995 E&M guidelines
2. 1997 E&M guidelines

The major difference between the two is that the examination section of Medicare's 1995 guidelines is more straightforward, providing a general description of a multisystem examination. The 1997 guidelines, on the other hand, give a more comprehensive description of a general multisystem exam, define the components of 10 single organ system exams, and result in much more extensive documentation of the examination. Medicare added the single multisystem examination guidelines in 1997 to allow specialists, who often focus an examination on a single organ system, to reach the highest **level of service**.

Providers may use their discretion when selecting which guidelines to use in documenting a visit. For purposes of this chapter, the 1995 guidelines are used.

1995 Guidelines

According to the 1995 general multisystem exam documentation guidelines, four types of exam are defined:

1. *Problem-focused:* A limited exam of the affected body area or organ system
2. *Expanded problem–focused:* A limited exam of the affected body area or organ system and other symptomatic or related organ system(s)
3. *Detailed:* An extended exam of the affected body area(s) and other symptomatic or related organ system(s)
4. *Comprehensive:* A general multisystem exam or complete exam of a single organ system

For purposes of exam, the following **body areas** are recognized:

- Head, including the face
- Neck
- Chest, including breasts and axillae
- Abdomen
- Genitalia, groin, and buttocks
- Back, including spine
- Each extremity

For purposes of the exam, the following **organ systems** are recognized:

- Constitutional (including vital signs, general appearance)
- Eyes
- Ears, nose, mouth, and throat
- Cardiovascular
- Respiratory
- Gastrointestinal
- Genitourinary
- Musculoskeletal
- Skin
- Neurologic
- Psychiatric
- Hematologic/lymphatic/immunologic

The extent of the examination performed and documented depends on the clinical judgment of the examiner and on the nature of the presenting problems. Exams range from a limited exam of a single body area to a general multisystem or complete single organ system examination.

1997 Guidelines

For a general multisystem examination under the 1997 guidelines, the peformance and documentation requirements for a given level of multisystem exam are as follows:

- *Problem-focused:* Should include one to five elements identified by a bullet in one or more organ system(s) or body area(s).
- *Expanded problem–focused:* Should include at least six elements identified by a bullet in one or more organ system(s) or body area(s).
- *Detailed:* Should include two bulleted elements for each of six organ system(s) or body areas(s). Alternatively, a detailed exam may include at least 12 elements identified by a bullet in two or more organ systems or body areas.
- *Comprehensive:* Should include all bulleted elements in at least nine organ systems or body areas. For each system or area selected, all elements of the examination identified by a bullet should be performed, unless specific directions limit the content of the exam. For each area or system, documentation of at least two elements identified by a bullet is expected.

The single organ systems or body areas for the 1997 multisystem examination are as follows:

- Constitutional
- Cardiovascular
- Chest (breasts)
- Ears, nose, mouth, and throat
- Eyes
- Gastrointestinal
- Genitourinary (female)
- Genitourinary (male)
- Hematologic/lymphatic/immunologic
- Musculoskeletal
- Neck
- Neurological
- Psychiatric
- Respiratory
- Skin

AUDITING

In an audit, the medical coder reviews the medical record documentation, which the provider has dictated, to verify that the codes reported for billing purposes accurately reflect the services dictated. When there is a discrepancy, the medical coder must correct the problem. If an overpayment resulted, the medical coder must process a refund to the payer. If the error resulted in an underpayment, the medical coder needs to submit a corrected claim. In addition to adjusting payment, the medical coder's responsibility includes addressing the problems with the provider and educating the staff regarding proper documentation.

> **Tip** *Problems discovered during an audit are usually a result of the provider's overcoding or undercoding.*

Determining Place and Type of Service

How does a medical coder audit the charges? First look at the notes to determine whether the patient is new or established and whether the services were provided in the **inpatient (Inpt)** or **outpatient (Outpt)** setting.

- A **new patient** is a patient who has not been seen in the office in the previous three years by someone of the same specialty.
- An **established patient** has been seen by a provider in the office within the past three years by someone in the same specialty.

This is an important distinction when you are coding for a large multispecialty group. Even though all the providers bill under the same tax identification number, each provider within a specialty who sees a new patient may report a new patient visit as long as no other provider within that specialty has seen the patient in the past three years. Therefore, the same group could report multiple new patient visits for the same patient as long as the visits are with providers of different specialties and the new patient criteria are met.

Then review the notes to make sure that they support the place of service (POS) (hospital, office, nursing home, etc.) and the type of service (TOS) as reported. Table 6-1 indicates E&M categories, code ranges, patient status, and POS.

TABLE 6-1   E&M Categories, Code Ranges, Patient Status, and POS

E&M Categories (Type of Service)	Code Range	New or Established Patient	Place of Service
Office and other Outpatient Service	99201–99205 99211–99215	New Established	Office or Outpatient
Initial Observation Care Observation Care Discharge	99218–99220 99217		Outpatient
Observation or Inpatient Hospital Care (same-day admit and discharge)	99234–99236		Inpatient or Outpatient (if Observation)
Initial Hospital Care Subsequent Hospital Care Hospital Discharge Service	99221–99223 99231–99233 99238–99239		Inpatient
Office or Other Outpatient Consultation Inpatient Consultation	99241–99245 99251–99255		Office or Outpatient Inpatient
Emergency Department Service	99281–99288		Outpatient

TABLE 6-1   **E&M Categories, Code Ranges, Patient Status, and POS** (Continued)

E&M Categories (Type of Service)	Code Range	New or Established Patient	Place of Service
Pediatric Critical Care Patient Transport	99289–99290		Outpatient
Critical Care Service			Inpatient or Outpatient
Adult	99291–99292		
Pediatric	99293–99294		
Neonatal	99295–99296		
Continuing Intensive Care Service for Low Birth Weight Babies	99298–99300		Inpatient
Nursing Facility Service			Skilled Nursing Facility, Nursing Facility
Initial Nursing Facility Care	99304–99306		
Subsequent Nursing Facility Care	99307–99310		
Nursing Facility Discharge	99315–99316		
Other Nursing Facility Services	99318		
Domiciliary, Rest Home, or Custodial Care Service	99324–99328 99334–99337	New Established	Custodial Care Facility
Domiciliary, Rest Home, or Custodial Care Service (Assisted Living Facility, Living Facility) or Home Care Plan Oversight Services	99339–99340		Custodial Care Facility, Assisted Living Facility
Home Services	99341–99345 99347–99350	New Established	Home
Prolonged Services			Inpatient or Outpatient
with Direct Patient Contact	99354–99357		
without Direct Patient Contact	99358–99359		
Physician Standby Service	99360		Inpatient or Outpatient
Medical Team Conferences			Outpatient
with Direct Contact with Patient and/or Family	99366		
without Direct Contact with Patient and/or Family	99367–99368		
Care Plan Oversight	99374–99380		Office or Outpatient
Preventive Medical Service	99381–99387	New	Office or Outpatient
Annual Physical Exam	99391–99397	Established	
Preventive Medicine			Inpatient or Outpatient
Individual Counseling	99401–99404		
Group Counseling	99411–99412		
Newborn Care	99431–99440		Inpatient
Non-Face-to-Face Physician Services			
Telephone Services	99441–99443		
On-Line Medical Evaluation	99444		Outpatient
Other Evaluation and Management Services Initial Hospital Care, Per Day, Intensive Observation, Neonate 28 days or less of age	99477		Inpatient

EXAMPLE: Consultation for Progressive Anemia

ADMISSION DATE: March 31, xxxx. **CONSULT DATE:** April 4, xxxx.

REASON FOR CONSULTATION: Progressive anemia.

HISTORY OF PRESENT ILLNESS: The patient is a pleasant 27-year-old gentleman with a known history of beta thalassemia trait who was evaluated in Hematology Clinic 2 days ago and was noted to have a high fever associated with chills and progressive anemia. Hence, hospitalization was recommended for further evaluation and recommendation. Dr. Jones from the clinic asked me to see him.

The patient states that he has been feeling poorly for the last 2 weeks and has had symptoms of fever, chills, and fatigue. He was evaluated by his primary care physician 2 days ago and further evaluation and therapy were initiated.

The patient states that his temperature was as high as 103°F to 104°F along with fatigue and night sweats. His symptoms decreased with Motrin or Tylenol, but recurred within a few hours. He has had some vomiting in the past as well as abdominal discomfort. He has had decreased appetite and reports a nearly 20-pound weight loss in the last 4 months. He also reports a similar episode several months ago and workup at that time yielded no obvious abnormality. He seemed to recover from his febrile illness, and his symptoms recurred 2 weeks ago as noted above.

He denies any symptoms of headache or dizziness other than when ambulating. He also had shortness of breath and chest pain last night, which seems to have resolved. He also had mild lower back pain, which also has resolved. He reports lower extremity edema bilaterally for the last 3 days, but since hospitalization the right lower extremity edema seems to have decreased. The left ankle edema persists. He denies any discomfort in his left leg or in his left groin. The patient denies any history of bleeding. He has noted no blood in his stool, denies dark colored stools; no blood in his urine.

His medical history is unremarkable except for the diagnosis of thalassemia.

MEDICATIONS: Tylenol and Motrin p.r.n.

DRUG ALLERGIES: None.

FAMILY HISTORY: His sister has a history of melanoma and brain tumor. Mother has fibromyalgia and has a history of thalassemia.

SOCIAL HISTORY: He is currently unemployed and lives with his wife and 2 children. No history of smoking. No history of IV drug abuse. He reports occasional alcohol use.

The patient is a Jehovah's Witness and would not accept any blood product support.

PHYSICAL EXAMINATION: The patient looks pale and is in no acute distress. He looks comfortable at rest.

HEENT: No evidence of cervical or supraclavicular adenopathy. No thyromegaly.

Lungs: Clear to both auscultation and percussion.

Cardiac: Tachycardia.

Abdomen: Soft, no evidence of hepatosplenomegaly. No evidence of free fluid. On exam of the axillae, the right axilla has no lymphadenopathy noted. The left axilla does have a 2-cm to 3-cm firm, tender lymph node present in the left medial aspect of the axilla. No other abnormality noted. No palpable inguinal adenopathy.

Extremities: He has left ankle edema, and no evidence of thigh or leg swelling is noted. No calf tenderness bilaterally. Homans' sign is negative.

DIAGNOSTIC DATA: Review of his blood tests: Hemogram from October 2005 shows a hematocrit of 34. His white count and platelets were normal. He did have red cell changes consistent with thalassemia trait.

His hemogram from April 2, 2006 showed a white count of 4.2, hematocrit 22.3, MCV 54, MCH 18, platelet count 142,000, and RDW 24. His reticulocyte count was 2 with an absolute reticulocyte response of 92 billion per liter. Iron studies showed a ferritin of 1586 but decrease in total iron, TIBC, and percent saturation was 8. His sedimentation rate was 66, LDH 423.

I reviewed his blood smear this morning, which showed significant hypochromia and target cells, and teardrop cells were present. No significant schistocytes or spherocytes were noted.

He had a chest x-ray done on admission, March 31, which showed slight scoliosis to the left. Heart, lung, and mediastinal structures appeared normal.

IMPRESSION: A 27-year-old gentleman with profound anemia.

The patient does have history of beta thalassemia trait. His mother is of Greek origin and has a history of thalassemia. The patient's hemoglobin electrophoresis done in October showed a hemoglobin A2 of 5.9, hemoglobin AI of 94.1, and hemoglobin F of 0. These findings were suggestive of beta thalassemia trait.

His baseline hematocrit seems to have been around 34 to 37 in October of 20X0, but he has had significant decline in his hematocrit to 27 and now 22. He also has associated increase in his RDW.

Though beta thalassemia trait is associated with profound hypochromia and mirocytosis, we would not expect RDW to be increased. Since this patient has significant increase in his RDW, this would be indicative of associated iron deficiency anemia. Sedimentation rate is significantly high, indicative of an inflammatory process. Presence of low iron, TIBC, and iron saturation is also suggestive of iron deficiency.

The patient has a decreased reticulocyte count disproportionate to his anemia. This is indicative of hypoproliferative microcytic hypochromic anemia consistent with iron deficiency. He does not have any evidence of hemolysis and no obvious bleed, but, given his findings, I would consider further GI evaluation when he is stable.

In the interim, I would recommend proceeding with an iron supplement to improve his red cell production.

The patient is a Jehovah's Witness and will not accept a blood transfusion, though he does have moderate symptoms associated with anemia. Respecting his wishes, we will hold off on blood transfusion but will initiate erythropoietin 40,000 to 60,000 units once or twice a week. One could use a higher dose of erythropoietin, but I would not recommend it until his iron deficiency is corrected.

The patient has palpable left axillary lymphadenopathy associated with fever. Though this could be indicative of an infectious etiology, the presence of the underlying hypoproliferative disorder could not be ruled out; hence I would recommend further evaluation with a CAT scan of the chest, abdomen, and pelvis prior to further intervention.

I have discussed these details with the patient. Will follow up in the a.m. and consider further recommendations.

continued

- *What kind of service was performed?* The first statement indicated that the patient was seen for a consultation. To bill for a consultation, the provider's documentation must include the reason for the consultation, who made the request, and a response to the requesting provider. This is know as the 3 Rs of a consultation.
- *Where was this consultation?* The medical notes state that the patient was hospitalized.

Now you have a place to start: You know the place of service (the hospital) and the type of service (an inpatient consultation). Look at your CPT codebook and find the inpatient consultation codes.

Leveling the Service

How do you level this service? The first step in leveling an E&M service is knowing its key components:

- History
- Exam
- Medical decision making

All E&M services must have these three key components.

Look in the E&M section of the *CPT Professional Edition.* All of the codes are listed with the requirements for choosing them.

Most medical or other third-party payers use an audit tool, which is a series of tables that enables the auditor to assess the information in the medical record. To choose a level of service, you must understand how to use these tables.

The first such table is the Patient Personal History Table. The elements of this table are:

- Chief Complaint
- History of Present Illness
- Review of Systems
- Past, Family, and/or Social History

This is a three-out-of-three table for new and established patients. "Three-out-of-three" means that, to meet a particular level of history, all three of the components of history must be met (see Table 6-2).

TABLE 6-2   History Table

Type of History	History of Present Illness	Review of Systems	Past, Family, and/or Social History
Problem Focused	Brief (1–3)	N/A	N/A
Expanded Problem Focused	Brief (1–3)	Problem Pertinent (1)	N/A
Detail	Extended (4)	Extended (2–9)	Pertinent (1)
Comprehensive	Extended (4)	Complete (10)	Complete (2/3)

Source: CMS Medicare Learning Network Evaluation & Management Service Guide (2006, revised 2007), p. 12.

CPT © 2007 American Medical Association. All rights reserved.

ELEMENTS OF HISTORY OF EVALUATION AND MANAGEMENT

Chief Complaint (CC): The Nature of the Presenting Problem

The **chief complaint** (**CC**) consists of the patient's statement describing symptoms, problems, and other factors that brought him or her to seek medical care. The CC statement is usually in the patient's or family member's own words. This is the subjective part of the visit. The CC must always be documented.

History of Present Illness (HPI)

The **history of present illness** (**HPI**) is a description of the patient's present illness, including any or all of the following eight elements:

1. Chronology, for instance, how long the patient has had the symptoms
2. Location, such as left ear pain
3. Quality, such as throbbing pain of the ear
4. Severity, such as pain on a scale of 1–10
5. Timing, specifically when the symptom occurs, when it was first noted, the time of day or after an activity or movement
6. Context, for example, after swimming
7. Modifying factors, for instance, better when warm ear drops are put into ears
8. Associated signs and symptoms related to the presenting problem, like a fever, head cold, headache

There are two types of HPI: brief and extended.

1. The documentation for a brief HPI must have one to three of the eight elements.
2. An extended HPI requires documentation of at least four of these elements.

Review of Systems (ROS)

The **review of systems** (**ROS**) is an inventory of the body systems that can be obtained by a patient questionnaire or taken by a nurse, medical assistant, medical student, or the provider. It is not necessary for the provider to comment on each system individually; the pertinent positives or negatives may be noted, and, if at least ten systems have been reviewed, the statement "all other systems negative" qualifies as a comprehensive (complete) ROS.

There are three levels of ROS:

1. *Problem pertinent:* Inquiries into the system are directly related to the CC.

> ### EXAMPLE
>
> A patient comes into the office for a sore throat. The provider asks about any other symptoms to the head and nasal sinus areas, color of mucus, ear pain, and headaches.

2. *Extended:* Inquiries into the system are directly related to the CC and limited to two to nine additional systems that could be related to the CC.

> ## EXAMPLE
>
> A patient comes into the office after a car accident for a follow-up to the treatment of broken leg bones. The provider asks the patient if there is any numbness associated with the reduction of the fracture to leg bone. The provider has reviewed two systems: the musculoskeletal system and the nervous system.

3. *Complete:* Ten body systems must be reviewed.

> ## EXAMPLE
>
> A patient comes into the office with bilateral numbness in both arms, under the breast, and down to the feet. The provider asks if there is any blurry vision or loss to peripheral vision, any trouble swallowing, speaking, any chest pains or shortness of breath, any nausea, bowel movement problems, urinary incontinence, skin changes, numbness when touched, any change in hot or cold sensations, any gait problems, any problems with memory loss, sleeping, any weight loss or gain of weight, or any fatigue.

Personal and Family History

The personal, family, and/or social history (PFSH) includes:

- *Personal medical history:* Past history of specific diseases, medications, and surgeries
- *Social history:* Whether the patient smokes, drinks alcohol, and is single or married
- **Family history**: The health status or causes of death of parents, siblings, and children

A complete history is very important for leveling a new patient. When the patient is new, the provider needs to take a complete history because the medical status is unknown.

When a CPT code description indicates that the code, such as the emergency department and hospital codes, is for either a new patient or an established patient, the new patient history requirements apply.

Only the detailed or comprehensive history requires the personal, family, and/or social history when leveling the services.

> ## EXAMPLE
>
> When a patient comes into the office with a sore throat, it is not necessary to obtain a patient history to treat the condition. However, if the patient's sore throat has not been resolved in a reasonable amount of time, the provider may then look into more of the PFSH and check to see if the problem is more than the usual viral or bacterial infection. Perhaps an earlier condition or part of the patient's social history, such as smoking, is causing the problem.

There are two types of (PFSH):

1. *Pertinent:* A review of the history directly related to the problem in the HPI

2. *Complete:* Documenting two of the three components for an established patient and all three for a new patient

Extent of Examination

The examination is the objective part of the E&M. This is the provider's observations of the patient's condition. Elements of the examination come from either the Medicare 1995 or 1997 guidelines.

The medical coder must understand the difference between body areas and organ systems because the number of body areas and/or organ systems is key to leveling the E&M. Table 6-3 illustrates the distinction between the two concepts.

Elements of the Examination

The examination might be of a single system or a multisystem, depending on the nature of the present illness and/or the well visit.

- Constitutional: vital signs, general appearance
- Eyes
- Ears, nose, mouth, and throat
- Gastrointestinal: Mouth, throat, esophagus, gall bladder, stomach, liver, small intestines, and large intestines
- Respiratory system: Nose and nasal passages, larynx, trachea, bronchi, and lungs
- Cardiovascular system: Heart, vascular structures
- Nervous system: Central nervous system (brain and spinal cord) and peripheral nervous system
- Genitourinary system: Kidney, ureter, urinary bladder, male genital system, and female genital system
- Integumentary system: Skin, breast

TABLE 6-3   Recognized Body Areas and Organ Systems

Body Areas	Organ Systems
Head, Including Face	Eyes
Neck	Ears, Nose, Mouth, and Throat (sinuses)
Chest, Including Breast and Axilla	Cardiovascular
Abdomen	Respiratory
Genitalia	Gastrointestinal
Back	Genitourinary
Each Extremity	Musculoskeletal
	Skin
	Neurologic
	Hematologic/Lymphatic/Immunologic
	Psychiatric

Source: CMS Medicare Learning Network Evaluation & Management Service Guide (2006, revised 2007), p. 17.

- Musculoskeletal: Muscles, skeleton (bones)
- Endocrine: Thyroid gland, pancreas, adrenal glands, ovary, and testes
- Hematologic/lymphatic: Blood and blood-forming organs, lymphatic tissue
- Allergy/Immunologic
- Psychiatric

Elements Required for Each Type of Examination

There are four types of examinations:

1. Problem-focused
2. Expanded problem–focused
3. Detailed
4. Comprehensive

Each type of examination is defined in terms of the body areas and/or organ systems affected:

1. *Problem-focused:* The exam is limited to the affected body area and/or organ system.

> **EXAMPLE**
>
> For ear pain, with no other symptoms noted, the exam is limited to the ears.

2. *Expanded problem–focused:* The exam is limited to the affected body area and/or organ system and includes any system-related body area or organ system.

> **EXAMPLE**
>
> For ear pain with a sore throat, the exam is limited to the ears and the head, neck, throat, and sinuses.

3. *Detailed:* The exam is limited to the affected body area and/or organ system and includes any system-related body area or organ system.

> **EXAMPLE**
>
> For ear pain with a sore throat, cough, high temperature, and chest pain on breathing, the examination is detailed and includes the ears and the head, neck, throat, sinuses, lungs, heart, and chest muscles.

4. *Comprehensive:* The exam is a general multisystem examination or a complete examination of a single organ system and includes any related body area or organ system.

> **EXAMPLE**
>
> For chronic fatigue, weight loss, muscle aches, and numbness in extremities, the examination would involve a full general system check including HEENT, neurological, lymph, musculoskeletal, cardiovascular, and respiratory.

TABLE 6-4   Medical Decision Making

Type of Decision Making	Number of Diagnoses or Management Options	Amount and/or Complexity of Data to Be Reviewed	Risk of Significant Morbidity and/or Mortality
Straightforward	Minimal	Minimal or none	Minimal
Low complexity	Limited	Limited	Low
Moderate complexity	Multiple	Moderate	Moderate
High complexity	Extensive	Extensive	High

Elements of Medical Decision Making

Some medical coding experts feel that the medical decision making element drives the level of the E&M coding process. **Medical decision making** consists of:

- Diagnoses and treatment options
- Amount and complexity of data to be reviewed
- Risk for complications, morbidity, or mortality

Table 6-4 is used to determine:

- How many different diagnoses the provider must consider
- How many tests, studies, or other forms of data must be reviewed

The risks of complications result from the treatment options, along with the morbidity or mortality risk to the patient.

When reading the medical notes, remember that the documentation must always support the level of service.

EXAMPLE

Let's look back at the example of the consultation for progressive anemia (page 110). The medical note is quite long, but you just take one element at a time.

- *What is the POS?* Inpatient
- *What is the TOS?* Consultation
- *New or established patient?* N/A

We know that this was an inpatient consult. Which code best describes the service rendered?

99251

Problem-focused history

Problem-focused examination

Straightforward medical decision making

99252

Expanded problem–focused history

Expanded problem–focused examination

Straightforward medical decision making

99253

Detailed history

Detailed examination

Medical decision making of low complexity

99254

Comprehensive history

Comprehensive examination

Medical decision making of moderate complexity

99255

Comprehensive history

Comprehensive examination

Medical decision making of high complexity

Again, look at the history in the medical notes. Table 6-5 shows that you have an extended HPI, an extended ROS, and a complete PFSH. Review Tables 6-6 and 6-7 to see how to arrive at the type of examination and medical decision making.

TABLE 6-5   History

	Key Components	Type of History
HPI	*Location:* Shortness of breath; chest pain previous night, which had resolved; mild lower back pain, which also had resolved; lower extremity edema bilaterally for the past 3 days	Extended HPI
	Quality: Symptoms decreased with Motrin or Tylenol, but recurred within a few hours	
	Duration: Feeling poorly for the last 2 weeks with fever, chills, and fatigue; chest pain previous night, resolved; edema past 3 days	
	Timing: Throughout the day	
	Associated signs and symptoms: Weight loss, night sweats, high fever, chills, and fatigue	
ROS	*HEENT:* Denies any symptoms of headache or dizziness other than when ambulating	Extended
	Respiratory: Shortness of breath and chest pain	
	Musculoskeletal: Mild lower back pain, which has resolved	
	Cardiovascular: Lower extremity edema bilaterally, with persistent left ankle edema; denies any discomfort in left leg or in left groin	
	Gastrointestinal and genitourinary: Denies any history of bleeding; has noted no blood in stool; denies dark colored stools, no blood in urine	
	Hematologic: Medical history unremarkable except for diagnosis of thalassemia	
PFSH	*Medications:* Tylenol and Motrin p.r.n.	Complete
	Drug allergies: None	
	Family history: Sister has a history of melanoma and brain tumor; mother has fibromyalgia and history of thalassemia	
	Social history: Currently unemployed, lives with wife and 2 children; no history of smoking; no history of IV drug abuse; reports occasional alcohol use; patient is a Jehovah's Witness and would not accept any blood product support	

TABLE 6-6   **Type of Examination**

	Description	Type of Examination
ROS	*HEENT:* No evidence of cervical or supraclavicular adenopathy; no thyromegaly	Expanded problem–focused
	Gastrointestinal: Abdomen: Soft, no evidence of hepatosplenomegaly; no evidence of free fluid	
	Respiratory system: Lungs: Clear to both auscultation and percussion	
	Cardiovascular system: Cardiac: Tachycardia, Homans' sign is negative; left ankle edema and no evidence of thigh or leg swelling noted; no calf tenderness bilaterally	
	Hematologic/lymphatic: Axillae: Right axilla has no lymphadenopathy noted. The left axilla has a 2-cm to 3-cm firm, tender lymph node present in the left medial aspect of the axilla. No other abnormality noted. No palpable inguinal adenopathy	

TABLE 6-7   **Medical Decision Making**

	Description	Medical Decision Making
Number of diagnoses or management options	Thalassemia trait Iron deficiency anemia Palpable left axillary lymphadenopathy associated with fever	Multiple
Amount and/or complexity of data to be reviewed	Reviewed lab tests; ordered CT scan; review of smear	Moderate
Treatment options and risk of significant morbidity and/or mortality	Chronic illness with severe exacerbation/progression	High

   A provider or medical coder does not have the time to set up these very long tables for every medical record when leveling a service. However, a leveling tool is very helpful to the provider in establishing the typical patient. Once this is done, the provider can use the tool as a guide for leveling other visits and consults that are either more or less complex. See the leveling tool in Table 6-8. Using that tool, let's level the service provided in the consultation for progressive anemia.

Leveling the Service

History

1. How many elements of the HPI are documented? _____
2. How many systems were reviewed (ROS)? _____
3. How many areas of the PFSH are documented? _____

TABLE 6-8   E&M Leveling Tool

History: Check all elements supported by the documentation in left column and mark the corresponding score in the right column. Circle the level of History from the right columns that corresponds to any box checked farthest to the left.

	Problem-Focused	*Expanded Problem–Focused*	*Detailed*	*Comprehensive*
☐ **Chief Complaint (Must Be There)**				
HPI				
☐ Timing ☐ Severity ☐ Context ☐ Duration ☐ Location ☐ Associated Signs and Symptoms ☐ Modifying Factors ☐ Quality ☐ Severity, pain on scale of 1–10	☐ 1–3 Elements	☐ 1–3 Elements	☐ 4–8 Elements	☐ 4–8 Elements
Review of Systems ☐ Constitutional ☐ Gastrointestinal ☐ Hematologic/Lymphatic ☐ Eyes ☐ Genitourinary ☐ Endocrine ☐ Integumentary ☐ Respiratory ☐ Allergic/Immunologic ☐ Cardiovascular ☐ Psychiatric ☐ Ear, Nose, Mouth, Throat ☐ Neurological ☐ Musculoskeletal ☐ All others negative	☐ None	☐ 1 System	☐ 2–9 Systems	☐ 10–14 Systems -or- ☐ One Complete Single System
PFSH (not needed for SH or FC codes) ☐ Past History ☐ Social History ☐ Family History	☐ None	☐ None	☐ Any one History	☐ All 3 or ☐ PFSH

Exam: Check all elements supported by the documentation in the level column and mark the corresponding score in the right column. Circle the level of exam from the right column that corresponds to any box checked.

	Problem-Focused	*Expanded Problem–Focused*	*Detailed*	*Comprehensive*
☐ Constitutional ☐ General Appearance ☐ Vital Signs ☐ Gastrointestinal ☐ Hematologic/Lymphatic ☐ Eyes ☐ Genitourinary ☐ Endocrine ☐ Integumentary ☐ Respiratory ☐ Allergic/Immunologic ☐ Cardiovascular ☐ Psychiatric ☐ Ear, Nose, Mouth, Throat ☐ Neurological ☐ Musculoskeletal ☐ All others negative	☐ 1 Limited exam of affected body area or organ system	☐ 2–7 Limited exam of affected body area or organ system and other symptomatic or related organ system(s)	☐ 2–7 Extended exam of affected body area or organ system and other symptomatic or related organ system(s)	☐ 8 or more General multisystem exam or complete exam of a single organ system

Medical Decision Making

Table of Risk (level of risk in any one category entered below. The highest level of any one of the three aspects of medical decision making will determine the overall *complexity level chosen for coding purposes.*)

Level of Risk	*Presenting Problem*	*Diagnostic Procedure(s) Ordered*	*Management Options Selected*
Low	☐ One or two self-limited or minor problems ☐ One stable chronic illness, e.g., well controlled hypertension, noninsulin-dependent diabetes, cataract, BPH ☐ Acute uncomplicated illness or injury, e.g., cystitis, allergic, rhinitis, simple sprain ☐ Low risk of complications, morbidity, or mortality	☐ Noninvasive or minimally invasive lab tests (urinalysis, venipuncture, etc.) ☐ Noninvasive diagnostic procedures (ECG, EEG, echocardiogram, ultrasound) ☐ Physiologic tests not under stress ☐ Non-CV imaging studies w/o IV or intrathecal contrast (upper GE barium enema) ☐ Superficial needle biopsies ☐ Clinical laboratory tests requiring arterial puncture ☐ Skin biopsies	☐ Rest or exercise, diet, stress management ☐ Medication management with minimal risk ☐ Referral not requiring detailed discussion or detailed care plan

TABLE 6-8   E&M Leveling Tool (Continued)

Level of Risk	Presenting Problem	Diagnostic Procedure(s) Ordered	Management Options Selected
Moderate	☐ Three or more self-limited problems ☐ One or more chronic mild and/or self-limited problem(s) with ongoing activity or side effects of treatment ☐ Two or three stable chronic illnesses or problems requiring evaluation ☐ Undiagnosed new illness, injury, or problem with uncertain progress ☐ Moderate risk of complications, morbidity, or mortality	☐ Physiologic tests under stress, e.g., cardiac stress test, fetal contraction stress test ☐ Diagnostic endoscopies for average risk patient ☐ Deep needle or incisional biopsy ☐ Interventional cardiovascular or radiological procedure for average risk patient (stable patient, low-risk procedure) ☐ IV contrast imaging ☐ Percutaneous removal of body fluid ☐ Data to be obtained/reviewed requiring at least 10 minutes of physician's time ☐ Therapeutic or diagnostic spinal, nerve injections	☐ Referrals requiring detailed discussion or detailed care plan ☐ Management of medications with moderate risk, requiring detailed discussion or limited laboratory monitoring (e.g., Coumadin, warfarin, IV heparin, IV anti-arrhythmic beyond 1 day) ☐ Surgery or procedure with ASA 1 risk status ☐ Discussion for psychotherapy and/or counseling ☐ Arranging hospitalization for noncritical illness/injury ☐ Initiation of total parenteral nutrition ☐ Referral for comprehensive pain management rehabilitation
High	☐ One or more acute or chronic illnesses with severe exacerbation ☐ Four or more stable chronic illnesses or problems requiring evaluation ☐ Acute, complicated injury with significant risk of morbidity or mortality ☐ One or more acute or chronic illnesses or problems that pose immediate threat to life or bodily function ☐ An abrupt change in bodily function (e.g., seizure, CVA, acute mental status change) ☐ High risk of complications, morbidity, or mortality	☐ Intra-arterial cerebral angiography (excludes MRA) ☐ Data to be obtained/reviewed requiring at least 20 minutes of physician's time ☐ Endoscopy for high-risk patient ☐ Interventionist cardiovascular or radiological procedure for high-risk patient (e.g., unstable condition)	☐ Emergency hospitalization ☐ Surgery or procedure with ASA 2 or higher risk status ☐ Mechanical ventilator management ☐ Medications requiring intensive monitoring, bearing untoward risks of serious morbidity if adverse effects occur (e.g., initiation of IV heparin, IV anti-arrhythmic, antineoplastics) ☐ Decision not to resuscitate or to deescalate care because of poor prognosis

Coding Based on Time

If the physician documents total time and the counseling and the coordinating care dominates (more than 50%) of the encounter, time may determine the level of service.

Total unit/floor time documented _____ (amount of time)

☐ Counseling and coordination of care should be greater than 50% of total time.

☐ Coding based on time should include documentation of topics discussed or coordination of care provided.

If all the above are documented, select the level of service in the appropriate E&M code section that results in the highest level, either by average time or by the components of History, Exam, and the Medical Decision Making.

Scenario Number _____
New or Established Patient _____   **POS** _____
Code _____

Examination

4. How many organ systems or body areas were documented? _____

Medical Decision Making

5. Based on the documentation, at what type of risk is this patient? _____

Answers

Let's take a look at the answers.

Level of Service

History

How many elements of the HPI are documented? You need four to eight for a comprehensive. In the consultation, you have five: (1) location, (2) quality, (3) duration, (4) timing, and (5) associated signs and symptoms.

How many systems are documented? You need two to nine for a detailed ROS. You have seven: (1) HEENT, (2) respiratory, (3) musculoskeletal, (4) gastrointestinal, (5) genitourinary, (6) cardiovascular, and (7) hematologic/lymphatic.

How many areas of the PFSH are documented? You need three for a comprehensive: (1) past—medications and drug allergies; (2) family—sister with history of melanoma and brain tumor, mother with fibromyalgia and thalassemia; and (3) social—currently unemployed, lives with his wife and 2 children; no history of smoking; no history of IV drug abuse; reports occasional alcohol use; is a Jehovah's Witness and would not accept any blood product support.

The level of history is detailed. Because this service requires three out of three key components (HPI, ROS, and PFSH), the lower level of the three is used to determine the level of history.

Examination

How many organ systems or body areas were documented? You need at least two and up to seven body areas or organ systems for an expanded problem-focused examination or detailed examination. The extent of the examination will determine which type of exam was provided. You have:

1. *HEENT:* No evidence of cervical or supraclavicular adenopathy. No thyromegaly
2. *Gastrointestinal:* Abdomen: Soft, no evidence of hepatosplenomegaly; no evidence of free fluid
3. *Respiratory system:* Lungs: Clear to both auscultation and percussion
4. *Cardiovascular system:* Cardiac: Tachycardia, Homans' sign is negative. Left ankle edema and no evidence of thigh or leg swelling noted. No calf tenderness bilaterally
5. *Hematologic/lymphatic:* Axillae: Right axilla has no lymphadenopathy noted. The left axilla has a 2-cm to 3-cm firm, tender lymph node present in the left medial aspect of the axilla. No other abnormality noted. No palpable inguinal adenopathy

Medical Decision Making

Based on the documentation, at what level of risk is the patient? Look at Table 6-5. This patient has one chronic illness, anemia, that could be thalassemia anemia, and, because of the patient's religious convictions, he will not take any blood products. The risk of death increases because the patient is refusing treatment through blood transfusion.

Now you put all the elements of the consult together to level the service. Keep in mind that in Table 6-6 all three elements must be met and in Table 6-7, two of the three elements must be either met or exceeded to select a particular level of service.

Using the levels of history, examination, and medical decision making, what consultation code would you use for this service?

- Detailed history
- Detailed examination
- High medical decision making

Given the documentation in the record, the level of service is 99253.

CHAPTER EXERCISES

Using the auditing tool, find the CPT code(s) for the following scenarios.

Scenario 6-1

OFFICE NOTE

Patient is here for follow-up of right knee pain.

The patient states that he did go to the Pain Clinic for his back and that he did receive an epidural steroid injection. He feels that there was no significant difference with the epidural steroid. He has a follow-up appointment in 2 weeks to receive another shot. He questions whether he should take this second shot or go to a chiropractor to see whether manipulation will help him with his symptoms. He also notes that since the Pain Clinic put him on Trilisate 1,000 mg twice a day, he has noticed some improvement in his back symptoms.

There is a remarkable improvement in his knee symptoms. He had complained of pain in his right knee especially with squatting. X-rays were done, which showed mild osteoarthritic changes. The patient states that he has been stretching regularly, trying to exercise and strengthen his quadriceps daily, and has taken the Trilisate regularly. Patient states that his knee feels quite good. He is still taking the Osteo Bi-Flex and feels it has resulted in a significant decrease in his knee pain. He was told that he could continue the same. He also informs me that he had seen Dr. Hajjar for his varicosities, and Dr. Hajjar has recommended against surgery for the varicosities and advised him to try compression stockings. He feels the compression stockings have worked very well for him, but he would like a prescription to get black colored stockings because he goes dancing on weekends. He states that he has been able to dance over the last couple of weekends now that his knee feels significantly better.

PHYSICAL EXAMINATION:

General: This is a pleasant white male who appears to be in no distress.

Vital Signs: Weight is 235 lb, pulse is 60/minute, and blood pressure is 112/72.

HEENT: No pallor or icterus.

Back: Does not reveal any vertebral tenderness to palpation today. There is no increased paraspinal muscle tone.

Extremities: Straight leg raising test is bilaterally negative today with intact strength in his lower extremities and intact reflexes. He has mild decreased pinprick sensation in his lower extremities, which has been noted in the past, suggestive of peripheral neuropathy. Examination of his knee does not reveal any erythema or

continued

effusion. There is slight tenderness to palpation over the patella, but no tenderness to palpation over the medial and lateral joint lines. Anterior and posterior drawer signs are negative. Gait appears to be normal.

ASSESSMENT AND PLAN:

1. Back pain due to spinal stenosis. He has received one epidural steroid injection, did not derive significant benefit. I recommended he try the second time before considering referral to another chiropractor because he may derive some benefits with the second shot. The patient is agreeable to that. He will continue the Trilisate 1,000 mg b.i.d. in the meantime.

2. Right knee pain improved since he has been on the Trilisate. He was told he could continue the Osteo Bi-Flex. He will continue to do regular strengthening exercises for his quadriceps and gentle stretching.

3. Varicose veins with a large varix, right leg. He was given a prescription for TED stockings per his request.

4. Events of peripheral neuropathy. He needs to have some baseline blood work done, which was recommended by Dr. Fine. He has not had it so far. He will be scheduled for the same today. He will follow up with me in 3 months for a comprehensive physical or sooner if needed.

Procedural code(s): _____

Scenario 6-2

OFFICE NOTE

This is a follow-up visit of this 52-year-old woman with metastatic malignant melanoma.

HISTORY OF PRESENT ILLNESS: Melanoma was found January 2005. A 2.2 mm lesion was removed from distal left leg. Sentinel node was negative. Stage IIA disease. She did not receive adjuvant therapy. Earlier this year routine screening CT scan showed liver lesions. Biopsy confirmed presence of metastatic malignant melanoma. She has been receiving DTIC as single agent.

PAST HISTORY: Diffuse large cell lymphoma, Stage IIIA, present since April 2003, treated with CHOP with Rituxan. In this regard, she remains in complete remission. She has tolerated her chemotherapy fairly well. Her next scheduled dose is in about 2 weeks. Routine medications include Lipitor, Fosamax, and alprazolam.

REVIEW OF SYSTEMS:

CNS: No headaches or lateralizing motor or sensory problems.

ENT: No sinus or epistaxis.

Metabolic: Benign.

Dermatologic: No rash or zoster.

Hematologic: No bleeding or easy bruising.

Cardiac and Pulmonary are both okay. No chest pain, palpitation, or dyspnea.

GI: No nausea, no diarrhea.

GU: Negative.

Musculoskeletal: Nonfocal.

Constitutional: Weight is 127 lb. Blood pressure is 162/78.

Good appetite. She has actually done quite well with her chemotherapy; no weight loss.

EXAMINATION: On exam, she looks well. Head and neck: No cervical or supraclavicular adenopathy.

Heart and lungs are okay.

Abdomen is benign.

Liver and spleen are not palpable.

Lymph nodes: No cervical, axillary, or inguinal adenopathy.

She recently underwent CT scan of the chest, abdomen, and pelvis. This revealed 3 well-defined lesions in the liver. The radiologist felt these to have increased slightly in size. In addition, they thought there might be a new hypodensity, but it was very difficult for them to ascertain this and so no conclusion was made. A small pericardial effusion was identified. Perhaps a little bit of pleural thickening on the right side could also be seen. A CT scan of the lower extremities showed no mass. No evidence of local recurrence.

Her white count is 4,100, hematocrit 39, platelets 266,000. ANC was 1,700. CHEM-7 normal. Creatinine 0.8, liver function tests normal. LDH 206.

IMPRESSION AND PLAN: Malignant melanoma, metastatic to the liver, status post 3 cycles DTIC. CT scan shows that there has really been no improvement; if anything, a slight degree of worsening. I discussed the findings with her. We could consider any of several clinical approaches. One would be to increase the dose of the DTIC, making it more aggressive. Another would be to switch the therapy, employ a combination program, perhaps Temodar and taxol. A third approach would be to go to chemoimmunotherapy with an IL-based regimen. We have discussed facets of different treatment plans. I favor preserving the DTIC-like activity with Temodar in this situation; it might give us better results. Also, in view of the evident growth, it might be reasonable at this point to place her on a combination. The combination of temozolomide plus a dose of taxol does seem to be effective. Temozolomide at a dose of 150 mg/m^2 days 1 to 5, every 4 weeks, along with Taxotere 80 mg/m^2 every 4 weeks seems to be a program that achieves responses in a larger number of patients. She is willing to try this and we will get her started on this switch in therapy.

Procedural code(s): _____

Scenario 6-3

HISTORY AND PHYSICAL

Emergency Room Visit

CC: Sam is here today after a fall off of his skateboard. He is complaining of a hurt foot and leg.

EXAMINATION: On examination, the foot and leg are both swollen and bruised. The patient is a 14-year-old who had to be helped into the office by his dad, because he could not put any weight on his leg or foot.

continued

> **IMPRESSION:** The x-ray showed that there is a Fx at the distal end of the femur.
>
> **PLAN AND TREATMENT:** A closed reduction was performed and a short cast was applied.

Procedural code(s): _____

Scenario 6-4

OFFICE NOTE

Mary comes in for a follow-up of hypertension and hyperlipidemia along with a physical exam. She reports she has been feeling well. Denies any polyuria, polyphagia, or polydipsia. Reports no paresthesias in the upper or lower extremities.

She is planning to go to Florida in 11/2006 and spend time until 04/2007. She is trying to cope better following the death of her husband. When she returns from Florida next year, she wants to sell her house and move into her daughter's place. She reports no chest pain or shortness of breath. She denies any cough, sputum, or hemoptysis. She denies any pedal edema or claudication pain in the lower extremities. She reports that her left ear has been blocked from wax accumulation. She cannot hear much on the left side. She tried to use eardrops without much success.

REVIEW OF SYSTEMS: She reports no ear discharge. Denies any blurred vision or diplopia. Denies any abdominal pain, hematemesis, melena, blood, or mucus in the stool. She reports no dysuria, frequency, or hematuria. Denies any joint pain, swelling, headache, syncope, weakness, or incoordination in the upper or lower extremities. She denies any skin rash or abnormal pigmentation on the skin. Reports no joint pain or swelling.

PAST MEDICAL HISTORY: Significant for:

1. Hypertension.

2. Hyperlipidemia.

3. Diabetes mellitus.

4. Status post appendectomy.

5. Status post tonsillectomy.

6. EKG showed bundle-branch block, echocardiogram in the past showed normal EF and valves, and she has had no chest pain.

7. She had a mammogram recently, which was unremarkable.

8. Status post right hemicolectomy for colon cancer in 08/2000.

She received therapy with 5-FU and leucovorin for one year. She had a repeat colonoscopy initially in 1996, another one in 2001, and more recently in 2006, which have all been normal.

CURRENT MEDICATIONS:

1. Hydrochlorothiazide 25 mg once daily.

2. Aspirin 1 per day.

3. Glyburide 2.5 mg once daily.

4. Adalat 90 mg once daily.

5. Atenolol 50 mg once daily.

6. Lipitor 10 mg once a daily.

7. Levothroid 0.05 mg once daily.

8. Calcium along with vitamin D.

ALLERGIES: She reports no allergies to any medication.

PERSONAL HISTORY: Unchanged from a previous dictation in 2005.

FAMILY HISTORY: Unchanged from a previous dictation in 2005. Her husband passed away last year.

PHYSICAL EXAMINATION:

Vital Signs: Temperature normal, blood pressure 130/58, pulse rate 60/minute and regular, weight 143 lb, and respiratory rate 16/minute.

HEENT: Normal tympanic membranes and external auditory canal on the right side. Left ear was occluded with cerumen. Pupils were equal and reactive. Eye movements were normal. Oral cavity exam showed normal posterior pharyngeal wall and tonsillar area.

Neck: No jugular venous distention, bruits in the neck, or thyromegaly.

Lungs: Clear to auscultation.

Heart: Heart sounds are normal. She has a 2/6 faint ejection systolic murmur in the aortic area.

Breasts: Normal-appearing nipples. She had no breast masses. No axillary adenopathy was noted. She had no nipple discharge.

Adbomen: Soft and nontender. No masses were palpable.

Pelvic: Pelvic exam and Pap smear were not performed.

Neurologic: Normal cranial nerves II through XII. Motor, sensory, and cerebellar system exam was normal.

Exremities: Lower extremity exam showed no edema.

Skin: No rash or abnormal pigmentation.

Musculoskeletal: Joint exam showed no swelling. Range of movement of joints was normal.

ASSESSMENT AND PLAN:

1. Occluded left external auditory canal with impacted cerumen leading to decreased hearing and discomfort. After discussion with her, her ear was syringed. Following syringing, considerable amount of wax was removed and her hearing improved. She had symptomatic relief after the procedure.

2. Diabetes mellitus. Her most recent glycohemoglobin was 6. She has no evidence of nephropathy. She does have regular eye exams. Clinically, she does not have any evidence of neuropathy.

3. Hyperlipidemia. Her LDL cholesterol is slightly above target. I have advised her to increase her Lipitor to 20 mg for better control of LDL cholesterol. Triglycerides and HDL were normal. If she experiences any muscle aches or pains, she was instructed to call me.

continued

4. Hypertension, controlled on the present combination of medication.

5. Hypertension. She is clinically euthyroid. She will continue the present dose of Levothroid.

6. Status post hemicolectomy for colon cancer. She had a colonoscopy in 2006, which was unremarkable. Her next colonoscopy will be in 3–4 years' time.

7. Health maintenance. States she received tetanus booster dose and Pneumovax in 1995. She was advised to get flu vaccine next week. She did not want to do a bone density scan. She had a mammogram in 08/2006, which was unremarkable. She has a follow-up with me in 04/2007 when she returns from her trip to Florida.

Procedural code(s): _____

Scenario 6-5

OFFICE NOTE

Today Amy's mother brings her in for a consult for a rash throughout her body.

HPI: Amy is a 3-year-old who has had this rash for about 2 weeks. The mother states that on or about the third day of the rash she brought Amy to her pediatrician where she gave her a topical over-the-counter cream for the rash and said that if it did not clear up in a few days to call. She did call back, and Amy's PCP referred her to me. There have been no fever cold symptoms or any other signs of illness, just the rash. Amy does not seem to be scratching the rash, nor does it seem to bother her in any way.

EXAM: On exam, Amy seems to be a very well taken care of child, well fed, and clean child. The rash is dry, red, scaly, and flaky. It appears on her face, arms, and back of her knees. The family has a cat and a dog that interact with Amy. The cat sleeps with her.

This looks like some kind of allergic reaction.

IMPRESSION: Contact dermatitis.

PLAN:

1. Do allergy testing.

2. Bathe in an oatmeal bath to remoisturize her skin.

3. Mom is to use unscented laundry detergent and fabric softener, and use unscented soap on Amy.

Procedural code(s): _____

Scenario 6-6

OFFICE NOTE

CHIEF COMPLAINT: CHF, chronic atrial fibrillation, dementia, and type 2 diabetes.

HISTORY OF PRESENT ILLNESS: Florence is here in follow-up of her CHF, atrial fibrillation, dementia, and diabetes. She is here today with her husband, doing well, having celebrated her 85th birthday earlier in the year.

MEDICATIONS: Glipizide 10 mg b.i.d., and atenolol 50 mg once a day. She has been off warfarin now for the last 4 months in a well-documented note related to the risk-benefit ratio of persisting with her anticoagulation with her chronic atrial fibrillation in which she had had very difficult to control protimes. She is on aspirin 325 mg a day, Lasix 80 mg b.i.d. She has been off the Zestril/lisinopril since last visit.

She apparently had been in Status 1 in the CHF program, but this has been unnoticed by the patient and they do not believe that they are actually in any case management. At any rate, she is doing well. She is using her cane. Denies any problems with activities of daily living and is quite happy and content. They are not checking home glucoses. She denies any symptoms of hyperglycemia.

REVIEW OF SYSTEMS:

ENT: Negative. Annual eye examinations are up to date, they state.

Cardiopulmonary: She denies any recent dyspnea, orthopnea, or PND. She does have peripheral edema. She does her daily weights, which she states have been stable. She is 135 lb here today and was 124 lb in 08/2004.

GI: Otherwise negative.

GU: Otherwise negative.

MS: Otherwise negative.

PHYSICAL EXAMINATION:

GENERAL: She is pleasant, alert, and oriented. Husband is helping her with some issues.

HEENT: Sclerae are clear.

Chest: Clear to auscultation.

Heart: Heart sounds are distant, but irregularly irregular with an apical rate of about 80.

Extremities: Show 1+ edema bilaterally. Skin is warm. Peripheral pulses are absent. There are no neurovascular changes.

IMPRESSION AND PLAN:

1. CHF. She has had a 9- or 10-pound weight gain over the last 4 months. I am presuming at least some of this is fluid related to her peripheral edema, although she has no symptoms of any CHF otherwise. We will reintroduce lisinopril 2.5 mg once a day, given her blood pressure being 160/80. We will recheck her CHEM-7 and watch for any worsening of her azotemia.

2. Chronic atrial fibrillation. She is currently taking a daily aspirin. Off of anticoagulation as noted with risk of stroke.

3. OBS/dementia, stable and early. Consider Aricept or other, not introduced at this juncture. She is doing well with her husband at home.

4. Type 2 diabetes, not monitored, but asymptomatic. Her glycohemoglobin was 7.6 in 09/2004. We will recheck today. She will have a CHEM-7, lipids, CBC, TSH, and glycohemoglobin today. She will recheck here in 3 months with her new primary care physician, Dr. Roger, because I will be departing to Salem, and transportation will be an issue to leave Newburyport where she has been a patient for 20 years. Her husband will continue to monitor weight and they will continue with the Status 1 program; they state they are getting nearly weekly calls from the nurse.

Procedural code(s): _____

Scenario 6-7

OFFICE NOTE

Mary Anne is here for a follow-up. It has been several months and she has been doing very well. She had a lot of trouble with the venous stasis dermatitis and a slow-to-heal ulcer on her left ankle in the fall. She required several Unna Boot applications, which finally helped resolve things. She is on an aggressive diuretic campaign of 68 mg of Lasix in the morning and 40 mg at night. She is troubled by how much urination she has to do. She has actually lost 17 lb since October and her peripheral edema has actually improved. I have decided to back off on her Lasix to 40 mg in the morning and 20 mg in the afternoon, and she will watch her weight; if she gains more than 5 pounds, she will increase the dose.

She has a history of gastric ulcer and anemia from GI blood losses. She was on aspirin at the time. Her ulcer has healed and her blood counts are normal. She asked about aspirin and I advised not to restart the aspirin again at this time. She does have a transient ischemic attack and of course she is at increased risk for stroke. Her recent blood work is all normal except for her blood sugar; cholesterol is in good shape. Her blood has increased dramatically from the summer and her Alc went from 5.8 to 9.4. She admits to a lot of dietary indiscretion and has been eating a lot of sweets. She was advised to cut down on the sweets and we are going to increase her glyburide to 2.5 mg b.i.d. and see how we do.

On review of systems, she denies chest pain, shortness of breath, paroxysmal nocturnal dyspnea, or orthopnea. Bowels are good.

OBJECTIVE: Weight 260 lb, blood pressure 140/72, pulse 72 and regular, and temperature 97.2°.

IMPRESSION:

1. Type 2 diabetes.

2. Hypertension, fair control.

3. Peripheral edema due to venous stasis. She also has a yeast infection in her skin folds.

PLAN:

1. Increase glyburide to 2.5 mg b.i.d.

2. Decrease Lasix to 40 mg in the morning and 20 mg in the afternoon.

3. Stop nystatin powder; try Monistat derm cream 2% b.i.d.

4. Advised her to cut back on sweets in her diet.

5. I will see her again in 3 months, sooner if problems.

Procedural code(s): _____

Scenario 6-8

OFFICE NOTE

Medical problems include hypertension, osteoporosis, and urinary incontinence.

HISTORY OF PRESENT ILLNESS: The patient comes in today for her usual follow-up. Her daughter and granddaughter accompany her and are concerned because the patient's hearing has deteriorated. She was due to have a hearing test done, but apparently the daughter was hospitalized and this never got done. Also, they are concerned because she has a lot of problems with pain in her knees and difficulty getting up the stairs. They are wondering about a home health aide to help her out. She lives with her son and daughter-in-law, but they are working and unable to assist her as much as is needed. They are also concerned because her memory has failed her and she is having continued urinary incontinence. When I asked the patient about all these symptoms, she denies having any problems whatsoever. She says she feels fine. Clearly she is hard of hearing.

REVIEW OF SYSTEMS: She denies headache. She denies chest pain, shortness of breath, or peripheral edema. She denies urinary incontinence. She denies memory dysfunction. Currently, she is on HCTZ 25 mg q.d., lisinopril 10 mg q.d., oxybutynin 5 mg q.d., and Fosamax weekly. She is allergic to Percocet.

PHYSICAL EXAMINATION: On physical examination, she is in no acute distress. Weight is 122 lb, up 6 lb. Blood pressure is 140/100. Pulse is 80 and regular. Right tympanic membrane is obscured by cerumen. Left appears normal. Neck is supple. No adenopathy. Heart reveals regular rhythm without murmurs. Her lungs are clear. Abdomen is benign, nontender, no masses. Extremities are without edema. Both her knees show scant amount of effusion and a lot of crepitus consistent with osteoarthritis. On a mini-mental status examination today, she scored 24/30. The rest of the neurologic is nonfocal.

ASSESSMENT AND PLAN:

1. Memory dysfunction consistent with early dementia. Some of this could be due to her poor hearing. I will, however, get a B12, CSC thyroic cascade. She will be booked for a CT scan of her head with and without contrast because she had a fall about 6 months ago and the family is unsure whether she struck her head or not. When I get those results I will mail them to the daughter and, if the CT is normal, will go ahead and start Aricept 5 mg daily. I will be planning on repeat mini-mental status examination when I see her in 6 months for her complete checkup.

2. Hard of hearing. She is going to use Debrox in the right ear and follow up in two weeks for removal of cerumen. Then if she is still having a hard time hearing, a hearing test will be scheduled.

3. Hypertension. She will have a follow-up blood pressure check in two weeks and, if it is still elevated, we will need to raise her lisinopril to 20 mg daily.

4. Urinary incontinence. She will get a urine culture done and increase the oxybutynin to 5 mg b.i.d. and continue with pads.

5. Osteoarthritis of her knees. She is going to use glucosamine over-the-counter. I talked to the family about considering getting a stair elevator to help her. They are going to meet with a social worker about getting a home health aide and some other help in the house.

Procedural code(s): _____

For the following scenarios, code procedure(s) and diagnosis(es).

Scenario 6-9

OFFICE NOTE

Anna is a new patient being seen today in the office without her complete medical record.

Anna is a 43-year-old female who comes into the office with complaints of right-sided mid- to low back pain. She is worried that she might have a kidney infection. She has not had any pyelonephritis. She states that in the 1980s, she used to get recurrent urinary tract infections. She states that at that time she found that she is allergic to sulfa drugs and she was given Macrodantin with good relief. She denies any dysuria or frequency. She has noted some slight increase in urgency recently. She does enjoy her low sugar cranberry juice and water. She tried some heat over her right low back yesterday evening, which helped her symptoms improve. However, because she had the heat on all night, she is left with a slightly red mark in that area of her back. She denies any fevers or chills. She denies any nausea or vomiting. She occasionally gets back pain from gas and constipation; however, she states she has had normal bowel movements lately. She has a good p.o. intake. She denies any worsening of her abdominal pain. She is scheduled for colonoscopy at the end of the month.

PAST MEDICAL HISTORY: DM and coronary artery disease, obesity, anxiety, paranoia, acne, rosacea, and chronic back pain.

CURRENT MEDICATIONS: Stool softeners, simethicone, Ativan 1 mg q.h.s. p.r.n. insomnia, Seroquel 25 mg q.h.s., doxycycline 100 mg q.d., lisinopril 20 mg q.d., aspirin, calcium, Lipitor 20 mg q.d., Isordil 10 mg t.i.d., lactulose 20 mg q.d. p.r.n., and OTC hydrocortisone p.r.n.

ALLERGIES: Sulfa.

The patient has a follow-up with her PCP, Dr. Bagga, on 05/17/2006. She denies any trauma to her back. She denies any numbness or tingling. She goes to Curves regularly to exercise to help her reduce weight.

PHYSICAL EXAMINATION:

General: No acute distress, obese female.

Vital Signs: Blood pressure is 130/80 and temperature is 99.3°.

HEENT: Normocephalic and atraumatic. Moist mucous membranes.

Neck: Supple.

Back: No spinal tenderness. No CVA tenderness. There is some mild erythema on the right lateral mid-lower to upper lower back. There is some minimal tenderness over the paraspinal muscles. No vesicles, pustules, or bullae appreciated.

ASSESSMENT AND PLAN: Back pain. Urinalysis is negative. Does not appear to be infectious at this time. Probably musculoskeletal. Recommend Tylenol or ibuprofen p.r.n. Can continue heat; however, reviewed importance of using warm, not hot temperature, to avoid burning. Can use heat t.i.d. to q.i.d. about 20 minutes at a time. Reviewed proper lifting. The patient will curtail going to Curves for a few days until symptoms improve. If she develops new symptoms such as rash or dysuria, she will return to the office for reevaluation.

Procedural code(s): _____

Diagnosis code(s): _____

Scenario 6-10

OFFICE NOTE

This 90-year-old woman is seen in consultation at the request of Dr. Smith. The patient has several complaints. First is that the right fourth and left third fingers have been locking on her. I had seen her over a year ago for injection of the right fourth finger with excellent results. These have been bothering her for months. Her second complaint is that her right shoulder bothers her. She fell and fractured that shoulder years ago. She has limited motion and it is moderately sore but does not wake her up at night. It is not red, hot, or swollen. She otherwise says from a musculoskeletal viewpoint, she has been feeling well. She is known to have osteoporosis and compression fractures and is taking nasal calcitonin and as far as I can tell has not had any recent fractures. She also has been found by Dr. Gilman to have a possible gastric malignancy, depression, asthma, and hypertension. She has been noted to have a nonhealing gastric ulcer but she has declined follow-up for that at this point.

PAST HISTORY: As above.

FAMILY HISTORY: Noncontributory.

BRIEF REVIEW OF SYSTEMS: Noncontributory. Medications per nursing note.

EXAM: Vital signs per nursing note include BP 154/80. She is alert, in no distress. Skin shows no nodules or tophi. TMJs, cervical spine, left shoulder negative. Right shoulder has only about 60° of motion in all directions with some tenderness over the subacromial bursa and some crepitus. Elbows, wrists, MCPs, PIPs, DIPs negative. The right fourth and left third flexor tendons are tender with some locking more on the left than tenderness, and some tenderness more than locking on the right. SCJs, costochondral junctions, thoracic spine, LS spine nontender. Some dorsal kyphosis. Hips, knees, ankles, and feet are okay. X-rays of the right shoulder were obtained today. There is evidence of the old fracture and some osteoarthritis of the glenohumeral joint.

ASSESSMENT:

1. Right shoulder pain. Probably both rotator cuff tendonitis and underlying osteoarthritis of the glenohumeral joint. After discussion, it was opted to treat her with local injections to see if that will give her some benefit. If not, we should not do this again.

2. Right fourth trigger finger.

3. Left third trigger finger. We will treat these with local injections.

4. Osteoporosis status post compression fractures. It is probably reasonable to continue nasal calcitonin, which is generally considered to be a fairly weak medicine. Given her non healing gastric ulcer, it is reasonable to avoid oral bisphosphonates.

PLAN: Right subacromial bursa and right shoulder anteriorly each injected with 0.75 ml of 1% lidocaine and 30-mg methylprednisolone acetate, and the right fourth and left third flexor tendon sheaths each with about 0.5 ml of 1% lidocaine and 20-mg methylprednisolone acetate, all after a sterile prep. The patient tolerated the procedures well. Follow-up call by my nurse in 2 weeks. She will follow up with Dr. Smith and return visit to me p.r.n.

Procedural code(s): _____

Diagnosis code(s): _____

Scenario 6-11

OFFICE NOTE

Sarah is here today for her first visit. She was born 7 days ago and is in for her 1-week PE.

EXAM: Today's weight is 7 lb 4 oz, length 22 in. She has gained 4 oz. The baby was very jaundiced a day after her birth and this has cleared up very nicely. Sarah's eyes are clear; she reacts to sounds. Her hips are not displaced. All other systems are negative.

IMPRESSION AND PLAN: Healthy baby. Will see her back in one month and at that time she will get her first series of shots.

Procedural code(s): _____

Diagnosis code(s): _____

Scenario 6-12

OFFICE NOTE

The patient is seen today for renal insufficiency, chronic V status post aortic valve replacement; chronic atrial fibrillation and history of melanoma twice, including a recently excised lentigo maligna (carcinoma in situ melanoma) of the left helix. He has not had any recurrent nosebleeds.

ALLERGIES: He has no allergies.

SOCIAL HISTORY: He lives at home with his wife. He is doing well. He is retired, stays active with yard work. Does not smoke or drink. No cough, chest pain, or shortness of breath. Has a chronic right pleural effusion, status post thoracoscopy and pleurodesis, probably related to his congestive heart failure. He has had recurrent epistaxis, which is no longer a problem since he is off Coumadin. He has had his aortic valve replaced with a tissue valve. Elevated creatinine. Mild memory disturbance and hypertension. No cough, chest pain, shortness of breath, orthopnea, PND, or dyspnea on exertion. No hemoptysis. No other masses. No nausea and no vomiting.

REVIEW OF SYSTEMS: No diarrhea, constipation, or rectal bleeding.

PHYSICAL EXAMINATION:

HEENT: Extraocular muscle movements intact. Pharynx normal. Healing wound in the left ear lobe. Small sebaceous cyst in the right submandibular area about 1 cm in diameter with a punctum.

Neck: Supple.

Heart: Heart sounds are irregular. There is a 2/6 systolic murmur. No diastolic murmur.

Lungs: Lung fields are clear with diminished breath sounds at the right base.

Abdomen: Soft, flat, and nontender.

Skin: Small, irregular, melanotic lesion on the right chest for which I am referring him to Dermatology for consult and/or treatment.

ASSESSMENT AND PLAN:

Labs were reviewed. Schedule complete physical in 3 months. Continue current medication with the exception of decreasing Lasix to half of a 40-mg tablet daily instead of 40 mg every other day. Continue atenolol 100 mg a day, lisinopril 20 mg a day, Lasix 20 mg a day, and potassium 10 mEq every other day, aspirin 81 mg a day, and multiple vitamins. Monitor systolic blood pressure; attempt to get this down below 130–140. Recheck in three months.

Procedural code(s): _____

Diagnosis code(s): _____

Scenario 6-13

OFFICE NOTE

The patient is here today for a consult for muscle invasive bladder cancer to discuss treatment options. The patient has always been really quite healthy. She recently presented with UTI symptoms and was found to have hematuria and bleeding. Multiple attempts with antibiotics were ineffective and she underwent urologic evaluation. She was found to have bladder cancer. Pathology showed papillary transitional cell carcinoma grade 3/3 with extensive necrosis and squamous differentiation. Treatment was suggested to be a cystectomy, but the patient declined as she did not wish to have a urostomy bag.

Staging has been okay. Lung scan and CAT scans do not show evidence of distant disease.

Past surgery includes hysterectomy for prolapse. She had surgery on her right shoulder with placement of prosthesis about 15 years ago. She has a history of breast cancer, managed with left lumpectomy and postoperative radiation.

FAMILY HISTORY: Sister had bladder cancer. Brother had colon cancer. One sister is diabetic. Her mother died of CHF at 90, father of a CVA and old age.

MEDICATIONS: Prilosec and multivitamins. She complains of a history of sulfa allergy, (?) hives. She also gets nauseous with codeine. She uses p.r.n. meclizine for occasional vertigo.

SYSTEM REVIEW:

CNS: No headaches or neuropathic symptoms.

ENT: She had a recent sinus infection, no lingering problems.

Metabolic: Benign. No thyroid or diabetic conditions.

Derm: No rash or zoster.

HEME: No bleeding or easy bruisability.

Pulmonary: She has never been a smoker. Denies asthma or TB.

Cardiac: No history of chest pain.

GI: Remote history of ulcers. Apparently, this was *H. pylori* positive. She got a brief period of antibiotic treatment, hence not had recurrent symptoms.

GU: As noted above. Bladder cancer.

continued

Musculoskeletal: Nonfocal apart from some arthritic problems.

Constitutional: Weight is stable. No weight loss. No fevers or night sweats. On exam, elderly woman in no acute distress. Weight is 106. Height is 56 in. Pulse is 64 and regular. Head and neck: No cervical or supraclavicular adenopathy. Jaundice not appreciated. Lungs are clear. Heart: Regular rhythm, no murmurs. Abdomen is benign. Liver and spleen are not palpable, no masses or tenderness.

Extremities: No clubbing or edema.

Lymph nodes: None appreciated. No cervical or axillary adenopathy.

IMPRESSION AND PLAN:

1. Muscle invasive bladder cancer.

2. Left breast cancer. I indicated to her that the best treatment option with the highest cure rate remains surgery. She is pretty much dead set against having a cystectomy and wishes to consider radiation and/or chemotherapy. Discussed with her bladder conserving radiation and chemotherapy. I pointed out that radiation in this situation is the cornerstone of the treatment and chemotherapy may add something to it. Various approaches exist. This can include induction chemotherapy, followed by radiation with concurrent chemotherapy or radiation alone or with concurrent chemotherapy. I pointed out to her that the cure rate and ultimate disease control rate with either chemoradiation or radiation alone are not ideal, and there is unfortunately a high relapse and progression rate. In addition, although it avoids surgery initially, it is quite common to have bladder-related symptoms with shrinkage of the bladder, nocturia, urinary frequency, and hematuria as a consequence of the treatment itself. She will be in touch soon regarding her thoughts on this.

Procedural code(s): _____
Diagnosis code(s): _____

Scenario 6-14

OFFICE NOTE

CC: Joe is here today for a bone marrow aspiration and Bx for lymphoblastic leukemia.

HPI: Joe is an 8-year-old with a present illness of lymphoblastic leukemia of about 4 months. He is now receiving treatment for his leukemia and is doing well with the treatment, but the side effects are hard on him.

PFSH: Joe's family lived near a Superfund Site when Joe's mom conceived him. Joe's sister also has leukemia, but a different form of the disease.

EXAM: Weight 70 lb, height just under 3 ft. Joe has lost 5 lb since the last visit, but does have the side effects of throwing up and being very lethargic. There is no bruising of his skin today and no other signs of bleeding. Joe had a blood transfusion yesterday and his appearance is great.

PROCEDURE: The hip is prepared for the aspiration. The fine needle is inserted into the hip and a small sample of bone marrow is aspirated. The sample is sent to the lab.

> **PLAN:** The patient will return after the Bx comes back from the lab. From there we will see how much longer the treatment will be or if we will need to change the treatment.

Procedural code(s): _____

Diagnosis code(s): _____

Scenario 6-15

OFFICE NOTE

Sue is a 69-year-old female here for a first-time visit.

PAST MEDICAL HISTORY: She has a history of hyperlipidemia; hypertension; atrial fibrillation, anxiety, and depression related to the death of a close friend about a year or so ago; history of osteoporosis.

PAST SURGICAL HISTORY: Appendectomy. She has had a history of kidney stones, the last one approximately 15 years ago.

SOCIAL HISTORY: She is a widow with no children. She is a retired clerk.

MEDICATIONS: Alprazolam 0.25 mg p.o. q.h.s. p.r.n. (she takes this rarely); Lipitor 10 mg q.d.; Fosamax 70 mg weekly; lisinopril 20 mg q.d.; chlorthalidone 50 mg q.d.; B-complex and vitamins.

ALLERGIES: Motrin, Naprosyn, Bactrim, and Penicillin.

REVIEW OF SYSTEMS: The patient feels otherwise healthy. She exercises daily. She denies any chest pain, shortness of breath, nausea, vomiting, diarrhea, or constipation. No change in bowel or bladder habits. She denies any numbness or weakness in her arms or legs.

PHYSICAL EXAMINATION: Otherwise healthy-appearing female who appears her stated age, in no acute distress. Blood pressure 120/70. Pulse regular at 72. HEENT exam: Unremarkable. PERLA, EOMI. Ears are clear. Tympanic membranes are negative. Throat is unremarkable. Neck is supple without adenopathy or bruits. Chest is clear. Heart is regular rhythm without murmurs, gallops, or rubs. Breast exam bilaterally is without masses. Axillary exam is negative. Abdomen is soft, no masses or tenderness. Pelvic exam is chaperoned by Donna Jordan, RN; normal external genitalia; normal appearing cervix; no adnexal masses or tenderness. Rectal exam: Brown, guaiac negative stool, no masses. Extremity exam: No clubbing, cyanosis, or edema. Sensory exam to light touch and pinprick is intact. Pulses are intact in the dorsal pedal pulses bilaterally.

ASSESSMENT:

1. Hyperlipidemia. Continue Lipitor and checking lipid profile. May consider reducing her medication to half a tablet per day if her cholesterol is under good control.

2. Hypertension. She remains on lisinopril 20 mg q.d. We are going to switch her to HCTZ 12.5 mg daily for her diuretic.

3. Osteoporosis. Continue Fosamax weekly.

4. Difficulty with sleep. This has actually pretty much resolved. She will continue alprazolam on a p.r.n. basis. She has no other complaints. Routine lab work

continued

ordered for health maintenance screening. She has had a bone density scan in the past and she is on Fosamax. She has had a lower GI endoscopy in the year 2000. She will do stool guaiac cards. In addition, she will have routine mammography scheduled. I will see her back in 4 months to check her blood pressure response and to adjust her medications as needed.

Procedural code(s): _____

Diagnosis code(s): _____

Scenario 6-16

OFFICE NOTE

CC: Patient comes in today for a recheck of her elevated blood pressure.

HPI: Patient has been on NSAIDs (Naprosyn) for about 10 years for chronic pain and now has elevated blood pressure. She was also on Vioxx for about 18 months, but has been off now for about a year. She did not want to go onto another medication and asked if she could cut out the NSAIDs. She wanted to do a trial run of being off of all NSAIDs to see if her BP would come down. The patient had also gained about 20 lb in the last year.

EXAMINATION: Weight 130, BP 140/98. She has lost about 10 lbs. Heart rate normal. Respiration normal.

IMPRESSION AND PLAN: The BP has not come down enough to go on without treatment. With both the weight loss and the absence of the NSAIDs, the BP should have come down more. Total time with the patient was 10 minutes in which more than half of the time was spent discussing the use of medication to help reduce her BP and she has agreed. We will start with lisinopril 5 mg and will see her back in 2 weeks.

Procedural code(s): _____

Diagnosis code(s): _____

Scenario 6-17

OFFICE NOTE

CC: George is here today for his well child PE; he is 10 years old.

HISTORY: George is an overweight child with a BMI in the 85th percentile. Last year at age 9, patient was Dx with diabetes and he has an elevated BP.

EXAM: Weight 140 lb. Height 3'24"3 ft 24 in. BP 126/87. Blood sugar reading 100. Home readings are normal.

HEENT: Normal.

Neck: Supple.

Heart: Heart sounds are normal.

Lungs: Clear.

Abdomen: Soft and nontender.

Skin: Acne on face and back.

ASSESSMENT AND PLAN: Overall George is doing well with his diet and he has lost some weight. He needs to lose about 20 lb more. He is in good health otherwise. I will see him back in 4 months for the diabetes and BP. He will continue his diet and do more exercise.

Procedural code(s): _____

Diagnosis code(s): _____

Scenario 6-18

OFFICE NOTE

DATE OF ADMISSION: 03/27/2006.

DATE OF DISCHARGE: 03/29/2006.

HISTORY: Patient is an 87-year-old white female resident of the Westbrook Nursing Facility who has a history of diabetes, of chronic venous stasis disease, and of seizure disorder. Patient at the nursing home was found to have a blood sugar of less than 30 and minimum responses. Glucagon was given, however, because of her unresponsiveness; patient was transferred to the emergency room where she was given 2 amps of D50. Blood sugar continued to decrease despite the D50 and as a result, the patient was admitted to the hospital. As stated, the patient is a long-term-care resident of the Westbrook Nursing Facility. She has a past medical history of hypertension, type 2 diabetes, seizure disorder, congestive heart failure, atrial fibrillation, and osteoarthritis.

ADMISSION MEDICATIONS:

1. Actos 30 mg daily.

2. Glyburide 10 b.i.d.

3. Paxil 30 daily.

4. Dilantin Extended Release 300 at bedtime.

5. Atenolol 50 daily.

6. Lasix 60 daily.

7. Zestril 5 daily.

8. Spironolactone 25 q 12.

9. Digoxin 0.125 alternating with 0.25.

10. Coumadin.

PHYSICAL EXAMINATION: On admission to the facility, she is an obese white female who is lying in bed, somewhat somnolent. Her pulse ox is 96% on room air. Blood pressure is 149/56. Ear, nose, and throat unremarkable. No JVD, no adenopathy. Clear lungs except for a few crackles at the bases. Heart was

continued

irregular/regular. Abdomen was obese, soft with good bowel sounds. No masses felt. Lower extremities showed edema of the feet and ankles with erythema over the anterior shins bilaterally.

HOSPITAL COURSE: Patient is an 87-year-old white female admitted from the nursing home secondary to hypoglycemia. Patient was unresponsive and diaphoretic in the nursing home. As stated, she was admitted to the hospital because of the hypoglycemia. In the emergency room, she was found to have abnormal urine and there was also a question of cellulitis.

LABORATORY DATA: On admission, showed a hemoglobin of 13, hematocrit of 38.9. White count 9,300. Sodium 136, potassium 3.8, chloride 94, CO_2 30, creatinine of 0.9, calcium 8.8. Troponin was less than 0.1. The BNP was 141. Chest x-ray showed cardiomegaly with slight effusions. Urine showed large leukocytes and many bacteria.

Patient was started on IV fluids, dextrose in normal saline. Started on IV Cipro and Ceftazidime to cover both the possible urinary tract infection and cellulitis of the lower extremities. Her Actos and glyburide were held and patient was continued on digoxin, spironolactone, atenolol, Dilantin, and Paxil. Later that day, patient was more awake, alert, and actually was starting to eat. Her blood sugar still remained low, in the 60–70s. By the following morning, the patient was more awake and basically at baseline. Her pulse ox remained stable. She was afebrile although she seemed to have a few more crackles in the bases. Her blood sugar was 70 in the morning and remained 70 at approximately noontime. Patient's appetite continued to improve, she denied shortness of breath or chest pains. The intravenous fluids were discontinued because patient was taking po. Because of the persistent hypoglycemia with a blood sugar in the morning of 70 and one prior of 70, it was decided to monitor the patient for another 24 hours. The patient will be discharged back to the nursing home on po Cipro pending urine culture. Patient will be restarted on her medications depending on her blood sugars. Blood sugars should be checked 4 times a day and depending on results possibly reintroduce her Actos and oral hypoglycemic glyburide. Unclear what caused the hypoglycemia as patient states she did not get any shots and she states the medication she received was her own. Nursing staff stated that they gave patient her medications. She did not receive any medications on the morning of admission because of her somnolence. Her INR remained stable on the Coumadin. INR will need to be monitored given the antibiotics.

FINAL DIAGNOSES:

1. Hypoglycemia.

2. Type 2 diabetes.

3. Congestive heart failure based per x-ray and crackles.

4. History of seizure disorder. Dilantin level was 5; however patient had no seizure disorder and given the antibiotic and changes we did not increase the Dilantin dose.

5. Possible urinary tract infection consistent with abnormal urine.

Procedural code(s): _____

Diagnosis code(s): _____

CHAPTER REVIEW

Using the *CPT* and *HCPCS* manuals and this textbook, complete the following exercises.

Define the following:

1. Medical records audits _____
2. Established patient _____
3. History of present illness (HPI) _____
4. Medical decision making _____
5. Level of service _____

Find the following E&M codes:

6. New patient office visit with:
   - Comprehensive history
   - Detailed examination
   - Medical decision making of moderate complexity

   Code: _____

7. Subsequent hospital care with:
   - Detailed focused interval history
   - Expanded problem–focused examination
   - Medical decision making of moderate complexity

   Code: _____

8. Observation or inpatient hospital care (admit and discharge on same day) with:
   - Detailed or comprehensive history
   - Detailed or comprehensive examination
   - Medical decision making that is straightforward or of a low complexity

   Code: _____

9. Nursing facility discharge day management of 30 minutes or less:

   Code: _____

10. Established patient with:
    - Periodic comprehensive preventive medicine
    - Patient under 1-year-old

    Code: _____

Chapter 7
Anesthesia Coding

LEARNING OBJECTIVES

Upon completion of this chapter, the student will be able to:

1. Code for anesthesia
2. Understand the modifiers used for anesthesia
3. Understand the different elements in coding for anesthesia

ANESTHESIA CODES

The following list presents the anesthesia-related ranges of codes:

Anesthesia codes	00100–01999
Qualifying circumstances for anesthesia (add-on codes)	99100–99140
Moderate (conscious) sedation codes:	
Codes for provider performing a procedure	99143–99145
Codes for providers only administering sedation	99148–99150
Nerve Blocks for Chronic Pain	64400–64530

ANESTHESIA FOR SURGERY: 00100–01999

Anesthesia is used to alter a patient's state of consciousness in order to perform a surgical procedure without pain. Anesthesia can also be used for postoperative pain, acute pain, and chronic pain.

Anesthesia coding is very different from the rest of CPT coding. When coding for anesthesia, the medical coder must have more information than just the procedure. The following information will also be needed:

- Type of surgery
- Where the surgery was performed
- The amount of time anesthesia was administered

143

- The physical status modifiers (patient condition **anesthesia modifiers**)
- The qualifying circumstances (if applicable anesthesia modifiers)

This information is needed to complete a formula for the pricing of anesthesia (which is explained later in this chapter). When an anesthesia procedure is performed, the amount of time can be different from person to person. The patient condition before the surgery is also a factor in how the anesthesiologist administers the anesthesia.

All of these factors may result in different charges for different patients, even though they may have had the same procedure performed.

Anesthesia codes are set up by body area as follows:

Head	00100–00222
Neck	00300–00352
Thorax (chest wall and shoulder girdle)	00400–00474
Intrathoracic	00500–00580
Spine and spinal cord	00600–00670
Upper abdomen	00700–00797
Lower abdomen	00800–00882
Perineum	00902–00952
Pelvis (except hip)	01112–01190
Upper leg (except knee)	01200–01274
Knee and popliteal area	01320–01444
Lower leg (below knee, includes ankle and foot)	01462–01522
Shoulder and axilla	01610–01682
Upper arm and elbow	01710–01782
Forearm, wrist, and hand	01810–01860
Radiological procedures	01905–01933
Burn excisions/debridement	01951–01953
Obstetric	01958–01969
Other procedures	01990–01999

Components for Calculating Anesthesia

The components needed to calculate anesthesia charges are:

- Base unit value
- Relative value modifiers

- Physical status modifiers
- Time
- Where the surgery was performed

Base Unit Value

Each surgical code involving anesthesia is given a **base unit value**, based on its complexity, by the **American Society of Anesthesiologists (ASA)** in the **Relative Value Guide (RVG)**. The values in this guide are used in the formula to price anesthesia services.

> ## EXAMPLE
> CPT code 95971 has an ASA base unit value of 3.

For the purpose of this book, all base unit values are given.

Relative Value Modifiers

Relative value modifiers come from two sources:

1. The qualifying circumstances
2. The physical status modifiers

These can be located in the Anesthesia guidelines of CPT within the CPT manual.

Qualifying Circumstances

Table 7-1 lists the code, description, and relative value for each qualifying circumstance.

TABLE 7-1 Qualifying Circumstances

Code	Description	Relative Value*
99100	Anesthesia for patient of extreme age, under 1 year and over 70	1
99116	Anesthesia complicated by the use of total body hypothermia	5
99135	Anesthesia complicated by the use of controlled hypotension	5
99140	Anesthesia complicated by an emergency condition	2

*These number values cannot be found in the CPT book; they can be located in an anesthesia crosswalk reference, such as *ASA Crosswalk* (Park Ridge, IL: ASA Publications). Updated annually in April, this book contains a complete listing of all Current Procedural Terminology (CPT) surgery codes with short descriptions (up to 28 characters), the CPT anesthesia codes to which the surgery codes are crosswalked, the American Society of Anesthesiologists (ASA) base unit values, and Medicare base unit values.

Physical Status Modifiers

Physical status modifiers are:

P1: A normal healthy patient	0
P2: A patient with mild systemic disease	0
P3: A patient with severe systemic disease	1
P4: A patient with severe systemic disease that is a constant threat to life	2
P5: A moribund patient who is not expected to survive without the operation	3
P6: A declared brain-dead patient whose organs are being removed for donor purpose	0

Time

The time for the procedure is reported by the anesthesiologist. The recording of time begins when the anesthesiologist begins to prepare the patient for the induction of the anesthesia and ends when the anesthesiologist is no longer in attendance. The time is reported in 15-minute units.

> **EXAMPLE**
>
> If the anesthesia time is listed as 2 hours, the coder reports 8 units of time.

Where the Surgery Is Performed

Where the surgery is performed is reported in terms of zip code and state. Insurance companies determine payment for a unit of anesthesia time based on the physical location in which the surgery was performed, that is, the geographical location of the provider. The reason is that the cost of practicing medicine in one state or in one part of a state can be very different than in another. Another payment factor is whether the provider participates in the plan (Par) or not (Nonpar). Table 7-2 presents a sampling of conversion factors.

TABLE 7-2   **2005 Medicare Anesthesia Conversion Factors**

State	Par	Nonpar	Limiting Charge
Kansas	$17.06	$16.21	$18.64
Nebraska	$16.63	$15.80	$18.17
Kansas City (Loc 00)	$17.06	$16.21	$18.64
Kansas City (Loc 02)	$17.61	$16.73	$19.24
Kansas City/Western Missouri (Loc 99)	$17.15	$16.29	$18.73

Formula for Calculating Anesthesia

Now we need to put this all together. The formula for calculating anesthesia charges is:

$$\text{Anesthesia charge} = (B + T + PSM + QCM) \times CF$$

where: B = base unit value

T = time of the procedure

PSM = physical status modifiers

QCM = qualifying circumstances modifiers

CF = conversion factor

EXAMPLE

Procedure: Anesthesia for open or surgical arthroscopic procedures on knee joint with a base value of 4

Time: 4 (15-minute) units

Modifiers: 99100 Anesthesia for patient of extreme age, under 1 year and over 70: **1**

P1: A normal healthy patient: **0**

Location: Kansas: $17.06

To calculate the anesthesia charge for this procedure:

- Add the basic value of 4 to the number of time units, 4.
- Add the sum to the modifiers: 1 and 0.
- Multiply the sum by the conversion factor ($17.06) for a resulting anesthesia charge of $153.54.

$$\text{Anesthesia charge} = (B + T + PSM + QCM) \times CF$$

$$= (4 + 4 + 1 + 0) \times \$17.06 = \$153.54$$

Qualifying Circumstances for Anesthesia as Add-on Codes

We used a qualifying circumstance in the formulation of the payment in the preceding example, but these codes can also be used as add-on codes. When there is a patient of extreme age, 99100 can also be billed. (See the Anesthesia Guidelines and Appendix D in the *CPT* manual.)

The add-on codes are as follows:

- +99100 Anesthesia for patient of extreme age, under 1 year and over 70
- +99116 Anesthesia complicated by the use of total body hypothermia
- +99135 Anesthesia complicated by the use of controlled hypotension
- +99140 Anesthesia complicated by emergency condition

Use these four add-on codes, if they are applicable, in addition to the primary anesthesia procedure.

ACUTE PAIN CODES (POSTOP PAIN) AND NERVE BLOCKS FOR CHRONIC PAIN: 64400–64681

Although many people think that anesthesia is administered only during a surgical procedure, an anesthesiologist administers anesthesia under two other circumstances:

- The postoperative management of pain
- For individuals with chronic pain (**nerve blocks**)

Note
Other types of providers also use these codes.

The related codes can be found in the surgical section of CPT in the nervous system codes and under the subheading of Introduction/Injection of Anesthetic Agent (Nerve Block), Diagnostic or Therapeutic; Neurostimulators, Destruction by Neurolytic Agent.

The coder who works with an anesthesiologist has to understand these codes.

Acute Pain Codes (Postop Pain)

The acute pain codes (postop pain) are:

Daily Hospital Management of Epidural or Subarachnoid	01996
Injection Including Cath Placement Epidural; Cervical, Thoracic	62318
Injection Including Cath Placement Epidural; Lumbar, Sacral	62319
Epidural Blood Patch	62273

Chronic Pain Codes

The chronic pain (nerve block) codes are:

Nerve Blocks for Chronic Pain	64400	64530
Neurostimulators	64550	64595
Destruction by Neurolytic Agent	64600	64681

Let's try coding some anesthesia procedures.

CHAPTER EXERCISES

Problem 7-1

Refer to the anesthesia log (Figure 7-1). What information do you see on this encounter form?

Mass College Medical Center
Anesthesia Log

Anesthesiologist: Dr. John Jones

DOS   1/23/2006

Surgery Performed: Repair of myelomeningocele < 5 cm

Diagnosis: Spina Bifida

Surgeon: Dr. Robert Smith

Time Start: 2:40 pm   Time End: 3:59 pm

Modifiers: AA, 23

Patient Mary Luo Harras

DOB   1/17/2006

MR#   55434

Address   123 St. Tomas Lane, London MA

Insurance and insurance number   HMO Blue- XXH 042324456-01

Physical Status Modifiers

- [x] P1- A normal healthy patient
- [ ] P2- A patient with mild systemic disease
- [ ] P3- A patient with severe systemic disease
- [ ] P4- A patient with severe systemic disease that is a constant threat to life
- [ ] P5- A moribund patient who is not expected to survive without the operation
- [ ] P6- A declared brain-dead patient whose organs are being removed for donor purpose

Qualifying Circumstances

- [x] 99100   Anesthesia for patient of extreme age, under 1 year and over 70
- [ ] 99116   Anesthesia complicated by the use of total body hypothermia
- [ ] 99135   Anesthesia complicated by the use of controlled hypotension
- [ ] 99140   Anesthesia complicated by emergency condition

Modifiers

AA- Anesthesia services performed personally by anesthesiologist
AD- Medically supervised by a physician for more than four concurrent procedures
QK- Medically directed by a physician: two, three, or four concurrent procedures
QX- CRNA with medical direction by a physician
QY- Medical direction of one certified registered nurse anesthetist (CRNA) by an anesthesiologist
QZ- CRNA without medical direction by a physician

2nd Modifiers
QS- Monitored anesthesia care service
23- Unusual anesthesia

Notes: Patient is a six day old infant. The procedure performed on this infant was longer and more difficult because of age.

Figure 7-1 Anesthesia Log

What is the procedure? _____
What is the number of units? _____
What are the modifiers? _____

Problem 7-1a

Code the anesthesia for this. Use the same information from Figure 7-1 to code the procedure(s).

What is the CPT code? _____
List any other codes and their category: _____

Problem 7-2

Use the information from Figure 7-2.

What is the CPT code? _____
List any other codes: _____
What is the time in units? _____
What are the modifiers? _____

Mass College Medical Center
Anesthesia Log

Anesthesiologist: <u>Dr. John Jones</u>

DOS   <u>1/23/2006</u>

Surgery Performed: <u>Laparoscopy surgical, with vaginal hysterectomy, for uterus > 250 grams</u>
Diagnosis: Dysfunctional Uterine Bleeding

Surgeon: <u>Dr. Lynn Carlson</u>

Time Start: <u>11:20 am</u>   Time End: <u>12:59 pm</u>

Modifiers: <u>AA</u>

Patient Ellen James

DOB   5/23/1950

MR#   12356

Address   345 Western Lane, Westland, MA

Insurance and insurance number   Cigna 554678

Physical Status Modifiers
- [x] P1- A normal healthy patient
- [ ] P2- A patient with mild systemic disease
- [ ] P3- A patient with severe systemic disease
- [ ] P4- A patient with severe systemic disease that is a constant threat to life
- [ ] P5- A moribund patient who is not expected to survive without the operation
- [ ] P6- A declared brain-dead patient whose organs are being removed for donor purposes

Qualifying Circumstances
- [ ] 99100 Anesthesia for patient of extreme age, under 1 year and over 70
- [ ] 99116 Anesthesia complicated by the use of total body hypothermia
- [ ] 99135 Anesthesia complicated by the use of controlled hypotension
- [ ] 99140 Anesthesia complicated by emergency condition

Modifiers

AA- Anesthesia services performed personally by anesthesiologist
AD- Medically supervised by a physician for more than four concurrent procedures
QK- Medically directed by a physician: two, three, or four concurrent procedures
QX- CRNA with medical direction by a physician
QY- Medical direction of one certified registered nurse anesthetist (CRNA) by an anesthesiologist
QZ- CRNA without medical direction by a physician

2nd Modifiers
QS- Monitored anesthesia care service
23- Unusual anesthesia

Notes: The patient was still vomiting and was admitted overnight, will check the patient tomorrow.

Figure 7-2 Anesthesia Log

Mass College Medical Center
Anesthesia Log

Anesthesiologist: <u>Dr John Jones</u>

DOS   <u>1/23/2006</u>

Surgery Performed: Embolectomy Carotid subclavian artery by neck incision

Diagnosis: Embolism of the carotid

Surgeon: <u>Dr. Dave Weeden</u>

Time Start: <u>10:00 am</u>   Time End: <u>3:59 pm</u>

Modifiers: <u>QK, 23</u>

Patient Helen Smith

DOB   11/11/1920

MR#   46578

Address   55 West End St., Wells, ME

Insurance and insurance number   Medicare 998468424A

Physical Status Modifiers
- [ ] P1- A normal healthy patient
- [ ] P2- A patient with mild systemic disease
- [ ] P3- A patient with severe systemic disease
- [x] P4- A patient with severe systemic disease that is a constant threat to life
- [ ] P5- A moribund patient who is not expected to survive without the operation
- [ ] P6- A declared brain-dead patient whose organs are being removed for donor purposes

Qualifying Circumstances
- [x] 99100 Anesthesia for patient of extreme age, under 1 year and over 70
- [ ] 99116 Anesthesia complicated by the use of total body hypothermia
- [ ] 99135 Anesthesia complicated by the use of controlled Hypotension
- [ ] 99140 Anesthesia complicated by emergency condition

Modifiers

AA- Anesthesia services performed personally by anesthesiologist
AD- Medically supervised by a physician for more than four concurrent procedures
QK- Medically directed by a physician: two, three, or four concurrent procedures
QX- CRNA with medical direction by a physician
QY- Medical direction of one certified registered nurse anesthetist (CRNA) by an anesthesiologist
QZ- CRNA without medical direction by a physician

2nd Modifiers
QS- Monitored anesthesia care service
23- Unusual anesthesia

Notes: This patient went through a longer surgical procedure because of complications.

Figure 7-3 Anesthesia Log

Problem 7-3

Use the anesthesia log in Figure 7-3.

What is the CPT code? _____

List any other codes: _____

What is the time in units? _____

What are the modifiers? _____

Problem 7-4

Now let's do the pricing for the previous three exercises. Using Table 7-3 for the anesthesia unit pricing and Table 7-4 for the relative value, look at Figure 7-1 and complete problems 7-4 through 7-6.

What is the base unit value (B) for the procedure? _____

What is the time (T) in units? _____

What are the values of any modifiers (M)? _____

What is the conversion factor (CF)? _____

What is the total charge? _____

Problem 7-5

Look at Figure 7-2.

What is the base unit value (B) for the procedure? _____

What is the time (T) in units? _____

What are values of any modifiers (M)? _____

What is the conversion factor (CF)? _____

What is the total charge? _____

Problem 7-6

Look at Figure 7-3.

What is the base unit value (B) for the procedure? _____

What is the time (T) in units? _____

What are the values of any modifiers (M)? _____

What is the conversion factor (CF)? _____

What is the total charge? _____

TABLE 7-3	Anesthesia Conversion Factor
Blue Shield	$49.37
Cigna	$45.80
HMO Blue	$42.00
Medicare	$18.66
United Health Care	$52.00

TABLE 7-4	Relative Value of the Surgery
Adjacent tissue transfer or rearrangement, trunk defect 10 sq. cm	3
Embolectomy carotid subclavian artery by neck incision	10
Laparoscopy, with vaginal hysterectomy	6
Myelomeningocele <5 cm	8

Scenario 7-1

OFFICE NOTE

CC: Patient presenting in the office with neck pain radiating down her left arm.

HPI: This new patient states that she has had the pain for about 6 months, but the pain has gotten worse in the last month. She denies any injury to the neck, back, or arm. She states that right now the pain is 7 out of 10, but at night it's about a 10. She states that the pain sometimes wakes her up.

EXAM: BP 139/90. The exam shows 3 palpable knots (trigger points) in the left trapezius muscle. The right side trapezius is negative for trigger points. When the trigger points were touched, the patient responded by jumping. The neck was flexible, without any tender points, no lumps or masses.

There is no numbness down the arm, but there is some sensory loss in the left hand.

IMPRESSION: Myofascial pain syndrome.

PLAN: Trigger point injections today for the myofascial pain syndrome.

Schedule an EMG for a later date to resolve the issue of the sensory loss in the left hand.

I also spent 20 minutes of a 30-minute visit explaining treatment and risk to the patient.

PROCEDURE: The patient was prepped for the procedure. I had identified 3 trigger points and proceeded with the injections using lidocaine. The patient tolerated the procedure well and was sent home with instructions to take an over-the-counter pain-reducing anti-inflammatory medication if the trigger point injection sites become inflamed. She was also told that she may experience soreness, bruising, or even an increase in pain for a few days until her body has time to recuperate from the injections. Heat and stretching exercises may help to lessen the discomfort. She was also told to call if the pain gets worse.

Look at Figure 7-4.

What did the doctor select for the procedure? _____

Does this match the clinic notes? _____

What E&M code was selected? _____

Do you agree with this selection? _____

Why or why not? _____

Scenario 7-2

OFFICE NOTE

CC: Patient comes into the office today complaining of TMJ pain. This is not a new problem, but he has been getting worse over the past 2 weeks. He complains that he is getting shooting pain from his jaw into his eyes and ears and has had migraine headaches that last for several days at a time. The pain level today is 7 out of 10, but during the migraines it is a 10. No tooth pain.

HPI: Mr. Jones has had TMJ for several years. This current episode started about 1 month ago but has gotten worse over the past 2 weeks. Patient denies any injuries to the face and denies eating any type of foods that can trigger an episode.

EXAM: There is no bruising or redness on the jaw or face. No redness in either tympanic membrane; eyes are clear without redness. The sinus cavities are clear. The patient does

Mass College Medical Center
CHRONIC PAIN CLINIC

ATTENDING M.D.   James Taylor, MD

OTHER PROVIDER (NON-BILLING) _____

TEACHING MOD: ☐ Resident Involved, w/MD presence (GC)   ☐ No Resident

LOCATION   ☒ OPD (2)
            ☐ OTHER _____   ☐ ADMIT TODAY

☐ POST OP VISIT   DATE OF SURGERY _____
                   DATE OF INJURY _____

TYPE OF INJURY: ☐ MVA State _____   ☐ WORKER'S COMP   ☐ OTHER _____
                   ☐ STATISTICAL VISIT

DATE   2/8/06

NAME   Anne Carpenter

MR #   349821

BIRTHDATE / AGE   Feb 27, 1954

STREET / TEL   59 Main St

CITY / STATE / ZIP   Millstone, MA, 02334

PRINT IN INK OR STAMP WITH PATIENT'S CARD

CASHIER	MODIFIER (MOD)	
AMOUNT _____	☐ 24 Unrelat E&M Service by Same Physician During Post-op Period	☐ 52 Reduced Services
RCPT# / CK# _____	☒ 25 Sep. Ident. E&M Same Day Proc. Same Physician	☐ 57 Decision for Surgery
	☐ 26 Professional Component	☐ 59 Distinct Procedural Service
CREDIT CARD# _____	☐ 50 Bilateral Procedural Service	☐ 74 Discontinued Procedure Prior to Administration of Anesthesia
☐ CASH ☐ CHECK	☐ 51 Multiple Procedures	☐ 75 Discontinued Procedure After to Administration of Anesthesia

VISITS

(Time = > 50% face to face time spent counseling/coordinating care of patient w/documentation)

	NEW MD		ESTAB MD		NON MD
LEVEL 1	☐ 99201	10 MIN	☐ 99211	5 MIN	☐
LEVEL 2	☐ 99202	20 MIN	☐ 99212	10 MIN	☐
LEVEL 3	☒ **99203**	**30 MIN**	☐ 99213	15 MIN	☐
LEVEL 4	☐ 99204	45 MIN	☐ 99214	25 MIN	☐
LEVEL 5	☐ 99205	60 MIN	☐ 99215	40 MIN	☐

☐ WC9157 WC - INITIAL EXAM W/REPORT
☐ INDEPENDENT MEDICAL EXAM

CONSULTS

	INITIAL	
LEVEL 1	☐ 99241	15 MIN
LEVEL 2	☐ 99242	30 MIN
LEVEL 3	☐ 99243	40 MIN
LEVEL 4	☐ 99244	60 MIN
LEVEL 5	☐ 99245	80 MIN

REFERRING M.D. _____
REFERRAL AUTH/PCC #: _____

Notes:

CODE	PROCEDURES	CODE	PROCEDURES	CODE	PROCEDURES	CODE	PROCEDURES
INJECTION NERVE BLOCKS		**INJECTION NERVE BLOCKS, cont.**		**RESERVOIR / PUMP IMPLANTATION, cont.**		**Supervision and Interpretation**	
☐ 20550	Tendon Sheath / Ligament		Transforaminal Epidural		Refilling / Maintenance of Pump /	☐ 72285	Diskography, Cervical / Thoracic
☐ 20551	Tendon Origin / Insertion	☐ 64479	Cervical or Thoracic, Single Level		Reservoir for Drug Delivery	☐ 72295	Lumbar
☐ 20552	Single / Multiple, Trigger Points	☐ 64480	____Each addti'l Cervical / Thoracic	☐ 95991	Physician	**Evoked Potential and Reflex Test**	
	1 or 2 Muscle(s)	☐ 64483	Lumbar or Sacral, Single Level	☐ 95990	Non Physician	Short-Latency Somatosensory Evoked Study	
☒ 20553	Multiple, Trigger, Points,	☐ 64484	____Each addti'l Lumbar / Sacral	**DESTRUCTION BY NEUROLYTIC AGENT**		☐ 95926	Lower Limbs
	3 + Muscle(s)			**Chem., Thermal, Electric or Radiofrequency CTR**		☐ 95927	Trunk or Head
☐ 20600	Small Joint / Bursa	**Sympathetic Nerves**		☐ 64680	Celiac Plexus	☐ 95925	Upper Limbs
☐ 20605	Intermediate Joint / Bursa	☐ 64520	Lumbar or Thoracic / Hypogastric	☐ 64613	Cervical Spinal	**NEUROSTIMULATORS**	
☐ 20610	Major Joint / Bursa		(Paravertebral Sympathetic)	☐ 64612	Facial Nerve	☐ 63650	Percutaneous Implantation of
☐ 27096	Sacroiliac Joint, w / Imaging	☐ 64530	Celiac Plexus	☐ 64620	Intercostal Nerve		Neurostimulator Electrodes
	Bilateral _____	☐ 64505	Sphenopalatine Ganglion		Paravertebral Facet Joint	☐ 63660	Revision / Removal of Spinal
Spine and Spinal Cord		☐ 64510	Stellate Ganglion	☐ 64626	Cervical / Thoracic, Single		Neurostimulator Electrode
☐ 62280	Subarachnoid	**Dental Blocks and Other Dental Procedures**		☐ 64627	____Each addti'l Cervical / Thoracic	☐ 63685	Insertion / Replacement of Spinal
☐ 62310	Epidural / Subarachnoid, Single	☐ 21110	Application of Interdental Fixation Device	☐ 64622	Lumbar / Sacral, Single		Neurostimulator Pulse
	Cervical / Thoracic	☐ 97703	Check for Orthotic, ea 15 Mins _____		Bilateral_____		Generator / Receiver
☐ 62311	Lumbar / Sacral (Caudal)	☐ 21480	Closed Tx of Temporomandibular	☐ 64623	____Each addti'l Lumbar / Sacral	☐ 63688	Revision / Removal of Spinal
☐ 62318	Epidural, Catheter Placement		Dislocation, Initial / Subsequent		Bilateral_____		Neurostimulator Pulse
	Cervical / Thoracic	☐ 21485	Complicated, Initial / Subsequent	☐ 64640	Other Peripheral Nerve		Generator / Receiver
☐ 62319	Lumbar / Sacral (Caudal)	☐ 20605	Intermediate Joint / Bursa	☐ 64630	Pudendal Nerve	☐ 95970	Electronic Analysis of
☐ 64412	Spinal Accessory Nerve		(Temporomandibular)	☐ 64600	Trigeminal Nerve		Neurostimulator Pulse System
Somatic Nerves		☐ 20550	Trigger Point Injection, Single	**MISCELLANEOUS PROCEDURES**			w/o Reprogramming
☐ 66417	Axillary Nerve			☐ 62287	Asp / Decomp Percutaneous	☐ 95972	Electronic Analysis, Complex
☐ 64415	Brachial Plexus, Single	☐ 64400	Trigeminal Nerve,		Nucleoplasty, Any Method		Neurostimulator Pulse System
☐ 64413	Cervical Plexus		Any Division / Branch	☐ 62273	Injection Blood or Clot Patch		w/ Programming 1st. Hr.
	Facet Joint Nerve	**CATHETER IMPLANTATION**			Injection for Diskography	**Electromyography / Nerve Conduction**	
☐ 64470	Cervical / Thoracic, Single Level	☐ 62350	Implant / Revision Spinal Catheter	☐ 62290	Lumbar: Each Level _____	☐ 95869	Needle EMG Thoracic
☐ 64472	____Each addti'l Cervical or Thoracic		w/o Laminectomy	☐ 62291	Cervical / Thoracic:		Paraspinal Muscles
☐ 64475	Lumbar / Sacral, Single Level	☐ 62355	Removal of Catheter		Each Level _____	☐ 95870	EMG Limited Study of
☐ 64476	____Each addti'l Lumbar / Sacral	**RESERVOIR / PUMP IMPLANTATION**		☐ 62284	Injection Procedure:		Muscles in One Extremity
☐ 64402	Facial Nerve	☐ 62360	Implant / Revision of Intrathecal		Myelography / CT, Spinal		or Non-Limb
☐ 64405	Greater Occipital Nerve		Subcutaneous Reservoir	**Intravenous Infusion Therapeutic / Diagnostic**		Other	
☐ 64425	Ilioinguinal , Iliohypogastric Nerves	☐ 62362	Implant Infusion Pump w/, w/o	☐ 90780	IV Administered up to 1 Hr		
☐ 64420	Intercostal Nerve, Single		Programming	☐ 97081	Each addti'l Hr. up to 8 Hr		
☐ 64421	Intercostal Nerve, Multiple	☐ 62365	Removal of Reservoir or Pump	**RADIOLOGY**			
☐ 64450	Other Peripheral Nerve	☐ 62367	Electronic Analysis of Programmable	**Fluoroscopic Guidance**			
☐ 64445	Sciatic Nerve, Single		Pump w/o Reprogramming	☐ 76003	Needle Placement		
☐ 64418	Suprascapular Nerve	☐ 62368	w/ Reprogramming	☐ 76005	With Epidural, SI, Root Blocks,		
☐ 64400	Trigeminal Nerve,				Facet, Medial Branch		
	Any Division / Branch						

Figure 7-4 Encounter Form

1°	2°	CODE	DIAGNOSIS	1°	2°	CODE	DIAGNOSIS	1°	2°	CODE	DIAGNOSIS	1°	2°	CODE	DIAGNOSIS
			HEADACHE				**NEOPLASM, cont.**				**PAIN / PAINFUL**				**MISCELLANEOUS**
☐	☐	784.0	Headache NOS	☐	☐	163.9	Pleura, Unspecified	☐	☐	789.00	Abdominal, Unspecified	☐	☐	322.9	Arachnoiditis / Meningitis, Unspecified
☐	☐	346.20*	Cluster	☐	☐	185	Prostate	☐	☐	789.09	Multiple Sites	☐	☐	714.0	Arthritis, Rheumatoid
☐	☐	346.90*	Migraine, Unspecified	☐	☐	154.1	Rectum	☐	☐	724.2	Back, Lower (Lumbago)	☐	☐	562.11	Diverticulitis w/o Hemorrhage
☐	☐	349.0	Spinal	☐	☐	151.9	Stomach, Unspecified	☐	☐	724.5	Postural	☐	☐	617.9	Endometriosis, Unspecified Site
☐	☐	307.81	Tension				**NEURALGIA / NEUROPATHY**	☐	☐	724.3	Sciatica	☐	☐	724.8	Facet Syndrome
			*w/o Mention of Intractable Migraine	☐	☐	353.0	Brachial Plexus	☐	☐	724.6	Sacroiliac	☐	☐	550.90	Hernia, Inguinal NOS, Unilateral
			SPONDYLOSIS w/ MYELOPATHY	☐	☐	354.0	Carpal Tunnel Syndrome	☐	☐	724.1	Thoracic	☐	☐	V08	HIV, Asymptomatic
☐	☐	721.1	Cervical Region	☐	☐	053.10	Herpes Zoster / Unspec. Complications	☐	☐	733.90	Bone	☐	☐	042	HIV, Symptomatic
☐	☐	721.42	Lumbar Region	☐	☐	053.13	Post Herpetic	☐	☐	611.71	Breast	☐	☐	340	Multiple Sclerosis
☐	☐	721.41	Thoracic Region	☐	☐	355.9	Mononeuritis, Unspecified Site	☐	☐	723.1	Cervical (Neck)	☐	☐	237.70	Neurofibromatosis, Unspecified
			SPONDYLOSIS w/o MYELOPATHY	☐	☐	354.1	Median Lesion	☐	☐	786.50	Chest, Unspecified	☐	☐	715.90	Osteoarthrosis, Unspecified
☐	☐	721.0	Cervical Region	☐	☐	355.3	Peroneal	☐	☐	724.79	Coccyx	☐	☐	715.97	Ankle
☐	☐	721.3	Lumbar Region	☐	☐	354.3	Radial Lesion	☐	☐	379.91	Eye, in or around	☐	☐	715.92	Elbow
☐	☐	721.2	Thoracic Region	☐	☐	354.2	Ulnar Lesion	☐	☐	350.2	Face (Atypical)	☐	☐	715.95	Hip
			DISK DEGENERATION	☐	☐	729.2	Neuralgia, Unspecified	☐	☐	784.0	Face, Facial	☐	☐	715.96	Knee
☐	☐	722.4	Cervical Region	☐	☐	350.1	Trigeminal	☐	☐	780.99	Generalized	☐	☐	715.99	Multiple Sites
☐	☐	722.52	Lumbar Region	☐	☐	729.2	Radiculopathy, Unspecified	☐	☐	625.9	Genital Organs (Female)	☐	☐	715.91	Shoulder Region
☐	☐	722.51	Thoracic Region	☐	☐	355.9	Neuropathy, Unspecified Site	☐	☐	608.9	Male	☐	☐	732.7	Osteochondritis Dissecans
☐	☐	722.6	Degenerative Disc. NOS	☐	☐	356.9	Polyneuropathy, Peripheral	☐	☐	719.40	Joint, Unspecified	☐	☐	732.9	Osteochondropathy, Unspecified
			DISK DISPLACEMENT w/o MYELOPATHY	☐	☐	356.4	Idiopathic Progressive	☐	☐	719.47	Ankle				**Osteomyelitis**
☐	☐	722.0	Cervical Region	☐	☐	337.21	RSD Upper Limp	☐	☐	719.42	Elbow	☐	☐	730.0_	Acute Site:_____
☐	☐	722.10	Lumbar Region	☐	☐	337.22	Lower Limb	☐	☐	719.45	Hip	☐	☐	730.1_	Chronic Site:_____
☐	☐	722.11	Thoracic Region	☐	☐	337.20	Unspecified	☐	☐	719.46	Knee	☐	☐	730.2_	Unspec. Site:_____
			SPINAL STENOSIS	☐	☐	355.5	Tarsal Tunnel Syndrome	☐	☐	719.49	Multiple Sites	☐	☐	577.0	Pancreatitis, Acute (Recurrent)
☐	☐	723.0	Cervical Region				**Diabetes / Neurological Manifestation**	☐	☐	719.41	Shoulder Region	☐	☐	577.1	Pancreatitis, Chronic
☐	☐	724.02	Lumbar Region	☐		250.6**_	Neurological Manifestation	☐	☐	524.62	TMJ	☐	☐	344.1	Paraplegia
☐	☐	724.01	Thoracic Region				**** Fifth Digits for Diabetes Codes	☐	☐	719.43	Wrist	☐	☐	344.00	Quadriplegia, Unspecified
☐	☐	724.00	Unspecified Region	Type I Controlled		1	Type II Controlled 0				Limb	☐	☐	282.62	Sickle Cell Crisis NOS
			MALIGNANT NEOPLASM	Type I Uncontrolled		3	Type II Uncontrolled 2	☐	☐	729.5	Arm / Hand / Finger	☐	☐	737.30	Scoliosis, Idiopathic
☐	☐	191.9	Brain, Unspecified				Use Additional Code to Identify Manifestation as	☐	☐	729.5	Leg / Foot / Toes	☐	☐	737.39	Paralytic
☐	☐	174.9	Breast Female, Unspecified				Diabetic:	X	☐	729.1	Muscle / Myalgia / Myositis	☐	☐	728.85	Spasm, Muscle
☐	☐	162.9	Bronchus and Lung, Unspecified	☐		713.5	Arthropathy	☐	☐	729.1	Neuromuscular				Other
☐	☐	180.9	Cervix Uteri, Unspecified	☐		337.1	Neuropathy, Autonomic,	☐	☐	472.1	Pharynx, Chronic				
☐	☐	153.9	Colon, Unspecified				Peripheral	☐	☐	786.52	Pleuritic / Respiration				
☐	☐	189.0	Kidney NOS except Renal Pelvis	☐		357.2	Polyneuropathy	☐	☐	569.42	Rectal				
☐	☐	199.1	Malignant, Site Unspecified	☐		Other	_____	☐	☐	786.50	Rib				
☐	☐	157.1	Pancreas, Body					☐	☐	784.1	Throat				

Figure 7-4 (Continued)

not have a temperature that could indicate an infection of the sinuses. There is prominent clicking of the jaw, and on examination the jaw moves out of the joint.

IMPRESSION: Worsening TMJ.

PLAN: First plan is to get some kind of relief for the pain. Treatment with a nerve block for the current pain was discussed with the patient. Patient cannot have the procedure during this appointment, but will come back tomorrow to have the nerve block of the trigeminal nerve.

Set up an appointment with an oral surgeon for long-term options. Also, order an MRI to R/O trigeminal neuralgia syndrome.

Procedure code(s): _____

Diagnosis(es): _____

Modifier(s)? _____

Scenario 7-3

HISTORY AND PHYSICAL

CC: This new patient complaining of lower back and right leg pain came into the clinic today. The patient states that one day he moved "just right" and started to get shooting pain down his right leg. Patient states that he is unable to get out of bed on most days because the pain is worse when sitting and the leg pain is worse than the back. Today is a good day; pain level is 8 out of 10 today.

HPI: The causative movement occurred about 1 month ago. He has been getting treatment for this pain by his primary care provider with 50 mg of Naproxen t.i.d.

and he states that this does not provide relief. He also has had an x-ray of the lumbar spine that was unremarkable and showed no injury. Patient denies any loss of bowel or bladder control. The patient also states that he has weakness in the right leg, with pins-and-needles numbness down the leg.

EXAM: The patient was helped up to the examination table and examined while lying on his back. A complete neurological evaluation was performed. He had an abnormal Babinski and when the right leg was raised the patient felt the pain before the 70° point. A sitting examination was also done. Other reflexes were unremarkable in this examination.

IMPRESSION: Sciatica.

PLAN: Schedule an MRI of the lumbar spine to find out why the patient has the sciatica. Also rule out a herniated disk or other lumbar radiculopathy. I will also give the patient an oral steroid and have the patient alternate between hot and cold packs to relieve the pain.

After the results of the MRI are available, we might think about an epidural steroid injection for the pain and also some physical therapy.

Procedure code(s): _____

Diagnosis(es): _____

Modifier(s)? _____

Find the anesthesia code and any physical status modifiers and qualifying circumstances for the remaining exercises. Don't let the length of the scenario put you off. Remember, when coding anesthesia, you need to know the following:

- The type of surgery
- Where the surgery was performed
- The amount of time anesthesia was administered
- The physical status modifiers (patient condition)
- The qualifying circumstance (if applicable)

Scenario 7-4

OPERATIVE NOTE

PREOPERATIVE DIAGNOSIS: Senile cataract, right eye.

POSTOPERATIVE DIAGNOSIS: Senile cataract, right eye.

PLANNED PROCEDURE: Phacoemulsification of cataract with implant of lens, right eye.

ACTUAL PROCEDURE PERFORMED: Phacoemulsification of cataract with implant of lens, right eye.

ANESTHESIA: Peribulbar local with monitored anesthesia care, Dr. Weeden.

DESCRIPTION OF PROCEDURE: An anesthetic mixture was formulated from a 50:50 ratio by volume of 2% Xylocaine and 0.75% Marcaine with 1 cc of Wydase per 10 cc of solution. The patient was given IV sedation. A peribulbar infiltration was given around

continued

the right eye. There was good akinesia and anesthesia. The procedure, site of surgery, and primary IOL parameters were confirmed with staff in the operating room.

The 85-year-old patient was prepped and draped in a sterile fashion. A speculum was placed in the right eye. A 3-min keratome was used to enter the anterior chamber through clear cornea with a beveled incision, just anterior to the limbal arcade at the 6 o'clock position. The anterior chamber was filled with viscoelastic. A limbal paracentesis was made at the 3 o'clock hour clockwise to the keratome incision. A continuous tear circular capsulorrhexis was completed with Utrata forceps. A balanced salt solution was used for hydrodissection of the lens nucleus. The phacoemulsification handpiece was found in proper working order and was used to sculpt the lens nucleus using a chopper as a second instrument for a total ultrasound time of 0.7 min at 8% power. The haptics deployed properly. The remnant cortical material was removed with the irrigation/aspiration handpiece. The capsular bag was found to be clear and intact and was inflated with viscoelastic. The lens implant, manufacturer Alcon, Model #SA60AT, Serial #985931.026, 19.5 diopter power, was rinsed, loaded into the C cartridge lubricated with viscoelastic and injected into the capsular bag. The trailing haptic was dialed into the capsular bag with a collar-button hook and centered. Residual viscoelastic was thoroughly removed with irrigation/aspiration handpiece. The keratome wound and paracentesis were hydrated with a balanced salt solution and found to be watertight to perilimbal compression. The eye was normotensive to palpation.

The speculum and draping were removed. The eye was dressed with 2 eye pads and a shield. The patient tolerated the procedure well and was escorted in good condition to the recovery area to await discharge later the same day. There were no complications.

Anesthesia code: _____

Physical status modifiers: _____

Qualifying circumstances: _____

Scenario 7-5

PROCEDURAL NOTE

This is a 73-year-old female patient referred for evaluation of mitral regurgitation.

PROCEDURE: Transesophageal echocardiogram in the operating room.

A transesophageal echocardiogram probe was placed by the anesthesiologist and conscious sedation was administered by the anesthesiologist.

PREOPERATIVE TRANSESOPHAGEAL ECHOCARDIOGRAM FINDINGS:

1. The left cavity appeared nondilated. There was concentric left ventricular hypertrophy. There is mild to moderately reduced LV systolic function with ejection fraction of 40%.

2. The left atrium was enlarged.

3. The right atrium and right ventricle appear normal.

4. There was thickening of mitral valve leaflets with hockey stick appearance of the mitral valve leaflet, consistent with rheumatic mitral valve disease, with severe mitral regurgitation noted.

5. The aortic valve appears calcified with moderate degree of aortic insufficiency noted.

6. The tricuspid valve leaflets appear unremarkable with mild tricuspid regurgitation noted.

7. There is no pericardial effusion or intracardiac mass seen.

8. The interatrial septum appeared intact on low flow Doppler examination.

9. There was atherosclerosis seen in the ascending aorta and the descending aorta.

POSTOPERATIVE TRANSESOPHAGEAL ECHOCARDIOGRAPHIC FINDINGS:

1. The overall left ventricular systolic function appeared to be unchanged.

2. There was a 23-mm St. Jude mitral valve in the mitral valve position, which appeared to be well seated.

3. No stenosis or insufficiency was seen.

4. The aortic insufficiency remained at a moderate level.

5. There was no other significant change.

Total time for this procedure was 45 min.

Anesthesia code: _____

Physical status modifiers: _____

Qualifying circumstances: _____

Scenario 7-6

OPERATIVE NOTE

PREOPERATIVE DIAGNOSIS:

1. Left volar wrist ganglion cyst.

2. Left carpal tunnel syndrome.

POSTOPERATIVE DIAGNOSIS:

1. Left volar wrist ganglion cyst.

2. Left carpal tunnel syndrome.

OPERATION:

1. Excision of left volar radial ganglion cyst.

2. Carpal tunnel release, left.

ANESTHESIA: Sedation plus local block.

PROCEDURE: After adequate sedation had been obtained, the patient was prepped and draped. The left upper extremity was exsanguinated and the tourniquet raised to 250 mmHg. 0.5 ml of 0.5% Bupivacaine was infiltrated into the left thenar crease and into the left volar radial wrist area in the area of the ganglion cyst. A 1.5-cm incision was made in the left thenar crease. The incision was carried down through the subcutaneous tissue, the superficial palmar fascia and the transverse carpal ligament. The transverse carpal ligament and distal portion of the antebrachial fascia were divided under direct vision. The incision line was closed using

4-0 nylon sutures. Attention was then turned to the left volar radial wrist, where a 1-cm longitudinal incision was made. The volar radial cyst was identified and traced back to its point of origin at the radioscaphoid joint. The cyst was excised in its entirety. Its base was cauterized. The incision line was closed using 4-0 nylon sutures. A dry sterile dressing was applied. The patient tolerated the procedure well.

Anesthesia code: _____

Diagnosis: _____

Scenario 7-7

OPERATIVE REPORT

PREOPERATIVE DIAGNOSIS: Failure to progress, previous low cervical transverse cesarean section.

POSTOPERATIVE DIAGNOSIS: Failure to progress, previous low cervical transverse cesarean section.

PROCEDURE: Repeat low cervical transverse cesarean section.

ANESTHESIA: Epidural.

FLUIDS: 2,000 cc.

ESTIMATED BLOOD LOSS: 500 cc.

DRAINS: Foley to gravity.

COMPLICATIONS: None.

FINDINGS: A viable male infant delivered from the vertex presentation. Apgars were 8 and 9 at 1 and 5 min, respectively. Weight 9 lb 0 ounces. Arterial cord pH 7.20.

TECHNIQUE OF PROCEDURE: After adequate epidural anesthesia was obtained, a Pfannenstiel incision was made at the site of her previous incision and extended down to the fascial layer. The fascia was scored in the midline and incised laterally. The fascia was then bluntly and sharply dissected off the underlying rectus muscles. The rectus muscles were bluntly and sharply dissected in the midline. The underlying peritoneum was identified and this was transected under direct visualization. The bladder was densely adherent to the anterior abdominal wall and this was dissected away using sharp dissection. The uterovesical flap was then formed horizontally across the lower uterine segment once the bladder was free and this was then incorporated into the Balfour blade. A horizontal incision was made in the lower uterine segment and the incision was extended laterally using blunt dissection. A single hand was placed into the lower uterine segment. The vertex portion of the infant was brought forward. The infant was bulb suctioned. The remainder of the infant was delivered in the usual fashion. The cord was clamped and cut. The infant was handed to the pediatric team in attendance.

The placenta was manually delivered. Normal configuration. The uterine cavity was cleaned of debris using a dry lap pad. The uterine incision was closed using a running interlocking suture of 0 Vicryl. A second imbricating layer was placed above the first using 0 Vicryl. The uterus was normal in appearance. There were some adhesions posteriorly as well. The tubes and ovaries appeared normal. The abdomen was irrigated. Hemostasis was assured. The uterus was returned to the abdominal cavity. The rectus muscles were plicated at three points in the midline using 0 Vicryl suture. The fascia was closed using 1 Vicryl in a running fashion. The subcutaneous tissue was then irrigated with saline. The skin was closed using 4-0 Vicryl in a subcuticular fashion, then supported with benzoin and Steri-Strips. All sponge, needle, and instrument counts were correct ×3.

The patient was taken to recovery in a stable condition.

Anesthesia code: _____

Diagnosis: _____

Scenario 7-8

OPERATIVE NOTE

POSTOPERATIVE DIAGNOSIS: Left breast pain with neuroma.

PROCEDURE: Left breast exploration with excision of mass neuroma.

ANESTHESIA: General.

SUMMARY OF PROCEDURE: After adequate anesthesia had been obtained, the patient was prepped and draped. The left inframammary fold incision line was incised. The incision was carried down through the subcutaneous tissue. The left capsule was encountered. A portion of capsule was excised. A mass close to the skin at the medial inferior margin of the left breast was encountered. It was excised through a 2-cm skin incision. A portion of the left capsule and the inferior portion of the left pectoralis major muscle was removed. As there appeared to be a mass in this area consistent with a neuroma, the inferior border of the muscle and the anterior portion of the capsule were all removed under direct vision. The area was irrigated with saline.

The incision lines were then closed using 4-0 Vicryl and 4-0 Monocryl. Steri-Strips and dry sterile dressing were applied. The patient tolerated the procedure well.

Anesthesia code: _____

Diagnosis: _____

Scenario 7-9

OPERATIVE NOTE

INDICATIONS FOR PROCEDURE: The patient is 2 years old. She has adenoid hypertrophy causing nasal obstruction. She is here for an adenoidectomy.

PREOPERATIVE DIAGNOSIS: Adenoid hypertrophy.

PROCEDURE: Adenoidectomy.

POSTOPERATIVE DIAGNOSIS: Adenoid hypertrophy.

ANESTHESIA: General endotracheal anesthesia.

continued

ESTIMATED BLOOD LOSS: Less than 10 cc.

FLUIDS: 100 cc lactated Ringer.

PROCEDURE: After the induction of adequate general endotracheal anesthesia, the patient is properly positioned on the bed. A McIvor mouth gag was put in place and suspended from a few towels on the patient's chest. Red rubber catheters were passed through the nostrils to retract soft palate. Tonsils were noted to be 2+ and nonobstructive. Adenoids were noted to be obstructing approximately 90% of the nasopharynx. Adenoids were removed using an adenoid curette and a St. Clair forceps, and the nasopharynx was packed with an Afrin-soaked tonsil pack. After 3 min this pack was removed and pinpoint suction electrocautery was performed and the area was repacked with an Afrin-soaked tonsil pack. After 3 min this pack was removed. There was no active bleeding noted. Oropharynx and nasopharynx were suctioned clean with no active bleeding. An orogastric tube was passed, the stomach emptied, and this tube removed. Red rubber catheters were removed. The patient was taken off suspension. The mouth gag was removed. She tolerated the procedure well. There were no complications. She was taken to recovery room extubated and in good condition.

Anesthesia code: _____

Diagnosis: _____

CHAPTER REVIEW

Using the *CPT* and *HCPCS* manuals and this textbook, complete the following exercises.

Define the following:

1. Relative Value Guide (RVG) _____
2. Nonpar provider _____
3. Nerve blocks _____
4. Physical status modifiers (PSM) _____
5. Moderate (conscious) sedation _____

Find the anesthesia codes for the following surgeries:

6. 27132 Conversion of previous hip surgery to total hip arthroplasty: _____

7. 23000 Removal of subdeltoid calcareous deposit, open, shoulder region: _____

8. 61680 Surgery of intracranial arteriovenous malformation; supratentorial, simple: _____

9. 59514 Cesarean delivery: _____

10. 52601 Transurethral resection of prostate, complete: _____

Chapter 8
Coding for Surgery

KEY TERMS

code range
diagnostic procedure
follow-up care

global period (days)
subsection notes
surgical package (global services)

Surgery section guidelines

LEARNING OBJECTIVES

Upon completion of this chapter, the student will be able to:

1. Utilize the tools of the *CPT*, *ICD-9*, and *HCPCS* manuals to enhance his or her coding abilities and to code surgical procedures accurately

SIZE AND ORGANIZATION OF THE SURGERY SECTION

The Surgery section of *CPT* is the largest section. This is further divided into subsections that are defined according to anatomic site. Each anatomic site is then organized by the surgical approach or type of procedure.

USING THE NOTES IN THE SURGERY SECTION

Many of the subsections have detailed notes that apply specifically to the use of the codes in those subsections. When coding surgical procedures, you must use these notes, as well as the numerous parenthetical notes throughout the sections. The parenthetical notes are especially helpful in reminding you of other codes that you should utilize in addition to the selected procedure. These notes also alert you to the codes that should not be reported in conjunction with a particular procedure.

> ### EXAMPLE
>
> The **code range** 12001–13160 is for Repair (Closure) within the Integumentary System. The related notes explain the types of closures and what the codes include. Without this information, the medical coder may code the procedures incorrectly, resulting in a claim that is either rejected or improperly reimbursed.

USING THE MODIFIERS WHEN CODING SURGERY

In the Surgery section you also find that many modifiers can be used to ensure correct reimbursement. Because major procedures are considered part of a **global surgical package or global service**, any services rendered during the **global period** that the provider feels warrants additional reimbursement requires a modifier. The modifier is used to identify the extenuating circumstances that led to the procedure, and it increases the possibility that the provider will receive additional reimbursement above and beyond the surgical package reimbursement.

A special report may also have to accompany the claim. The special report gives the payer the necessary information regarding the procedure so that it can determine the correct reimbursement.

■ *Find the Code 8-1*

OFFICE NOTE

Patient is here to re-excise the site of the basal cell cancer on the left cheek that had been treated with curettage and electrodesiccation. The reason for the re-excision is that the lesion had a very infiltrative pattern and I feel the recurrence rate will be too high with simply a curettage and electrodesiccation.

After verbal and written informed consent was obtained, I explained at considerable length that we cannot guarantee the cosmetic results of the scar removal. After also confirming the site of the lesion with the patient, the scar lesion measuring 1.5 cm was anesthetized with 1% lidocaine with epinephrine and excised as an ellipse down to the frontalis fascia. There is significant tension on the wound and closing the wound required extensive undermining and closure with double-pulley 4-0 PDS 2 subcutaneous suture and 2 horizontal mattress 4-0 nylon cuticular sutures and 2 interrupted 4-0 nylon cuticular sutures in running 6-0 nylon cuticular suture.

Suture removal will be in 7 days, and he is scheduled for follow-up in about 6 months.

From the scenario, does the documentation support both an E&M and a procedure? _____

What procedure(s) would you code? _____

List them: _____

Would you use a modifier? _____ If so, which one? _____

From the scenario, does the documentation support both an E&M and a procedure? No. What procedure(s) would you code? Excision of malignant lesion. List them: 11642, 12051. Would you use modifier? Yes. If so, which one? 51.

The medical coder knows that a simple repair of an excised lesion is included in the excision code. However, when more complex closure is required, the rules stated in the Excision section and the rules in the Repairs section must be reviewed. Not all sections have special rules or conventions, but the medical coder must always be aware of these sections and consult them when needed.

When looking at a medical note, the medical coder must always be sure of what is being documented. If a procedure is not documented, it was not done. The provider stated how large the lesion was, but he did not state the margin he took. If he had, the medical coder could have coded for a higher level of service.

Let's change Find the Code and code it.

Find the Code 8-2

OFFICE NOTE

Patient is here today for a follow-up to a basal cell cancer lesion, which seems to have come back. After a problem-focused exam and low medical decision making, I have decided to re-excise the site of the basal cell cancer today.

The history of this lesion is on the left cheek and had been treated with curettage and electrodesiccation about 6 months ago.

The reason for the re-excision is that the lesion had a very infiltrative pattern and I feel the recurrence rate will be too high with simply a curettage and electro-desiccation. I explained the procedure and the risk of scarring.

After verbal and written informed consent was obtained, I explained the approximate length of the scar and that we cannot guarantee the cosmetic results. After also confirming the site of the lesion with the patient, the scar lesion measuring 1.5 cm was anesthetized with 1% lidocaine with epinephrine and excised with margins of 1 cm all around the lesion as an ellipse down to the frontalis fascia. There is significant tension on the wound and closing the wound required extensive undermining and closure with double-pulley 4-0 PDS 2 subcutaneous suture and 2 horizontal mattress 4-0 nylon cuticular sutures and 2 interrupted 4-0 nylon cuticular sutures in running 6-0 nylon cuticular suture.

Suture removal will be in 7 days, and he is scheduled for follow-up in about 6 months.

From the scenario, does the documentation support both an E&M and a procedure? _____

What procedure(s) would you code? _____

List them: _____

Would you use a modifier? _____   If yes, which one? _____

From the scenario, does the documentation support both an E&M and a procedure? Yes. What procedure(s) would you code? E&M and removal of lesion. List them: 99212, 11643, 12051. Would you use a modifier? Yes. If yes, which one? 25 and 51.

The medical documentation dictates which codes the medical coder uses for the procedure. Understanding the documentation and how to get the information from the documentation is the key for coding. Another tool a medical coder can use when abstracting medical information from a note is to underline or highlight the key elements on a copy of the record. Never highlight or write on the original record.

The medical coder will also find office-based surgeries on the encounter forms. When coding, you sometimes need to check the office notes regarding the surgery to see if there is missing information, that is, no diagnosis to support the procedure, a missing modifier, or any other procedure done in addition to another procedure.

Let's further modify the note and see how this impacts the coding of it.

Find the Code 8-3

> **OFFICE NOTE**
>
> After verbal and written informed consent obtained, discussed permanent scar and that we cannot guarantee cosmetic results. After also confirming the site of the lesion with the patient, the biopsy-proven basal cell cancer on the right lateral forehead, which measures 0.9 cm in diameter, was anesthetized with 1% lidocaine with epinephrine and excised as an oval into the subcutaneous fat. The lesion plus margins measured 1.5 cm.
>
> It became apparent that a side-to-side closure resulting in a horizontal scar would have significant tension. At that point, I discussed with the patient that we could close it side-to-side, but that in my opinion it may be advantageous to close it with an A-to-T flap. He agreed to the A-to-T flap and I explained that it will be a T-shaped scar.
>
> Laterally based flaps were excised and undermined. There was extensive undermining to the area. Care was taken to avoid the underlying neurovascular bundles. The wound was then closed in a layered fashion with interrupted 3-0 PDS 2 subcutaneous sutures followed by multiple interrupted 6-0 nylon cuticular sutures. A corner stitch was placed at the point of the T where the 3 arms connect. The total flap area was 10 cm^2. Sutural removal will be in 4 days and I am scheduling a checkup in 6 months to check the final healing appearance.

From the scenario, does the documentation support both an E&M and a procedure? _____

What procedure(s) would you code? _____

List them: _____

Would you use a modifier? _____ If so, which one? _____

For all of these scenarios, what would the diagnosis be? _____

What would the diagnosis code be? _____

From the scenario, does the documentation support both an E&M and a procedure? No. What procedure(s) would you code? Excision of malignant lesion and T-flap. List them: 11642, 14040. Would you use a modifier? Yes. If so, which one? 51. For all of these scenarios, what would the diagnosis be? Basal cell cancer—forehead. What is the diagnosis code? 198.2.

When abstracting from the surgical notes, the new medical coder must not get overwhelmed by the length of the medical note. Read through a *copy* of the notes and underline or highlight any and all pertinent information for coding purposes.

Now, try your hand at coding scenarios within each anatomic site of the Surgery section.

CHAPTER EXERCISES

Scenario 8-1

> **OPERATIVE REPORT**
>
> **PREOPERATIVE DIAGNOSIS:** Approximately 2.9 cm composite length of a stellate laceration of the right helix and the antihelix of the ear including skin and cartilage.

POSTOPERATIVE DIAGNOSIS: Approximately 2.9 cm composite length of a stellate laceration of the right helix and the antihelix of the ear including skin and cartilage.

PROCEDURE: Complex repair, layered closure including skin and cartilage of 2.9-cm laceration of helix and antihelix of right ear.

ANESTHESIA: General.

COMPLICATIONS: None.

INDICATIONS FOR SURGERY: This 5-year-old young lady suffered trauma to the right ear at school today. Apparently a little boy threw a building block of some sort at her. She came to the emergency room and I was consulted by the emergency room. She has the aforementioned laceration of her ear. It goes through the cartilage of the helix and antihelix. I have advised closure. Her mother is advised of the risks and benefits of surgery including risks of having scarring, infection, and need for possible further surgery. No guarantees have been given as to final functional or aesthetic results.

PROCEDURE: Under satisfactory general anesthesia with the patient intubated and after prepping and draping in the usual fashion, the skin in the ear around the laceration was infiltrated with 1% Xylocaine 1:100,000 epinephrine. The cartilage of the helix and antihelix was repaired with two sutures of 5-0 PDS. The skin edges were then carefully approximated and closed with 6-0 fast-absorbing gut. The wound was approximately 2.9 cm long. Dermabond glue was applied to the wound to protect it, and a protective ear dressing was applied. The patient was awakened from anesthesia and taken to the recovery room in satisfactory condition. She tolerated the procedure well. There were no complications and no significant blood loss.

Procedure code(s): _____

Diagnosis code(s): _____

Scenario 8-2

OPERATIVE REPORT

Patient came in for 2 excisions of biopsy-proven basal carcinoma on the neck (1.5 cm) and 1 on the chest (2.0 cm).

After informed consent obtained and time-out procedures observed, the areas numbed with lidocaine and epinephrine, 1-cm margins obtained around each site. Elliptical excision made. Subcutaneous sutures with 4-0 Vicryl placed. Epidermal sutures with 4-0 Ethilon placed.

The patient given wound care instructions. Return to clinic for suture removal of the lesion on the neck in 7 days and in 10 to 14 days we will do suture removal on the chest.

At that time, we will do another body check.

Procedure code(s): _____

Diagnosis code(s): _____

Scenario 8-3

OFFICE NOTE

This is a 6-month follow-up for a patient who has a history of melanoma in situ removed from the left forearm in November 2005. This was a lentigo maligna. Patient comes in today for routine surveillance. He has no new areas that he is concerned about. Also had an area of lichen simplex chronicus on the left buttocks medial region that has been present for quite some time. His treatment for that had been fluocinonide cream mixed with Bacitracin ointment once or twice a day. He does tell me that that area is improved.

He has no medication allergies. Medication list is reviewed in the paper chart. He has no new lesions that he is concerned about. His medical history is reviewed.

On exam, he is in no acute distress. Today's exam included scalp, face, neck, chest, abdomen, back, upper extremities, hands, buttocks, and portions of his lower extremities. The patient seems mildly depressed today. The thing that bothers him the most is the loss of his vision. He has an essentially clear exam today with very few nevi noted.

One in particular, however, on his back is quite deeply pigmented. Measures only about 4 mm, brown, smooth-edged papule; however, it does appear to be very deeply pigmented. Its location is in the midline about 15 to 17 cm above his waistline region. It is also adjacent to a flesh-colored, compound nevus, which is slightly below and to the right of midline. I reviewed the risks and benefits including permanent scar, doing a shave removal of this atypical nevus. He wished to proceed. I explained that, in view of his history of lentigo maligna, it would be worth checking this lesion.

After verbal informed consent was obtained and the site was confirmed with him, the area was anesthetized with 1% lidocaine with epinephrine and a shave removal was performed.

Specimen was sent to Pathology. Aluminum chloride was used for hemostasis. Bacitracin and Band-Aid were applied. Left arm shows no evidence of recurrence of lentigo maligna.

IMPRESSION AND PLAN: The patient with a history of lentigo maligna has an atypical nevus on the back today. This was removed by shave. I will call him with the results of the pathology and arrange needed follow-up. Routine surveillance for 6 months will also be established today.

Note
Pathology report indicates tissue negative for malignancy.

Procedure code(s): _____

Diagnosis code(s): _____

Scenario 8-4

OFFICE NOTE

This patient has been referred to me by nurse practitioner, Kelly Mason, regarding 2 neoplastic skin lesions noted on her left foot. She is here today for skin neoplasm excision and tissue reconstruction.

PAST MEDICAL HISTORY: Hypothyroidism.

MEDICATIONS: Levothyroxine 50 mcg per day.

ALLERGIES: Erythromycin.

PAST SURGICAL HISTORY: Left foot surgery in which she had tendon reconstruction and joint fusions as a result of polio.

SOCIAL HISTORY: Negative tobacco. Negative alcohol. Occupation: She is a graphic artist.

FAMILY HISTORY: Mother positive for hypertension.

REVIEW OF SYSTEMS: The patient denies chest pains. Denies shortness of breath. Denies dizziness or headaches. Denies history of hepatitis. Denies GI ulcers and denies history of stroke.

PHYSICAL FINDINGS:

General: This is a well nourished, well developed, white female who is awake, alert, and oriented ×3.

VASCULAR: Her pedal pulses are palpable; however, skin temperature is warm to cool going proximal to distal. Capillary filling time is less than 3 sec to all 10 digits.

Dermatological: The skin is smooth and supple. No open lesions or macerations noted. There is a hyperpigmented skin lesion that is flattened and the borders are irregular noted to the left lateral foot as well as the medial arch region. The first lesion measures approximately 9 mm, and the second lesion measures approximately 8 mm in diameter.

Musculoskeletal: Muscle strength is weakened upon dorsiflexion and plantar flexion of the ankle.

Neurological: Protective threshold is intact.

ASSESSMENT: Skin neoplasm ×2 left foot, rule out malignancy.

PLAN: A surgical consent was obtained and the 2 lesions were anesthetized and excised together, followed with rotational skin flap closure and tissue rearrangement. The patient tolerated the procedure well without complications. Also noted is that approximately a 3.5- to 4-mm border of regular tissue was included in the excision. She is to keep the area clean and dry and bandaged at all times. Vicodin 5/500 mg was prescribed for pain, and she is to return to the clinic on Monday for a wound check. The tissue is to be sent to Pathology to rule out malignancy and I will call her with the results.

Addendum: The pathology report came back positive for skin malignancy. A follow-up appointment will be needed.

Procedure code(s): _____

Diagnosis code(s): _____

Scenario 8-5

OFFICE NOTE

This is a new patient referred by Dr. Helen Lang for a consultation regarding his basal cell carcinoma on the right side of his nose, which was biopsied in August

continued

2005. The pathology showed nodular basal cell carcinoma. At that time, it measured about 4 mm; it now measures at least 8 mm. He takes allopurinol, lisinopril, and aspirin. He has no known drug allergies. Examination was limited to the skin, which shows a large basal cell carcinoma on the right side of the nose. Excision will require a bilobed flap closure. This was explained to him and to his wife. Risks of bleeding, infection, scarring, pincushioning, recurrence, and need for additional surgery were described. This will be done with frozen section in the near future under local anesthetic. A 60-minute slot has been requested.

Procedure code(s): _____

Diagnosis code(s): _____

OPERATIVE REPORT

PREOPERATIVE DIAGNOSIS: Basal cell carcinoma, right alar groove.

POSTOPERATIVE DIAGNOSIS: Basal cell carcinoma, right alar groove.

PROCEDURE: Excision of basal cell carcinoma with bilobed flap closure.

SURGEON: Dr. Susan Barry, M.D.

ANESTHESIA: Local.

FINDINGS: Basal cell carcinoma, peripheral margins negative, deep margins positive, additional deep margins sent for final pathology.

EDL: 5 cc.

COMPLICATIONS: None apparent.

DISPOSITION: Stable to home.

TECHNIQUE: The patient was brought to the operating room and placed supine on the operating room table. The patient marked the lesion preoperatively. The area was infiltrated with 1% lidocaine with 1:100,000 of epinephrine. A bilobed flap closure was designed around the lesion subtending a 100° angle. The lesion itself (1.0 cm plus a margin of 1.0 cm) was sharply excised and sent for frozen section marked at 12 o'clock. The transposition flap was then incised and elevated from the surrounding tissue. Hemostasis was obtained with the bipolar electrocautery. Frozen section showed negative margins peripherally, but deep margins were positive. Significant amounts of additional deep tissue were removed and the deepest tissue was then sent for permanent section. The flaps were then transposed and sutured in place with interrupted 4-0 Vicryl sutures to approximate the wound edges. The wound edges were closed using a running 5-0 fast-absorbing gut. He tolerated the procedure well. Steri-Strips were placed over the wounds. A compression dressing was placed over the nose. The patient will follow up in 1 week with Dr. Helen Lang and in 6 weeks with me.

Procedure code(s): _____

Diagnosis code(s): _____

Scenario 8-6

OPERATIVE REPORT

PREOPERATIVE DIAGNOSIS: Right breast cancer.

POSTOPERATIVE DIAGNOSIS: Right breast cancer.

PROCEDURES: Right breast lumpectomy with needle localization ×2, sentinel lymph node biopsy, injection of vital dye.

ATTENDING SURGEON: Dr. Paul Artist.

ANESTHESIA: General.

INDICATIONS: The patient is a 43-year-old female who presents with biopsy-proven right breast cancer. The patient presents for a right breast lumpectomy with needle localization ×2, sentinel lymph node biopsy, injection of vital dye.

PROCEDURE PERFORMED: The patient was placed in a supine position. The patient was prepped and draped in the usual sterile fashion. The isosulfan blue dye was injected in a subdermal, as well as periareolar region and massaged into the breast for 5 min. Once this was performed, an 8-cm skin incision was made in the lateral right breast. The superior skin flap was raised to the axilla and the axillary fascia was incised. Using the gamma probe, 2 lymph nodes were identified. These were both bluntly and sharply dissected and completely removed. They were confirmed to contain both the radioactive material as well as the blue dye. Once this was performed, the inferior skin flap was raised. Both wires were delivered into the wound. The area in question was grasped with a Lahey clamp. Circumferential dissection was made around this area using the electrocautery. The area was completely excised. The wound was thoroughly irrigated. Hemostasis was obtained. The skin was reapproximated using interrupted 3-0 Vicryl sutures. The skin was then closed using 4-0 Vicryl subcuticular sutures.

The patient tolerated the procedure well.

Procedure code(s): _____

Diagnosis code(s): _____

Scenario 8-7

OPERATIVE REPORT

PREOPERATIVE DIAGNOSIS:

1. Right silicone breast prosthesis rupture

2. Right breast ptosis, Grade 2

3. Silicone breast prosthesis, left

4. Scar contracture left inframammary fold

OPERATION:

1. Explant bilateral silicone breast prostheses

2. Bilateral capsulectomies

continued

3. Bilateral capsulorrhaphies

4. Scar revision of left inframammary fold

5. Mastopexy, right breast

POSTOPERATIVE DIAGNOSIS:

1. Right ruptured breast implant

2. Left intact breast implant

ANESTHESIA: General anesthesia. 0.5% Marcaine with epinephrine. 0.5%. Marcaine infusion to bilateral breast pockets.

OPERATIVE TIME: 4 hr.

1. Skin left breast

2. Left breast prosthesis intact

3. Right breast prosthesis ruptured

ESTIMATED BLOOD LOSS: 100 cc.

INTRAVENOUS FLUIDS: 3.4 L of lactated Ringer's solution.

URINE OUTPUT: 500 cc.

INDICATIONS FOR SURGERY: The patient is a 40-year-old woman with a history of breast cancer on the left status post external beam radiation and lumpectomy for breast conservation who had previously undergone bilateral breast prosthesis placement. She recently had an exchange of her breast implants in 2000 with silicone implants. A recent mammogram of the right breast was complicated by pain and MRI confirmed rupture. She presents with the above diagnoses for the proposed procedure.

PROCEDURE: After receiving adequate preoperative consent, a discussion of the risk factors as well as preoperative antibiotics, namely vancomycin, she was taken to the operating room after markings had been performed. She was placed in the supine position at which time general anesthesia was adequately induced endotracheally without incident. All pressure points were sufficiently padded and Venodyne therapy was initiated. Her arms were abducted to 90°, padded, and Kerlix wraps were placed. She was positioned above the break of the bed for intraoperative elevation to 90°. Her chest was prepped and draped in the usual sterile fashion after a Foley catheter was sterilely inserted. Venodynes were inflated prior to general anesthesia and functioned throughout the case. Once her chest was prepped and draped in the usual sterile fashion, staples were placed along the inframammary folds bilaterally to mark them. Attention was placed over the left breast, at which time the previous scar was excised with a 10-blade scalpel and sent to Pathology. The soft tissue was dissected down to the level of the prosthesis with Bovie electrocautery. The intact breast prosthesis was removed and sent to Pathology. The cavity was irrigated with copious amounts of saline and a capsulectomy was performed. The capsule was left over the anterior chest wall. The position was confirmed to be in a submuscular position. Next, capsulorrhaphy sutures of 3-0 Vicryl were placed laterally as well as inferiorly to recreate the inframammary fold. The medial border of the breast cavity was also plicated with 3-0 Vicryl. Next, a breast sizer was placed and inflated to 300 cc. This was done after hemostasis was obtained with Bovie electrocautery. Once this was inflated, attention was then placed over the right breast.

A circumareolar incision was performed and the skin was deep ithelialized. Access to the breast pocket was obtained inferiorly.

Of note: The previous access for her augmentation mammoplasty was from an inframammary fold incision. Next, the breast pocket was breeched and ruptured silicone was seen. Liposuction machine tubing was placed into the cavity and silicone was aspirated. The implant was removed and sent to Pathology. The cavity was irrigated with copious amounts of normal saline.

Next, a capsulectomy was performed with Bovie electrocautery. Bleeding was controlled with electrocautery as well. The implant was found to be in a subpectoral position. Capsulorrhaphy sutures were placed laterally using 3-0 Vicryl. The soft tissue was dissected medially to help medialize the breast pocket. Next, the sizer was placed in the breast cavity. This was stapled into place, as was the contralateral side, and the patient was raised to a 90° angle. Additional skin and breast tissue was felt to be present in the inferior and lateral poles of the right breast.

At that time, a completion of the vertical reduction mammoplasty incision was performed. Bleeding was stopped with Bovie electrocautery and 3-0 Vicryls were used to reapproximate the breast pillars. Once this was completed, the patient was then raised to a sitting position once again and volumes were checked. She was then placed again in the supine position. The sizers were removed and the pockets were irrigated with Bacitracin irrigation. 270 cc smooth, round implants were brought to the surgical field, soaked in Bacitracin saline solution and steriley placed in each breast pocket. These were inflated to 310 cc on the left and 275 cc on the right. The pockets were closed. The patient was raised to a sitting position and volumes were checked once again.

Of note: Prior to the breast prosthesis placement, 15 round Blake drains were placed through transaxillary incisions and sutured in place with 3-0 nylon. Both pockets were irrigated with Bacitracin containing antibiotic saline solution.

The left wound was closed in a 3-layer fashion with 3-0 Vicryl, followed by 4-0 Monocryl, followed by 5-0 Monocryl, and the drain was placed on suction after instillation of 10 cc of 0.5% Marcaine into the pocket. The right breast was closed with interrupted 3-0 Vicryl, followed by 3-0 Monocryl and 4-0 Monocryl. 5-0 Monocryl was used to pursestring the vertical limb approximately 9 cm down to 6.5 cm. Circumareolar sutures were placed using 3-0 Monocryl, followed by 4-0 PDS, and a running subcuticular 5-0 PDS was used to close the skin. The right areola measured approximately 4 × 4 cm in diameter, the right 3.5 × 3.5. An additional 10 cc of Marcaine was placed in the pocket on the right breast as well.

The needle, sponge, and instrument count was correct at the end of the case. There were no intraoperative complications. Drains were placed on negative bulb suction. She was transferred once extubated and wrapped with Kerlix and Ace wraps to the postanesthesia recovery room. There were no complications. All specimens were sent as dictated above.

Procedure code(s): _____

Diagnosis code(s): _____

Scenario 8-8

OPERATIVE REPORT

Verbal and written informed consent was obtained and the location of the site to be removed was confirmed with the patient. The approximate length of the scar

continued

that would result was discussed. Patient was also informed that there is no guarantee of cosmetic results and that, due to the size of the lesion, I will be taking narrow margins. Because of the narrow margins, there is a possibility of positive margins and if so, one could simply observe the remainder or do a second procedure in the future.

The 2.3-cm basal cell cancer over the sternum was anesthetized with 1% lidocaine with epinephrine, total volume 17 cc. During the informed consent, possible closures of side-to-side closure, O-to-Z flap, or incomplete closure with secondary healing were discussed. The wound was excised as a circle with 2-mm margins resulting in a wound that measured 2.7 cm.

To close this wound, extensive undermining was done and it was found that this would close side-to-side resulting in horizontal scar. This was discussed with the patient that a horizontal scar would be closed in vertical, and the wound was then closed in a layered fashion with interrupted 3-0 PDS II subcutaneous suture followed by running 3-0 nylon cuticular suture.

Due to the length of the procedure, which was 16 min, and the significant size of the open wound, cephalexin 500 mg 4 times a day for 5 days was prescribed and side effects were discussed.

He will return in 7 to 8 days in the nursing schedule just to check on the wound healing. He is willing to avoid swimming and other rigorous physical activity over the next 2 weeks. Again, he is also scheduled for a follow-up appointment in September.

Procedure code(s): _____
Diagnosis code(s): _____

Scenario 8-9

OPERATIVE REPORT

PREOPERATIVE DIAGNOSIS: Breast cancer.

POSTOPERATIVE DIAGNOSIS: Breast cancer.

OPERATION: Bilateral transverse rectus abdominis myocutaneous flap reconstruction (TRAM flap).

ANESTHESIA: General anesthesia.

SURGEON: Phil E Kelly, M.D.

ASSISTANT: Mary Ann Smith, P.A.

PROCEDURE: After adequate anesthesia had been obtained, the patient was prepped and draped. Bilateral mastectomies were performed by Dr. Potter. This is dictated under a separate note. An elliptical incision in the lower abdominal area was made extending from superior just above the umbilicus to an inferior point at the suprapubic fold and extending laterally just beyond the anterior superior iliac spine on each side.

The incision was carried down through the subcutaneous tissue. The lateral border of each rectus sheath was incised. The inferior epigastric artery and veins were identified, ligated, and divided. The rectus abdominis muscle, subcutaneous tissue, and skin on each side of the abdomen were then raised out of the rectus bed and a midline incision in the tissue was made in order to achieve reconstruction for each side. A subcutaneous tissue tunnel was then made in the epigastric region after undermining. The undermining was extended to the breast area in the lateral portion on each breast.

The anterior abdominal wall defect was then repaired using mesh, which was secured using 2-0 Prolene sutures. These were running sutures placed at the margin of each rectus sheath. Two 0 Prolene sutures were used to secure the mesh in the umbilical area. These were placed on the lateral aspect of the umbilicus on each side. The caudal margin of the superior flap was brought to the cephalad margin of the inferior flap and secured by first approximating Scarpa's fascia using 2-0 Vicryl sutures. The skin was then closed in layers using 2-0 Vicryl and 3-0 Monocryl sutures. Prior to closure, two #15 BLAKE Drains were brought out through separate incisions. The umbilicus was then brought out through a separate incision and secured using 4-0 Vicryl and 5-0 fast-absorbing. The abdominal tissue was then sculpted on each side to recreate the appearance of the breast tissue. These were then inset using 4-0 Vicryl and 3-0 Monocryl.

Prior to closure, a #15 BLAKE Drain was brought out through a separate incision at the lateral margin of the mastectomy incision lines. Dry sterile dressings were applied. The patient tolerated the procedure well.

Procedure code(s): _____

Diagnosis code(s): _____

Scenario 8-10

OPERATIVE REPORT

PREOPERATIVE DIAGNOSIS: Facial trauma.

POSTOPERATIVE DIAGNOSIS: Facial trauma.

OPERATION: Facial reconstruction using fat transfer.

ANESTHESIA: Sedation plus local.

PROCEDURE: After adequate sedation had been obtained, the patient was prepped and draped. The right malar area and periumbilical area were both infiltrated with 0.5% bupivacaine. A transverse incision was made in the umbilical area. Fat was removed using a Coleman cannula. The fat was then separated from the surrounding liquid, blood, and local anesthetic. A 3-mm incision was then made in the right nasolabial fold. Fat was injected into the area of the right malar region, which was slightly depressed secondary to fat atrophy following facial trauma. A 6-0 fast-absorbing was placed in the right nasolabial fold incision. The umbilical incision was closed using 5-0 Vicryl. He tolerated the procedure well.

Procedure code(s): _____

Diagnosis code(s): _____

Scenario 8-11

OPERATIVE REPORT

PREOPERATIVE DIAGNOSIS: Sacral pressure ulcer, osteomyelitis of the coccyx.

POSTOPERATIVE DIAGNOSIS: Sacral pressure ulcer, osteomyelitis of the coccyx.

NAME OF PROCEDURE: Coccygectomy, debridement and irrigation of sacrum, with sacral bone biopsy, excision of pressure ulcer.

ANESTHESIA: General.

DESCRIPTION OF PROCEDURE: After adequate anesthesia had been obtained, the patient was prepped and draped. The sacral pressure ulcer was excised widely. The coccyx was then removed. Half of it was sent to Pathology and half was sent to the Laboratory for culture. The sacrum was then debrided and a biopsy was taken. Again, half was sent to the Laboratory for culture and half to Pathology for evaluation of osteomyelitis. The wound was then irrigated with a pulse lavage using antibiotic solution. The area was then packed with a damp dressing. She tolerated the procedure well.

Procedure code(s): _____
Diagnosis code(s): _____

Scenario 8-12

OPERATIVE REPORT

PREOPERATIVE DIAGNOSIS: Left hemothorax with multiple rib fractures (fall from stairs at home, 6 weeks ago).

POSTOPERATIVE DIAGNOSIS: Left hemothorax with multiple rib fractures (fall 6 weeks ago) and associated hemothorax (4 L of fluid).

PROCEDURE: Left thoracoscopy, drainage of 4 L of fluid.

PROCEDURE DESCRIPTION: Under adequate general endotracheal anesthesia with a double-lumen tube in place, the patient positioned and prepared and draped in the usual manner for left thoracoscopy. An incision was made anterolaterly after a needle was inserted into the chest and dark old blood was withdrawn. The suction device was then inserted and 4 L of dark bloody fluid was removed. Thoracoscopy was performed and the lung did not appear to be trapped. There was no obvious evidence of malignancy. It seems as if the whole process was related to fractured ribs and was a hemothorax. A single-size 32 chest tube was directed posteriorly into the middle of the chest behind the lung. This was anchored to the skin with heavy silk suture. Occlusive dressing was applied. He tolerated the procedure well.

Procedure code(s): _____
Diagnosis code(s): _____

Scenario 8-13

OPERATIVE REPORT

PREOPERATIVE DIAGNOSIS: Osteoarthritis left knee.

POSTOPERATIVE DIAGNOSIS: Osteoarthritis left knee.

PROCEDURE: Left total knee arthroplasty using a cruciate retaining fixed bearing implant system with a DePuy PSC Sigma size 3 cruciate retaining femoral component, modular size 3 tibial tray with a 10-mm PLI insert and a 35 nonsurface patellar replacement.

ANESTHESIA: Femoral nerve block with spinal.

INDICATIONS: This 82-year-old presents for a second-side total knee arthroplasty.

PROCEDURE: After informed consent was obtained, the patient was properly identified. She was brought to the operating room and given a spinal anesthesia after administration of femoral nerve block. The leg was prepped and draped after application of a tourniquet. A midline approach was carried down through the subcutaneous tissue and any bleeders were cauterized. A medial parapatellar arthrotomy was created over the patella and flexing the knee. Marginal debridement was performed with Smiley retractors to protect the collateral ligaments.

An IM guide was placed for the distal femoral cut, an IM guide placed for the proximal tibial cut, and a block used to confirm the adequacy of extension of resection.

Anterior and posterior vertical cuts and chamfer cuts were made to accept the size 3 femoral component. This was followed by preparation of the tibia for the modular tibial tray and followed by sagittal resection of the patella.

The above implants were placed as trials before final selection was made. Pulsatile debridement was followed by methacrylate fixation of all 3 components. Final trial of various spacers was performed with final selection and placement of the spacer after release of the tourniquet at 57 min. A deep ConstaVac drain was placed below the extensor mechanism before it was closed with #1 suture. A layered closure was brought up to subcuticular skin and Dermabond used as the final skin seal. There were no complications. Blood loss was 150 cc.

Procedure code(s): _____

Diagnosis code(s): _____

Scenario 8-14

OPERATIVE REPORT

PREOPERATIVE DIAGNOSIS:

1. Right knee anterior cruciate ligament tear

2. Right knee medial meniscus bucket-handle tear

continued

POSTOPERATIVE DIAGNOSIS:

1. Right knee anterior cruciate ligament tear

2. Right knee medial meniscus bucket-handle tear

OPERATION:

1. Right knee arthroscopically assisted ACL reconstruction

2. Right knee arthroscopic medial meniscus repair

COMPLICATIONS: None.

TOURNIQUET TIME: 56 min.

INDICATIONS: The patient is a 15-year-old gentleman who sustained a sports-related injury to the right knee with resultant tear of the anterior cruciate ligament and medial meniscus. He has a bucket-handle tear of the posterior one half of the medial meniscus. I have reviewed with him and his parents the risks, benefits, and alternatives of operative intervention. They have agreed to proceed. Informed consent has been obtained and is in the chart.

FINDINGS: Examination of the right knee under anesthesia demonstrated full passive range of motion, no capsular restriction. No evidence of an effusion.

The suprapatellar pouch demonstrated the synovium to be normal. The patellofemoral joint was pristine with no evidence of articular cartilage injury appreciated.

The medial meniscus demonstrated a bucket-handle tear, which was flipped into the intercondylar notch. The overall quality of the meniscus was soft. There appeared to be some fraying of the inner lip of the meniscal tear itself. However, based upon his age and despite this being a somewhat complex tear, he was still indicated for repair. The tear was located in the red zone of the meniscus. It involved the posterior one half. It could easily be reduced and stay reduced without dislodgement with range of motion. The intercondylar notch demonstrated complete disruption of the anterior cruciate ligament. There was a positive empty wall sign. There was a preoperative 2+ Lachman, 2+ pivot shift and no instability to varus or valgus stress testing. The lateral compartment demonstrated the articular cartilage to be intact. The lateral meniscus was stable to probing. No tears were noted.

PROCEDURE: The patient was brought to the operating room and placed in the supine position on the operating table. After the induction of general anesthesia by the anesthesia team, the patient's right knee and lower extremity were prepped and draped in the usual manner. A tourniquet had been placed over Webril padding to the right upper thigh. A leg holder was utilized to aid in varus and valgus manipulation of the knee. A Linvatec arthroscopic pump was used to aid in inflow and outflow. A diagnostic arthroscopy was then performed with standard parapatellar portals. A superomedial portal was established for outflow. The findings were noted as previously dictated in the findings section. At the conclusion of diagnostic arthroscopy, I directed my attention to the medial meniscus. I utilized my meniscal rasp and I freshened the meniscal tear itself. I then reduced the meniscus. I utilized the Smith & Nephew fast fix meniscal repair system. I inserted 2 vertical mattress sutures over the superior aspect of the meniscus and inferior vertical mattress over the inferior aspect of the meniscus. Once all sutures were in place with my all inside meniscal repair technique, I excised the excess suture and I probed my repair. It was now secure. I brought the knee through a full range of motion. There was no evidence of instability of the repair. I then directed my attention to the ACL.

I elevated the leg and exsanguinated it with an Esmarch bandage. I inflated the tourniquet to 300 mm Hg. A 4-cm vertical incision was made over the pes anserine bursa and tendons. I carried this down through the subcutaneous tissues.

Hemostasis was obtained with electrocautery. The overlying sartorius fascia was elevated, and the underlying semitendinosus and gracilis tendons ASA Publications were identified. These were then harvested in the usual manner without difficulty. I folded these over, giving me a quadrupled hamstring autograft. I then passed them through tubular sizers and the tightest that I could get was an 8-mm tibial socket, 8-mm femoral socket.

I kept the graft moist with saline lavage. I directed my attention to the interior of the knee. I utilized straight and angled curettes to debride the remnant of the ACL from the intercondylar notch, identified the over-the-top position at 2 o'clock on the femur. I utilized a motorized shaver to debride the ACL stump off the tibia. I inserted my ACL drill guide at a 55° angle, and I drilled my guide pin up through the tibia, giving me a 45-mm tibial socket aimed at the 11 o'clock position on the femur. This entered 7 mm anterior to the posterior cruciate ligament. I utilized my 8-mm solid drill and drilled my tibial socket. I then flexed the knee to 90°. I placed my 5-mm femoral offset guide at the 2 o'clock position on the femur. I drilled my Beath pin up through the femur, exiting superolateral aspect of the thigh.

My EndoButton drill followed by depth gauge was utilized. Preoperatively, I planned for 30 mm of graft within the femur. The patient was measured for a 50-mm femoral socket. I utilized my 8-mm acorn drill and I drilled to a depth of 40 mm to allow deployment of my EndoButton for femoral fixation.

I then utilized a 20-mm continuous loop EndoButton and passed this around the graft. I tubularized my graft. I then attached my graft to the Beath pin. I pulled the Beath pin through the knee and deployed the EndoButton. I set the graft and cycled the knee 10 times in full extension and full flexion.

Prior to graft passage, I inserted an impingement rod into the knee joint through the tibial socket and brought the knee through a full range of motion. No evidence of notch impingement at the conclusion of my notchplasty.

Once this was done, the graft was set into position. I cycled the knee 10 times for full extension and full flexion. I placed the knee in 15° of knee flexion. I applied 15 lb of tension to the tibial portion of the graft and I inserted a 9 × 35–mm Delta bioabsorbable interference screw with good torque upon insertion appreciated. I then probed my graft. There was excellent resting tension. The patient had full terminal extension. Full range of motion was noted. I then let the tourniquet down. Total tourniquet time was 56 min. I attained hemostasis in the knee joint with my bipolar cautery. Once this was done, I repaired the sartorius fascia. I then closed the wound in layers with an absorbable suture, and a subcuticular closure was applied to the skin. A dry sterile dressing was applied. The patient tolerated the procedure well, was extubated in the operating room, and transported to recovery room in a stable condition.

Sponge and needle count were correct.

Procedure code(s): _____

Diagnosis code(s): _____

Scenario 8-15

OPERATIVE REPORT

PREOPERATIVE DIAGNOSIS: Right middle finger mucous cyst.

POSTOPERATIVE DIAGNOSIS: Right middle finger mucous cyst.

continued

PROCEDURE: Right middle finger mucous cyst excision.

ANESTHESIA: Sedation plus local.

DESCRIPTION OF PROCEDURE: After adequate sedation had been obtained, the patient was prepped and draped. One cc of 0.5% bupivacaine was infiltrated into the eponychial area of the right middle finger. The right upper extremity was exsanguinated and a tourniquet raised to 250 mm Hg.

An elliptical incision over the cyst was made. The cyst was excised in its entirety and traced back to its origin at the DIP joint. The DIP joint was rongeured. The incision line was closed using 4-0 nylon suture. A dry sterile dressing was applied. The patient tolerated the procedure well.

Total procedure time 30 min.

Procedure code(s): _____

Diagnosis code(s): _____

Scenario 8-16

OPERATIVE REPORT

PREOPERATIVE DIAGNOSIS:

1. Left volar wrist ganglion cyst
2. Left carpal tunnel syndrome

POSTOPERATIVE DIAGNOSIS:

1. Left volar wrist ganglion cyst
2. Left carpal tunnel syndrome

OPERATION:

1. Excision of left volar radial ganglion cyst
2. Carpal tunnel release, left

ANESTHESIA: Sedation plus local.

PROCEDURE: After adequate sedation had been obtained, the patient was prepped and draped. The left upper extremity was exsanguinated and the tourniquet raised to 250 mm Hg. 0.5 ml of 0.5% bupivacaine was infiltrated into the left thenar crease and into the left volar radial wrist area in the area of the ganglion cyst. A 1.5-cm incision was made in the left thenar crease. The incision was carried down through the subcutaneous tissue, the superficial palmar fascia, and the transverse carpal ligament. The transverse carpal ligament and distal portion of the antebrachial fascia were divided under direct vision. The incision line was closed using 4-0 nylon sutures. Attention was then turned to the left volar radial wrist, where a 1-cm longitudinal incision was made. The volar radial cyst was identified and traced back to its point of origin at the radioscaphoid joint. The cyst was excised in its entirety. Its base was cauterized. The incision line was closed using 4-0 nylon sutures. A dry sterile dressing was applied. The patient tolerated the procedure well.

Total procedure time 60 min.

Procedure code(s): _____

Diagnosis code(s): _____

Scenario 8-17

OPERATIVE REPORT

PREOPERATIVE DIAGNOSIS:

1. Right ring finger trigger
2. Right ring finger mass ×2

POSTOPERATIVE DIAGNOSIS:

1. Right ring finger trigger
2. Right ring finger mass ×2

OPERATION:

1. Right ring finger trigger release
2. Excision of right ring finger mass ×2

ANESTHESIA: Sedation plus local.

PROCEDURE: After adequate sedation had been obtained, the patient was prepped and draped. The right upper extremity was exsanguinated and the tourniquet raised to 250 mm Hg. 0.5% bupivacaine was infiltrated into the operative site of the cutaneous region of the right ring finger A1 pulley. There was a proximal right ring finger mass, which was located at the DIP joint, dorsal radial surface and verrucous-type mass on the radial and distal aspect of the right ring fingernail. A chevron incision was made over the A1 pulley of the ring finger and carried down through the subcutaneous tissue. The A1 pulley was then divided under direct vision. The incision was closed using 4-0 nylon sutures. Attention was then turned to the right ring finger mass on the DIP joint dorsoradial surface. This was excised in its entirety. The defect was closed using 4-0 nylon sutures. The verrucous-appearing mass on the radial border of the right ring fingernail as well as the distal aspect of the finger were excised. The defect was closed using 3-0 Vicryl sutures. The patient tolerated the procedure well.

Total procedure time 30 min.

Procedure code(s): _____
Diagnosis code(s): _____

Scenario 8-18

OPERATIVE REPORT

PREOPERATIVE DIAGNOSIS:

1. Right shoulder rotator cuff tear supraspinatus tendon
2. Right shoulder impingement

continued

POSTOPERATIVE DIAGNOSIS:

1. Right shoulder 3-cm anterior-posterior tear

2. Rotator cuff supraspinatus tendon

OPERATIVE PROCEDURE:

1. Right shoulder arthroscopic rotator cuff repair supraspinatus tendon

2. Right shoulder arthroscopic acromioplasty

SPECIMENS: None.

COMPLICATIONS: None.

INDICATIONS: The patient is a 73-year-old gentleman who has persistent pain and dysfunction from the right shoulder with a symptomatic tear of his rotator cuff.

I have reviewed with him the risks and alternatives of the surgery. He has agreed to proceed. Informed consent has been obtained and is in the chart.

PROCEDURE: The patient was brought to the operating room and placed in a supine position on the operating room table. After the induction of general anesthesia by the anesthetic team, the patient's right shoulder and upper extremity were prepped and draped in the usual manner.

A modified beach chair position was utilized. All bone prominences were well padded.

A standard posterior arthroscopic portal was established. An anterior portal was created in an interlocked fashion lateral to the coracoid process. Through these 2 working portals, diagnostic glenohumeral arthroscopy was performed. The synovium was unremarkable. The articular cartilage intact. No evidence of degenerative arthritis.

The subscapularis tendon demonstrated mild to moderate fraying but no significant tearing. The supraspinatus tendon demonstrated a large 3-cm anterior-posterior tear with retraction of 1 cm. Infraspinatus was not involved. The subacromial space demonstrated significant thickening and fraying of the coracoacromial ligament. There was a large hook type 3 acromion appreciated.

I then directed my attention to the subacromial space. A midacromial lateral portal was established and a bipolar cautery was inserted. The coracoacromial ligament was debrided from the undersurface of the acromion extending from the midacromial portal lateral to the acromioclavicularjoint medially. I then utilized a 4.0 acromionizer and performed an arthroscopic acromioplasty with a cutting block technique from a posterior to an anterior direction. The portals were switched. The acromioplasty was completed working from a lateral-to-medial direction. The undersurface was left completely smooth. I debrided the subacromial bursa. I mobilized the subdeltoid bursa and I was able to get an anatomic reduction of the rotator cuff supraspinatus tendon.

I then utilized the Opus AutoCuff rotator cuff repair system. I inserted 3 inverted inclined mattress sutures of #2 FiberWire into the leading edge of the rotator cuff tear. I then inserted 3 Opus magnum anchors into the greater tuberosity beginning at the anterior margin of the greater tuberosity and extending 1 cm for each anchor posteriorly. I attached each suture to its respective anchor and as I reduced the suture into the anchor, the supraspinatus tendon came anatomically back down to the greater tuberosity. An anatomic reduction was obtained. Once all sutures were tightened into the anchor, the anchor was fully deployed, and the excess suture excised.

Once this was completed, I probed my rotator cuff repair. An anatomic repair was obtained. I then inserted a DonJoy PainBuster catheter into the subacromial space. I preloaded the subacromial space with 20 cc of 0.25% Marcaine with epinephrine and hooked this up to a 100-cc pump of 0.25% Marcaine with epinephrine preset to run at 2 cc/hr.

A dry sterile dressing was applied to the right shoulder. The arm was put into a shoulder abduction sling pillow. He tolerated the procedure well. He was extubated in the operating room and transported to the recovery room in stable condition.

Sponge and needle counts were correct.

Procedure code(s): _____

Diagnosis code(s): _____

Scenario 8-19

OPERATIVE REPORT

PREOPERATIVE DIAGNOSIS: Nasal trauma.

POSTOPERATIVE DIAGNOSIS: Nasal trauma.

PROCEDURE: Septorhinoplasty.

SURGEON: Dr. Theodore Kelly.

ANESTHESIA: General.

DESCRIPTION OF PROCEDURE: After adequate anesthesia had been obtained, the patient was prepped and draped. The nose was infiltrated with 8 cc of 0.5% bupivacaine. A V-shaped transcolumellar incision was then made extending into an infracartilaginous incision. The nasal dorsum was then skeletonized. A small portion of the dorsal nasal cartilage was then excised with a 415 blade in the cartilaginous portion and a 110-mm osteotome in the bony portion.

Attention was then turned to the septum, which was straightened. The turbinates were obliterated with a nasal speculum and then cauterized using a needle-tip Bovie. A cephalic trim from the lower lateral alar cartilages was then performed. A medial crural fixation suture was then placed using 5-0 PDS. The nasal tip was then advanced in an anterior direction using another 5-0 PDS suture. A portion of the soft tissue from the nasal dorsum was then removed with the cautery turned down to 7.

The incision lines were then closed using 5-0 chromic in the infracartilaginous incision and a 6-0 nylon in the transcolumellar incision. An alar wedge excision was then performed on each side.

The resulting defect was then repaired using 5-0 Vicryl and 5-0 fast-absorbing suture. An internal Doyle Splint was then placed on each side. Steri-Strips and an external thermoplast splint was placed. The Doyle Splints were secured using a 2-0 nylon suture. The patient tolerated the procedure well.

Procedure code(s): _____

Diagnosis code(s): _____

Scenario 8-20

OPERATIVE REPORT

PREOPERATIVE DIAGNOSIS: Hemothorax.

POSTOPERATIVE DIAGNOSIS: Hemothorax (1,350 cc of bloody fluid and clot).

NAME OF PROCEDURE: Right thoracoscopy and evacuation of hemothorax, removal of old chest tube, placement of new chest tube.

PROCEDURE: Under adequate general endotracheal anesthesia with double-lumen tube in place and after the patient was positioned, prepped, and draped in the usual manner, and after the old chest tube was removed and the lung collapsed, a small incision was made anterolaterally and deepened until the pleural cavity was entered. Suction device was inserted and about 1,350 cc of bloody fluid, including clot, was removed. Thoracoscopy was performed. There was some irritation in the pleura, but no obvious tumor or other abnormalities noted. Irrigation was carried out for about 0.5 hr until returns were clear, and then a size 32 Bard chest tube was put in, placed through the incision. This was anchored to skin with heavy silk suture. Occlusive dressing was applied. Patient tolerated the procedure well.

Procedure code(s): _____

Diagnosis code(s): _____

Scenario 8-21

OPERATIVE REPORT

PROCEDURE: Percutaneous tracheostomy.

INDICATION FOR PROCEDURE: Prolonged mechanical ventilation and inability to wean from the ventilator.

INFORMED CONSENT: Obtained from the patient's spouse. This was done over the telephone on the day prior to the procedure by me. The risks, including hemorrhage, pneumothorax, tearing of the posterior wall of the trachea, and cardiopulmonary compromise, were explained in detail to the patient's wife. She clearly understood these risks and agreed to the procedure. This was witnessed. She was given an opportunity to ask questions and I answered her questions to the best of my ability. The patient also had a bronchoscopy during the procedure that was performed by Dr. Short.

DESCRIPTION OF PROCEDURE: The anterior neck was cleansed with Betadine solution. The neck was extended as much as possible by placing a pillow beneath the shoulder blades. The patient received sedation with propofol, which was instilled via a continuous infusion, and also Versed 2 mg and fentanyl for a total of 50 mcg. The drapes were placed and, under sterile technique, the area over the anterior trachea was anesthetized with 2% lidocaine. The cuff of the endotracheal tube was deflated and a 14-gauge needle was inserted into the anterior trachea. The position of the needle was confirmed bronchoscopically to be in the midline between the first and second tracheal rings. The wire was then inserted through the needle and the needle removed. Following this, a small horizontal incision was made along the wire. Following this, the punch dilator was inserted. This was then removed and the Blue Rhino dilator was inserted. Using a to-and-fro motion, the tissues were stretched to accommodate the #8 percutaneous tracheostomy tube, which was easily inserted. Following the insertion of the tracheostomy tube, correct placement was determined via the bronchoscope. It was found to be several centimeters superior to the carina. The endotracheal tube was then removed. The patient was connected to the ventilator and appropriate exhaled volumes were obtained. The new tracheostomy tube was then sutured at all 4 corners. The trache collar was applied. The patient tolerated the procedure well. He will be having a chest x-ray post procedure, which is pending at the time of this dictation. The procedure went very well.

IMPRESSION: Placement of a percutaneous tracheostomy tube. The patient will remain on mechanical ventilation until such time as he can be safely weaned.

Procedure code(s): _____

Diagnosis code(s): _____

Scenario 8-22

OPERATIVE REPORT

PREOPERATIVE DIAGNOSIS: Nodule, right upper lobe, metastatic renal cell carcinoma.

POSTOPERATIVE DIAGNOSIS: Metastatic renal cell carcinoma to the right upper lobe and also to right hilum.

PROCEDURE: Right thoracotomy with excision of nodule and frozen section, and then biopsy of right hilar node (from main pulmonary artery), also likely positive for metastatic renal cell carcinoma.

BLOOD LOSS: Less than 50 cc.

DESCRIPTION OF PROCEDURE: Under adequate general endotracheal anesthesia with a double-lumen tube, arterial line, Foley catheter, and epidural catheter in place, the patient was positioned, prepared, and draped in the usual manner for right thoracotomy. Incision was made in the posterolateral position, sparing the serratus anterior muscle and entering the chest through the fifth interspace. There were some adhesions between the lung and the chest wall, which were taken down by sharp dissection. The minor fissure was incomplete. The nodule was readily palpable, posterior aspect of the upper lobe in the fissure area quite close to the junction of the minor and major fissures. The minor fissure was developed to allow us to get better exposure of the nodule, and then the nodule was excised using electrocautery and scissors to remove it.

Hemostasis was obtained with the Bovie. Frozen section confirmed likely renal cell carcinoma metastatic deposit. On further palpation, there was a tiny nodule also removed from the upper lobe, just less than 2 mm in size, the only other one that we could feel, and it was excised and sent for permanent section. In addition, there was a suspicious node on top of the main pulmonary artery in the hilum area, which was biopsied and was very vascular; histology also most likely consistent with renal cell carcinoma. Check was made for hemostasis and found to be satisfactory. A single chest tube was put through a separate stab incision and directed

continued

posteriorly and superiorly. The ribs were approximated with 5 pericostal sutures of #1 PDS, muscle layer closed with running 0 Vicryl, subcutaneous tissue with 2-0 Vicryl, and the skin with staples. Blood loss was less than 50 cc. She tolerated the procedure well. Biopsy was performed and came back positive for metastatic renal cell carcinoma of the lung.

Procedure code(s): _____

Diagnosis code(s): _____

Scenario 8-23

OPERATIVE REPORT

INDICATIONS FOR PROCEDURE: This is a patient who presents to be evaluated for aspiration of a foreign body. The patient aspirated a Q-tip into the right mainstem bronchus.

DESCRIPTION OF PROCEDURE: After obtaining an informed consent from the patient, the Olympus Video bronchoscope was passed via his stoma into the right mainstem bronchus, where the Q-tip was easily seen. After multiple attempts with biopsy forceps and wires and grasping instruments, the Q-tip could not be dislodged. I requested that the patient be evaluated by thoracic surgery for a rigid bronchoscopy and removal of the foreign body.

Procedure code(s): _____

Diagnosis code(s): _____

Scenario 8-24

OPERATIVE REPORT

INDICATION: Left pneumothorax, quite large, in a patient with mechanical ventilation, status post bronchoscopy for left upper lobe collapse.

CONSENT: Again, the family could not be reached for consent and the procedure needed to be done in an urgent fashion. Therefore, the procedure was accomplished.

PROCEDURE IN DETAIL: The left chest was prepped with Betadine solution. Following this, local anesthesia was applied to the interspace between the 8th and 9th ribs. This area had been identified as the area by ultrasound prior to the procedure in which there was a very large pocket of air. Following local anesthesia, a 14-gauge needle was inserted into the left chest and a wire was inserted through the needle. Following that, the needle was removed.

A small skin incision was made along the wire and a series of three dilations were performed. Following this, a #14 French chest tube was inserted without difficulty. It was sutured in place and a StatLock was also placed. This was connected to suction and a large amount of air was removed. There was a continuous small air leak following that. The area was bandaged with an occlusive dressing. The patient tolerated the procedure very well. A chest x-ray has been ordered post procedure but is pending at the time of this dictation.

IMPRESSION: Large left pneumothorax.

PLAN: The patient will have a chest tube in place until there is no longer any significant air leak, and then the chest tube may be removed.

Procedure code(s): _____

Diagnosis code(s): _____

Scenario 8-25

OPERATIVE REPORT

PREOPERATIVE DIAGNOSIS: Recurrent tonsillitis.

POSTOPERATIVE DIAGNOSIS: Recurrent tonsillitis.

PROCEDURE: Tonsillectomy.

SURGEON: Dr. Mary Ellen Tomas.

ANESTHESIA: General.

FINDINGS: Severe tonsillitis.

SPECIMENS: Tonsils.

ESTIMATED BLOOD LOSS: 150 cc.

FLUIDS: Per record.

COMPLICATIONS: None apparent.

DISPOSITION: Stable to recovery room.

TECHNIQUE: The 5-year-old patient was brought to the operating room and placed supine on the operating room table. Patient was put to sleep by a general technique of anesthesia and intubated without difficulty. A Crowe-Davis retractor was inserted into the oral commissure to retract the tongue and mandible. The patient was placed in gentle neck extension and suspended from towels on his chest. The palate and uvula were inspected and palpated. There were no submucous cleft nor bifid uvula appreciated. A red rubber catheter was inserted through the nostril to retract the soft palate. A towel was placed over the eyes. The left tonsil was grasped and retracted from its fossa. Attempts to develop a capsular plane failed due to severe scarring superiorly. At this point in time, the tonsil had fragmented making resection difficult. The tonsil subsequently was removed in pieces, developing a plane as I went. Hemostasis was obtained simultaneously. Essentially the inferior pole had a more normal plane, but the superior pole suggested chronic abscess. The right tonsil was then grasped and medialized. The resection was started inferiorly and a plane was easily developed. As I worked up to the superior pole, significant scarring was again encountered and the tonsil started to fragment again, although I was able to maintain the integrity of the tonsil and remove the tonsil intact. There was substantial bleeding on both sides. In particular on the right side, which bled from the superior pole. The left side bled from all areas. All areas were cauterized at the end and hemostasis was assured. Approximately

continued

1.5 cc of 0.5% Marcaine with 1:200,000 epinephrine was injected into each anterior tonsillar pillar. The stomach was suctioned. The wounds were irrigated and the patient was awakened from anesthesia and extubated without difficulty.

Procedure code(s): _____

Diagnosis code(s): _____

Scenario 8-26

OPERATIVE REPORT

PREOPERATIVE DIAGNOSIS: Bilateral lower extremity deep venous thrombosis.

POSTOPERATIVE DIAGNOSIS: Bilateral lower extremity deep venous thrombosis.

OPERATION: Insertion of percutaneous cannulation of the left femoral vein with an IVC venacavogram, initiation and completion, and IVC filter placement, infrarenal.

ANESTHESIA: Local sedation.

ESTIMATED BLOOD LOSS: Minimal.

COUNTS: Sponge count checked and verified.

COMPLICATIONS: No complications.

BRIEF HISTORY: This is an 85-year-old patient who developed bilateral lower extremity DVTs. Heparin and Coumadin anticoagulation is contraindicated and the plan is for an IVC filter. The risks and benefits of the procedure were explained to the patient, including bleeding, infection, hematoma formation, possible pulmonary embolism. He consented to the operation.

DESCRIPTION OF PROCEDURE: The patient was brought to the operating room and placed in a supine position. After good IV sedation was achieved by the anesthesiologist, the left groin was prepped and draped in the usual sterile fashion. Lidocaine 1% was infiltrated into the skin and subcutaneous tissue 2 finger breadths medial and inferior to the femoral pulse. The femoral vein was cannulated with a 22-gauge and with an 18-gauge single wall-puncture needle, venous outflow was obtained. A wire was inserted under fluoroscopic guidance into the IVC. An incision was made through skin, and subcutaneous tissue was dilated and then the dilator and introducer sheath were inserted over the wire into the IVC. The dilator and the wire were removed. The sheath was flushed with heparinized saline. A venogram was performed with Conray ×2. This revealed the patient had two renal veins at L1 and L2 level and a single left renal vein at the L3 level; both were patent. The WC was patent.

We proceeded to insert the sheath and placed that at L2-1-3. The filter was inserted into the sheath and then the sheath was pulled back. It deployed nicely at 1-2-3. A completion venogram revealed adequate good placement of the filter below the renal vein. The procedure was completed. The sheaths were removed. Pressure was held. Hemostasis was achieved. The patient left the operating room in stable condition.

Procedure code(s): _____

Diagnosis code(s): _____

Scenario 8-27

OPERATIVE REPORT

PREOPERATIVE DIAGNOSIS: Three-vessel coronary artery disease, unstable angina.

POSTOPERATIVE DIAGNOSIS: Three-vessel coronary artery disease, unstable angina.

PROCEDURE PERFORMED: Coronary artery bypass grafting ×5 (left internal thoracic artery to left anterior descending artery, saphenous vein graft to ramus, saphenous vein graft to diagonal artery, saphenous vein graft to posterolateral ventricular artery, and left radial artery to posterior descending artery).

INDICATIONS FOR PROCEDURE: Patient is a 65-year-old gentleman who had two episodes of unstable angina; the most recent one being the day of admission, whereupon he was awakened while sleeping at home. He was seen in the emergency room and admitted after being ruled for an acute myocardial infarction. Further workup, however, revealed significant cardiac catheterization demonstrating severe coronary artery disease (50% to 60% left main, 80% LAD, 80% RCA, and 50%–60% circumflex). He was seen and evaluated by cardiothoracic surgery and the indications, benefits, risks (2% mortality) were discussed with the patient. He understood and wished to proceed with the coronary artery bypass grafting.

SURGICAL FINDINGS: Normal left ventricular function. Normal great vessels. The LAD was 1.5 mm, the diagonal was 1.5 mm, the ramus was 1.5 mm. The TLV was 2 mm, and the PDA was 1.5 mm. Patient had no complications coming off the cardiopulmonary bypass.

DESCRIPTION OF PROCEDURE: Patient was identified in the holding area, brought back to the operating room. He was placed on the operating room table in the supine position. Following the placement of a Swan-Ganz catheter and an arterial line, patient was then placed under general anesthesia. The chest, abdomen, legs, and left arm were prepped in the usual fashion. A median sternotomy was performed. Simultaneous harvesting of the left internal thoracic artery and left radial artery was performed at this time. The patient was started on nitroglycerin to reduce spasm in the radial artery during harvesting. Once the left internal thoracic artery and left radial artery were harvested, we then harvested the right greater saphenous vein. Both the radial and saphenous vein harvesting were done using endoscopic technique using the Vasoview System. Once all the conduits were harvested, the patient was heparinized. The aorta and right atrium were cannulated in the usual fashion. A retrograde catheter was then placed in the coronary sinus.

Once an appropriate ACT was achieved, patient was placed on cardiopulmonary bypass. The distal targets were then identified and marked. An antegrade cardioplegic cannula was placed. The aortic cross clamp was placed and the heart arrested using both antegrade and retrograde cold cardioplegia. Myocardial temperature was measured throughout the whole procedure and remained under 18° Celsius. Once we had full arrest of the heart, we then proceeded with our anastomoses. The left radial artery was anastomosed to the PDA. The reverse saphenous vein grafts were used for the PLV, diagonal, and ramus distal anastomoses. All 4 of these anastomoses were performed using 7-0 Prolene suture in a running fashion. Following completion of each distal anastomosis, the patient was given cold retrograde cardioplegia as well as additional cardioplegia down each vein graft and the radial arterial graft.

We then turned our attention to the LAD. The left internal thoracic artery was then prepped and incised appropriately and then anastomosed at the LAD using 8-0

continued

Prolene suture in running fashion. Once all of our distal anastomoses were performed, we then performed the proximal anastomoses. The diagonal vein graft and the ramus vein graft were anastomosed to the aorta using 6-0 Prolene suture in a running fashion. The PLV vein graft was also anastomosed to the aorta directly using 6-0 Prolene suture. The radial vein graft to the PDA was anastomosed onto the hood of the PLV vein graft proximally. This was performed using 7-0 Prolene. Once the proximal anastomoses were accomplished, hot shot retrograde cardioplegia was delivered. The aortic cross-clamp was removed. Two atrial and two ventricular pacing wires were placed. The patient was then weaned off cardiopulmonary bypass. While coming off cardiopulmonary bypass and with the heart more filled, it was noted that the saphenous vein graft to the diagonal coronary artery was a little taut. Therefore the decision was made to redo this anastomosis. Patient was then placed back on full cardiopulmonary bypass. The proximal portion of this vein graft to the diagonal artery was ligated and reanastomosed in an end-to-side fashion onto the vein graft to the ramus using 7-0 Prolene suture. Once this revision of the proximal anastomosis was performed, patient was then weaned back off of cardiopulmonary bypass uneventfully without incident. The heart was decannulated and protamine was administered. Once adequate hemostasis was ensured, we then placed bilateral pleural and two mediastinal chest tubes. Once we were satisfied with our hemostasis, the chest was then closed with #6 sternal wires. The fascial tissue was then closed using 0 Vicryl, 2-0 Vicryl, and 3-0 Vicryl, in respective order. The patient tolerated the procedure well. The closed chest cardiac output was 6.0. Patient had a total bypass time of 183 min (163 for the initial bypass run and then an additional 20 for revision of the anastomosis). Total cross clamp time was 129 min.

Procedure code(s): _____

Diagnosis code(s): _____

Scenario 8-28

OPERATIVE REPORT

PREOPERATIVE DIAGNOSIS: Right carotid stenosis.

POSTOPERATIVE DIAGNOSIS: Right carotid stenosis.

OPERATION: Right carotid endarterectomy, bovine pericardial patch angioplasty.

ANESTHESIA: General anesthesia.

ESTIMATED BLOOD LOSS: Less than 50 cc.

REPLACEMENT: Crystalloids.

Sponge count checked and verified. No complications.

BRIEF HISTORY: This is a 75-year-old patient with a high-grade stenosis right carotid artery, asymptomatic. The plan was endarterectomy with patch angioplasty. The patient understood the risks and benefits of the procedure including the risks of bleeding, infection, hematoma formation, possible stroke, death, respiratory complications, cardiac nerve damage, dysphagia, for feeding tube, need for repeat surgery for hematoma, and he consented for the operation.

OPERATIVE NOTE: The patient was wheeled into the operating room and placed in the supine position. After adequate general anesthesia was achieved by the anesthesiologist, a Foley catheter was placed and perioperative antibiotics were given. His right neck was prepped and draped in the usual sterile fashion.

An incision was made on the anterior border of sternocleidomastoid through skin and subcutaneous tissue. The platysmal muscle was incised, and the carotid sheath was entered. Sternocleidomastoid muscle was mobilized in the medial-to-lateral fashion. The jugular vein was identified and dissected. The venous structures were taken down between ligatures. The vagus nerve and hypoglossal nerves were identified and spared. The carotid bulb was noted to be more proximal. We needed to extend the incision more proximally. Then we dissected all the way down to the strap muscles. We proceeded to dissect the common carotid, the soft area controlled with tourniquets. Internal carotid was dissected up to the level of the hypoglossal, controlled with vessel loops. The external carotid was dissected and controlled with vessel loops. 1% lidocaine was given to the carotid sinus nerve and the patient was given 5,000 units of heparin intravenously to make sure the ACT was above 250.

We proceeded to clamp the internal, common external and common sequentially. Arteriotomy was made into the common carotid; it extended to high grade. Calcified stenosis at the carotid stump extended all the way into normal internal carotid artery. Back-bleeding was adequate. EEG revealed no evidence of ischemia.

We proceeded with the endarterectomy using the Freer Elevator to elevate the track at the proper medial level and followed it down to the common carotid. Transected flush with the arterial wall. Then we followed it up into the internal where it feathered nicely. We performed an eversion endarterectomy of the external carotids and superior thyroid artery with good back bleeding from these branches. Removed all debris and made sure that we did not have an intimal flap. After irrigating with heparin and dextran, we proceeded to perform a bovine pericardial patch angioplasty with 6-0 Prolene sutures. After nearly completing the anastomosis, we retrograde and antegrade flushed out into the field, and then we irrigated with heparin saline and completed the anastomosis. Resumed antegrade flow first in the external and then into the internal. At this point, we had good pulses in the common, internal, and external; good biphasic Doppler signals throughout. Hemostasis was achieved with Gelfoam, thrombin and Surgicel.

After achieving good hemostasis, flushed with antibiotic. Skin was closed with sutures. Dressed with sterile dressings.

The patient tolerated the procedure well, was noted to be neurologically intact. Left the operating room in stable condition.

Procedure code(s): _____

Diagnosis code(s): _____

Scenario 8-29

OPERATIVE REPORT

PROCEDURE: Bone marrow aspirate and biopsy.

Mrs. Johnson is an 84-year-old female patient who presented because of diffuse large cell B-type non-Hodgkin lymphoma involving the chest wall. A bone marrow aspirate and biopsy was scheduled as part of the staging workup.

continued

After obtaining informed consent and explaining the procedure to the patient, its complications, which include bleeding and pain, using aseptic measures and under local anesthesia with lidocaine, a bone marrow aspirate and biopsy were done through the right posterosuperior iliac crest.

Patient tolerated the procedure fairly well with no complications. After the procedure was done, I had a lengthy discussion with the patient in the presence of her daughter about the Pathology finding, about the rest of the staging workup, which included CT of the neck, chest, abdomen, and pelvis.

Procedure code(s): _____

Diagnosis code(s): _____

Scenario 8-30

OPERATIVE REPORT

PREOPERATIVE DIAGNOSIS: Anterior mediastinal tumor.

POSTOPERATIVE DIAGNOSIS: Anterior mediastinal tumor (rule out thymoma).

PROCEDURE: Sternotomy with removal of mediastinal tumor.

DESCRIPTION OF PROCEDURE: Under adequate general endotracheal anesthesia with a Foley catheter in place, the patient was positioned, prepared, and draped in the usual manner for a sternotomy. Incision was made in the skin over the middle of the sternum and deepened until the bone was encountered. The sternum was then opened with a sternal saw exposing the anterior mediastinum. By palpation there was a firm mass measuring 2 to 3 cm in diameter in the upper right parasternal area just where the innominate vein and vena cava joined. It appeared to be attached to the pleura in this location, and after some dissection for 10 to 15 min, it became clear that we had to enter the pleural cavity to get around the tumor. On entering the pleural cavity, there was some inflammatory response between the lung itself and the mass, which was easily dissected. The lung was quite easily dissected off from the tumor to which it was attached by flimsy inflammatory adhesions. We got a good margin around the tumor using the Bovie; some pleura and the tumor were excised in total. The specimen was opened on the table and it seemed like much of it was necrotic, almost like encasing material. Pathology showed encasing material and some epithelial cells around it. In my opinion, the gross findings are most consistent with a thymoma, which was completely excised by surgery. A check was made for hemostasis and found to be satisfactory. A single chest tube was put through a separate stab incision below the sternal incision and directed upward and into the pleural cavity toward the apex via the opening in the pleura. The sternum was approximated with 5 sternal wires. The fascia was closed in layers with 0 Vicryl and 2-0 Vicryl. The skin was closed with a subcuticular Vicryl suture. Biopsy was done and returned positive for cancer. Patient tolerated the procedure well. Blood loss was less than 25 cc.

Procedure code(s): _____

Diagnosis code(s): _____

Scenario 8-31

OPERATIVE REPORT

PREOPERATIVE DIAGNOSIS: Abdominal wall abscess.

POSTOPERATIVE DIAGNOSIS: Abdominal wall abscess.

NAME OF PROCEDURE: Debridement of abdominal wall abscess.

ANESTHESIA: General.

DESCRIPTION OF PROCEDURE: After adequate anesthesia was obtained, the patient was prepped and draped. The abdominal wall abscess was incised. A segment of the skin and surrounding tissue in the abscess area was removed. The area was irrigated with a pulse lavage irrigator using 1 L of triple antibiotic solution. The incision line was closed with a small opening in the central portion for drainage. A dry sterile dressing was applied. She tolerated the procedure well.

Procedure code(s): _____

Diagnosis code(s): _____

Scenario 8-32

OPERATIVE REPORT

PREOPERATIVE DIAGNOSIS: Perforated viscus.

POSTOPERATIVE DIAGNOSIS: Perforated Meckel diverticulum with abscess.

ANESTHESIA: General endotracheal.

ESTIMATED BLOOD LOSS: 200 ml.

REPORT OF PROCEDURE: This is a 79-year-old nursing home resident who actually underwent coronary artery bypass 2 weeks ago. While recuperating, she developed some abdominal discomfort, which has worsened over the course of about a week. She presented to the emergency room today with peritonitis, free air under the diaphragm, and an elevated white blood count. She does normally take prednisone for temporal arteritis and has had several prior abdominal surgeries. We discussed with her, as well as with her sons, the risks of operating, including bleeding, infection or abscess formation, damage to other structures, need for retention sutures, sepsis, prolonged ICU course, DVT, PE, MI and others and they understood, and they wished to proceed with the surgery.

Thus she was taken to the operating room. She was placed supine on an operating room table after the induction of adequate general anesthesia. Her abdomen was prepped with Betadine solution and draped in a sterile fashion. We then made a vertical incision just below the umbilicus in her old scar in order to place a Hasson cannula. This was introduced into the abdominal cavity and we insufflated to 15 mm Hg CO_2 pressure. There was a dense row of adhesions obliterating the right lower quadrant and the midline. I was able to get out into a clear space and

continued

on the left side of the abdomen; I did not see any obvious bile staining or purulent fluid.

The bowel looked slightly edematous but did not appear compromised or ischemic. On examination of the liver, it did have a slightly cirrhotic appearance of fatty liver. The stomach looked normal and the anterior aspect of the duodenum seemed to be free from any scarring. In the right gutter, which was as far down toward the cecum that we could visualize, there was some air present in the retroperitoneum and edema. In sweeping back around, we did examine the sigmoid colon and there was no obvious perforation or stool present in the abdomen. It did appear slightly thickened; thus we decided to convert to a laparotomy.

A midline incision was made from the mid-upper abdomen down to the mid-lower abdomen. This was carried down through the subcutaneous tissue and the fascia was divided. Numerous adhesions were encountered and the abdominal wall musculature was elevated with Kocher clamps, and these were taken down carefully by means of electrocautery and sharp dissection. Eventually, we freed up the entire midline. We then explored off to the right side of the abdomen. Here, the adhesions seemed slightly more flexible and broke apart fairly easily with finger dissection. I traced the right colon down to the level of the cecum and this was freed up from the right gutter and peritoneal sidewall. I visualized the appendix after a fair amount of dissection in the retroperitoneum and this appeared normal. We did control it with a 0 Vicryl tie and the mesentery was controlled with the Bovie and hemostats. The appendix was amputated and passed off the field as a specimen. The appendiceal stump was cauterized and then buried using a Z stitch.

Next, we followed the terminal ileum from its junction to the right colon. There were numerous inflammatory and fairly thick adhesions in the pelvis overlying the sigmoid colon. At one point, I did enter into an abscess cavity, which was quickly suctioned free. Once this was evacuated, we were able to pull up the small intestine and there did appear to be an inflammatory mass with small bowel heaped up on itself, though fairly free on its mesentery at this point. My suspicion, given its location near the terminal ileum, was for a perforated Meckel diverticulum. Certainly being in the pelvis and with the thickening of the sigmoid, abscess was also a possibility. As we could not safely separate the small bowel loops, and as they comprised only about a foot of small intestine, I elected to resect these and perform an anastomosis of the small bowel for expediency sake. Thus, I made 2 small holes in the small intestine on the antimesenteric side. A GIA stapler was inserted and fired between the bowel loops. I then used another load of the GIA stapler to amputate these enterotomies and the diseased bowel.

Next, we came across the small intestinal mesentery. Using clamps and ties, eventually this was separated completely and we were able to pass this intestine off the field as a specimen. We then irrigated the abdomen. We closed the mesenteric rent with a 3-0 Vicryl running suture. The staple line crotch was also reinforced with a 3-0 Vicryl stitch. We then continued to run the small bowel all the way up to the ligament of Treitz. This appeared to be uninvolved with any disease process and there was no pneumatosis or bile staining in the remainder of the intestine.

Finally, we turned our attention to the large intestine. The cecum was immobilized further and the hepatic flexure taken down. There was no evidence of disease or perforation throughout this area. The duodenum was inspected in its position below the transverse mesocolon. It was kocherized and tactile evidence was obtained for intactness. We continued to follow the transverse colon around and inspected the descending and sigmoid colon. There was an area of thickening of the sigmoid colon in its distal aspect down near the pelvis. There was no evidence of an acute process here aside from the small abscess, which had been liberated previously, though this was removed from the actual lumen of the colon. There were more chronic adhesions here to the pelvic sidewall and the bladder. We took these down carefully with sharp dissection and mobilized the sigmoid from its attachments. We then attempted to fill the pelvis with fluid and subjected it to an intra-abdominal leak test. There was no evidence of air leakage or any obvious stool contamination. As it did not appear to be acutely involved, we deferred resection of this segment of the colon. We then made a quick inspection of the stomach and upper abdomen. Finally, a thorough irrigation of the abdominal cavity was carried out. We then checked the sponge count, which was accurate.

The abdomen was then closed with retention sutures of 2-0 nylon, buttressed by Davol drains on either side of the incision, as well as with a running 2-0 nylon fascial closure. The skin was closed with staples and Telfa wicks were placed down into this area due to the contamination from the perforation and her obesity. A dry sterile dressing was placed over this. The patient was transferred to the ICU in stable condition but still intubated.

As the attending, I was present throughout the entire procedure.

Procedure code(s): _____

Diagnosis code(s): _____

Scenario 8-33

OPERATIVE REPORT

ANESTHESIA: General.

PREOPERATIVE DIAGNOSIS: Multiple colonic polyps in the right colon.

POSTOPERATIVE DIAGNOSIS: Multiple colonic polyps in the right colon, with ventral hernia.

PROCEDURE: Exploratory laparotomy, lysis of adhesions, right colectomy, and repair of ventral hernia.

INDICATIONS: This is a 70-year-old female who has multiple colonic polyps in the right colon that cannot be retrieved with a colonoscope, and she was scheduled for right colectomy. The option of continued observation with follow-up colonoscopy and expected observation was discussed. The risk of this surgery including the risk of infection, bleeding, fistulization, intestinal injury, intestinal obstruction, wound complication, need for reoperation, sepsis, pneumonia, MI, DVT, and perioperative death were clearly discussed. The family and the patient understand that she is at higher risk due to her age, morbid obesity, and diabetes. They desire the surgery, which is scheduled today.

PROCEDURE: The patient was placed on the operating room table in the supine position. The abdomen was prepped and draped in a sterile fashion. Due to the multiple previous abdominal incisions, it was elected to use a midline approach. Midline incision was carried out. There was a proximal 4-cm ventral hernia above the umbilicus. This was incorporated into the midline incision. The abdomen was filled with numerous adhesions from her prior abdominal surgeries. The adhesions were

continued

carefully taken down with sharp dissection and with the electrocautery. The Bookwalter device was placed into the field and used for retraction. The abdomen was explored. There was no obvious liver abnormality, although there were numerous adhesions to the liver. It appears that the patient has had a prior cholecystectomy but again she was not aware of this fact.

The right colon was mobilized by incising the lateral peritoneal reflection. The ureter and duodenum were identified and preserved. The terminal ileum was divided with a GIA stapling device. The transverse colon was divided with the GIA stapling device. The mesentery was divided between hemostats and ligatures of 2-0 and 0 Vicryl. The colon was divided up to the second area of India ink, which was present in the transverse colon.

The anastomosis was carried out between the terminal ileum and the transverse colon with a GIA stapling device. The anastomosis was done in the side-to-side functional end-to-end fashion. The anastomosis is closed with a TA-90 stapling device. The rent in the mesentery was repaired with interrupted 3-0 Vicryl. The abdomen was lavaged with warm saline, carefully inspected for hemostasis, which was noted to be complete.

Due to the patient's ventral hernia, her morbid obesity, and her diabetes, it was elected to use stay sutures to reinforce the abdominal closure. Number 2 nylon stay sutures of Silastic drain bolsters were placed. A running #2 nylon with large on mesh suture technique was used for the midline closure.

The wound was irrigated with an antibiotic solution and closed with staples.

The patient tolerated the procedure well and was brought to the recovery room in a stable condition. Sponge, needle, and instrument counts were correct. I was present throughout the entire procedure.

Procedure code(s): _____

Diagnosis code(s): _____

Scenario 8-34

OPERATIVE REPORT

INDICATIONS FOR SURGERY: A 50-year-old gentleman with previous removal of large villous adenoma from the proximal rectum/rectosigmoid area. Repeat flexible sigmoidoscopy showed some abnormal tissue, which was biopsied and came back as villous adenoma. All the visible abnormality was at that time removed with cold biopsy bites.

OPERATIVE NOTE: Informed consent was obtained. Risks including bleeding, perforation, missed lesions, and necessity for surgery in case of complication were explained. No sedation was given because the patient did not have a ride. The scope was advanced to proximal ascending colon to the ileocecal valve area. The cecum was full of stool. There was also solid stool in the right colon and in patches in the transverse colon. Bowel preparation was fair in the rest of the colon. There was no obvious polyp.

On close inspection of the polypectomy site, at 15 cm from the anal verge in the proximal rectum/rectosigmoid junction area, there was scarring and nodularity especially behind a fold. Visualization of this area was difficult and had to be done with change in patient position and rotation of the scope to an extreme angle. This area was again biopsied. It was not technically possible to snare and cauterize this flat nodular area behind a fold. The portion of the rectum just lateral to and distal to this area was marked with India ink. The rest of the rectum looked normal. This area was inspected multiple times.

RECOMMENDATIONS: Check Pathology report. If biopsy still shows adenomatous tissue, the patient will need surgical resection of this area as complete endoscopic removal of the adenomatous tissue has not been possible and he is showing evidence of recurrence of adenomatous tissue on multiple examinations. If he has surgical resection, he will need surveillance colonoscopy in 3 years after surgery.

Procedure code(s): _____

Diagnosis code(s): _____

Scenario 8-35

OPERATIVE REPORT

PREOPERATIVE NOTE: A 72-year-old lady with incidental finding of dilated common bile duct on CT scan and on MRCP. MRCP showed a 2.2-cm common bile duct with a possible retained stone in the distal duct or a filling defect in the wall of the common bile duct distally. Patient has normal liver function tests and does not have any abdominal pain, weight loss, or jaundice.

OPERATIVE NOTE: Informed consent obtained from the patient. Risks including pancreatitis, infection, bleeding, perforation, necessity for surgery, and possible complications in case of stent placement were discussed in detail. ERCP information material was provided to the patient at the time of clinic visit. Alternatives including no intervention and surgery and PTC discussed. The patient requested sedation by anesthesia. Hence, the patient was sedated with propofol by the anesthesiology service. She was placed in semiprone position. Scope was advanced under direct vision to the second portion of the duodenum. The ampulla was identified and was normal with no evidence of periampullary tumor or diverticulum. The common bile duct was selectively cannulated in one attempt. The pancreatic duct was not cannulated or injected. There was significant dilatation of the common bile duct particularly in the proximal common bile duct of approximately 2 cm. Intrahepatic ducts were also visualized and slightly dilated. The distal common bile duct was visualized with continuous injection with sphincterotome just inside the ampulla. No filling defect or definite stricture was seen; however, it was relatively narrow compared to the proximal duct, which was dilated. Even before cannulation, there was spontaneous free flow of bile visualized from the ampulla. Brushing was obtained from the distal common bile duct. Sphincterotomy or stent placement was not performed because of the absence of any definite stricture, asymptomatic patient, normal LFTs, and free flow of bile visualized during ERCP. There was also free drainage of contrast visualized on fluoroscopy.

IMPRESSION: Dilated common bile duct and intrahepatic duct of unclear etiology. No definite stricture or filling defect visualized on ERCP, except relative narrowing in distal CBD.

continued

RECOMMENDATION: The patient should follow up with her other appointments including workup for hematuria. Will follow her in gastroenterology clinic with repeat liver function tests and repeat imaging. She will call if she is symptomatic. Will follow common bile duct brushing result, and consider surgical opinion.

Procedure code(s): _____

Diagnosis code(s): _____

Scenario 8-36

OPERATIVE REPORT

NAME OF PROCEDURE: Esophagoscopy.

INDICATIONS: Dysphagia.

MEDICATIONS: Demerol 50 mg IV, Versed 3 mg IV. Informed consent was obtained. The video endoscope was introduced without difficulty. Again there was a recurrent stricture at the gastroesophageal junction. I was able to enter the stomach without difficulty. Wire was left in the stomach. A #51 French Savary dilator was passed over the wire without difficulty.

FINAL IMPRESSION: Successful dilatation to 51 French. Will repeat in approximately 4 weeks.

Procedure code(s): _____

Diagnosis code(s): _____

Scenario 8-37

OPERATIVE REPORT

OPERATION: An upper endoscopy with Savary dilation.

PREOPERATIVE DIAGNOSIS: The patient is a 34-year-old woman here for an upper endoscopy for evaluation of dysphagia and abnormal upper GI series, which identified a mural-based filling defect with some margin irregularity at the C5–C6 level.

POSTOPERATIVE DIAGNOSIS:

1. Abnormal x-ray

2. Dysphagia

3. Normal-appearing mucosa in the cervical esophagus, hypopharynx, and upper esophageal sphincter

4. 54 French Savary dilator passed

MEDICATIONS: Versed 3 mg IV, fentanyl 75 mcg IV.

PROCEDURE: After the risks, benefits, and alternatives of the procedure were thoroughly explained, informed consent was obtained. The endoscope was introduced into the mouth and past the cervical esophagus under direct visualization.

The endoscope was then advanced down the esophagus to the gastroesophageal junction. The esophageal mucosa and the gastroesophageal junction appeared normal. The cervical esophagus, hypopharynx, and upper esophageal sphincter were carefully inspected, and there was no evidence of any mucosal abnormality. The endoscope then advanced into the gastric cardia, fundus, body, and antrum, and retroflexion was performed in the stomach. The stomach mucosa appeared normal. The endoscope was then advanced to the pylorus into the duodenal bulb and descending duodenum, all of which appeared normal. The endoscope was then withdrawn from the patient. Using standard technique, a 54 French Savary dilator was passed. The patient tolerated the endoscopy and the Savary dilation well.

RECOMMENDATIONS: If the patient continues to have dysphagia, she may benefit from PPI treatment for possible reflux causing dysphagia, and should have indirect laryngoscopy examination by ORL.

Procedure code(s): _____

Diagnosis code(s): _____

Scenario 8-38

OPERATIVE REPORT

PREOPERATIVE DIAGNOSIS: Status post end colostomy, Hartmann pouch for perforated diverticulitis, with pelvic abscess.

POSTOPERATIVE DIAGNOSIS: Status post end colostomy, Hartmann pouch for perforated diverticulitis, with pelvic abscess.

PROCEDURE: Partial colectomy, enterolysis, reversal of colostomy with EEA pelvic anastomosis.

DESCRIPTION OF PROCEDURE: The patient was taken to the OR, prepped, and draped in the usual manner after anesthesia was induced. She was placed in the lithotomy position.

The risks and benefits had been discussed preoperatively.

We began by making an elliptical incision around the previous end colostomy with a 15 blade through skin and subcutaneous tissue. Hemostasis was achieved with Bovie electrocautery. Dissection was carried down to the fascia. The wall of the colon was identified. It was carefully dissected from surrounding tissue. We entered the peritoneal cavity. We then oversewed the colostomy with Vicryl suture to avoid spillage of stool. We opened the midline and removed the previous scar, incising this with cautery.

We then used a knife to incise the fascia. The peritoneal cavity was entered. Some adhesions were taken down to facilitate exposure. We then proceeded with mobilizing the colon of the end colostomy back into the peroneal cavity.

Once we had achieved taking down multiple adhesions, which took a considerable amount of time, we needed to completely mobilize the left colon. The splenic flexure was taken down in order to facilitate our anastomosis in the pelvis.

We subsequently copiously irrigated the peritoneal cavity to assure good hemostasis. We placed a Buchwalter retractor for adequate exposure. On exposing

continued

the pelvis, we found the significant inflammatory changes secondary to the pelvic abscess at the original operation. This was carefully dissected from the surrounding tissue using Metzenbaum Scissors.

We excised a portion of the proximal rectum to facilitate our anastomosis. This was done using the reticulating gun. We gave the patient glucagon.

We opened up the proximal staple line. We placed a 29-mm trocar after sizing the proximal colon and brought the anvil of the EEA through the side of the colon. We then stapled off the colotomy with a TA 60 staple gun. This was brought down into the pelvis. We then performed the standard EEA anastomosis with a 29-mm gun in the pelvis. At the end of the procedure we had no tension on the anastomosis, with a good blood supply. We then insufflated the rectum with air and clamped it superiorly.

There was no evidence of leak in the peritoneal cavity. We then copiously irrigated the pelvis again to assure good hemostasis. We closed the fascia with a running #2 nylon, followed by closure of the skin with staples. The patient tolerated the procedure well.

Sponge count was correct. Blood loss was minimal. The patient was sent to the recovery room in a stable condition.

Procedure code(s): _____

Diagnosis code(s): _____

Scenario 8-39

OPERATIVE REPORT

PREOPERATIVE DIAGNOSIS: Infected mesh.

POSTOPERATIVE DIAGNOSIS: Infected mesh.

PROCEDURES: Exploratory laparotomy, removal of infected mesh, insertion of retention sutures 30 cm in length.

ANESTHESIA: General.

INDICATIONS: The patient is a 40-year-old male who is status post laparoscopic repair of incarcerated ventral hernia with mesh. Postoperatively, the patient did well, but returned 10 days postoperatively with a large erythematous area along his previous laparotomy incision. The patient presents for an exploratory laparotomy.

Risks and benefits of exploratory laparotomy, possible bowel resection, possible ostomy, with removal of infected mesh were discussed with the patient. Possible complications discussed. Bleeding, infection, possible bowel injury, possible bladder injury, possible ureter injury, possible anastomotic leak, possible ostomy, possible recurrence, possible missing lesion, possible incomplete excision, possible need for further surgery, possible DVT, possible PE, possible CVA, possible MI, possible perioperative death were all discussed with the patient. The patient understands these risks and wishes to proceed.

PROCEDURE PERFORMED: The patient was placed in a supine position. The patient was prepped and draped in the usual sterile fashion. A midline laparotomy was made. Dissection was carried down through the subcutaneous tissue using electrocautery. The hernia sac was opened. There was gushing of a large amount of purulent fluid. This was foul smelling, but there was no appearance of enteric contents. The hernia sac was opened along its entire length and the fascia was opened to a smaller extent in order to completely visualize the previous mesh. The mesh was dissected in a circumferential manner around the entire fascial defect and removed. Care was taken to remove all the pieces of the mesh, as well as the tacks supporting the mesh. This was done in a circumferential manner around the entire fascial defect. Once this was performed, exploration of the abdomen revealed no evidence of bowel injury. There were no enteric contents. There was a matted area of scar tissue deep to the mesh, which was not adherent to the mesh, but there was no gastroenteric contents that could be expressed from the small bowel.

The entire abdomen was thoroughly explored. Given this finding, the abdomen was closed using running #2 nylon full-thickness suture. Retention sutures were also placed using #2 nylon horizontal mattress sutures buttressed with Davol drains. The wound was left open and packed using saline soaked Kerlix sponges. The patient tolerated the procedure well.

Procedure code(s): _____

Diagnosis code(s): _____

Scenario 8-40

OPERATIVE REPORT

PREOPERATIVE DIAGNOSIS: A 52-year-old female with urinary stress incontinence and rectocele.

POSTOPERATIVE DIAGNOSIS: A 52-year-old female with urinary stress incontinence and rectocele.

PROCEDURE: Posterior extraperitoneal sacral colpopexy.

INDICATIONS FOR PROCEDURE: The patient had urinary stress incontinence with a posterior rectocele requiring definitive correction of her incontinence and rectocele with a posterior Prolift mesh. The cosurgeon was Dr. Jones.

DESCRIPTION OF PROCEDURE: After assuring informed consent, the patient was taken to the operating room where general anesthesia was administered. The patient was placed in the dorsal lithotomy position and prepared and draped in the usual sterile fashion. Dr. Jones and I as cosurgeons proceeded with the transvaginal obturator tape and cystoscopy. Her dictation will follow.

At this point, attention was placed to the posterior vagina, where the vaginal mucosa was grasped with Allis clamps in the midline. Using 1% lidocaine with epinephrine, we injected approximately 6 cc infiltrating the subfascial space. An incision was made approximately 4 cm and the subfascial space was identified. Using Metzenbaum Scissors, this space was created and using a Breisky-Navratil retractor, the ischiorectal fossa was identified on both sides. Dissecting away the fat, the sacral spines were identified on both sides and the sacrospinous ligament was identified as well and dissected out. At this point, irrigation was applied in both areas. The stab incisions were made 3 cm laterally to the anal verge and 3 cm caudal. The trocars were then placed serially on each side, sublevator, up through the levators medially about 1.5 cm to the sacral spine and through the sacrospinous ligament where the cannula was left in place. The trocar was removed, and the

continued

suture retrieval device was placed through the cannula on both sides and these were strapped to the drape. At this point, the mesh that was fixed for the posterior repair was sewn in distally to the subvaginal tissue, and the straps were then delivered using the retrieval devices through the cannulas. The straps were held on tension free. The proximal portion of the mesh was sewn in with 3-0 Monocryl. The vaginal mucosa was closed with 2-0 Monocryl in an interlocking running fashion, the cannula was removed, and excess mesh from the straps was cut at the skin. The skin was closed with Dermabond. The patient tolerated the procedure well. Vaginal pack with Premarin cream was placed. The Foley catheter was draining clear urine. The patient was taken to the recovery room in stable condition.

COMPLICATIONS: None.

DISPOSITION: Stable.

Procedure code(s): _____
Diagnosis code(s): _____

Scenario 8-41

OPERATIVE REPORT

PREOPERATIVE DIAGNOSIS: A 50-year-old female with cystocele, rectocele, and stress incontinence.

POSTOPERATIVE DIAGNOSIS: A 50-year-old female with cystocele, rectocele, and stress incontinence.

PROCEDURE: Anterior extraperitoneal sacral colporrhaphy with Prolift mesh.

FINDINGS AT SURGERY: Examination under anesthesia revealed a stage III cystocele.

DESCRIPTION OF PROCEDURE: After assuring informed consent, the patient was taken to the operating room where general anesthesia was administered. The patient was placed in the dorsal lithotomy position, and prepared and draped in the usual sterile fashion. At this point Xylocaine and epinephrine were used to inject the anterior vaginal wall. A catheter was placed and the bladder was completely drained.

Using Allis clamps, the anterior vaginal wall was grasped, grasping the mucosa. A midline incision was made approximately 4 cm and in the subfascial plane Metzenbaum Scissors were used to create the plane into the paravesical space on both sides. At this point, adequate space was created and the ischial spines were palpated bilaterally. Using a marking pen, a mark was made on the inferior aspect of the ischial rami 1 cm laterally and 2 cm caudal. Another marking was made for the deep strap. These markings were made for the superficial straps and the deep straps on both sides of the patient's perineum.

Using a #15 blade, incisions were made at those sites. Using long trocars and palpating the ischial spine on one side, the trocar was placed up to the ischial spine approximately 1 cm and removed. While the cannula was remaining in place, the retrieval suture was placed through the cannula and this was then articulated and strapped to the drape. The same procedure was done for the deep strap on the contralateral side. The superficial straps were placed by placing the trocars through the superficial landmark and through the obturator foramen. The trocar was removed. The cannula remained in place, the suture retrieval device was placed through the cannula, and this was strapped to the drape. The same procedure was done on the contralateral side.

The catheter was removed. Under direct visualization of the bladder there were no injuries or perforations or punctures noted. The bladder was normal. UOs were normal bilaterally and the dome was normal. The cystoscope was withdrawn. The catheter was placed once again. The mesh that was fashioned for the anterior wall was then fixed anteriorly and posteriorly with 3-0 Monocryl. The arms of the mesh were then placed through the straps using the looped Prolene retrieval suture wire. These were pulled through the cannulas while the cannulas remained in place. By using the 4 straps, the mesh was then placed on tension free, pulling on the straps in all 4 quadrants.

The spaces were then irrigated with triple antibiotic. The mesh was laying flat and the vaginal mucosa was closed with 2-0 Vicryl in an alternating locking fashion. The excess mesh at the skin was trimmed away and those incisions were closed with Dermabond.

A vaginal pack with Premarin cream was placed. The patient tolerated the procedure well. Needles, sponges, and instruments were correct ×2 and the patient was taken to the recovery room in stable condition.

COMPLICATIONS: None.

DISPOSITION: Stable.

Procedure code(s): _____

Diagnosis code(s): _____

Scenario 8-42

OPERATIVE REPORT

PREOPERATIVE DIAGNOSIS:

1. Duplicated left collecting system

2. Left ureterocele

3. Left ureteral stones

POSTOPERATIVE DIAGNOSIS:

1. Duplicated left collecting system

2. Left ureterocele

3. Left ureteral stone

OPERATION:

1. Left ureterotomy

2. Left ureteroscopy with laser lithotripsy of stones

3. Left ureteral stent placement

continued

INDICATIONS: This is a 53-year-old man who came to the urology clinic for evaluation of microscopic hematuria. A CT scan demonstrated a duplicated left collecting system with upper pole ureterocele in the distal ureter, just behind opening of the ureterocele, with 2 large stones.

PROCEDURE: The patient was brought to the operating room and placed in a supine position on the operating table. After adequate general anesthesia had been established, he was placed in the lithotomy position, and prepped and draped in a standard sterile fashion. A cystoscope was introduced transurethrally into the bladder. On inspecting the left side of the trigone, there was a large bulge consistent with a ureterocele with a very small punctate opening of the ureter. Behind this, more lateral on the bladder wall, was the second opening consistent with the lower pole moiety ureter. At this point, the guidewire was placed through the ureterocele opening up into the upper pole renal pelvis. The cystoscope was removed and the resectoscope was then placed into the bladder. The hot knife was then used to make an incision in the anterior aspect of the ureterocele therefore opening up the opening quite widely.

The resectoscope was then removed and a semirigid ureteroscope was then placed easily through the widened opening into the distal left ureter where 2 large stones were seen. The 365-μ holmium fiber was used at a power setting at 22.5 W to break up the stones into many smaller fragments. The fragments were then basketed and removed and some were passed off as specimens. A 6 French 28 cm double-j ureteral stent was then placed over the wire with one end in the renal pelvis and the other end in the bladder. The bladder was emptied. The cystoscope was removed. The patient tolerated the procedure well. He was extubated in the operating room and transported to the recovery room in stable condition.

ESTIMATED BLOOD LOSS: Minimal.

INTRAVENOUS FLUIDS: Crystalloid only.

SPECIMENS: Stone fragments.

DRAINS: 6 French 28 cm double-J ureteral stent on the left.

COMPLICATIONS: None.

Procedure code(s): _____

Diagnosis code(s): _____

Scenario 8-43

OPERATIVE REPORT

PREOPERATIVE DIAGNOSIS: Microscopic hematuria.

POSTOPERATIVE DIAGNOSIS: Bladder calculi, enlarged median lobe.

PROCEDURE: Cystourethroscopy, cystolitholipexy.

ANESTHESIA: General anesthesia.

CLINICAL NOTE: The patient is a 51-year-old man whom I had seen in consultation for metastatic prostate cancer. He is on maximal androgen blockade with Zoladex and Casodex but was complaining of some irrigative and obstructive lower urinary tract symptoms. He also was found to have microscopic hematuria. He was advised to undergo cystoscopy; however, he refused to have it done under local anesthesia and wanted general anesthesia. The risks and benefits of the cystoscopy were explained to the patient, and they included risks of reaction to general anesthetic, infection, bleeding, and bladder injury. He has consented to have the procedure done.

OPERATIVE NOTE: The patient was brought to the operating room in stable condition and put under general anesthetic, then put in the dorsal lithotomy position and prepped and draped in the usual fashion. I inserted the 22 French Storz sheath and 30° telescopic lens as the assembled cystoscope into the patient's urethral meatus and advanced the scope under direct vision into the patient's bladder. The urethra appeared to be somewhat noncompliant. It was difficult to manipulate the scope but it was able to gradually go into the bladder, and he did have a very enlarged and prominent median lobe. He was also found to have a number of bladder calculi in his bladder. These were flushed out through the sheath of the cystoscope. The entire bladder mucosa was visualized. There were no tumors seen. No diverticula seen. The entire bladder itself appeared to be somewhat noncompliant with the impression of decreased bladder capacity. Since he had consented to have only cystoscopy done, I will see how his symptoms are after the bladder calculi have been removed to see if there is any improvement in his voiding dysfunction. Ultimately, I suspect he may require a TURP to shave down the median lobe in order to open up the bladder outlet.

The patient was awakened from general anesthesia and sent to recovery room in stable condition. I will follow up with him in the urology clinic.

Procedure code(s): _____

Diagnosis code(s): _____

Scenario 8-44

OPERATIVE REPORT

DATE OF OPERATION: 07/26/2006.

PREOPERATIVE DIAGNOSIS: Bladder tumor.

POSTOPERATIVE DIAGNOSIS: Invasive bladder tumor.

ANESTHETIC: LMA.

PROCEDURE: TUR bladder tumor large size.

INDICATIONS: This is a gentleman who had gross painless hematuria on positive cytology and a large filling defect on IVP. He is here for further evaluation and possible resection of a bladder tumor.

INTRAOPERATIVE FINDINGS: EUA, no evidence of fixation, prostate not indurated, no rectal masses appreciated. Urethra, unobstructed, prostatic urethra bilobar hypertrophy with fronds of superficial bladder tumor at the bladder neck and just beginning within the prostate. The bladder has huge mounding sessile bladder tumor with mucosal erythema. Part of the tumor is necrotic. It extends from the right trigone onto the wall. There is approximately 8 cm or more of tumor burden.

continued

PROCEDURE: In the cystolithotomy position, after sterile prep and drape with LMA anesthetic, the patient underwent cystourethroscopy under camera vision using the 22 French cystoscope with a 30° lens. After visualization of the urethra, prostatic urethra, and bladder, the patient was catheterized with a 27 French continuous flow resectoscope with obturator without difficulty. The left UO was identified, the right UO was not because it was covered with tumor. However, he was given indigo contrast and there was some looseness on that side even the UO was not identified. Representative cuts of the tumor were taken, approximately 5 cc in all. The area was then inspected. Mild bleeding was fulgurated, the resectoscope was withdrawn, replaced with a 24 French Foley inflated to 10 cc and attached to a leg bag. He was sent to the recovery room in satisfactory condition.

DISPOSITION: This was clearly a very aggressive, most likely invasive, bladder tumor. This gentleman will need a cystectomy.

Procedure code(s): _____

Diagnosis code(s): _____

Scenario 8-45

OPERATIVE REPORT

PREOPERATIVE DIAGNOSIS: Prostate cancer.

POSTOPERATIVE DIAGNOSIS: Prostate cancer.

PROCEDURE: Robotic laparoscopic retropubic prostatectomy.

ANESTHESIA: General.

INDICATIONS: This is a 54-year-old gentleman who was recently diagnosed with prostate cancer after having prostate biopsies, which showed bilateral Gleason grade 3 + 3 disease. On rectal exam, he has a 30-gm prostate without any nodules. He therefore has clinical stage T1 disease. He elected to undergo robotic prostatectomy.

PROCEDURE: The patient was brought to the operating room and placed in supine position on the operating table. After adequate general anesthesia had been established, he was placed in lithotomy position, and prepped and draped in the standard sterile fashion. A small incision was made above the umbilicus with a scalpel. The Veress needle was placed into the abdominal cavity, which was then insufflated to a pressure of 18. The Veress needle was removed and a 12-mm trocar was placed through the supraumbilical incision into the abdominal cavity. The rest of the trocars were placed in the usual configuration.

Dissection was initiated by incising the peritoneum overlying the bladder. The retropubic space was entered and developed bluntly. The endopelvic fascia was incised with cautery lateral to the prostate on both sides. There did not appear to be much dorsal venous complex above the urethra; so no stitch was placed around the dorsal venous complex at this time. Instead a stitch was placed in the anterior surface of the prostate as a backbleeding stitch, and this was a figure-of-eight 0 Vicryl suture. The anterior bladder neck was then opened with electrocautery. The catheter was identified and brought out through the opening in the bladder neck, and then the posterior bladder neck was divided with electrocautery. The dissection was carried down to the plane of the seminal vesicles. The vas deferens were identified, and these were skeletonized and transected with cautery. The seminal vesicles were dissected carefully and completely using electrocautery. The scissors were then used to open up the Denonvilliers' fascia and get into the retroprostatic fat plane, which was developed bluntly.

Attention was turned to the left side where the pedicle was identified and clamped with a Week clip. The pedicle was then transected beyond the clip. An antegrade nerve-sparing dissection along the left lateral surface of the prostate was then undertaken with scissors. No electrocautery was used. The same procedure was carried out on the right side where a clip was used to secure the pedicle and then an antegrade dissection along the lateral surface of the prostate with scissors was undertaken in a nerve-sparing fashion. The scissors were then used to transect through the small amount of dorsal venous tissue that was there. This was partially coagulated with the cautery and there was no significant bleeding. The anterior urethra was opened with scissors. The catheter was retracted and the posterior urethra was transected with scissors as well. The rectourethralis muscle was divided with scissors, and then the prostate was put into a laparoscopic bag. There was no significant bleeding identified after removal of the specimen.

At this point an anastomosis was performed. The bladder neck was a little bit large and opening; so it was reduced in size by placing a figure-of-eight suture at the 12 o'clock position. The bladder neck and urethra were then brought back together with 2 running 3-0 Monocryl sutures, one running from 3 o'clock to 10 o'clock along the posterior urethra and one running from 3 o'clock to 11 o'clock around the anterior urethra and bladder neck. The two sutures were tied down to each other.

Following this, a new catheter was placed and the bladder was insufflated with 200 cc of fluid. With some pressure on the bladder, there was a small amount of leakage at the site of the figure-of-eight suture in the anterior bladder neck but no other leakage was noted at the site of the anastomosis. A BLAKE Drain was placed through the left-sided trocar and draped over the area of the bladder neck. The laparoscopic ports were removed. The bag was retrieved through the supraumbilical port and the specimen was removed. The fascia at the supraumbilical port as well as the right-sided 12-mm trocar site were closed with interrupted Vicryl suture. The subcutaneous tissue was closed at all sites with interrupted Vicryl suture and the skin was closed with Dermabond. A clean dressing was placed around the drainage site.

The patient tolerated the procedure well. He was extubated in the operating room and transported to the recovery room in stable condition.

ESTIMATED BLOOD LOSS: 300 cc.

FLUIDS: Crystalloids only.

SPECIMENS: Prostate and seminal vesicles.

DRAINS: BLAKE Drain in the pelvis and a Foley catheter in the bladder.

COMPLICATIONS: None.

Procedure code(s): _____

Diagnosis code(s): _____

Scenario 8-46

OPERATIVE REPORT

PREOPERATIVE DIAGNOSIS: Fluid in the uterus with cervical stenosis, unable to sample in the office.

PROCEDURE: Cervical dilatation, biopsy, hysteroscopy.

DESCRIPTION OF PROCEDURE: On bimanual examination, small uterus, no adnexal masses. The anterior lip of the cervix and posterior lip of the cervix grasped with a tenaculum. Because of quite marked stenosis, normal dilators would not pass. A lacrimal probe was used to gradually dilate the cervix. The cervix was dilated to 8 Hegar. A hysteroscope was then entered. The cavity was entirely atrophic. It had a slight bicornuate appearance with both ostia visualized. An attempt at curettage was performed but no tissue obtained. The fluid from distention was submitted for cytology. There was no intraoperative bleeding or complications. The patient was taken to the recovery room in good condition.

Procedure code(s): _____

Diagnosis code(s): _____

Scenario 8-47

OPERATIVE NOTE

PREOPERATIVE DIAGNOSIS: Uterine septum, uterine fibroids, submucous.

PROCEDURE: Resection of fibroid, partial division of septum.

DESCRIPTION OF PROCEDURE: Under general anesthesia, the patient was placed in the lithotomy position, prepped and draped in the usual fashion. The cervix was grasped with a tenaculum and the canal gently dilated to 10 Hegar. The operative hysteroscope was then entered into the cavity. A fibroid as expected was noted in the left horn of the uterus coming from the septal wall toward the fundus; it was fairly large. The right horn appeared narrowed but otherwise unremarkable The 20 cc of vasopressin was injected into the cervix using mannitol for distention. The fibroid was resected because of the shape of the fibroid. Basically the base of the fibroid was difficult to reach and it was serially resected into small bites. A small rim of the outside of the fibroid was left at the end of the procedure. This should become atrophic and regress on its own. The resectoscope was also used to define the lower third of the uterine septum; subsequent to this the right horn of the uterus appeared more normal. The left cornua was noted to appear normal, as did the lateral wall of the uterus. Because of the resected surface on the medial aspect of the septum, left horn, the patient may be at increased risk for abnormal presentation. Fluid bath was 500 cc.

ESTIMATED BLOOD LOSS: Minimal.

COMPLICATIONS: Nil.

NOTE: The patient will be placed on Premarin to treat the endometrium in her hypoestrogenic state.

Procedure code(s): _____

Diagnosis code(s): _____

Scenario 8-48

OPERATIVE REPORT

PREOPERATIVE DIAGNOSIS: Endometrial polyp.

POSTOPERATIVE DIAGNOSIS: Endometrial polyp.

PROCEDURE: Hysteroscopy, polypectomy, dilatation, and curettage.

COMPLICATIONS: Nil.

ANESTHESIA: Sedation.

PROCEDURE: Under IV sedation, the patient was placed in the lithotomy position, prepped and draped in the usual fashion, straight catheterized. A UA revealed a small mobile anteverted uterus. The uterus sounded to 10 cm, canal dilated to 8 to 9 Hegar. The hysteroscope was entered using saline and the cavity was visualized. There was a polypoid mass anterior right fundal. This was grasped with a polyp forceps and removed. Subsequent to that, dilatation and curettage were performed for minimal tissue. With minimal bleeding the patient was taken to recovery in good condition.

Procedure code(s): _____

Diagnosis code(s): _____

Scenario 8-49

OPERATIVE REPORT

PREOPERATIVE DIAGNOSIS: Uterine fibroids with bleeding.

POSTOPERATIVE DIAGNOSIS: Uterine fibroids with bleeding.

NAME OF PROCEDURE: Laparoscopic hysterectomy, right salpingo-oophorectomy.

ANESTHESIA: General.

ESTIMATED BLOOD LOSS: 500 cc.

INTRAVENOUS FLUIDS: 2,000 cc lactated Ringer's solution.

FINDINGS: At surgery, examination under anesthesia revealed a large, bulbous, global fibroid uterus with a pedunculated fibroid anteriorly. Intraoperative findings revealed a 12-week-sized uterus with a large fundal fibroid and an additional pedunculated exophytic fibroid coming off of the fundus anteriorly. The ovaries were noted bilaterally. The right ovary was adhered to the fundal fibroid on the patient's right side.

DESCRIPTION OF PROCEDURE: After assuring informed consent, the patient was taken to the operating room, where a general anesthesia was administered. The patient was placed in dorsal low lithotomy position for laparoscopy, and prepped and draped in the usual sterile fashion. A Foley catheter was placed in the bladder. Attention was then placed on the vagina, where the cervix was well visualized utilizing a weighted speculum. Utilizing a tenaculum, this was used to grasp the

continued

anterior lip of the cervix, and the cervix was dilated to accommodate a roomy uterine manipulator. The pneumoballoon was then backloaded on the roomy manipulator as well as the coring. This was then articulated to the cervix utilizing the help of the tenaculum, and the roomy manipulator balloon was then insufflated with 5 cc of saline. At this point, attention was then placed on the abdomen, where an infraumbilical incision was made to accommodate the 5-mm trocar. A Veress needle was introduced with confirmation of the saline-drop test, and CO_2 gas was turned on with the opening pressure of 5 mm Hg. At this point, EPI gas is used to expand the abdominal cavity. The Veress needle was removed and the 5-mm trocar was used to advance the laparoscope. The laparoscope was entered and confirmed entry. At this point, in Trendelenburg position, the uterus was identified using the manipulator.

There was a large exophytic fibroid as well as the large fundal fibroid, which was noted, and the uterus was severely rotated to the right. At this point, an incision was made on the patient's right side 2 cm medial to the ischial rami and in an avascular plane. An incision was made and the 12-mm trocar was placed. The 5-mm trocar was placed on the contralateral side in a similar fashion in an avascular plane. At this point, using the atraumatic grasper, the round ligament was grasped on the right side using the bipolar gyrus cutting instrument. This was cauterized and cut. The vesicoperitoneum was then opened using the gyrus mechanism. At this point, since the ovary was adhered to the fundus on the right side, the infundibulopelvic ligament was identified. The ureter was identified below and infundibulopelvic ligament was grasped with the gyrus and cauterized in several places and then cut. Hemostasis was assured. Skeletonization of the broad ligament was performed using the gyrus and down to the uterine vessel on the patient's right side. The uterus was identified throughout the course of the skeletonizing of the uterine artery. The uterine artery was identified and cauterized with the gyrus. At this point, the decision was to start on the contralateral side. The round ligament was grasped with the gyrus, cauterized on both sides, and then cut in the midline, and hemostasis was assured. The bladder flap was created by using the gyrus on both the cautery and cutting mechanism. The grasper was used to dissect the bladder off of the cervix in the midline, and using blunt dissection this was easily performed. At this point, the ovarian ligament attached to the uterus on the patient's left side was serially cauterized and cut with the gyrus. The ovary was then freed easily from the fundus as well as the fallopian tube with the same gyrus cautery and cutting mechanism.

At this point, the ureter was identified on the patient's left side, opening up the posterior leaflet of the broad ligament. The internal iliac vessel was identified and the origin of the uterine artery was identified as well, coursing over the ureter on the left side. The uterine artery was cauterized and desiccated at the level of its origin on the left side, and hemostasis was assured.

At this point, an additional trocar was placed in the midline for manipulation and suction irrigation. Also the 5-mm scope was changed and upgraded to a 10-mm scope during the case. Continuous suction irrigation of the abdomen occurred and hemostasis was assured.

At this point, using the spatula for the gyrus, the exophytic fundal fibroid was amputated from the fundus for better manipulation. The uterus was then grasped and meticulously using the spatula, the uterus was amputated from the cervix at the coring. The vaginal cuff was cauterized with the spatula. There was a notable fibroid posteriorly on the lateral left side, which was grasped several times and lifted up so that adequate amputation could occur on that side. The posterior peritoneum along that vaginal cuff on that left side was continually cauterized and cut at the gyrus until the uterus was completed amputated from its vaginal cuff.

The pneumoperitoneum was obtained at this point using the Storz morcellator. This was then placed after removing the 12-mm trocar. This was placed on the patient's right side opening the incision a few more millimeters to accommodate the morcellator. Morcellation continued, morcellating the exophytic fibroid as well as the multiple fibroids in the uterus, and the uterus was taken out in pieces. Warm irrigation was applied once again and suctioned. Indigo carmine was then given intravenous, and the uterus was noted intact. We saw peristalsis on both sides and the patient was making adequate urine.

At this point, the decision was made after suctioning and irrigating the blood that there was hemostasis. The morcellator was removed and the 15-mm incision on the right was closed, closing the fascia with 0 Vicryl and then closing the skin with 4-0 Vicryl. The rest of the gas was expelled since the decision was made to close the vaginal cuff vaginally. The other instruments were removed. The gas was expelled and the other incisions were closed, closing with 2-0 Vicryl and then 4-0 Vicryl and Dermabond. Attention was then placed on the vagina, where the roomy manipulator was removed as well as the coring. A weighted speculum was placed, and the vaginal cuff was well visualized and grasped with Allis clamps. Using a series of figure-of-eight 0 Vicryl sutures, the cuff was closed with ease. No active bleeding was noted. Sponge, instruments, and needle counts were correct ×2.

The patient was taken to the recovery room in stable condition with a Foley catheter placed.

Complications none. Disposition stable. Specimens were uterus, cervix, and right fallopian tube and ovary.

Procedure code(s): _____

Diagnosis code(s): _____

Scenario 8-50

OPERATIVE REPORT

PREOPERATIVE DIAGNOSIS: Pelvic prolapse.

POSTOPERATIVE DIAGNOSIS: Pelvic prolapse.

PROCEDURE: Cystoscopy, tension-free obturator tape, and total Prolift.

INDICATIONS FOR OPERATION: This 50-year-old female, who has significant uterine descensus, has been using a pessary for quite some time. She is now brought for surgical correction by total Prolift and tension-free obturator tape.

OPERATIVE FINDINGS: A tension-free obturator tape was placed without incident and a posterior Prolift was performed without incident.

After completion of placement of the mesh for the anterior Prolift by Dr. Jones, the obturator fossae and anterior vagina were infiltrated with local anesthesia.

continued

A 1-cm incision was made in the midline and a submucosal tunnel was created to the endopelvic fascia bilaterally. The wing guide was inserted first in the right side and then in the left side. After passing the trocar each time, the bladder was inspected to make sure there was no evidence of perforation. After this had been completed, the tape was advanced out through the endopelvic fascia and clamped.

The anterior Prolift was then completed by Dr. Jones.

The tension-free obturator tape was then tensioned using an 8-Hegar dilator between the tape and the urethra containing the Foley catheter. Appropriate tension was applied. The cellophane wrapping was removed and the excess tape was then excised. The midurethral incision was closed using a figure-of-eight 2-0 Vicryl suture.

Attention was directed toward the posterior vaginal wall. The rectovaginal space was infiltrated with local anesthesia. An incision was made into the rectovaginal space. This was then gently dilated. The trocars were then placed 3 cm dorsally and 3 cm laterally to the anal verge through the sacrospinalis ligaments bilaterally. The Gynemesh was then sutured to the apex of the rectocele. The tags of the Gynemesh were then passed through the lumens of the cannulas. Appropriate tension was applied. The excess Gynemesh was excised from the perineum.

This was sutured to the posterior fourchette with 3-0 Monocryl suture ×2. The posterior vaginal wall was then closed using a running alternating locking 2-0 Vicryl suture. The excess mesh was cut from the perineal incisions.

The vagina was then packed with Premarin-coated vaginal packing. The puncture sites in the perineum were closed with Dermabond.

The patient was then awakened from general anesthesia and transferred to the PACU having tolerated the procedure well.

Procedure code(s): _____

Diagnosis code(s): _____

Scenario 8-51

OPERATIVE REPORT

PREOPERATIVE DIAGNOSIS: Previous cesarean section, pregnancy at term.

POSTOPERATIVE DIAGNOSIS: Previous cesarean section, pregnancy at term.

PROCEDURE: Repeat low cervical transverse cesarean section.

ANESTHESIA: Spinal.

FLUIDS: 2,000 cc.

ESTIMATED BLOOD LOSS: 500 cc.

COMPLICATIONS: None.

DRAINS: Foley to gravity.

FINDINGS: Delivered was a viable male infant weighing 7 lb, 2 oz. Apgars were 8 and 9 at 1 and 5 min, respectively. Arterial cord pH 7.30, hypospadias noted on initial exam.

TECHNIQUE AND PROCEDURE: Patient attended through entire pregnancy and now at full term. After adequate spinal anesthesia was obtained, the patient was placed in the supine position, prepped and draped in the usual sterile fashion with a Foley catheter draining to gravity. A Pfannenstiel incision was made at the site of a previous incision. This was extended down to the fascial layer. The fascia was scored in the midline, the incision was extended to the right and the left sides using sharp dissection. The fascia was then bluntly and sharply dissected off the underlying rectus muscles. The rectus muscles were bluntly and sharply dissected in the midline. The underlying peritoneum was identified and this was transected using sharp dissection extended superiorly and inferiorly. Uterovesical flap was performed horizontally across the lower uterine segment and incorporated into a Balfour blade. A horizontal incision was made across the lower uterine segment and the incision was extended laterally using blunt dissection. A single hand was placed in the lower uterine segment, a vertex portion of the infant was brought forward. Amniotic fluid was clear, the cord was clamped and cut, and the infant was handed to the pediatric team in attendance.

Delivered was a viable male with Apgars of 8 and 9 at 1 and 5 min, respectively. Weight 7 lb 2 oz. Arterial cord pH 7.30, placenta manually delivered, found to be of normal configuration. There was a nuchal cord noted at the time of delivery, which was easily reduced. The uterus was exteriorized into the abdominal wall. Uterus, tubes, and ovaries were all normal. There were absolutely no intra-abdominal adhesions whatsoever. Uterine incision was closed using 0 Monocryl from the left to the right in a running interlocking fashion. A second imbricating layer was placed above the first using 0 Monocryl. The abdomen was irrigated, the uterus was returned to the abdominal cavity, the rectus muscles were plicated to the midline using 0 Vicryl suture after hemostasis was assured. The fascia was then closed using #1 Vicryl from the left to the right in a running fashion. Subcutaneous tissue was irrigated with saline. Skin was closed using 4-0 Vicryl in a subcuticular fashion, then supported with benzoin and Steri-Strips. All sponge, needle, and instrument counts were correct ×3.

The patient was taken to the recovery room in stable condition.

Procedure code(s): _____

Diagnosis code(s): _____

Scenario 8-52

OPERATIVE REPORT

PREOPERATIVE DIAGNOSIS: Nonreassuring fetal heart rate tracing.

POSTOPERATIVE DIAGNOSIS: Nonreassuring fetal heart rate tracing.

PROCEDURE: Primary low cervical transverse cesarean section.

BLOOD LOSS: 500 cc.

FLUIDS: 2 L of crystalloid.

INDICATION FOR PROCEDURE: The patient was being induced at 39-weeks gestation for a history of recurrent variable decelerations. The patient had been

continued

started on Pitocin and developed prolonged decelerations on 2 ml of Pitocin. Given the positive contraction stress test, the patient consented to a cesarean section.

TECHNIQUE: The patient was brought to the operating room and placed on the operating table in the dorsal supine position. After adequate anesthesia, the patient had a Foley catheter placed to gravity drainage and was sterilely prepped and draped in the usual fashion. The scalpel was taken to make a transverse skin incision 2 cm above the pubic symphysis and carried down through the subcutaneous tissue to the fascia, which was opened in the midline. The fascial incision was extended bilaterally using Mayo Scissors. Kocher clamps were used to elevate the fascia from the underlying rectus muscle and the rectus muscle was dissected from the overlying fascia using Mayo Scissors. The rectus muscles were separated in the midline. The peritoneum was entered in a clear area using blunt dissection. The peritoneal incision was extended superiorly and inferiorly, taking care to avoid the bladder. The bladder blade was placed. The peritoneum overlying the lower uterine segment was grasped and entered with Metzenbaum Scissors and the bladder flap was created. The scalpel was taken to make an incision transversely in the lower uterine segment. This was carried down through the uterine layers bluntly and the uterus was entered bluntly. The uterine incision was extended with bandage scissors. Clear fluid was noted. The head was delivered and a bulb was used for nose and mouth suction. The infant was delivered without difficulty. There was noted to be a cord around the legs. The cord was doubly clamped and cut and the infant was handed off to the awaiting pediatric staff. The infant was a male infant with Apgars of 9 and 9. Cord pH was 7.26. Cord bloods were drawn. The placenta was manually removed. The uterus was delivered through the incision. The uterine incision was marked with the ringed forceps and it was closed with 0 Vicryl in a running fashion using a single length of suture. The incision was closed with a second layer of 0 Vicryl. Good hemostasis was noted. The tubes and ovaries were normal. The pelvis was irrigated. Good hemostasis was again noted. The uterus was returned through the uterine incision and the fascia was closed using number 0 Vicryl. The subcutaneous tissue was irrigated. It was noted to be hemostatic and the skin was closed using skin staples. The patient tolerated the procedure well and was taken to the recovery room in stable condition.

COMPLICATIONS: None.

DRAINS: Foley to gravity.

SPECIMENS: None.

Procedure code(s): _____

Diagnosis code(s): _____

Scenario 8-53

OPERATIVE REPORT

INDICATIONS FOR PROCEDURE: The patient is a 15-year-old girl who has had thyroid nodules for quite some time. Needle biopsy revealed lymphocytes and histiocytes that continued to stay enlarged. We are here for removal. Mother and child understand the operative risks and benefits.

PREOPERATIVE DIAGNOSIS: Nodules, right lobe of thyroid.

PROCEDURE: Right hemithyroidectomy.

POSTOPERATIVE DIAGNOSIS: Nodules, right lobe of thyroid.

ANESTHESIA: General endotracheal anesthesia with an NIM monitoring tube.

ESTIMATED BLOOD LOSS: 25 cc.

FLUIDS: 1,400 cc of lactated Ringer's.

FINDINGS: Smooth and encapsulated multinodular right lobe thyroid gland. One parathyroid was reimplanted into the medial portion of the right sternocleido-mastoid muscle.

PROCEDURE: After the induction of adequate general endotracheal anesthesia with the NIM monitoring tube, which was noted to be hooked up appropriately and functional. The patient was sterilely prepped and draped. A standard thyroidectomy incision was made in the low anterior neck using a #15 blade. Hemostasis was maintained with bipolar electrocautery. The platysma and subcutaneous tissue were transected using electrocautery. A subplatysmal flap was raised superiorly to the level of the hyoid bone and inferiorly to the level of the sternal notch. The skin and platysma were retracted by being sewn to the drapes. The midline was identified and opened with electrocautery. The strap muscles were carefully dissected off the right lobe of the thyroid gland using bipolar electrocautery. The midline was identified. The isthmus was dissected off the trachea at the midline, clamped, transected, and tied with a suture ligature bilaterally with 3-0 Vicryl.

Dissection was then continued on the right lobe of the thyroid gland, taking it off the trachea and off Berry's ligament and a second from inferior to superior, exposing the inferior thyroid artery and the associated parathyroid gland, which was left in its bed. The artery was tied and cut. No significant middle thyroid vein was identified. There was one vessel superior to this that was tied and cut. The recurrent laryngeal nerve was identified in its bed and stimulated and was functioning normally. It was left intact in its bed. The superior vasculature was dissected out of surrounding tissue. The superior laryngeal nerve was identified and left intact. The superior vasculature was clamped. The thyroid was cut off of this stem. At this point, it was noted that a parathyroid gland was on the medial surface of the upper portion of the thyroid lobe. This was taken off the thyroid. A portion was sent for frozen section evaluation. It was confirmed that it was parathyroid and the remainder was implanted into the medial portion of the right sternocleidomastoid muscle. The fascia was opened. Macerated, minced gland was put in place and the fascia was closed with two 4-0 Prolene sutures. Attention was then turned back to the thyroid vasculature, which was tied. A frozen section of the thyroid lobe revealed benign nodular disease. The wound was irrigated. All hemostasis was maintained. A BLAKE Drain was put in place and brought out a separate skin puncture. The midline was closed with running 3-0 Vicryl suture. The platysma was closed with interrupted 3-0 Vicryl suture, and the skin was closed with running subcuticular Monocryl.

The patient tolerated the procedure well. There were no complications. She was taken to the recovery room extubated and in good condition.

Procedure code(s): _____

Diagnosis code(s): _____

Scenario 8-54

OPERATIVE REPORT

DIAGNOSIS: Symptomatic lumbar spinal stenosis.

POSTOPERATIVE DIAGNOSIS: Symptomatic lumbar spinal stenosis.

PROCEDURE PERFORMED: L2 through L5 bilateral decompressive laminectomies.

ANESTHESIA: General endotracheal anesthesia.

ESTIMATED BLOOD LOSS: 300 cc.

COMPLICATIONS: There were no complications during the case.

HISTORY AND INDICATIONS: The patient is a 62-year-old male with symptomatic lumbar spinal stenosis that failed conservative measures and was considered for surgical intervention. For further detail, please review the patient's chart.

OPERATIVE PROCEDURE: I met with the patient in the holding unit. All questions and concerns were addressed. Following that, the patient was taken to the operating theater, given preoperative antibiotics, and after adequate general anesthesia was achieved by the anesthesia team, the patient was placed prone on a Camden frame on the operating table. All pressure points were examined and padded. The lower back was then shaved, prepped, and draped in the usual sterile surgical fashion. Incision was made at the midline and carried down through the subcutaneous tissues in the lumbosacral fascia to expose the laminae at L3 to S1 bilaterally in a subperiosteal fashion. Following that, self-retaining retractors were placed to maintain the exposure. Meticulous hemostasis was achieved using bipolar and Bovie cautery, and a localization x-ray was obtained to confirm the correct levels. The spinous processes of L4 and partially of L3–L5 were removed using a Leksell Rongeur. The lamina of L4 was completely drilled bilaterally, and the laminae of L3 and L5 were drilled halfway to remove bilaterally. The Kerrison Rongeurs were used to remove the laminae bilaterally and remove the stenosis at L4–L5 and L3–L4 bilaterally. Meticulous foraminotomies were carried out at the foramina of L3, L4, and L5 bilaterally. Meticulous hemostasis was achieved using Surgiflo and the wound was irrigated with copious amounts of antibiotic irrigation. The dental instrument was used to confirm that all the foramina were widely patent. Marcaine was placed subcutaneously for postoperative pain control. A round Hemovac drain was placed epidurally, externalized from the skin, and secured with 3-0 nylon stitch. The incision was then closed using interrupted Vicryl stitches and a dry sterile dressing was applied. The patient was extubated in the operating room and transferred in stable condition to the recovery room. There were no complications during the case.

Procedure code(s): _____

Diagnosis code(s): _____

Scenario 8-55

OPERATIVE REPORT

PREOPERATIVE DIAGNOSIS: Right carpal tunnel syndrome.

POSTOPERATIVE DIAGNOSIS: Right carpal tunnel syndrome.

OPERATION: Right carpal tunnel release.

ANESTHESIA: Sedation plus local.

PROCEDURE: After adequate sedation had been obtained by the anesthesiologist, the patient was prepped and draped. The right upper extremity was exsanguinated and the tourniquet raised to 250 mm Hg. Five milliliters of 0.5% bupivacaine were then infiltrated into the right thenar crease. A 1-cm incision was then made and carried down through the subcutaneous tissue. The superficial palmar fascia, transverse carpal ligament, and distal portion of the antebrachial fascia were all divided under direct vision. The incision line was closed using 4-0 nylon sutures. A dry sterile dressing was applied. He tolerated the procedure well.

Total procedure time 30 min.

Procedure code(s): _____

Diagnosis code(s): _____

Scenario 8-56

OPERATIVE REPORT

PREOPERATIVE DIAGNOSIS: Normal pressure hydrocephalus.

POSTOPERATIVE DIAGNOSIS: Normal pressure hydrocephalus.

PROCEDURE PERFORMED: Right VP shunt placement, with a programmable Medtronic Strata 2 valve set at 1.5 Doppler.

ANESTHESIA: General endotracheal anesthesia.

ESTIMATED BLOOD LOSS: 75 cc.

COMPLICATIONS: There were no complications during the case.

OPERATIVE PROCEDURE AND FINDINGS: I met with the patient in the holding area and all questions and concerns were addressed.

Following that, the patient was taken to the operating theater and after adequate general anesthesia was achieved by the anesthesia team, preoperative antibiotics were given and the patient was placed supine on the operating table with a shoulder roll under the right shoulder and the head turned to the left. The head was then shaved. The head, neck, and torso were prepped and draped in the usual sterile surgical fashion. A curvilinear incision was made at the Dandy point in the right parieto-occipital area and was carried down through the subcutaneous tissues. A pocket was made under the galea, leaving the pericranium intact. A small piece of pericranium was removed using a Bovie cautery, and the high-speed drill was used to place a burr hole at the Dandy point.

Following that, attention was turned to the abdominal part, where an incision was made at the midclavicular line in a transverse fashion approximately 2 finger breadths below the rib cage. The incision was carried through the subcutaneous tissues with sharp and blunt dissection.

Meticulous hemostasis was achieved using bipolar and Bovie cautery. The anterior rectus fascia was opened using a scissor and the muscle was retracted medially. The posterior rectus fascia was opened using a scissor and the peritoneum was

continued

found and retracted using snaps. The peritoneum was entered using a #15 blade and the intraperitoneal space was confirmed using a #4 Penfield instrument. Following that, the shunt passer was used to connect the 2 incisions and the unitized Strata system was passed through. The Strata valve was preset at 1.5 Delta prior to the surgery. Following that, the Strata valve and the distal catheter were primed using gentamicin irrigation.

Following that, the Bovie and bayonet forceps were used to make a small opening into the dura mater and pia mater. A ventricular shunt was then placed into the right occipital ventricle at 5 cm and moved to 9 cm. The catheter was trimmed at 10 cm and connected to the proximal aspect of the valve. The valve was placed into the premade pocket and the connection was secured using 2-0 silk ties. The valve was secured to the pericranium using two 4-0 Nurolon stitches. Good spontaneous flow was seen distally, and the distal part of the catheter was placed into the peritoneum. Both incisions were closed using interrupted Vicryl stitches and staples were placed on the skin. A dry sterile dressing was applied.

The patient was extubated in the operating room and transferred in stable condition to the recovery room. There were no complications during the case.

Procedure code(s): _____

Diagnosis code(s): _____

Scenario 8-57

OPERATIVE REPORT

PREOPERATIVE DIAGNOSIS: Uncontrolled glaucoma in the left eye.

POSTOPERATIVE DIAGNOSIS: Uncontrolled glaucoma in the left eye.

PROCEDURE: Left eye trabeculation with Mitomycin C.

COMPLICATIONS: None.

INDICATIONS FOR PROCEDURE: The patient's intraocular pressure was inadequately controlled on maximum tolerated medications and following laser treatment.

DESCRIPTION OF PROCEDURE: Under retrobulbar block anesthesia, the patient was prepared and draped in the normal ophthalmic fashion. The area was selected to perform trabeculation superiorly. A fornix-based conjunctival flap was raised from 11 o'clock to 1 o'clock and then dissected back slightly. Hemostasis was obtained using wet-field cautery. Mitomycin C in a concentration of 0.3 mg saline was applied to the scleral surface and subconjunctival space for a total of 3 min. The conjunctival sponge was removed and the area was irrigated with balanced salt solution copiously. A triangular shape of half-thickness scleral flap was raised superiorly and dissected down to the surgical limbus using a crescent blade knife. Hemostasis was again obtained with the wet-field cautery. The anterior chamber was entered at the base of the scleral flap using a 75° Superblade. Trabeculectomy was created with a Kelly punch. The iris prolapsed freely and a peripheral iridectomy was performed without having entered the anterior chamber. The iris fell back into the anterior chamber nicely. The scleral flap was then repositioned into its original bed. The conjunctival flap was then pulled tightly across the cornea below the scleral flap. The scleral flap was closed with 10-0 nylon in interrupted fashion. The conjunctiva was closed with Number 9-0 Vicryl in horizontal mattress fashion.

At the end of the procedure, a bleb was seen to form nicely and the conjunctival flap site was negative. The anterior chamber was well formed and the pupil was round with iridectomy patent. Maxitrol ointment and 1% atropine were applied to the left eye. The eye was patched in a normal sterile ophthalmic fashion and the patient then returned to the recovery room in good condition with no complications.

Procedure code(s): _____

Diagnosis code(s): _____

Scenario 8-58

OPERATIVE REPORT

PREOPERATIVE DIAGNOSIS: Visually significant cataract of right eye.

POSTOPERATIVE DIAGNOSIS: Visually significant cataract of right eye.

PROCEDURE: Cataract extraction with phacoemulsification and intraocular lens implantation of right eye.

ANESTHESIA: MAC.

COMPLICATIONS: None.

PATHOLOGY: None.

PROCEDURE IN DETAIL: The risks and benefits of the cataract surgery were discussed at length with the patient, including bleeding, infection, retinal detachment, reoperation, lost vision, lost eye. Informed consent was obtained. On the day of surgery the patient received medication in the right eye including 2.5 phenylephrine, 1% Cyclogyl, Ocuflox, and Acular. The patient was sent to the waiting area and retrobulbar block was performed by anesthesiologist, and then the patient was taken to the operating room and placed in the supine position. The right eye was prepped and draped in the normal ophthalmic fashion.

A Liberman lid speculum was placed to provide exposure. The Thornton Fixation Ring and the Superblade were used to create a paracentesis at 3 o'clock. Viscoat was injected through the paracentesis into anterior chamber. A 3.0-mm keratome blade was used to create a 2-step full-thickness clear corneal incision at 12 o'clock. The cystitome was used to open anterior capsule back to create a capsular flap. Utrata forceps were used to create a continuous capsulorrhexis in the anterior lens capsule. BSS on a cannula was used to perform gentle hydrodissection as well as hydrodelineation. With the nucleus now found to be free moving, a phacoemulsification handpiece was used to remove the nuclear material. An FA handpiece was used to remove the remaining cortex material. Provisc was injected to peel the capsule back in anterior chamber. A 19.5 intraocular lens was injected in the capsular bag without difficulty. A Kuglen hook was used to rotate it into the proper position into capsular bag. The FA handpiece was used to remove the remaining viscoelastic from the anterior chamber. BSS on a 30-gauge cannula was used to hydrate the wound. The wound was checked and was watertight.

continued

The lid speculum and drapes were carefully removed. Several drops of Ocuflox were applied to the eye. The eye was covered and patched with the shield. The patient was taken to the recovery room in good condition. There were no complications.

Procedure code(s): _____

Diagnosis code(s): _____

Scenario 8-59

OPERATIVE REPORT

PREOPERATIVE DIAGNOSIS: Chronic serous otitis media and adenotonsillar hypertrophy.

POSTOPERATIVE DIAGNOSIS: Chronic serous otitis media and adenotonsillar hypertrophy.

OPERATION: Bilateral myringotomy and tympanostomy tube placement. Tonsillectomy and adenoidectomy on a 6-year-old.

SURGEON: Dr. Latent.

ANESTHESIA: General.

FINDINGS: Bilateral mucopurulent fluid.

SPECIMENS: Tonsils and adenoids.

ESTIMATED BLOOD LOSS: 5 cc.

COMPLICATIONS: None apparent.

DISPOSITION: Stable to recovery room.

TECHNIQUE: The patient was brought to the operating room and placed supine on the operating room table. The patient was put to sleep by a general technique of anesthesia and intubated without difficulty. The ears were inspected under an otologic microscope with a 250 focal length lens at 6× magnification. Wax was curetted from the canal. Myringotomy incisions were made in the anterior-inferior quadrants in a radial fashion on each side. Mucopurulent fluid was aspirated from each side. Collar button tubes were atraumatically inserted on each side. Cortisporin drops were then instilled on each side. The patient was then positioned for adenotonsillectomy. She was placed in gentle neck extension on a shoulder roll.

A Crowe-Davis retractor was inserted in the oral commissure to retract the tongue and mandible. She was suspended from Mayo stand. A towel was placed over her face. The palate and uvula were inspected and palpated. There was no submucous cleft or bifid uvula appreciated. A red rubber catheter was inserted through the nostril to retract the palate. The nasopharynx was inspected and showed a mild adenoid hypertrophy. This was Bovie ablated and then debulked with the Sinclair forceps. Hemostasis was obtained with the bipolar electrocautery in conjunction with tonsil sponges with Afrin. The tonsils were grasped and medialized. Each tonsil was resected from its fossa in a capsular plane, preserving the anterior and posterior tonsillar pillars. Hemostasis was obtained simultaneously. Each tonsil pillar was injected with 1 cc of 0.25% Marcaine and 1:200,000 epinephrine. The wounds were irrigated and the stomach was suctioned. The patient was awakened from anesthesia and extubated without difficulty. She was brought to the recovery room in stable condition.

Procedure code(s): _____

Diagnosis code(s): _____

Scenario 8-60

OPERATIVE REPORT

PREOPERATIVE DIAGNOSIS: Adenotonsillar hypertrophy and chronic serous otitis media.

POSTOPERATIVE DIAGNOSIS: Adenotonsillar hypertrophy and chronic serous otitis media.

PROCEDURE: Adenoidectomy and bilateral myringotomy and tympanostomy tube placement.

SURGEON: Anna Jones, M.D.

ANESTHESIA: General.

FINDINGS: Severe adenoid hypertrophy, moderate tonsillar hypertrophy and mucoid fluid right ear, serous fluid left ear.

SPECIMENS: Adenoids.

ESTIMATED BLOOD LOSS: 10 cc.

COMPLICATIONS: None apparent.

DISPOSITION: Stable to recovery room.

TECHNIQUE: The 11-year-old patient was brought to the operating room and placed supine on the operating room table. The patient was put to sleep by a general technique of anesthesia and intubated without difficulty. The ears were inspected under an otologic microscope at 6× magnification. Wax was curetted from the canal. Myringotomy incisions were made in the anterior-inferior quadrant on each side. Mucoid fluid was suctioned from the right and serous fluid was suctioned from the left. Collar button tubes were inserted. Cortisporin drops were then instilled. Next, the patient was repositioned for adenoidectomy and possible tonsillectomy. A small shoulder roll was placed beneath the shoulder blades. She was placed in gentle neck extension. A Crowe-Davis retractor was inserted in the oral cavity to retract the tongue and mandible. She was suspended from the Mayo stand. The palate and uvula were inspected and palpated. There was no submucous cleft or bifid uvula appreciated. The tonsils were moderately enlarged but not enough so that the adenoid could not be addressed. A red rubber catheter was inserted through the nostril to retract the palate. The nasopharynx was inspected. This showed a severe adenoid hypertrophy completely blocking the nasopharynx. A curette was used to scrape the adenoid until the choana could be seen. Bovie electrocautery was used for initial hemostasis and hemostasis was completed with Afrin-soaked tonsil sponges. The wound was irrigated. There was no further bleeding. The stomach was suctioned and the patient was awakened from anesthesia and extubated without difficulty.

Procedure code(s): _____

Diagnosis code(s): _____

CHAPTER REVIEW

Using the *CPT* and *HCPCS* manuals and this textbook, complete the following exercises.

Define the following:

1. Global days _____
2. Subsection notes _____
3. Surgery section guidelines _____
4. Diagnostic procedure _____
5. Code range _____

Find the following CPT codes and identify what coding rule or symbol the medical coder would use.

6. A patient comes into the ER with 5 lacerations: (1) 1 simple repair of 5 cm on the side of the face, (2–3) 2 on the hand requiring a simple repair of 3.5 cm, and a complex repair of 4 cm, (4) 1 complex repair of 3 cm on the trunk, and (5) 1 intermediate on the leg of 5 cm.
   _____

7. Patient comes into the ER with a dislocation of 3 metacarpal bones of the right hand. A closed treatment of the index and middle finger bones with manipulation and an external fixation without manipulation of the thumb are performed.
   _____

8. Patient comes in for a diagnostic proctosigmoidoscopy, but during the procedure the physician found a bleeding tumor and he removed it with the snare technique.
   _____

9. The physician performed a laryngoscopy to remove a tumor of the vocal cords with the use of the operating microscope. Would the code 69990 be used?
   _____

10. When a physician sees a maternity case throughout the pregnancy and delivers the baby by any method, then sees the patient 6 weeks after the delivery, would the medical coder bill for all of these services separately? _____

Chapter 9
Radiology, Laboratory, Pathology, and Medicine Coding

LEARNING OBJECTIVES

Upon completion of this chapter, the student will be able to:

1. Utilize the tools of the *CPT*, *ICD*-9, and *HCPCS* manuals to enhance his or her ability to code laboratory, radiological, and other medical procedures accurately

RADIOLOGY

The radiology chapter has four major sections:

1. **Diagnostic Radiology** (70010–76499), which includes:
   - **Computerized tomography (CT)**
   - **Magnetic resonance imaging (MRI)**
   - Interventional radiology procedures
2. **Diagnostic Ultrasound** (76506–76999)
3. **Radiation Oncology** (77261–77799)
4. Nuclear Medicine (78000–79999)

There are also 19 subsections:

1. Aorta and Arteries	75600–75790
2. Veins and Lymphatics	75801–75893
3. Transcatheter Procedures	75894–75989
4. Diagnostic Ultrasound	76506–76999
5. Abdomen and Retroperitoneum	76700–76778
6. Obstetrical	76801–76828

7. Non-Obstetrical	76830–76857
8. Radiation Oncology	77261–77799
9. Function MRI	70554–70555
10. Delivery	77520–77525
11. Clinical Treatment Planning	77261–77299
12. Radiation Treatment Management	77427–77499
13. Proton Beam Treatment Delivery	77520–77525
14. Hyperthermia	77600–77620
15. Clinical Brachytherapy	77750–77799
16. Nuclear Medicine	78000–78299
17. Musculoskeletal System	78300–78399
18. Cardiovascular System	78414–78499
19. Therapeutic	79005–79999

Codes are divided according to anatomic site and body system.

General Diagnostic Radiology

Coding diagnostic radiology in a simple step-by-step method:

1. Determine the number of views taken and then code accordingly. Minimum views allow the coder to use the code even if you have done more.

EXAMPLE

Four views of the hand were taken. The medical coder finds the code that is closest to the number of views taken.

73120 Radiologic examination, hand; two views
73130 minimum of three views

In this case the code is 73130. If the medical coder used 73120 twice, that is not correct coding.

2. Determine whether the procedure is bilateral (two-sided) or unilateral (one-sided).
   - Some procedure descriptions are unilateral, but if they are performed on both sides, then use modifier 50.
   - Some procedures already have the term "bilateral" in the description. Read the description carefully to be sure it is describing the exact procedure performed.

EXAMPLE

71040 Bronchography, unilateral, radiological supervision and interpretation
71060 Bronchography, bilateral, radiological supervision and interpretation

---

Computerized Tomography (CT) and Magnetic Resonance Imaging (MRI)

When coding for computerized tomography (CT) and magnetic resonance imaging (MRI), remember that the two procedures are not interchangeable or part of each other. The services and technology are very different.

When contrast material is used, be sure to use the appropriate code.

EXAMPLE

70486 Computer tomography, maxillofacial area; without contrast material

70487 with contrast material

70488 without contrast material followed by contrast material

---

Mammography

A mammography can be either:

- Bilateral (77056) or
- Unilateral (77055)

The coder also needs to know if the mammogram is a diagnostic or a screening mammogram.

- Diagnostic mammograms are performed because the patient is experiencing symptoms, such as a breast lump or a discharge from the breast, and the procedure can be unilateral (77055).
- Screening mammograms are bilateral and are asymptomatic (77057).

Diagnostic Ultrasound (76506–76999)

Several methods of diagnostic ultrasound (76506–76999) are used. The medical coder needs to pay close attention to the different display modes and scans.

- A-mode
- Amplitude modulation
- A-scan
- B-mode (brightness mode)
- B-scan
- M-mode (motion mode)
- Real time

PECULIARITIES OF CODING FOR RADIOLOGY

Coding for radiology is different from that of other services. Not only are there many specialists in radiology who are qualified and credentialed to perform and interpret radiological procedures, but many of these specialists have their own equipment in their offices. So it is important for the medical coder to understand how to code for these services.

Some key points to be aware of when coding radiological services are:

- Who owns the equipment?
- Is the provider credentialed by the payer?
- Who is reading, interpreting, and reporting on the images taken?

Knowing who owns the equipment is important because there are two components for radiology coding:

- The **professional component:** The physician's interpretation and report of radiological, cardiovascular, therapeutic, and diagnostic services.
- The **technical component:** A report that describes the services of the technologist, as well as the use of the equipment, film, room, and other supplies.

When the provider owns the equipment, most insurance companies pay for both the professional component and the technical component, that is, a **global fee**. A global code that includes both the professional and technical components is used without modifiers.

EXAMPLE

Patient goes to the orthopedic doctor's office after a fall on the ice.

CC: Patient, age 4, slipped on some ice and fell on his hand.

EXAM: The hand is bruised and swollen. The child is unable to move his index finger as well as his thumb.

RADIOLOGIC EXAM: Three views of his hand, taken in the office, reveal that both metacarpals are broken.

ASSESSMENT AND PLAN: There are 2 broken metacarpals, both greenstick. After the swelling goes down in a day or so, a cast will be applied. In the interim a splint was placed on his hand to keep it stable until a cast can be put on.

How would you code for the radiology service for this patient? In this case, because the provider owns the equipment, you code for the three-view x-ray for the hand:

73130 TOS 4, with no modifier.

The professional and technical components, when billed separately, are used with modifiers: modifier 26 for the professional component and TC (technical component) if the provider only took the images.

The third-party payer (TPP) will not pay a global fee if the medical coder reports only the "reading," or interpretation, of the radiological images. The provider who reads the images uses modifier 26, and the facility that owns the equipment bills for the technical component by adding the **modifier TC**.

EXAMPLE

Patient goes to the ER after a fall on the ice.

CC: Patient, age 4, slipped on some ice and fell on his hand.

EXAM: The hand is bruised and swollen. The child is unable to move his index finger as well as his thumb.

RADIOLOGIC EXAM: Three views of his hand were taken and reveals that both metacarpals are broken.

ASSESSMENT AND PLAN: There are 2 broken metacarpals, both greenstick. In the interim a splint was placed on his hand to keep it stable until he sees the orthopedist. A referral to an orthopedist was given.

Here the ER provider read the x-ray images, and the hospital technician took the images. The medical coders would code these services as follows:

The ER coder: 73130-26

The hospital coder: 73130-TC

Some third-party payers want the providers who own their equipment to split the codes as follows:

- X-rays three views of hand interpretation   73130-26
- X-rays three views of hand technical   73130-TC

EXAMPLE

Patient goes to the ER after a fall on the ice, then to the orthopedic a day later.

CC: Patient, age 4, slipped on some ice and fell on his hand.

EXAM: The hand is bruised and swollen, but the swelling has come down well enough to place a cast on it today.

RADIOLOGIC EXAM: Three views of his hand were taken yesterday at the ER and reviewed. The films revealed that both metacarpals are broken.

ASSESSMENT AND PLAN: There are 2 broken metacarpals, both greenstick. A cast was placed on the child's hand without having to reduce the Fx.

In this situation, the x-ray was read by another provider. Even if the radiologist also reads the x-ray images, the service would not be reported again.

| Tip | *Many surgeons, orthopedists, OB/GYNs and other specialists have special training to read radiological images. Some of these providers like to read the images themselves. They may also have these images in the OR as a guide during the procedure.* |

ABSTRACTING THE DIAGNOSIS IN RADIOLOGY CODING

When coding for radiological procedures, where do you get the diagnoses? The diagnoses can be found in the impression or findings. But what happens when the impression states negative? The medical coder must look for the indications, or the signs and symptoms.

■ *Find the Code 9-1*

RADIOLOGY REPORT

EXAMINATION DESIRED: Chest film, 2 views, frontal, and lateral.

REASON FOR EXAM: Chronic respiratory problems.

REPORT: CHEST, PA AND LATERAL, 10/8/06: an approximately 2- to 3-cm irregular, poorly marginated mass is located in left midlung laterally. A few strands are seen extending from it toward the left hilum. The patient is noted to have a low diaphragm, and an increased AP diameter. This is suggestive of chronic obstructive pulmonary disease. The lungs are clear of any infiltrate and any other definite mass lesions. The heart is not enlarged.

IMPRESSION: A 2- to 3-cm irregular, poorly marginated mass, left midlung laterally, probably adenocarcinoma. There are some dense streaky strands extending from this mass toward the left hilum. Chronic obstructive pulmonary disease.

RECOMMENDATION: Tomogram might be helpful.

What would the medical coder code for the procedure? _____

What would be the diagnosis? _____

What would the medical coder code for the procedure? The procedure is chest film, two views frontal, and lateral. The code is 71020. What would be the diagnosis? The diagnosis would be the lung mass and COPD. The codes are 213.2 for the lung mass (benign) and 496 for the COPD.

Tip *Remember: The medical coder never codes a probable. If the interpretation was adenocarcinoma, then the medical coder can code for the cancer.*

LABORATORY

Most medical laboratory tests are not done in the physician's office. The reason is that doctors' offices now need a **Clinical Laboratory Improvement Amendment (CLIA)** number from the federal government. The objective of the CLIA program is to ensure quality laboratory testing in the medical office as well as in the laboratories. The CLIA number must be reported on the claim in order for payment to be received.

A *CLIA-waived test* is one that is free from most of the regulatory standards associated with CLIA and requires only that the test be performed in accordance with the manufacturer's instructions. A certificate of waiver is issued to laboratories in a physician's office that perform only waived tests and is valid for a two-year period. Append **modifier QW** to all codes that represent waived tests, with the exception of the following CPT-coded tests, which do not require the QW modifier:

- 81002 Urinalysis by dip stick
- 81025 Urine pregnancy test
- 82270 Blood occult, by peroxidase activity qualitative, feces

- 82272 Blood occult, by other sources
- 82962 Glucose, blood by glucose monitoring device
- 83026 Hemoglobin, by copper sulfate method, non-automatic
- 84830 Ovulation test, by visual color for human luteinizing hormone
- 85013 Spun microhematocrit
- 85651 Sedimentation rate, erythrocyte; non-automatic

> **Tip** *The list of CLIA-waived tests, which doctors can perform in the medical office, can be found on the following Web site: www.cms.hhs.gov/clia. A sample of this list is shown in Table 9-1.*

TABLE 9-1   **Tests Granted Waived Status Under CLIA**

CPT Code(S)	Test Name	Manufacturer	Use
81002	Dipstick or tablet reagent urinalysis – non-automated for bilirubin, glucose, hemoglobin, ketone, leukocytes, nitrite, pH, protein, specific gravity, and urobilinogen	Various	Screening of urine to monitor/ diagnose various diseases/ conditions, such as diabetes, the state of the kidney or urinary tract, and urinary tract infections
81025	Urine pregnancy tests by visual color comparison	Various	Diagnosis of pregnancy
82270 82272 G0394 (Contact your Medicare carrier for claims instructions.)	Fecal occult blood	Various	Detection of blood in feces from whatever cause, benign or malignant (colorectal cancer screening)
82962	Blood glucose by glucose monitoring devices cleared by the FDA for home use	Various	Monitoring of blood glucose levels
83026	Hemoglobin by copper sulfate – non-automated	Various	Monitors hemoglobin level in blood
84830	Ovulation tests by visual color comparison for human luteinizing hormone	Various	Detection of ovulation (optimal for conception)
85013	Blood count; spun microhematocrit	Various	Screen for anemia
85651	Erythrocyte sedimentation rate – non-automated	Various	Nonspecific screening test for inflammatory activity, increased for majority of infections, and most cases of carcinoma and leukemia

Courtesy of the Centers for Medicare and Medicaid, Department of Health & Human Services

In the medical office, the laboratory services are often not reported because:

- Either the nurse does them and the charge slip is already at the front desk
- Or the doctor forgets to note the test in the record

The loss of revenue is twofold:

1. The cost of the test
2. The time that it took to perform the test

How does the medical coder know that the encounter form is missing a lab? One way is by noting the diagnosis.

EXAMPLE

If the patient has a strep infection, chances are that a rapid strep test was done.

The other way is if a value is stated.

EXAMPLE

A patient's glucose level is at 100. This might mean that the patient had a test done in the office. The medical coder should check the office notes or ask the provider whether a test was performed.

The last thing the medical coder must remember about coding for laboratory tests done in the medical office is that the diagnosis must always be linked to the service. Many payment denials occur when the procedure is not linked to an accurate diagnosis.

MEDICINE

The last chapter of *CPT*, Medicine, includes all the other procedures and services that are not appropriate for inclusion in any of the other chapters. These are mostly nonsurgical diagnostic and therapeutic procedures, although some procedures, such as cardiac catheterizations, are invasive. The Medicine chapter contains all the other services that may be provided during an office visit, such as children's immunizations, allergy testing, EKGs, EMGs, and the like.

EXAMPLE

The medical coder who works for a cardiologist might be dealing with services in the code range of 93303–93990: echocardiography, cardiac catheterization, intracardiac electrophysiological procedures/studies, peripheral arterial disease rehabilitation, and noninvasive vascular diagnostic studies.

Such services can be done in any setting and can be the only services that the provider might render, such as osteopathic manipulative treatment, physical medicine, and rehabilitation services, or services done in combination with other services.

CHAPTER EXERCISES

Scenario 9-1

RADIOLOGY REPORT

EXAMINATION DESIRED: Esophagram.

REASON FOR EXAM: Carcinoma of esophagus.

REPORT: Esophagram.

The swallowing mechanism was observed at fluoroscopy and spot films were obtained. Overhead views were then done in AP lateral and oblique positions while the patient was swallowing barium. There was an irregular narrowed area in the midportion of the esophagus at the approximate level of the aortic knob. This has tapering margins and measures approximately 5.5 cm in length. It is consistent with the clinical information of carcinoma of the esophagus.

IMPRESSION: There is no obstruction at this time and the lumen measures 1.3 cm in its most narrow region.

Procedure code(s): _____

Diagnosis code(s): _____

Scenario 9-2

RADIOLOGY REPORT

EXAMINATION DESIRED: Ultrasound of abdomen.

REASON FOR EXAM: Retroperitoneal mass.

REPORT: Ultrasound of abdomen.

Examination of the left kidney was performed in both supine and prone positions. There is evidence of a mass lesion in the superior pole causing a bulbous superior pole of the kidney, which is fairly homogeneous in consistency but not cystic. The mass is mainly in the superior pole but also seems to be somewhat more posteriorly placed, displacing the normal midportion of the kidney slightly anteriorly. An examination of the right kidney is within normal limits.

IMPRESSION: Mass lesion, superior portion, and posterior portion of the left kidney. Not cystic.

Procedure code(s): _____

Diagnosis code(s): _____

Scenario 9-3

RADIOLOGY REPORT

EXAMINATION DESIRED: Mammogram of the remaining breast (right).

REASON FOR EXAM: Carcinoma of breast.

REPORT: Mammogram of the remaining breast (right).

There is no evidence of skin thickening. In the upper outer quadrant, there is noted a small area of increased opacification with radiating fibrotic strands. There is at least 1 large vein leading out of this area, as well as 2 smaller venous channels that are dilated in comparison with the remaining vasculature of this breast. No calcifications can be detected. Incidentally, also in the axilla on this side are 2 rounded opacities suggesting lymph nodes.

IMPRESSION: Possibility of an upper outer quadrant carcinoma is surely to be considered. However, I would suggest a repeat mammogram in 2 or 3 months.

Procedure code(s): _____

Diagnosis code(s): _____

Scenario 9-4

RADIOLOGY REPORT

CLINICAL INFORMATION: Mr. Baker is a 43-year-old with a long history of nasal congestion, facial pain, and failure to improve on antibiotic treatment. CT of the paranasal sinuses was requested to evaluate for acute/chronic sinusitis.

PROCEDURE: Coronal thin-sectioned CT scan was obtained through the paranasal sinuses without intravenous contrast. There are no prior cross-sectional image studies available for comparison at the time of this dictation.

FINDINGS: The frontal sinuses are clear. The ethmoid sinuses show mucosal thickening on both left and right sides. The maxillary sinus shows mucosal thickening on both sides with an air fluid level on the right side. The osteomeatal complex on the right side is narrowed secondary to a Haller cell and the mucosal thickening. The osteomeatal complex on the left side is narrowed but patent. The sphenoid sinus shows a minimal air fluid level. The nasal septum is deviated to the right with a nasal septum spur.

IMPRESSION: Acute and chronic sinusitis involving all paranasal sinuses. Blockage of the right osteomeatal complex. Narrowing of the left osteomeatal complex.

Procedure code(s): _____

Diagnosis code(s): _____

Scenario 9-5

RADIOLOGY REPORT

CLINICAL INFORMATION: Mrs. Kelly is 55 years old and presents with neck pain and neurologic symptoms indicating a left C6 radiculopathy. MRI was requested to evaluate for an anatomic explanation for her signs and symptoms.

PROCEDURE: Sagittal T1- and T2-weighted images were obtained through the cervical spine, as well as axial proton density and T2-weighted images.

FINDINGS: The alignment, vertebral body, and disk space height are normal. There is decreased signal from the C3/C4, C4/C5 disks indicating desiccation. The signal intensity from the remainder of the disks and vertebral bodies are normal.

C2/C3: No stenosis of the neural foramina or central canal.

C3/C4: Mild narrowing of the right neural foramina secondary to facet hypertrophy and uncovertebral arthropathy. The central canal is normal and the left neural foramen is normal.

C4/C5: No narrowing of the neural foramina or central canal.

C5/C6: Moderate to severe narrowing of the central canal secondary to a posterior spondylotic ridge. There is moderate to severe narrowing of the right neural foramina secondary to uncovertebral arthropathy and facet hypertrophy. The left neural foramen is patent.

C7/T1: No narrowing of the central canal or neural foramina.

IMPRESSION: C5/C6: Moderate to severe narrowing of the central canal and moderate to severe narrowing of the right neural foramina secondarily compressing the right C6 nerve caused by a tumor of the cervical spine.

Procedure code(s): _____

Diagnosis code(s): _____

Scenario 9-6

RADIOLOGY REPORT

CLINICAL INFORMATION: Mr. Grant is 46 years old and presents after a car accident with injury to the lower back. There is a clinical suspicion of a fracture of the lumbar spine since he has pain and neurologic symptoms.

LUMBAR SPINE CT PROCEDURE: Contiguous axial tomographic sections were obtained through the lumbar spine without intravenous contrast.

2D Reconstruction: Sagittal and coronal 2D reconstructions were performed to evaluate vertebral height and alignment, neural foramina, and intervertebral disk spaces.

FINDINGS: The alignment is normal. The vertebral body and disk space height are normal. There is a fracture of anterior lower endplate of L1 without significant

continued

reduction in height. The posterior elements and the posterior wall of the vertebral body is intact. The soft tissues surrounding the lumbosacral spine are normal.

IMPRESSION: L1 inferior endplate fracture.

Procedure code(s): _____

Diagnosis code(s): _____

Scenario 9-7

OFFICE NOTE

This is a 78-year-old gentleman who is in for a follow-up on his diabetes. The patient feels well in general. He says he had been eating a lot of ice cream, and he wants to just try diet alone to control his diabetes. We will certainly give him a chance.

PRESENT MEDICATIONS: At present, he remains on atenolol 50 mg q.d., lorazepam 1 mg b.i.d. for chronic anxiety and Trusopt solution for his glaucoma. He is also taking multivitamins. The patient is also on aspirin as a protective against his atrial fibrillation.

VITAL SIGNS: His blood pressure today is 130/82, apical rate is 84, peripheral rate is 60, temperature is 97.4°F, and weight is 190 lb.

PHYSICAL EXAMINATION:

General: The patient looks good and does not look in any acute distress.

HEENT: Normocephalic.

Lungs: Breath sounds are distant.

Heart: There is an irregularly regular beat.

Abdomen: Soft.

Extremities: There is no evidence of any joint swelling or ankle edema.

LABS: His blood sugar today was a little high at 154. Creatinine is slightly high also at 1.6, but he has no evidence of microalbuminuria. The patient's hemoglobin was 18.7 and hematocrit was 54.6.

I think this is consistent with his COPD. These tests were done previous to this appointment.

IMPRESSION: Diabetes mellitus status could be better. He did get his flu shot, so I feel more comfortable with that, and his glaucoma is followed carefully by Dr. Bleakley.

PLAN: To get him back in 3 months. We will recheck and see his parameters for his diabetes at that time as well as his cholesterol. He will call if there are problems in between.

A glucose test was performed on the patient and should also be coded.

Procedure code(s): _____

Diagnosis code(s): _____

Scenario 9-8

OFFICE NOTE

CC: An established patient of 45 comes into the office for a sore throat.

HPI: The patient states that the sore throat started a couple of days ago and that he has had a low fever of 101° for the last 3 days. He also states it has been hard eating anything other than hot soups.

EXAMINATION:

General: The patient looks well nourished and healthy, other than the sore throat.

VITAL SIGNS: BP 120/80, temperature 101°F.

HEENT: See below.

Neck: Swollen glands.

Chest: Clear.

Heart: Normal, no murmurs.

Abdomen: Soft without any masses.

Extremities: Normal pulses, color, and muscle tone.

Neurologic: Normal and within limits.

A strep test was performed and it came back positive for strep.

ASSESSMENT: Strep throat.

A prescription for penicillin and instructions were given to the patient. If the sore throat persists after 5 days, he is to call me.

Procedure code(s): _____
Diagnosis code(s): _____

Scenario 9-9

OFFICE NOTE

CC: Painful when urinating.

Hx: A 25-year-old woman, recently married, has burning pain and urgency when she urinates. She also has itching and a white discharge in the vagina. She has been running a 101° Fahrenheit temp for 2 days. She also states that she has been very tired for the past week.

EXAM: A GYN exam was performed and a sample was taken and placed on a microscope slide. The vaginal walls were very red, with white to yellow discharge.

LABS: The urine dip showed blood and nitrates in the urine.

The slide shows the classic *Candida* yeast.

ASSESSMENT: UTI and yeast infection.

continued

A prescription of a single-dose treatment vaginal suppository and instruction were given to the patient. An antibiotic that should not worsen the yeast infection was also prescribed.

Procedure code(s): _____

Diagnosis code(s): _____

Scenario 9-10

OFFICE NOTE

CC: B/P Check.

Hx: 51-year-old woman here for her 6-month B/P check due to recent history of hypertension.

Urine dip was taken and showed that she had microalbumin in the urine. Glucose was normal.

Because of the abnormal urine dip I felt it appropriate to ask if she had any problems with urgency or urinating more often, which she denied. She had no extreme thirst or weight gain or lost. She did state that she had been sick with vomiting and diarrhea with a temp of 100° Fahrenheit about a week ago. She also stated that her urine was very dark, almost red, but she did not think it was blood.

EXAM: B/P 124/86. She did not seem to be in distress. On exam, I did notice a rash on her arm. She states that it had been there for about a month, but was not itchy. There was no back pain over the kidneys.

ASSESSMENT AND PLAN: Microalbumin, r/o lupus, liver disease.

I will have a 24-hr microalbumin urine test, a hep panel, and creatinine tests done. I will have her return to the office in 2 days to go over the results.

Procedure code(s): _____

Diagnosis code(s): _____

Scenario 9-11

OFFICE NOTE

CC: Rheumatoid arthritis.

Hx: 35-year-old woman here for a follow-up for her rheumatoid arthritis.

Patient states that the pain is still bad enough to keep her up at night. She states that the medication has not worked at all. She is on Rituxan infusion treatment. She has only had 1 treatment.

EXAM: B/P 124/86. She seemed to be in a lot of pain. On exam, I did notice that her joints were very swollen and inflamed on her hands and elbows. Her knees and feet were not as bad.

A sedimentation rate was performed and was still very high at 40 mm, with the normal value for her age group being 0–20 mm.

> **ASSESSMENT AND PLAN:** She will have the last treatment, and we will have her come back to the office after the treatment to see how she is getting along.

Procedure code(s): _____

Diagnosis code(s): _____

Scenario 9-12

OPERATIVE REPORT

PROCEDURE NOTE: Intraoperative transesophageal echocardiogram.

INDICATIONS: Mitral valve disease.

PROCEDURE IN DETAIL: In the cardiac OR with the patient under general anesthesia, the transesophageal probe was introduced into the esophagus by anesthesia. After initial imaging by anesthesia, the additional imaging was done by Dr. Mark of Cardiology with the assistance of Dr. Mercer, Cardiology fellow.

FINDINGS:

1. The aortic valve leaflets are thickened but separate well with no evidence of aortic stenosis or aortic insufficiency.

2. The mitral valve has a typical rheumatic appearance with thickening of the leaflet tips and doming. The mean gradient across the mitral valve is about 4.0 mm; however, it should be noted that this was done with a cardiac index of 1.9. It was not possible to planimeter the mitral valve area. By color Doppler, there is a moderate degree of mitral regurgitation even with the patient's intra-aortic balloon pump at 1:1. Overall findings are consistent with moderate mitral regurgitation and mild mitral stenosis done at a time when the patient was on the intra-aortic balloon pump 1:1. Therefore, the degree of mitral regurgitation may be greater.

3. The tricuspid valve appeared grossly normal from a morphologic standpoint. Trace tricuspid regurgitation was noted.

4. There is a significant area of thinning involving the inferoposterior wall, which had been noted previously. This area is akinetic. Global LV systolic function appears mildly depressed, with an ejection fraction of about 50%.

5. The ascending aorta and proximal segments of the aortic arch appear grossly normal. The upper descending thoracic aorta appeared grossly normal. The intra-aortic balloon pump is visible in the upper descending thoracic aorta.

6. There is no evidence of shunting at the atrial septal level by color Doppler. There may be lipomatous hypertrophy of the atrial septum.

7. The right atrium and right ventricle appeared to be of normal dimensions.

8. The left atrium is mildly dilated. There is no evidence of thrombus within the atrial appendage or body of the left atrium. Mild spontaneous echo contrast is present.

The findings were discussed in the cardiac OR with the patient's cardiac surgeon.

Procedure code(s): _____

Diagnosis code(s): _____

Scenario 9-13

OFFICE NOTE

This is a new patient, a 75-year-old female with a history of emphysema. She is coming in today for a complete evaluation of her emphysema.

HPI: Patient was diagnosed 3 years ago with emphysema and COPD. In the past several weeks, she has developed more trouble breathing even at rest. Any physical activity results in a need to rest every 10 min in order to "catch her breath."

ALLERGIES: Trimox, question rash but does not know what happened. Other medications include lorazepam as needed for anxiety 0.5 mg p.o.

PAST MEDICAL HISTORY: No surgeries. She has never been intubated and has no significant history of other illness except for her emphysema and COPD.

SOCIAL HISTORY: Patient lives alone. She has had 3 kids of her own in good health. She has a history of smoking for 30 years. She smoked at least 1 pack a day for 30 years. No history of alcohol abuse. Her daughter, Anna, is her health proxy. She filled in the paperwork in the past.

REVIEW OF SYSTEMS: She has been losing weight for about 20 years. She used to be around 130 pounds 25 years ago. Now she weighs only 102 pounds. She denies any loss of appetite. She denies having any night sweats.

General: Patient denies any significant weight change, chronic malaise, fever, or chills.

ENT: Denies hearing change but does have persistent hoarseness.

LUNGS: She does have a chronic cough and dyspnea, no sputum production.

Cardiac: Denies chest pain, palpitations, edema.

GI: Denies chronic dysphagia, chronic heartburn, change in bowel habits, nausea, vomiting, rectal bleeding.

GU: Denies dysuria, urgency, hematuria.

Neuro: Denies chronic headaches, weakness, or numbness. All other systems negative.

EXAM: The physical examination reveals the characteristic sounds in the lungs, rales, and crackles. A peculiar rounding of the fingernails is observed. A spiromety was performed and a determination of lung volume of the patient was classified as moderate to severe obstructive. An O_2 was taken and shows that she has an O_2 saturation reading of only 85% and a PO_2 level of 56–59 on room air.

IMPRESSION: COPD and emphysema.

PLAN: Patient will begin using oxygen as needed when she becomes breathless. She will return to this office for follow-up in 1 month or sooner if needed.

Procedure code(s): _____

Diagnosis code(s): _____

Scenario 9-14

OFFICE NOTE

Patient's first visit for her reactive depression related to her husband's death September 1. This visit is just to assess her depression and to see if she would like to continue coming to therapy. She is still having trouble dealing with her husband's death. Her good friend Mrs. Costa has just lost her husband, so she has been trying to help her at the same time. She thinks that she can help herself while she helps others.

Her medications at this time include hydrochlorothiazide and Bentyl.

She is still smoking a pack a day; she thinks about stopping. Alcohol intake is light.

GENERAL: Patient states that she lost about 10 lb, has chronic malaise, and all she wants to do is sleep all day. She is 5 ft 5 in. Her weight is 117 lb. Pulse is 72. Blood pressure is 112/60. The patient states that she does not want to feel this way anymore.

ASSESSMENT: Reactive depression. I have advised the patient that she would benefit from a little talk therapy and also a short-term antidepression medication.

Note

It must be noted that in most cases the medical coder would never see a note from a psychiatric provider. This is an example to show that these visits would be coded from the medicine section.

CPT code(s): _____
ICD-9: _____

Scenario 9-15

OFFICE NOTE

Emily is a 24-year-old female who comes into this chiropractic office with complaints of mid to low back pain. She is worried that she might have a slipped disk. She states that at this time she finds that she is allergic to sulfa drugs and she was given Macrodantin with good relief. She denies any dysuria or frequency. She has noted some slight increase in urgency recently. She does enjoy her low-sugar cranberry juice and water. She tried some heat over her right low back yesterday evening, which did help her symptoms improve. However, because she had the heat on all night, she is left with a slightly red mark in that area of her back. She denies any fevers or chills. She denies any nausea or vomiting. She occasionally gets back pain from her gas and constipation; however, she states she has had normal bowel movements lately.

PAST MEDICAL HISTORY: Chronic back pain.

ALLERGIES: Sulfa.

The patient has a follow-up with her PCP, Dr. Bagga, on 05/17/2004. She denies any trauma to her back. She states that she has numbness and tingling down her leg. She goes to Curves regularly for exercise to help her reduce weight.

continued

PHYSICAL EXAMINATION:

General: She is in acute distress from the pain.

Vital Signs: Blood pressure is 130/80 and temperature is 98.6°.

Neck: Supple.

Back: Spinal tenderness. No CVA tenderness. There is some mild erythema on the right lateral lower middle to upper lower back. There is tenderness over the paraspinal muscles.

ASSESSMENT: Back pain; probably musculoskeletal.

TREATMENT: I started the back manipulation and was able to do two regions of the spine until the patient was unable to tolerate the pain.

Recommend Tylenol or ibuprofen p.r.n. Can continue heat; however, reviewed importance of using warm, not hot, temperature to avoid burning. Can use heat t.i.d. to q.i.d. about 20 min at a time. Reviewed proper lifting. The patient will hold off going to Curves for a few days until symptoms improve. If she develops new symptoms, such as rash or dysuria before her next visit, she will return to the office for reevaluation. She will return in 1 week.

Procedure code(s): _____

Diagnosis code(s): _____

Scenario 9-16

OFFICE NOTE

Martha Conlon is a 19-year-old nulliparous patient who presents today without complaint. Her past history is reviewed and is little changed, other than that she has now graduated from high school and will be a freshman at Clark University. Of note is that she has an unpleasant reaction to milk and she was advised to use calcium supplementation. There is no family history of cancer.

Review of systems is negative with the exception that she wears glasses and suffers from constipation and diarrhea. She attributes this to nerves about going to college and moving out of home for the first time.

On physical examination, weight is 114 lb. Blood pressure is 98/68. Last menstrual period was July 25. HEENT is within normal limits. Neck is supple. No thyromegaly. Heart has regular rate and rhythm. Lungs are clear to auscultation bilaterally. Breasts are symmetrical without suspicious masses, nipple discharge, or axillary or supraclavicular lymph nodes. Abdomen is soft and nontender. She has a pierced navel. On GYN exam, she has normal external female genitalia. Vagina and cervix are within normal limits. Pap was done. GC and chlamydia were done. On bimanual examination, the uterus is anteverted, smooth, and nontender. She has a palpable right ovary with what is likely a functional cyst. No palpable left ovary. Rectovaginal exam was not done. The college requires her to have an updated immunization, which includes the meningicoccal vaccine, and she also asked about the HPV vaccine.

IMPRESSION: Normal GYN exam on teenager.

PLAN:

1. GC and chlamydia done; the patient will be notified by letter.

2. Both the meningicoccal vaccine and HPV vaccine were given to her.

3. The patient is using condoms as well as birth control pills.

4. Rx: Tri-Sprintec Lo, 1 pack with 12 refills.

5. Return in one year.

Procedure code(s): _____

Diagnosis code(s): _____

Scenario 9-17

OFFICE NOTE

Sarah is here today for her 2-week visit. I saw her at her birth, and she had no problems except a little jaundice, which has cleared.

EXAM: Today's weight is 9 lb 4 oz, length 27 in. She has gained 2 lb. The baby was very jaundiced a day after her birth, and this has cleared up very nicely. Sarah's eyes are clear; she reacts to sounds. Her hips are not displaced. All other systems are negative.

Spoke to mom regarding the baby's sleep position; the baby should be placed on her back. Asked her if the baby is in a car seat at all times while driving and that it should never be placed in the front seat. Also pointed out that seat should always be facing backward in the back seat. Mom does not smoke but the dad does, but mom states that he only smokes outside. I let her know that babies of parents who smoke have a higher incidence of asthma, ear infections, and colds. The baby does not have any feeding issues.

The baby will get her first series of shots today. I let her know about the side effects and to give the baby Tylenol for pain and any fever associated with the shots. If the fever persists, she should call me. I reassured her.

Diphtheria-Tetanus-Acellular-Pertussis (DTaP), the Inactive Polio Vaccine (IPV), Haemophilus influenzae type b (Hib), and Hep B #1 were given to the baby.

IMPRESSION AND PLAN: Healthy baby. Will see her back in 1 month, and at that time she will get her second series of shots.

Procedure code(s): _____

Diagnosis code(s): _____

Scenario 9-18

OPERATIVE REPORT

ANESTHESIA: Sedation.

PREOPERATIVE DIAGNOSIS: Rectal mass, carcinoma.

POSTOPERATIVE DIAGNOSIS: Rectal mass, carcinoma.

OPERATION: Limited colonoscopy.

INDICATIONS: This is a 46-year-old male with a large symptomatic rectal mass who is scheduled for colonoscopy. The risk of bleeding, perforation, and missing malignant lesions was discussed. He understands the risks.

PROCEDURE: The patient was placed on the endoscopy table in the decubitus position. A digital exam was performed that revealed a large fungating rectal mass. The patient did not follow his colonoscopy prep fully and therefore the colonoscope is not able to be advanced out of the sigmoid colon. His colon is filled with solid stool because it is largely unprepped. The rectal mass is easily identifiable. It is occupying at least two-thirds of the circumference, and it is fairly large in size. It is palpable easily with an examining finger. I am able to get the colonoscope through this without difficulty and therefore there is no obstruction. Bx was taken of the mass and sent down for reading. When the Bx came back postitive, I spoke to the family and it was decided to try the chemotherapy and radiation first. Again, due to poor prep, the exam was then discontinued at that point. The patient has a follow-up next week to see radiation and medical oncology for preop chemo radiation.

Procedure code(s): _____
Diagnosis code(s): _____

Scenario 9-19

OPERATIVE REPORT

DATE OF OPERATION: 02/27/2006.

PROCEDURE: Preliminary catheterization report.

Informed consent was obtained from the patient preoperatively for cardiac catheterization, possible intervention, and IV conscious sedation. ASA classification 3.

Cardiac catheterization included Swan-Ganz catheter, right heart catheter, which showed cardiac output of 4.7, cardiac index 2.7, right atrial pressure 4, wedge pressure 13, PA pressure 27/5, RA saturation 68, PA saturation 65. Ventriculogram showed ejection fraction of 65%, no gradient across the aortic valve.

Coronary angiogram showed right coronary artery 60%–70% midstenosis with diffuse irregularities, anterior descending artery 90%–95% proximal to midstenosis, which is consistent with a culprit lesion. Circumflex luminal irregularities up to 30%. Left main: No stenosis.

COMPLICATIONS: None.

ASSESSMENT: Systolic heart failure.

The case was discussed via telephone with Dr. Mikelson. Patient and family notified. Intervention by Dr. Davidson. See separate note for intervention to the anterior descending artery.

Procedure code(s): _____
Diagnosis code(s): _____

Scenario 9-20

PULMONARY PROCEDURE NOTE

NAME OF PROCEDURE: Postoperative transesophageal echocardiogram.

PROCEDURE: The transesophageal echocardiogram probe was placed back into the heart postoperatively to check the mitral valve.

FINDINGS: Postoperative transesophageal echocardiogram findings: There was a 27-mm bioprosthetic mitral valve, which appeared to be well seated in the mitral valve portion. There was mild mitral regurgitation seen. No significant stenosis was evident. Aortic valve was atherosclerotic without any stenosis.

The left ventricular function appeared to be preserved. No significant wall motion abnormalities were seen. The left atrium appeared enlarged. There was no clot seen in the left atrial appendage.

Right atrium is normal. There was mild tricuspid regurgitation seen. The pulmonary valve was not well seen. There was no pericardial effusion seen. There was no intracardiac mass seen. There was an intra-aortic balloon pump in place and there was a pacer wire seen in the right-sided chambers.

Procedure code(s): _____

Diagnosis code(s): _____

CHAPTER REVIEW

Using the *CPT* and *HCPCS* manuals and this textbook, complete the following exercises.

Define the following:

1. Technical component _____
2. Nuclear medicine _____
3. Modifier 26 _____
4. Clinical Laboratory Improvement Act (CLIA) _____
5. Modifier QW _____

Find the following CPT codes and identify what coding rule or symbol the medical coder would use.

6. When moderate (conscious) sedation is administered, would the medical coder always report this service separately? _____
7. A 6-year-old child comes in for an annual exam. As part of that exam, the physician discusses the benefits and risks of the planned immunizations

with the parent. Can the administration of the immunization be reported in addition to the visit code? _____.
What code would be used? _____

8. Must modifier QW be appended to every lab test performed in the medical office? _____

9. True or false: The Medicine chapter of *CPT* has all of the procedures that do not fit into the other chapters in *CPT*. True or False? Why or why not?
_____

10. What section of the Medicine chapter includes a sleep test subsection?
_____

When abstracting from medical records, here are some things to remember:

- Always look for a *what* and a *why*. What procedure was done (*CPT*), and why it was done (*ICD-9*).
- The *why* is the medical necessity for what was done; so linking the *what* and *why* is the key to medical coding.
- Follow the rules in the manuals closely.
- Don't let the length of the medical note prevent you from being able to code it. With your pencils, highlighters, and rulers, mark up a *copy* of the notes.
- One last thing: Have a medical dictionary, a book of medical abbreviations, or any other reference materials that can help you get the correct information. You cannot code a diagnosis or procedure if you don't know what you are coding.
- Double-check all the information you are given. If you make assumptions and you are wrong, then you have coded incorrectly.

CHAPTER EXERCISES

Scenario 10-1

OPERATIVE REPORT

PREOPERATIVE DIAGNOSIS: Pelvic organ prolapse.

POSTOPERATIVE DIAGNOSIS: Pelvic organ prolapse.

PROCEDURE: Examination under anesthesia, total vaginal hysterectomy, anterior repair.

ANESTHESIA: General.

COMPLICATIONS: None.

EBL: 150 cc.

IV FLUIDS: 1,400 cc.

FINDINGS: On exam under anesthesia, the patient was noted to have a large cystocele grade 2 to 3 with uterine prolapse. The posterior wall of the vagina was well supported. She was noted to have a small uterus that was anteverted, no adnexal mass.

continued

SPECIMENS:

1. Uterus with cervix weighing 200 g

2. Vaginal mucosa

PROCEDURE: The patient was taken to the operating room where she was placed in high dorsal lithotomy position. When she was comfortable, she was then placed under general anesthesia without any difficulty. Exam under anesthesia was performed with the findings noted above. She was then prepped and draped in the normal sterile fashion in the dorsal lithotomy position. A weighted speculum was placed in the vagina, and the cervix was grasped with 2 sweetheart tenaculums. The cervix was circumferentially incised with the scalpel, and the bladder was dissected off the pubovesical cervical fascia anteriorly with a sponge stick and the Metzenbaum Scissors. The same procedure was performed posteriorly and the posterior cul-de-sac was entered sharply without difficulty. A Heaney clamp was placed over the uterosacral ligaments on either side. These were used to transect and suture ligated the uterosacral ligaments with 1 chromic. Hemostasis was assured. The anterior cul-de-sac was then entered bluntly. The cardinal ligaments were then fulgurated using the gyrus curved clamp. The cauterized areas were then cut using Mayo scissors. This procedure was repeated until we reached the cornuae, which were clamped with Heaney clamps, transected and the uterus delivered. The pedicles were suture ligated with excellent hemostasis. The vaginal cuff angles were closed with figure-of-eight stitches of 1 chromic on both sides and transfixed to the ipsilateral cardinal and uterosacral ligaments. The posterior vaginal cuff was closed with 1 chromic in a running locked stitch. Attention was then turned to the anterior wall of the vagina, which was incised along the dependent portion of the cystocele from approximately 1 cm below the urethra down to the cut edge of the anterior vaginal cuff. The anterior wall mucosa was sharply and bluntly dissected off of the bladder. The submucosal tissue on the bladder was then plicated using 3-0 chromic. This offered good support to the bladder. The vaginal mucosa was then trimmed and closed using 3-0 chromic in a running locked fashion. Two pieces of surgical sponge were placed between the anterior and posterior cuffs of the vaginal wall, and the anterior and posterior cuffs were tacked together. The vagina appeared hemostatic. All instruments were removed from the vagina. The patient was taken out of high lithotomy position, then awakened from anesthesia.

She tolerated the procedure well. Sponge, lap, needle, and instrument counts were correct ×2. The patient was taken to recovery awake and in good condition.

Procedure code(s): _____

Diagnosis code(s): _____

Scenario 10-2

OPERATIVE REPORT

PREOPERATIVE DIAGNOSIS: Displaced right femoral neck fracture.

POSTOPERATIVE DIAGNOSIS: Displaced right femoral neck fracture.

PROCEDURE: Noncemented herniarthroplasty right.

ANESTHESIA: Spinal.

HISTORY: The patient is an 86-year-old white male who used to be extremely active. It was about a month ago that he began complaining of right-sided hip pain which gradually has become debilitating. He apparently has some normal x-rays from August 11, but he presented to the hospital on August 24, 2006 with a significant increase in hip pain and at that time x-rays showed a significantly displaced femoral neck fracture. It was a possibility that the fracture had been displaced for some time and the soft tissues might be tight. The decision was made to proceed with a right herniarthroplasty, which could be converted to a total hip arthroplasty should it dislocate. The patient was medically cleared.

PROCEDURE: He was brought to the operating room on August 25, 2006. He received 1 g of Ancef preoperatively. He was brought to the operating room and after induction of spinal anesthesia was positioned on the table and held in place with a beanbag and kidney bars. There was noted to be no evidence of bruising over the thigh. He did have a decubitus ulcer on the left buttock. The right hip was sterilely prepped and draped. All bony prominences were padded. The incision was made over the greater trochanter heading posteriorly. The soft tissues were dissected through. A large liquefied hematoma was identified. There was scarring in the soft tissues. The fascia was opened in the direction of its fibers. The short external rotators were identified. The piriformis was noted to be significantly scarred to the capsule. It was tagged and cut. It could not be separated from the capsule. A T was made in the capsule and the femoral head was removed. It was measured and found to be approximately 55 mm. The trials were utilized and a 55 mm was found to fit best. A hip skid was placed under the femoral neck. The trial was utilized to ascertain the neck cut, which was made approximately 1 cm above the lesser trochanter. The oscillating saw was used to complete the cut and then the box osteotome was utilized followed by the femoral canal locator. The distal reamers were utilized and a size 14 fit well. Then the broaches were utilized. A size 4 broach had an excellent fit with no micromotion. The components were trialed, and it was possible to reduce them although he initially was quite tight. He had no evidence of a knee flexion contracture in full extension. He had full flexion with 70° of internal rotation and 40° of adduction prior to any levering. The wound was irrigated. The calcar reamer was utilized. The trial components were then removed. A #4 reliance stem with the distal taper of 14 was then press-fit into place. It was extremely stable. A 26-mm head with the standard neck and a 55 Universal head component was then cold welded into place. The acetabulum was ascertained to make sure that there was no soft tissue interposition. The hip was reduced. The hip was stable. The capsule was approximated with 0 Vicryl. The piriformis structure along with the capsule was attached to the lateral femur. The soft tissues were approximated with a running suture proximally and a figure-of-eight inverted interrupted 0 Vicryl distally. The soft tissues were approximated with 2-0 Vicryl and 3-0 Vicryl, and the skin was closed with staples. Xeroform was placed over the incision. Soft tissues were placed followed by foam tape. An abduction pillow was placed between the legs and the bean bag was then let down and he was turned into the supine position. His leg lengths were checked and he was noted to have equal leg lengths. His version was equal. He was then transferred to his bed and taken to the recovery room. He received 1 g of Kefzol, 800 cc of fluid and had approximately 100 cc of blood loss. He tolerated the procedure well.

Procedure code(s): _____

Diagnosis code(s): _____

Scenario 10-3

OPERATIVE REPORT

PROCEDURE PERFORMED: Upper endoscopy with biopsies.

PREOPERATIVE DIAGNOSIS: Abdominal pain, gastroesophageal reflux disease, and failure to thrive. Rule out celiac disease.

POSTOPERATIVE DIAGNOSIS: Esophagitis, gastritis.

EQUIPMENT USED: Adult video Lipper endoscope.

ANESTHESIA: General endotracheal anesthesia.

INFORMED CONSENT: History and physical examination were performed. Indications and complications (bleeding, infection, perforation, adverse reaction to medication) and alternatives available were explained to the patient and his mother who appeared to understand and indicated this. Opportunity for questions was provided and informed consent was obtained.

PROCEDURE: After the patient was placed in the left lateral decubitus position, the endoscope was inserted into the oral cavity and Linder direct visualization achieved, the esophagus was intubated. The endoscope was advanced through the esophagus to the stomach and duodenum. A careful inspection was made as the endoscope was withdrawn. The patient tolerated the procedure well. There were no complications.

FINDINGS: Esophageal mucosa revealed linear ridges and erythema in the mid and distal esophagus. No ulcerations were noted. No hiatal hernia was noted. Biopsies were obtained along with photo documentation from the mid and distal esophagus.

Gastric mucosa revealed erythema in the antrum. No ulcerations were noted. Biopsies were obtained along with photo documentation.

Duodenal mucosa appeared to be normal. Biopsies were obtained from the duodenum and duodenal bulb.

IMPRESSION: Gastritis, esophagitis. Possible eosinophilic esophagitis.

PLAN: Shall await biopsy results. Will continue current medications.

Procedure code(s): _____

Diagnosis code(s): _____

Scenario 10-4

OFFICE NOTE

Mrs. Bleakley lives in Florida. She visits here in the summer. She is seen here today with 2 areas of erythema and scaling with some peripheral papery appearance on her nose.

Lesions have been biopsied in the past and treated on several occasions by her physician in Florida with liquid nitrogen. I am planning quick curettage and desiccation for the next visit to obtain a tissue for pathology again. She is leaving for Maine and her procedure will be scheduled for a later date. She is also concerned about a lesion of her left breast where, on examination, seborrheic keratosis is seen and reassurance is given to her as to the benign nature of this lesion.

Procedure code(s): _____

Diagnosis code(s): _____

OPERATIVE REPORT—SURGICAL VISIT

Mrs. Bleakley is seen here today for her surgical visit. Two lesions of the nose were curetted and desiccated today. The patient tolerated the procedure very well. She identified the lesions. Operative note is attached and specimen is sent to the Pathology laboratory. The patient is leaving for Fort Myers where she lives most of her time, and the pathology report will be called in to her at this location.

Procedure code(s): _____

Diagnosis code(s): _____

Scenario 10-5

PROCEDURE NOTE

PROCEDURE: Traction removal of percutaneously placed endoscopic gastrostomy tube.

INDICATION: Patient had a PEG placed by another physician on 5/27/2006 when he was on a ventilator and had a tracheostomy following colectomy and ileostomy. Patient has now recovered and is eating normally. He is not using the PEG.

PROCEDURE IN DETAIL: The PEG site is cleaned with Betadine and alcohol. Anesthesia of 1% Xylocaine was injected around the PEG site. The PEG was then removed with traction without difficulty. There was minimal bleeding after the procedure. Bacitracin dressing was applied. Postprocedure orders sent to the nursing home.

FINAL IMPRESSION: Successful PEG removal. Post procedure orders sent to the nursing home.

Procedure code(s): _____

Diagnosis code(s): _____

Scenario 10-6

OPERATIVE REPORT

PREOPERATIVE DIAGNOSIS: Foreign body in left eye.

POSTOPERATIVE DIAGNOSIS: Foreign body in left eye.

PROCEDURE: Magnetic extraction of metallic foreign body.

COMPLICATIONS: None.

PROCEDURE IN DETAIL: The risks and benefits of the surgery were discussed at length with the patient including bleeding, infection, retinal detachment, reoperation, lost vision, lost eye. Informed consent was obtained.

Superior limbal clear corneal 3.2 mm incision was made at least 90° away from the IOFB site. After injecting Healon GV to maintain the anterior chamber, a 20 g intravitreal foreign body magnet (Synergetics) was introduced into the anterior chamber and IOFB was gently dislodged and extracted via the incision. Residual Healon GV was expressed out by irrigation. No intraoperative bleeding or iridodialysis was noticed.

The lid speculum and drapes were carefully removed. Several drops of Ocuflox were applied to the eye. The eye was covered and patched with the shield. The patient was taken to the recovery room in good condition. There were no complications.

The postoperative follow-up at 1, 2, 6, and 12 weeks revealed minimal inflammation with both eyes retaining their preoperative BCVA. No development of cataract was seen.

Procedure code(s): _____

Diagnosis code(s): _____

Scenario 10-7

OPERATIVE REPORT

DIAGNOSIS: Subacute subdural hematoma on the right.

PROCEDURE PERFORMED: Right craniotomy for evacuation of subdural hematoma.

ANESTHESIA: General endotracheal anesthesia.

ESTIMATED BLOOD LOSS: 200 cc.

COMPLICATIONS: There were no complications during the case.

BRIEF HISTORY AND INDICATIONS: The patient is an 84-year-old female with a history of hitting her head approximately a week prior and developing acute problems with confusion today. The patient was found to have a large right subacute subdural hematoma. It was decided to take the patient to surgery.

OPERATIVE PROCEDURE AND FINDINGS: I met with the patient and family in the preoperative area. All questions and concerns were addressed. The patient was then given preoperative Dilantin, Decadron, and antibiotics and was taken to the operating theater where, after adequate general anesthesia was achieved by the anesthesia team, the patient was placed supine on the operating table with a shoulder roll under the right shoulder and the head turned to the left. The right side of the head was shaved, prepped, and draped in the usual sterile surgical fashion. Incision was made at the coronal suture in a linear fashion and was carried down through the subcutaneous tissues and the self-retaining retractors were placed to maintain the exposure. Meticulous hemostasis was achieved using bipolar Bovie cautery. A single burr hole was placed in a high frontal area at the coronal suture and was carried down to the dura. The high-speed drill was used to turn a small craniotomy flap. The dura was tacked circumferentially to the bone and the dura was opened in a cruciate fashion. A large amount of subacute blood was expressed and irrigated using bulb irrigation. A 7-mm flat JP drain was placed subdurally, externalized from the skin, and secured with 3-0 nylon stitch. A piece of Gelfoam was placed. The dura was reapproximated using 4-0 Nurolon stitches and a piece of Gelfoam was placed on the dura. The bone flap was reapproximated using 3 cranial clamps, and a subdural Hemovac drain was placed and externalized from the skin and secured with 3-0 nylon stitch. The incision was then closed using interrupted Vicryl stitches and staples were placed on the skin. A dry sterile dressing was applied. The patient was taken intubated to the intensive care unit. There were no complications during the case.

Procedure code(s): _____

Diagnosis code(s): _____

Scenario 10-8

OPERATIVE REPORT

OPERATION: Proctoileoscopy with biopsy.

INDICATION: Patient is status post total colectomy with J pouch ileoanal anastomosis. The patient comes for surveillance but is also having diarrhea and possible pouchitis.

MEDICATIONS: No sedatives were given.

PROCEDURE: With the patient in the left lateral position, rectal examination was performed. This was normal. The Olympus PCF-160AL colonoscope was then introduced into the anal sphincter and advanced into the colon through the residual rectum into the J pouch. The scope was then advanced into the blind loop of the J pouch as well as the terminal ileum. The scope was then withdrawn from the J pouch. Biopsies were obtained of the J pouch. Biopsies were also obtained of the residual rectum for dysplasia surveillance.

ENDOSCOPIC FINDINGS: Terminal ileum is normal. There is proctitis involving the pouch, especially the blind end of the pouch. The rectum appears uninflamed.

FINAL IMPRESSION: Pouchitis in a patient who is status post colectomy and J pouch creation. There is no endoscopic involvement of the native terminal ileum and the rectum itself. The anal sphincter is also normal.

It is recommended that the patient take Flagyl 500 mg 3 times a day for 2 weeks. The patient should call me at the end of 2 weeks in follow-up.

Procedure code(s): _____

Diagnosis code(s): _____

Scenario 10-9

OPERATIVE REPORT

PREOPERATIVE DIAGNOSIS: Right breast cancer.

POSTOPERATIVE DIAGNOSIS: Revision of right reconstructed breast, scar revision, right axillary mastectomy incision (8 cm).

ANESTHESIA: General.

PROCEDURE: After adequate anesthesia had been obtained, the patient was prepped and draped. An 8 cm segment of the lateral aspect of the right mastectomy incision line was excised and passed off the field for specimen. The incision was carried medially. An incision was then made in the upper outer quadrant of the right capsule. The implant was removed. The inferior aspect of the right capsule at the inframammary fold was incised. A sizer was placed and filled to 625 ml. The patient was placed in the upright sitting position. This was slightly larger than what appeared to be symmetric, and the volume was reduced to 600 ml. This appeared to achieve good symmetry. The original implant was then reinserted (the original implant was a 575 cc implant inflated to 600 cc of normal saline). The incision lines were then closed using a combination of 3-0 Vicryl, 4-0 Vicryl, 3-0 Monocryl, and 3-0 nylon. Steri-Strips and a dry sterile dressing were applied. The patient tolerated the procedure well.

Procedure code(s): _____

Diagnosis code(s): _____

Scenario 10-10

OPERATIVE REPORT

PROCEDURE PERFORMED: Upper endoscopy with biopsies.

PREOPERATIVE DIAGNOSES: Abdominal pain, GERD.

POSTOPERATIVE DIAGNOSES: Esophagitis, gastritis.

ANESTHESIA: General endotracheal anesthesia.

DESCRIPTION OF PROCEDURE: Informed consent, history, and physical examination were performed. Indications and complications (bleeding, infection, perforation, adverse reaction to medication) and alternatives available were explained to the patient and his mother who appeared to understand and indicated this. Opportunity for questions was provided and informed consent was obtained.

PROCEDURE: After placing the patient in the left lateral decubitus position, the endoscope was inserted into the oral cavity and under direct visualization the esophagus was intubated. The endoscope was advanced to the esophagus, stomach, and duodenum. A careful inspection was made as the endoscope was withdrawn. The patient tolerated the procedure well. There were no complications.

FINDINGS: Upper endoscopy: Esophageal mucosa revealed question of a ring in the junction of the mid and distal esophagus. Erythema in the antrum and body was observed. No ulcerations were noted. Biopsies were obtained along with photo documentation. The duodenal mucosa appeared to be normal. Biopsies were obtained along with photo documentation.

IMPRESSION: Gastritis, esophagitis.

PLAN: Shall await biopsy results.

Procedure code(s): _____

Diagnosis code(s): _____

Scenario 10-11

OPERATIVE REPORT

DIAGNOSIS:

1. Lumbar spondylolisthesis

2. Lumbar stenosis

ANESTHESIA: General endotracheal.

ESTIMATED BLOOD LOSS: 300 cc.

COMPLICATIONS: There were no complications during the case.

PROCEDURE PERFORMED: Bilateral L4-L5 and S1 decompressive laminectomies and L4-L5 pedicle transarticular screw fixation bilaterally.

BRIEF HISTORY AND INDICATIONS: The patient is a 61-year-old gentleman with lumbar spondylolisthesis and severe lumbar stenosis at L4-L5 and L5-S1 and history of severe bilateral leg pain and lower back pain. The patient was considered for surgical intervention at that time. For further details, please refer to the hospital chart.

OPERATIVE PROCEDURE AND FINDINGS: I met with the patient in the holding area and all questions were addressed. Following that, the patient was taken to the operating theater, given preoperative antibiotics and, after adequate general anesthesia was achieved by the anesthesia team, the patient was placed prone on a Camden frame and all pressure points were examined and padded. The lower back was then shaved, prepped, and draped in the usual sterile surgical fashion. Incision was made at the midline and was carried down through the subcutaneous tissues and the lumbosacral fascia to expose the lamina of L4-L5 and S1 bilaterally in a subperiosteal fashion. Self-retaining retractors were placed to maintain exposure. Meticulous hemostasis was achieved using bipolar and cautery, and the localization x-ray was obtained to confirm the correct level. Internal, external, and radiographic landmarks were used to place the pedicle screws in L4-L5 bilaterally. Bilateral laminectomies of L4-L5 and S1 were carried out by removing the spinous process using a Leksell Rongeur and the lamina were drilled down using a high-speed drill and removed using 3- and 4-mm Kerrisons. A durotomy was found in the dural surface, which was repaired using running 5-0 Prolene stitch. Two Valsalva maneuvers following that revealed no significant spinal fluid leak. Following that, the meticulous arthrodesis was carried out at L4-L5 and L5-S1, and the bone laterally was decorticated using a high-speed drill. The left hip was accessed through a separate incision and bone marrow was obtained for the Healos graft. The allograft, autograft, and bone marrow were then mixed together with the Healos and placed into the lateral gutters. A piece of DuraGen was placed on the dural repair and was covered with Tisseel. Meticulous hemostasis was achieved using bipolar Bovie cautery. The incision was then closed using interrupted Vicryl stitches, and a running locked nylon stitch was placed on the skin.

continued

The patient was extubated in the operating room and transferred to the recovery room in stable condition. There were no complications during the case.

Procedure code(s): _____

Diagnosis code(s): _____

Scenario 10-12

OPERATIVE REPORT

PREOPERATIVE DIAGNOSIS: Right knee medial meniscus tear.

POSTOPERATIVE DIAGNOSIS: Right knee medial meniscus tear.

PROCEDURE: Right knee arthroscopic partial medial meniscectomy.

INDICATIONS: The patient is a 45-year-old woman who has persistent pain and dysfunction from the right knee. She has failed a thorough conservatively managed rehabilitation program and I have reviewed with her the risks, benefits, and alternatives of surgery. She has agreed to proceed. Informed consent has been obtained and is in the chart.

FINDINGS: Examination of the right knee under anesthesia demonstrated full passive range of motion, no capsular restriction. The patellofemoral joint demonstrated the articular cartilage of the patella to have grade 3 chondromalacia of the central facet with deep fissuring. No significant signs of osteoarthritis within the patella. The trochlear groove demonstrated grade 3 chondromalacia appreciated with minimal osteoarthritis. The medial compartment demonstrated maceration of most of the medial meniscus to within 3 mm of the capsular rim. There was exposed bone over the peripheral medial tibial plateau and peripheral medial femoral condyle. The majority of the compartment had grade 3 chondromalacia. Only a small area of grade 4 chondromalacia was noted. The intercondylar notch demonstrated ACL and PCL to be visualized and intact. The lateral compartment demonstrated articular cartilage to be intact. No evidence of osteoarthritis.

PROCEDURE: The patient was brought to the operating room and placed in a supine position on the operating table. After induction of general anesthesia by the anesthetic team, the patient's right knee and lower extremity were prepped and draped in the usual manner. A tourniquet was placed over Webril padding to the right upper thigh. A leg holder was utilized to aid in varus and valgus manipulation of the knee. A Linvatec arthroscopic pump was used to aid in inflow and outflow. A diagnostic arthroscopy was then performed with standard parapatellar portals. A superomedial portal was established for outflow. Findings were noted as previously dictated in the finding section. At the conclusion of diagnostic arthroscopy, I directed my attention to the medial meniscus.

Utilizing a combination of handheld instruments and a motorized shaver, a partial medial meniscectomy was carried out until a smooth contour was left. The portals were switched and a partial medial meniscectomy was completed. I removed all meniscal debris with the motorized shaver. I then injected the knee with 10 cc of 0.25% Marcaine with epinephrine and 5 mg of Duramorph. Portals were closed with interrupted nylon sutures.

Procedure code(s): _____

Diagnosis code(s): _____

Scenario 10-13

OPERATIVE REPORT

PREOPERATIVE DIAGNOSIS: End-stage renal disease requiring hemodialysis.

POSTOPERATIVE DIAGNOSIS: End-stage renal disease requiring hemodialysis.

PROCEDURE: Right upper extremity arteriovenous fistula using cephalic vein and radial artery.

BLOOD LOSS: Minimal.

FINDINGS: Very diminutive cephalic vein. There was, however, at the end of the case, a strong Doppler signal throughout the course of the cephalic vein and a bruit as well.

INDICATIONS AND HISTORY: Ms. Morison is a very pleasant 58-year-old woman who has end-stage renal disease. She is currently receiving hemodialysis through a Hickman catheter. Previously, she had had a transplant that unfortunately failed. She is currently back on the waiting list for a transplant and required access in the meantime for dialysis. Therefore, after obtaining informed consent, the above procedure was performed.

INFORMED CONSENT: Ms. Morison understood that the risks include but are not limited to bleeding, infection, failure of the fistula, steal syndrome causing hand ischemia, radial nerve damage, scarring, and postoperative discomfort.

DESCRIPTION OF PROCEDURES AND FINDINGS: Patient was brought to the operating room and placed in the supine position on the table. Cardiopulmonary monitoring devices were placed and antibiotics were administered. She was then prepped and draped in the standard sterile fashion. One percent lidocaine with 0.5% Marcaine was then infiltrated in the right wrist for a local field block. An incision was made over the radial pulse and brought down through the skin and subcutaneous tissues. The radial artery was easily identified, and proximal and distal control was obtained with Vesseloops. Subsequently, the cephalic vein was identified and was noted to be very small in its caliber. The vein was mobilized, ligated at its distal end, and then transected. The vein was then spatulated. Ms. Morison was administered 5,000 units of intravenous heparin, and then the Vesseloops were tightened. An arteriotomy was made with an 11 blade and carried proximally and distally with the Potts scissors. The fistula was then created and the anastomosis performed using a running 7-0 Prolene suture. Prior to completion of the anastomosis, the arteries were allowed to backbleed and flush, and the area was copiously irrigated with heparinized saline. The anastomosis was then completed and the distal loop was loosened. There were 2 areas of hemorrhage, which were oversewn with figure-of-eight sutures of 7-0 Prolene. Subsequently, there was no more hemorrhage. The vein did distend and there was a good Doppler signal along the course of the cephalic vein in the forearm, which disappeared when the vein was pinched off. The more proximal loop was also loosened, and there was noted to be a good radial Doppler signal as well as a good u1nar Doppler signal of the right hand. Her right hand was warm and pink also. The wound was then irrigated and the skin reapproximated with vertical mattress sutures of 3-0 nylon. The sponge, needle, and instrument counts were correct at the end of the case ×2, and I was present and scrubbed through the entire procedure.

Procedure code(s): _____

Diagnosis code(s): _____

Scenario 10-14

OPERATIVE REPORT

PREOPERATIVE DIAGNOSIS: Right ankle instability.

POSTOPERATIVE DIAGNOSIS: Right ankle instability.

PROCEDURE: Right ankle stabilization.

ANESTHESIA: General.

HISTORY OF PRESENT ILLNESS: The patient is a 44-year-old white female who sustained an injury while running. She has been unable to run. She has strengthened up her peroneal muscle and we have completed conservative intervention. The majority of her discomfort is gone, but she has persistent discomfort over the ankle ligaments. The patient has noted that when she is sleeping at nighttime, if she does not put a pillow underneath her ankle, she has a significant amount of pain over the anterior aspect of her ankle, which is consistent with an anterior drawer maneuver causing pain. She has a positive anterior drawer. The decision was made to proceed with ankle stabilization.

PREOPERATIVE EXAMINATION: Preoperatively in the holding area, she was noted to have no pain to palpation over the peroneal tendons. She has only scant pain over the medial aspect of the ankle. The majority of the pain was along the lateral aspect of the ankle and slightly anteriorly. She had negative Tinsel's over the superficial nerve. She had some discomfort to palpation over the deep peroneal nerve. She received her 1 g of Ancef and was brought to the operating room.

PROCEDURE IN DETAIL: After induction of anesthesia, a bump was placed underneath her right hip, and her right leg was sterilely prepped and draped in the usual fashion. An incision was made over the anterior and distal aspect of the fibula, curving over the extensor retinaculum. The soft tissues were dissected through. The ankle ligaments were noted to be attenuated. The ankle ligaments were dissected free from the distal fibula. The ankle joint was evaluated. There were no osteochondral lesions identified. There was some synovitic ligamentous debris, especially in the anterior superior gutter. A rongeur was utilized to make a bony trough in the anterior and distal aspects of the fibula. The calcaneal fibular ligament was identified and it was noted to be significantly attenuated. Then four #1 Ethilons were placed through the lateral aspect of the fibular cortex out through the bony trough; 2 were placed into the calcaneal fibular ligament area and 2 were placed into the anterior talofibular ligament area. The sutures were then brought back through the trough and out the lateral side of the fibula. The soft tissue covering over the fibula had been dissected free so as to provide a covering over the sutures because the patient was very slender. A bump was placed underneath the distal tibia to prevent an anterior drawer. The foot was then placed into maximum dorsiflexed everted position and the sutures were tied down. The extensor retinaculum had been identified and dissected free and this was then brought up and over the repair and sewed in place with 0 Vicryl. This led to a very stable repair. She had full dorsiflexion and plantar flexion. She no longer had a positive anterior drawer. She had limitation of inversion. The wound was irrigated and then approximated with 3-0 Vicryl followed by 3-0 nylon. Marcaine was injected. Xeroform was placed over the incision, followed by a soft dressing, sterile Webril, a U splint and a posterior splint holding the foot and ankle in neutral. She received 800 cc of fluid, 1 g of Kefzol, 30 mg of Toradol and had

> minimal blood loss. She was extubated and taken to the recovery room in stable condition.

Procedure code(s): _____

Diagnosis code(s): _____

Scenario 10-15

OPERATIVE REPORT

PREOPERATIVE DIAGNOSIS: Left shoulder impingement syndrome.

POSTOPERATIVE DIAGNOSIS: Left shoulder impingement syndrome, glenohumeral osteoarthritis.

OPERATIVE PROCEDURE: Left shoulder arthroscopic acromioplasty.

COMPLICATIONS: None.

INDICATIONS: The patient is a 49-year-old gentleman who has persistent pain and dysfunction of the left shoulder. He has failed a thorough conservatively managed rehabilitation program and I have reviewed with him the risks, benefits, and alternatives of surgery. He has agreed to proceed. Informed consent has been obtained and is in the chart.

FINDINGS: Examination of the left shoulder under anesthesia demonstrated an excellent passive range of motion. No evidence of frozen shoulder was noted. The glenohumeral joint demonstrated grade 4 osteoarthritis of the posterior third of the glenoid down to exposed bone. Approximately a quarter of the humeral head was devoid of articular cartilage secondary to osteoarthritis. He had a moderately sized kissing lesion of the humeral head and glenoid. Biceps tendon was unremarkable. Biceps anchor was normal. Subscapularis demonstrated moderate fraying consistent with partial-thickness tearing. The supraspinatus demonstrated no significant tearing. Subacromial space demonstrated significant subacromial inflammation, curved type 2 acromion. Thickening and fraying of the coraco-acromial ligament was noted. No evidence of bursal articular sided supraspinatus full-thickness tearing.

PROCEDURE: The patient was brought to the operating room, placed in the supine position on the operating table. After induction of general anesthesia by the anesthetic team, the patient's left shoulder and upper extremity were prepped and draped in the usual manner. A modified beach chair position was utilized. All bony prominences were well padded. The left shoulder and upper extremity were prepped and draped. A standard posterior arthroscopic portal was established. An anterior portal was created in an interlocked fashion lateral to the coracoid process. Through these 2 working portals, diagnostic glenohumeral arthroscopy was performed. The findings were noted as previously dictated in the finding section. At the conclusion of diagnostic arthroscopy, I directed my attention to the subacromial space. A midacromial lateral portal was established. A bipolar cautery was inserted. The coraco-acromial ligament was debrided from the undersurface of the acromion extending from the midacromial portal laterally to the acromioclavicular joint

continued

medially. I then utilized a 4.0 acromion and performed an arthroscopic acromioplasty with a cutting block technique from a posterior to anterior direction. The portals were switched. The acromioplasty was completed working from a lateral to medial direction. The undersurface was left completely smooth. Once this was completed, I debrided the subacromial bursa. I then inserted DonJoy Pain Buster catheter into the subacromial space. I preloaded the subacromial space with 20 cc of 0.25% Marcaine with epinephrine and hooked this up to a 100-cc pump of 0.25% Marcaine with epinephrine preset to run at 2 cc/hr.

A dry sterile dressing was applied to the left shoulder. The arm was put into a sling. He tolerated the procedure well. He was extubated in the operating room and transported to the recovery room in stable condition. Sponge and needle counts were correct.

Procedure code(s): _____

Diagnosis code(s): _____

Scenario 10-16

OPERATIVE REPORT

PREOPERATIVE DIAGNOSIS: Facial trauma.

POSTOPERATIVE DIAGNOSIS: Facial trauma.

OPERATION: Facial reconstruction using prosthetic material.

ANESTHESIA: Sedation plus local.

PROCEDURE: After adequate sedation had been obtained, the patient was prepped and draped. The right malar area was infiltrated with 0.5% Bupivacaine. A 3 mm incision was then made in the right nasolabial fold. The prosthetic material was injected into the area of the right malar region, which was slightly depressed secondary to fat atrophy following facial trauma. A 6-0 fast-absorbing was placed in the right nasolabial fold incision. He tolerated the procedure well.

Procedure code(s): _____

Diagnosis code(s): _____

Scenario 10-17

OPERATIVE REPORT

OPERATION: Cystoscopy, vaginoscopy, left retrograde pyelogram, attempted left ureteral stent insertion, and methylene blue cystogram.

PREOPERATIVE DIAGNOSIS: Left ureterovaginal fistula.

POSTOPERATIVE DIAGNOSIS: Left ureterovaginal fistula.

INDICATIONS: This is a 35-year-old female who is now in her third week following a laparoscopic supracervical hysterectomy. Postoperatively, she developed significant discharge of urine from her vagina. A Foley catheter was placed but the significant amount of urine persisted, requiring 9 to 10 pads per day. Otherwise, she was feeling well, tolerating a regular diet, and having normal bowel movements, without fever, left flank pain, or chill. CAT of her abdomen and pelvis demonstrated no hydronephrosis but a probable left ureterovaginal fistula. She was brought to the operating room today for assessment and for further management of this problem. She understood the nature of the procedure, what was to be accomplished, specifically to attempt to perform conservative placement of a left double-J ureteral stent if the leak was small; if not, she would subsequently undergo insertion of a left percutaneous nephrostomy and subsequent left psoas-hitch and left ureteral reimplantation in the near future. We would also perform a methylene blue cystogram and assess the possibility of a vesicovaginal fistula. She understood the possible risks and complications of the procedure and the general anesthetic.

PROCEDURE: The patient was taken to the operating room, placed in the dorsal lithotomy position. After satisfactory general endotracheal anesthesia, intravenous Kefzol was administered. Her entire external genitalia were prepped with Betadine solution and draped in the usual sterile fashion. Panendoscopy was carried out with 22 French Storz pariendoscope and with the 30° lens. The urethra and bladder neck appeared to be unremarkable. There was some squamous metaplasia of the trigone. Both ureteral orifices appeared to be normal in size, position, and configuration. The bladder mucosa throughout was entirely normal and there did not appear to be any extrinsic masses effacing the bladder. With the Albarran attachment, an 8 French cone-tipped catheter was inserted into the left ureteral orifice and water soluble contrast material instilled under fluoroscopic control. This demonstrated a 1.5-cm normal intramural ureter and then extravasation of dye extravesically at the left ureterovesical junction with some media displacement, no evidence of any intact ureter was visualized nor of the dye entering the vagina. We therefore attempted to pass 0.038 Sensorcaine guidewire without success, as it coiled in this inflammatory area extravesically. We then emptied the bladder.

Vaginoscopy was limited because of inability to extend the vagina. By palpation, I did not palpate any masses and intact vaginal cuff. Her indwelling Foley catheter was removed after the anesthesia was induced. We, therefore, inserted a 16 French Foley catheter into the bladder, placed 10 cc of water in the balloon, placed the balloon on traction at the bladder neck, and instilled 400 cc of water-soluble contrast material stained with methylene blue. We had packed the vagina with a lubricated vaginal pack and then removed the vaginal pack with the bladder under distention, and there was no evidence of any vesicovaginal fistula, i.e., no blue staining of the vaginal pack. We, therefore, drained the bladder entirely and obtained a postdrainage film, which demonstrated again no evidence of extravasation of dye or contrast material from the bladder and the retained small amount of dye within the left uretero extravesical area.

We decided no Foley catheter was necessary and the patient will now undergo a left percutaneous nephrostomy at least an antegrade nephrostomy, although I doubt it will be technically possible to insert an antegrade stent. She will most probably need a left ureteral reimplantation with a psoas-hitch in the near future to correct this problem.

Procedure code(s): _____

Diagnosis code(s): _____

Scenario 10-18

OPERATIVE REPORT

PREOPERATIVE DIAGNOSIS: Carcinoma of the left lower lobe, adenocarcinoma.

POSTOPERATIVE DIAGNOSIS: Carcinoma of the left lower lobe, adenocarcinoma.

PROCEDURE:

1. Bronchoscopy

2. Mediastinoscopy (negative after mediastinoscopy)

PROCEDURE: Under adequate general endotracheal anesthesia, bronchoscopy was performed. The carina was sharp. Both sides of the tracheobronchial tree were examined. All segments seen to be widely patent and free of obvious tumor. Scope was removed. The patient was next positioned, prepared, and draped in the usual manner for cervical mediastinoscopy. A transverse incision was made in the neck just above the suprasternal notch and deepened in the midline until the trachea was encountered. The finger was advanced along the anterior surface of the trachea, separating it from surrounding structures, and it separated quite easily. A large scope was advanced inward and downward, and all nodal sites searched for suspicious or enlarged nodes and none identified. Mediastinal evaluation was felt to be negative. Checks made for hemostasis were found to be satisfactory. The scope was removed. The wound closed in layers using interrupted Vicryl on the deeper tissue, closing the skin with a subcuticular stitch. He tolerated the procedure well.

Prior to surgery the patient had a bronchoscopy by Dr. Ross, and this was positive for adenocarcinoma of the left lower lobe.

Procedure code(s): _____
Diagnosis code(s): _____

Scenario 10-19

OPERATIVE REPORT

PREOPERATIVE DIAGNOSIS: Postoperative acquired nasal deformity and nasal vestibular stenosis.

POSTOPERATIVE DIAGNOSIS: Postoperative acquired nasal deformity and nasal vestibular stenosis.

PROCEDURE:

1. Harvesting of septal cartilage

2. Repair of nasal vestibular stenosis of left nasal sidewall with septal cartilage grafts subcutaneously in lower sidewall of nose

3. Excision of nasal labial flap left side of nose, cheek, and upper lip, approximately 2.5 sq. cm

4. Advancement flap of cheek, adjacent tissue transfer to approximately 2.0 sq. cm defect

5. Rotation flap of soft tissue triangle of left upper lip, adjacent tissue transfer, to approximately 0.5 sq. cm defect

ANESTHESIA: General.

COMPLICATIONS: None.

INDICATIONS FOR PROCEDURE: This patient had Moh's micrographic surgery with reconstruction by another surgeon a number of months ago. She has a nasal labial flap that is rounded and she would like it removed. She also has nasal vestibular stenosis on the left side of the nose secondary to scar formation with the flap. In addition, the apex of the soft tissue triangle of the left upper lip has been lateralized by the nasal labial flap. The patient is desirous of improvement in the appearance of her nose and upper lip. In addition, I will treat the nasal vestibular stenosis. Although the nasal vestibular stenosis is mild to moderate at this point, I am concerned about further scar formation of the nose making it worse. The patient has been advised of the risks and benefits of surgery including risks of scarring and bony infection and need for possible further functional or aesthetic surgery. No guarantee has been given with regard to functional or aesthetic results. She has also been advised of the risks of cerebrospinal fluid leak, anosmia, and septal perforation.

PROCEDURE: Under satisfactory general anesthesia with a gastric tube in place and an endotracheal tube in place and after prepping and draping in the usual fashion, a Killian incision was made on the right side of the nasal septum. A mucoperichondrial flap was elevated and a portion of quadrilateral cartilage was harvested leaving a very adequate L-shaped strut. The patient had a very short quadrilateral cartilage. The septal flaps were then reapproximated with a running quilting suture of 4-0 plain gut. The drainage hole was created posteriorly on the left side. Doyle splints were placed on either side of the septum and sutured in place with 3-0 Prolene. The tubes were filled with Bactroban.

The nasal labial flap of the left side of nose was then carefully excised. An incision was also made from the apex of the soft tissue triangle about 1.5 cm down the nasal labial crease. A rotation flap was undermined and rotated into position in order to place the apex of the soft tissue triangle back up at a more appropriate level. This rotation flap was sutured in place deeply in the subcutaneous and subcuticular layers with 4-0 PDS. The cheek was then undermined for a distance of approximately 2 cm laterally. An advancement flap of the cheek was then brought medially. Prior to suturing the flap in place, a subcutaneous pocket was placed underneath an area of retraction of the sidewall just above the alar subunit. Two pieces of cartilage were placed in this area, one more medially and one more laterally. The pieces of cartilage measured about 1.5 cm × 1 cm each. The cheek flap was then advanced medially and thinned and trimmed as needed. A dart was placed above the alar to get the correct shape of the alar as much as possible. The patient's alar had been shortened by the original surgery. She did not want a total alar reconstruction so she understands the alar will still be a bit shorter. The advancement flap was then sutured in subcutaneous layers with 4-0 PDS. The skin was closed with 6-0 fast-absorbing gut along the advancement flap and along the rotation flap of the upper lip. Steri-Strips were applied. The patient was then awakened from anesthesia and taken to the recovery room in satisfactory condition. She tolerated the procedure well. There were no complications and no significant blood loss.

Procedure code(s): _____

Diagnosis code(s): _____

Scenario 10-20

OPERATIVE REPORT

PREOPERATIVE DIAGNOSIS: Left cholesteatoma.

POSTOPERATIVE DIAGNOSIS: Left cholesteatoma.

NAME OF PROCEDURE: Left tympanomastoidectomy with NINIS monitoring.

DESCRIPTION OF PROCEDURE: Under general endotracheal anesthesia, the ear was injected with 11% Xylocaine with 1:100,000 epinephrine. The patient was prepped with Betadine. NINIS monitoring was hooked up and the patient was sterilely draped. The ear was examined. The Betadine was flushed free from the canal. Canal injections were used to augment the preoperative injections of local and the ear was examined. There was found to be an attic retraction pocket filled with cholesteatoma. A tympanomeatal flap was incised and turned partially laterally after which attention was directed to the postauricular area. An incision was made with the cutting Bovie and dissection was continued down to the temporalis fascia where fascia graft was obtained and set aside to dry. Bleeders were controlled with cautery. The soft tissues were elevated from the mastoid periosteum, after which the ear was turned forward after canalplasty and meatoplasty had been created. The drum was elevated posteriorly. It was found to be a sac of granulation and cholesteatoma extending just below the chordae tympani nerve. The chorda tympani was sacrificed during the course of the dissection. The cholesteatoma involved the head of the malleus. The incus body could not be identified, and at this point I decided to proceed with a simple mastoidectomy. The cholesteatoma sac was encountered at the aditus, the antrum, and just below this. The dura was buried in one location. The cholesteatoma sac was removed from the attic area after the epitympanum had been widely opened with a cutting burr. The cholesteatoma was removed from the epitympanum and down onto the malleus. The malleus snipper was used to remove a small residual portion of malleus head. The incus body, as previously noted, could not be identified. There was a small piece of a lenticular process attached to the stapes head, and that was freed after the cholesteatoma had been removed from this area. The facial nerve ridge was taken down to a level compatible with the safety of the nerve. The oval window appeared to be clear and the stapes superstructure was displaced posteriorly from this. Although there was some scarring in the area, I elected not to disturb the stapes further. The facial canal was palpably intact. A fascia graft was placed over the stapes head and under the drum remnant and brought up into the attic area. This was packed in place with Gelfoam laterally. The Gelfoam was placed in Ciloxan. The postauricular wound was closed with interrupted 4-0 Vicryl after which the Korner flap was reapproximated to the posterior mastoid and packed in place with half-inch gauze coated with Bacitracin, after which the mastoid dressing was applied. The NINIS monitor was used through 2 hr of the 2.5- to 3-hr case. She tolerated this well and was allowed to awaken and sent to the recovery room in good condition.

Procedure code(s): _____

Diagnosis code(s): _____

Scenario 10-21

OFFICE NOTES

This is a 39-year-old female who is a new patient to my practice. Her previous PCP was Dr. Day. She has 3 concerns today: One is that of headache, second is that of fatigue, and last is that of the sharp pain in her breast.

She notes that she has been having headaches since she has been a teenager, but over the last 6 months, she has been having almost daily headaches. The headaches are predominantly right-sided and then they radiate into the right side of the neck and into the shoulder. The neck and shoulder are very sore and it is painful to move. Patient denies any photophobia or sonophobia. She also admits that she gets migraine headaches, which she gets only around the time of her periods and that is associated with photophobia, sonophobia, and nausea. The other daily headaches that she has been having are not associated with those symptoms, so she feels they are not migraines. She questions whether this can be muscle contraction headaches or tension headaches and if anything can be done regarding those.

Second issue is that of fatigue, which has been ongoing for about one and a half years. She was evaluated for this by her previous PCP, was diagnosed to have B12 and vitamin D deficiency reportedly, and was advised to use over-the-counter vitamin D supplement and B12. She states that she took it for a few weeks diligently and then has not been very regularly taking those medications, and she questions whether her fatigue could be related to that. She also notes that she has a 2-year-old who does not still sleep through the night, so she is waking up several times and this also interrupts her sleep. She does not feel rested when she wakes up in the morning.

Last concern is that of a sharp pain in her right breast. This happens usually before her period, and she has breast discomfort and soreness just before the week of her period and then once she has her period, the soreness goes away. It is there on both breasts, but it appears to be more prominent on the right. She did not know whether this is significant and also states that she is due for a mammogram, so she would like to have that scheduled.

PAST MEDICAL HISTORY:

1. Dust allergies

2. Migraine headaches

3. Vitamin D and vitamin B12 deficiency documented in 2005

SURGICAL HISTORY: None.

CURRENT MEDICATIONS: None.

DRUG ALLERGIES: None.

FAMILY HISTORY: Father is 64 and has hyperlipidemia. Mother is 64 and has asthma and B12 deficiency. There is no family history of diabetes, hypertension, premature heart disease, or stroke. She had two brothers who are healthy. Her maternal first cousin was diagnosed to have breast cancer at age 36. No history of colon cancer. She is not sure whether her maternal grandmother had ovarian cancer.

continued

SOCIAL HISTORY: She is married. Her husband, Henry, is 40 years of age and healthy. Two children: David, 6, and Diane, 2. Children are healthy. Denies any tobacco use, alcohol use, or drug use. She works at American Bank as an analyst.

HEALTH MAINTENANCE: Tetanus toxoid more than 10 years. Pap smear was less than a year ago. She had a baseline mammogram at age 35. On review of systems, no changes in her weight or appetite. No fever, chills, or rigors. She notes that she has a lot of dry skin around her neck and a rash relating to that, but that appears to be getting better. Headaches as already mentioned in the HPI. She states that, indirectly, her ears feel a little blocked, so she would like to have them checked. She also notes that she has been having problems with reading. She needs to move things further away to be able to read clearly. She has not had an eye examination recently. Denies any persistent rhinorrhea, sore throat, or hoarseness of voice. No chronic cough, sputum production, hemoptysis, dyspnea, orthopnea, or PND. No chest pain, palpitations, swelling in her feet, or intermittent claudication. No dysphagia or abdominal pain. No nausea or vomiting. No recent alteration of bowel habits. No hematemesis, melena, or hematochezia. No urinary urgency, frequency, dysuria, or hematuria. Denies any specific arthralgias. No numbness, weakness, or tingling in her extremities. She denies any tick bites to her knowledge.

On physical examination, height is 62 in. Weight is 118 lb. Pulse is 68. Blood pressure is 106/70. This is a pleasant Indian female who appears to be in no acute distress. Skin examination is unremarkable.

HEENT Examination: No pallor and no icterus. Pupils are round and reactive to light. Extraocular movements are intact. Ear canals are normal with normal tympanic membranes. Nasal mucosa is normal. Oral mucosa is moist. Oropharynx is clear. Neck examination reveals tight neck muscles with tenderness to palpation over the paraspinal neck muscles and trapezial ridge on both sides, the right greater than the left. No lymphadenopathy, bruit, or thyromegaly. No jugular venous distention. Cardiovascular system: With normal S1 and S2. Regular rate and rhythm. No murmurs, rubs, or gallops. Lungs are clear to auscultation bilaterally. Breast examination reveals nipples to be everted. No discrete breast masses. No nipple discharge. No axillary adenopathy. Abdomen is soft and nontender. No organomegaly. Bowel sounds are well heard. Inguinal hernial orifices are free. Pelvic rectal examinations are deferred. Extremities: Without cyanosis, clubbing, or edema. Pedal pulses are well felt. Good range of movement in her cervical and in her lumbar spine with good range of movement in her hips, knees, ankles, shoulders, elbows, and wrists. No evidence of active synovitis in her joints. Neurologically alert and oriented to time, place, and person. Motor strength is 5/5 in her extremities with intact reflexes. Gait and coordination are normal.

ASSESSMENT AND PLAN:

1. Headaches. She appears to have perimenstrual migraines, which is baseline for the patient. More recently, she has been having muscle contraction headaches. We talked about using amitriptyline to decrease the intensity and frequency of headaches. She is agreeable to a trial of amitriptyline. We will start her on 10 mg p.o. q.h.s. Common side effects of amitriptyline are discussed with the patient and she was instructed to cut down the amitriptyline to 5 mg if she felt very sedated with the 10 mg. She will give me a call in 2 weeks' time to let me know how she is doing on the 10 mg and, if need be, we can titrate her medication upward for optimal control.

2. Fatigue with history of vitamin D and B12 deficiency. Check CBC, B12, and vitamin D levels. We will also check a thyroid cascade to make sure that that is

within normal limits. She has not had any tick bites to her knowledge, but we will also check a Lyme titer for completeness sake.

3. Premenstrual breast discomfort. I explained to the patient that this can be normal in some women and it is not uncommon to have breast soreness or tenderness prior to periods. She was instructed to cut down her intake of coffee and caffeine of any kind as that could also cause aggravation of her symptoms.

Health maintenance: Tetanus toxoid is updated today. She will let us know about the Pap smear. She will be scheduled for a baseline mammogram. She is given a lab requisition slip for a fasting lipid profile, CBC, CHEM-7, TSH, vitamin D, vitamin B12, and a Lyme titer.

Procedure code(s): _____

Diagnosis code(s): _____

Scenario 10-22

OPERATIVE REPORT

PREOPERATIVE DIAGNOSIS: Menorrhagia.

POSTOPERATIVE DIAGNOSIS: Menorrhagia.

PROCEDURE: Total abdominal hysterectomy.

ANESTHESIA: General endotracheal.

COMPLICATIONS: None.

CONDITION: Stable.

INTRAVENOUS FLUIDS: 2,800 ml of crystalloid.

URINARY OUTPUT: 350 ml of clear yellow urine.

ESTIMATED BLOOD LOSS: 150 ml.

FINDINGS: Small uterus with normal tubes and ovaries bilaterally. Otherwise normal abdominopelvic anatomy.

DESCRIPTION OF PROCEDURE: After informed consent was obtained, the patient was taken to the operating room where general anesthesia was performed without any complications. The patient was then prepped and draped in the normal sterile fashion in the dorsal supine position. The universal protocol was followed and documented.

A low transverse skin incision was then made with a scalpel where a prior incision was. This incision was then carried down to the fascia and the fascia was incised in the midline with a scalpel. The fascial incision was then extended laterally with Mayo scissors. This superior aspect of the fascial incision was grasped with Kocher clamps and elevated, and the underlying rectus muscles dissected off bluntly. In a similar fashion, the inferior aspect of the fascial incision was grasped with Kocher clamps, elevated, and the underlying rectus dissected off bluntly. The rectus was

continued

then separated in the midline and the peritoneum was entered atraumatically and the peritoneal incision was then extended superiorly and inferiorly. The bowel was then packed away with moist laparotomy sponges and the O'Connor-O'Sullivan retractor was then placed. Curved Kocher clamps were used to grasp the cornual region to provide retraction. The round ligaments on both sides were then grasped with Kocher clamps, ligated with chromic and transected with a Bovie. The bladder flap was then created. The utero-ovarian ligaments again bilaterally were identified, doubly clamped with Heaney clamps, and transected with Mayo scissors. These ligaments were doubly ligated with chromic suture. The uterine arteries were then skeletonized and doubly clamped with Heaney clamps, transected, and doubly ligated with 0 chromic. The ligation of the uterine arteries was performed bilaterally. With straight hysterectomy clamps, the remaining broad ligament was clamped and cut up to the level of the cervix. The cervix was then amputated from the vagina with Jorgenson scissors. The vaginal angles were then closed following the Richardson stitches. Also, modified Marchetti stitches were used in the vaginal angles to provide elevation of the cuff. The rest of the vaginal cuff was closed with 0 chromic. A Hysterovac drain was then left in place to be removed in 24 hr. The pelvis was copiously irrigated with warm saline solution and suctioned. There was a small area of bleeding on the left side next to the utero-ovarian pedicle, which was properly controlled with 2-0 Vicryl stitches. Good inspection of the pelvis showed again good hemostasis. The previously introduced laparotomy sponges were then removed and the rectus muscles were then reapproximated with chromic stitches. The fascia was then closed with 0 PDS suture in a running fashion. The skin was then closed with a 4-0 Vicryl in a subcuticular fashion. The patient tolerated the procedure well. Sponge, lap, needle, and instrument counts were all correct. The patient was awakened and extubated inside the operating room and taken to PACU in stable condition.

Dr. John Farris was present for the entire procedure.

Procedure code(s): _____

Diagnosis code(s): _____

Scenario 10-23

OPERATIVE REPORT

PREOPERATIVE DIAGNOSIS: Right upper pole renal calculus.

POSTOPERATIVE DIAGNOSIS: Right upper pole renal calculus.

PROCEDURE:

1. Right ESWL

2. Placement of right double-J ureteral stent

ANESTHESIA: Conscious sedation.

CLINICAL NOTE: Mr. Mason is a 48-year-old man whom I had previously seen in consultation for nephrolithiasis. He was found to have a large 1 cm × 5 mm right renal upper pole calculus. He consented to have it treated with ESWL. Risks and benefits of the procedure were explained to the patient and are outlined in my previous office notes. He has consented to have the procedure done.

OPERATIVE NOTE: The patient was brought to the operating room in stable condition, put under conscious sedation and put in the dorsal lithotomy position, prepped and draped in the usual fashion. I first proceeded to place the stent, inserting the 22 French Storz sheath and 30° telescopic lens as the assembled cystoscope into the patient's urethral meatus and advanced the scope under direct vision into the patient's bladder. The entire bladder wall was visualized, and there were no stones, tumor, or diverticula. The right ureteral orifice was visualized. It was cannulated using the sensor-tip guidewire and the guidewire was advanced under fluoroscopic guidance all the way up to the kidney. Over the guidewire, I advanced a 6 French variable-length double-J stent under fluoroscopic guidance and the proximal end of the stent could be seen at the level of the upper pole of the kidney. The guidewire was then gradually withdrawn at a point so the proximal end of the stent could be seen coiling in the kidney. Then the distal end of the stent was advanced until the marker at the tip of the follower was seen at the level of the bladder neck. At that point, the guidewire was withdrawn entirely and the distal coil of the stent could be confirmed under direct vision with the cystoscope. The patient was then flipped back to the supine position and he proceeded to receive ESWL to the right upper pole calculus using a power of 5 and 2,500 impulses. There was some evidence of stone fragmentation during the ESWL. Overall, the patient tolerated the procedure well. He was then taken to the recovery area in stable condition. The patient will be discharged home today with oral antibiotics and analgesia. He will follow up with me in 2 weeks' time with a repeat KUB x-ray to reassess the right renal stone burden, and, if there has been a reduction in stone burden, then the stent will be removed at that time.

Procedure code(s): _____

Diagnosis code(s): _____

Scenario 10-24

OPERATIVE REPORT

PREOPERATIVE DIAGNOSIS: Foreign body in right mainstern bronchus.

POSTOPERATIVE DIAGNOSIS: Foreign body in right mainstern bronchus (brush).

PROCEDURE: Bronchoscopy with removal of foreign body via tracheostomy.

Under adequate general endotracheal anesthesia and after the endotracheal tube was removed from the tracheostomy stoma, a rigid scope was advanced downward into the right mainstern bronchus where the foreign body was identified and grasped and then pulled out through the stoma without difficulty. It was about 4 in. long and was a brush that he was using for cleaning his tracheostomy stoma. He tolerated the procedure well and was taken to the recovery room in a satisfactory state.

Procedure code(s): _____

Diagnosis code(s): _____

Scenario 10-25

OPERATIVE REPORT

PREOPERATIVE DIAGNOSIS: Adenocarcinoma in situ of cervix.

POSTOPERATIVE DIAGNOSIS: Adenocarcinoma in situ of cervix.

PROCEDURE: Total vaginal hysterectomy.

FINDINGS: Small anteverted uterus with little cervical tissue, status post cone biopsy, normal adnexa bilaterally.

COMPLICATIONS: None.

ESTIMATED BLOOD LOSS: 150 ml.

IV FLUIDS: 1,200 ml LR.

SPECIMENS: Uterus with cervical remnant weighing 258 g.

DISPOSITION: Stable to recovery. Note: IV Kefzol prior to surgery.

PROCEDURE IN DETAIL: After establishing general anesthesia, the patient was placed, prepped, and draped in normal sterile fashion in modified dorsal lithotomy position. Exam prior to surgery confirmed a small anteverted uterus with only a very small amount of cervical tissue left status post cervical cone biopsy.

The bladder was initially not drained for easier location and the plan was to enter the peritoneal cavity posteriorly. A weighted speculum was placed into the patient's vagina and the cervical remnant was grasped with a triple-tooth tenaculum. The tissue was notably friable and appeared inflamed due to recent surgery. Careful dissection posteriorly was performed using Mayo scissors. After identifying the peritoneum, which again appeared also thickened and inflamed, a rectal exam was performed to confirm the correct location, and subsequently the peritoneum was entered using Metzenbaum Scissors. At this point 2 Heaney clamps were positioned on both uterosacral ligaments, which were bluntly cut and suture ligated using 0 Vicryl. Continued from here, both cardinal ligaments were identified, clamped, and Heaney suture ligated. At this point, the bladder was carefully dissected off the anterior uterine wall and after completing this step successfully the bladder was drained. Then, the utero-ovarian pedicle was easily identified and in a similar fashion clamped, transected, and then tied and suture ligated. Inspection of both adnexa confirmed normal-appearing ovaries and tubes bilaterally, and excellent hemostasis was confirmed. At this point, all instruments were removed from the peritoneal cavity. The uterosacral ligaments were tied to each other and the vaginal cuff was closed using 0 Vicryl in a running locked fashion. The procedure was concluded at this point and the patient returned to recovery in stable condition.

Procedure code(s): _____

Diagnosis code(s): _____

Scenario 10-26

OFFICE NOTE

Kurt is a 28-year-old patient who is here for a comprehensive physical. He had a recent left ankle injury, Achilles tendon tear. He has been seen by Dr. Roy. He also saw Dr. Summers recently. He is going to undergo physical therapy. He is requesting some pain medication. He said that he is on his feet every day. He gets increased pain because of that. No other concerns or complaints. Past medical history is significant for:

1. Asthma

2. Allergic rhinitis

3. Achilles tendon injury and ankle sprain on the left ankle

Past surgical history is foreign body removal from his chest wall.

ALLERGIES: No known drug allergies.

MEDICATIONS: Advair 50/500, albuterol, and Vicodin.

SOCIAL HISTORY: The patient lives with his girlfriend. He has a 2-year-old son. No smoking. Social alcohol use. He works for a collagen company.

FAMILY HISTORY: No history of prostate or colon cancer in the family. Positive diabetes mellitus.

HEALTH MAINTENANCE: The patient had a tetanus shot in 07/2007. He received a flu shot today.

REVIEW OF SYSTEMS: Weight has been stable. Appetite good. Sleeps okay. He informed that he has been having loss of hearing, bilaterally for more than a year. He feels that when he has to talk on the phone, he has to amplify it and he usually increases his TV volume. He would like to get a hearing test. He has history of hearing too loud music when he was a teenager. No vertigo. No syncope. No sore throat. No cold, cough, dyspnea, chest pain, angina, palpitation, edema, or claudication. No abdominal pain or bloating. No nausea, vomiting, constipation, or diarrhea. No frequency or urgency. No incontinence. Positive pain in his left ankle.

PHYSICAL EXAMINATION: The patient is a pleasant male, not in any distress. Blood pressure is 122/80. Pulse rate of 74. Temperature is 97.9°F. Weight of 220.

HEENT Examination: Pupils equally reactive to light. Tympanic membranes clear.

Neck: Supple.

Lungs: Clear.

CVS: S1 and S2. Regular rate and rhythm. Abdomen: Soft and nontender. Bowel sounds present.

External genitalia: Normal male. Hernial orifices free. Testicles descended bilaterally.

Extremities: Positive ankle swelling on the left ankle. Pulses 2+.

ASSESSMENT AND PLAN:

1. Health maintenance. Advised self-testicular exam. We will check a fasting sugar and cholesterol level. Received flu shot. Up-to-date with tetanus shot. Advised skin care and seatbelt safety.

2. Hearing loss for almost more than a year. We will get a baseline hearing test today.

3. Ankle sprain, followed by Podiatry.

continued

4. Asthma, stable. Continue Advair and albuterol. Received flu shot. We will also make an appointment for him to see Dermatology for skin evaluation.

Procedure code(s): _____

Diagnosis code(s): _____

Scenario 10-27

OPERATIVE REPORT

PREOPERATIVE DIAGNOSIS: Encrusted left ureteral stent.

POSTOPERATIVE DIAGNOSIS: Left ureteral stenosis, post ESWL.

PROCEDURE:

1. Cystoscopy

2. Removal of left ureteral stent

3. Holmium laser lithotripsy

4. Left retrograde pyelogram

5. Placement of dangling left ureteral stent

ANESTHESIA: General anesthesia.

CLINICAL NOTE: Mr. Harris is a 54-year-old man who had undergone bilateral ESWL 2 weeks ago. He had a left renal pelvis stone that appeared to have been treated successfully with ESWL. He was supposed to have stent removed yesterday; however, at the time of stent removal with flexible cystoscopy in the office, the stent could not actually be removed. It appeared to be stuck. The distal end of the stent was actually pushed back into the patient's bladder. The urethral catheter was placed. The patient comes today to have stent removal in the operating room, possibly with the assistance of the holmium laser to vaporize the presumed encrustation. Risks and benefits of the procedure were explained to the patient. Risks of infection, bleeding, ureteral injury including perforation, avulsion, intussusceptions and stricture, and perforation were discussed with the patient. He also may require another stent depending on the operative findings. He consented to have the procedure done and he comes in on the emergency list today to have the procedure done.

OPERATIVE NOTE: The patient was brought to the operating room in stable condition, put under general anesthesia after receiving perioperative IV antibiotics, and put under general anesthesia. He was put in the dorsolithotomy position and prepped and draped in the usual sterile fashion. I first did a cystoscopy inserting the 22 French Storz sheath and the 30° telescopic lens as the assembled cystoscope into the patient's urethral meatus and advanced the scope into the patient's urethra and into the bladder. In the proximal urethra, the stent could be seen. It was further pushed into the bladder. I then visualized the left ureteral orifice and cannulated it with a 5 French flexible-tipped ureteral catheter and guide wire. The guide wire was able to go up to the level of the kidney without any difficulty. We then removed the cystoscope and, alongside the guidewire and stent, advanced a rigid ureteroscope without any difficulty through the ureteral orifice, all the way up to the UPJ. The stent could not come out because the patient actually had multiple stone fragments from the right renal pelvis stone that had been previously treated with ESWL. This was now occluding the left proximal ureter. These stones were vaporized using the holmium laser at a setting of 10 J and a frequency of 15 Hz. Stones were successfully vaporized into smaller fragments that could be passed on their own. No encrustations were seen from the stent to the ureteral wall throughout the length of the stent itself. Once this was done, I removed the ureteroscope and then grasped the distal end of the stent with the rigid grasping forceps. I was able to remove the stent without any difficulty in its entirety. I then advanced a 5 French flexible catheter over the guidewire and did a retrograde pyelogram. The entire left pelvic caliceal system and proximal ureter were opacified. There was evidence of some hydronephrosis but no extravasation was seen. There did not appear to be any ureteral injury. I then put the guide wire back through the ureteral catheter and over the guidewire advanced a 6 French variable-length double-J dangling stent. The proximal end of the stent was advanced until the stent could be seen at the level of the renal pelvis. We then gradually withdrew the guide wire and could see the proximal end of the stent coiling in the renal pelvis. I then advanced the distal end of the stent using the follower until the radiopaque marker at the tip of the follower was seen at the level of the mid symphysis pubis. At that point, I withdrew the guide wire in its entirety. The distal end of the stent could be seen coiling in the bladder. I then verified the distal end of the stent position by doing cystoscopy. Indeed the distal coil of the stent could be seen in the bladder. The string at the end of the stent was then taped very carefully with Steri-Strips to the glans penis after I drained the patient's bladder of irrigate through the sheath of the scope. The patient was awakened from anesthesia and taken to the recovery room in stable condition.

He will be discharged home today with a prescription for prophylactic antibiotics and pain medication. He will follow up in 3 to 5 days' time for removal of the stent.

Procedure code(s): _____

Diagnosis code(s): _____

Scenario 10-28

RADIOLOGY REPORT

Screening Mammography Bilateral (2-View Film Study of Each Breast)

Results Bilateral mammogram:

Exam compared to previous 2/25/2007

Spot view left included.

There has been some interval weight gain. Parenchymal density pattern is fairly stable. There is no dominant or distinctly separable mass. A focal opacity initially seen left does not persist with spot compression. There are a few scattered benign calcifications noted. A few microcalcifications in the inferior left breast are stable. There are no suspicious calcifications or secondary signs of malignancy. There is no significant interval change. There are subtle architectural distortions from prior biopsies. Conclusion: Some stable microcalcifications left likely benign. There is no interval change to suggest malignancy. One-year follow-up recommended. The FDA, in accordance with the Mammography Quality Standards Act, requires that this letter be sent to the patient by the interpreting radiologist.

continued

> BT-RADS Category 3: Probably Benign Finding, follow-up suggested.
>
> **LETTER SENT:** A mammogram letter type El P was printed on 01/16/2007

Procedure code(s): _____

Diagnosis code(s): _____

Scenario 10-29

RADIOLOGY REPORT

US, Limited—Renal Kidney Stones

Results Renal ultrasound 08/29/2007:

Both kidneys are normal in size and configuration, with the right kidney measuring 11.9 cm in length and the left kidney 13.7 cm in length. There is an echogenic focus in the lower pole of the right kidney with strong posterior acoustic shadowing consistent with a renal calculus or calculi. There is no evidence of right renal mass or hydronephrosis. On the left side there are small echogenic foci in the midpole and lower pole of the left kidney with a suggestion of posterior acoustic shadowing. These are consistent with small renal calculi. There is also evidence of left hydronephrosis, and there is a suggestion of duplication of the left collecting system. No left renal mass is seen.

IMPRESSION: Bilateral renal calculi. Left hydronephrosis.

Procedure code(s): _____

Diagnosis code(s): _____

Scenario 10-30

OFFICE NOTE

SUBJECTIVE: The patient is sent by Dr. Hockins for my opinion regarding painful fungal toenails due to his diabetes and diabetic foot care in general. He also has a sliver in his left extremity.

PAST MEDICAL HISTORY: Positive for AODM ×2 years.

MEDICATIONS: Nasarel, lisinopril, Flovent, Combivent.

ALLERGIES: Positive to penicillin.

PAST SURGICAL HISTORY: Positive for gallbladder surgery.

SOCIAL HISTORY: Negative for tobacco use, negative for alcohol use. He is retired.

FAMILY HISTORY: Positive for diabetes.

REVIEW OF SYSTEMS: Denies claudication.

OBJECTIVE: Dermatological exam reveals that he has elongated toenails, both feet, some callus on his heels bilaterally. He has a splinter in his left extremity.

Vascular exam reveals palpable pedal pulses. His feet are warm to touch bilaterally. CRT was 1 sec × 10 toes.

Neurologic exam revealed sharp, dull, light touch, and proprioception sensation was decreased to the feet and toes bilaterally. Constitutional exam revealed this is an adult male in NAD.

ASSESSMENT:

1. Elongated toenails, both feet, and callus on his heels bilaterally

2. Sliver, left extremity

3. Adult-onset diabetes mellitus ×2 years with good vascular supply but he does have some peripheral neuropathy

PLAN:

1. Debrided the toenails ×10, callus on his heels bilaterally.

2. I removed the sliver, which was a splinter from the left extremity, and applied some Betadine solution and a Band-Aid.

3. I went over diabetic foot care with him, instructing him to inspect his feet daily. Call if there is any trouble.

4. I will see the patient back in 3 months, sooner if needed.

Procedure code(s): _____

Diagnosis code(s): _____

Scenario 10-31

OFFICE NOTE

This is a 20-year-old female who is here for a follow-up. Her depression is doing much better. She is seeing a counselor at her church and is taking her Prozac. She is able to feel happy, able to sleep better. She feels like a different person. She had some workup done for her hypertension, and she had some elevated metanephrines and normetanephrines. Her CT of the abdomen was done, which was negative for any adrenal mass; however, a radionucleotide study has been recommended to rule out any extraintestinal lesion. The patient has an appointment coming up with Renal. I will see what their recommendation is if we need to proceed with that. Her other concern is that, for the last 2 days, she has been having some rectal bleeding. It was initially bright red with the stools. Lately, now, it is maroon mixed with the stool. Certain times, she feels like she has to go to the bathroom and only blood comes out. She is feeling a little bit weak and dizzy. She has been having some cramping just before she needs to go to the bathroom; otherwise, no persistent abdominal pain. No nausea, no vomiting. She is eating fine.

On physical exam, she is sitting comfortably. Blood pressure is 138/90. Sitting comfortably in no acute distress. Chest: Clear to auscultation and percussion. CVS: S1 and S2 normal. Regular rate and rhythm. Abdomen: Obese, soft, and nontender. Rectal exam: No external hemorrhoids. I do think I felt internal hemorrhoids. There was no stool. There was some maroon-colored blood on my finger.

continued

ASSESSMENT AND PLAN:

1. The patient has lower GI bleed. Sigmoidoscopy has been arranged for tomorrow. Hemoglobin, hematocrit done today was stable. Hemoglobin at 30 and hematocrit at 39.7.

2. Hypertension. Increase Norvasc to 5 mg. Blood pressure is doing much better, however.

3. We will wait for Renal appointment; recommendation for further workup for this possible pheochromocytoma.

Procedure code(s): _____

Diagnosis code(s): _____

Scenario 10-32

OPERATIVE REPORT

PREPROCEDURE DIAGNOSIS: Mediastinal adenopathy.

POSTPROCEDURE DIAGNOSIS: Sarcoidosis.

PROCEDURE:

1. Bronchoscopy with washing

2. Mediastinoscopy, biopsy of R-2, with frozen section confirming sarcoidosis

DESCRIPTION OF PROCEDURE: Under adequate general endotracheal anesthesia, a bronchoscopy was performed. The carina was quite sharp. Both sides of the tracheobronchial tree were evaluated and there were no obstructing lesions identified. There was, however, an inflammatory process throughout the tracheobronchial tree, which in my opinion was most consistent with sarcoidosis. Washings were obtained for cytology. The scope was removed and the patient was next positioned, prepared, and draped in the usual manner for a cervical mediastinoscopy.

A transverse incision was made in the neck just above the suprasternal notch and deepened in the midline until the trachea was encountered. A finger was advanced along the anterior surface of the trachea, separating it from surrounding structures, and the nodes were palpable and enlarged in the right paratracheal space just in the R-2 position. The scope was advanced to this location, the nodes isolated from surrounding tissue, and multiple biopsies obtained from the R-2 nodes. Frozen section on one of these confirmed granulomatous disease consistent with sarcoidosis. Two other specimens were sent for permanent section. A check was made for hemostasis and found to be satisfactory. The scope was removed. The wound was closed in layers using interrupted Vicryl on the deeper tissue, closing the skin with a subcuticular stitch.

Procedure code(s): _____

Diagnosis code(s): _____

Scenario 10-33

OFFICE VISIT

Mr. Stony comes in for his first visit here as a new patient. He is 31 years old. He has a benign past history.

Medications are Naprosyn p.r.n.

ALLERGIES: NKDA.

PAST MEDICAL HISTORY:

1. T and A

2. Fractured collarbone as a child

FAMILY HISTORY: Uncle with a CVA. Father with hypertension. Parents otherwise doing well.

SOCIAL HISTORY: He is single. He works in a warehouse filled with government materials. He is a nonsmoker. He has had a rash in the lower part of his face intermittently over the last few months. It happens after he shaves. They started out as small pustules.

On exam, he has small clusters of erythematous bumps with some honey-colored crusting.

ASSESSMENT AND PLAN: Folliculitis/impetigo. I will put him on Keflex 500 mg q.i.d. He will try antibacterial soaps when he shaves. He will call p.r.n.

Procedure code(s): _____

Diagnosis code(s): _____

Scenario 10-34

VISIT SUMMARY

This is a 36-year-old woman here for her first preventative visit. She is also followed by Dr. Power in Gynecology and she has seen her less than a year ago. She does not have any acute concerns, but wishes to follow up on several previous issues.

PAST MEDICAL HISTORY:

1. She had gestational diabetes with her last child, who is now 2 years old. She actually had a premature rupture of the membranes and was hospitalized for 6 weeks. She delivered at 35 weeks.

2. History of lipomas. No significant change in the shape or size, but she does want them rechecked.

3. History of some nasal congestion and allergy symptoms, but currently minimal.

CURRENT MEDICATIONS: Birth control pills.

continued

ALLERGIES TO MEDICATIONS: None.

PAST SURGICAL HISTORY: Childhood appendix removal, adenoids removal, and bilateral ear tubes. Socially, the patient is currently not working outside the home, but she was working in accounting until 2 months ago. She is a mother of a 2-year-old and a 5-year-old. She is married. Social alcohol intake and no tobacco. She tries to go to aerobics twice a week and walk frequently.

FAMILY HISTORY: Mother 60, affected by borderline lipids. Father 60, borderline hypertension. One brother 32, alive and well. Review of systems is essentially negative with the exception of rare sense of some dyspnea with exertion, but no associated wheezing, cough, chest pains, or light-headedness. It also has not occurred in some time and currently she feels fine. She does admit she is fighting a cold currently.

ROUTINE HEALTH MAINTENANCE: Gynecologic exam less than a year ago. Does not recall last tetanus or lipid profile. She states she did have a history of borderline iron deficiency.

PHYSICAL EXAMINATION:

General: Generally well appearing young woman. Normal body habits.

Vitals: Weight is 118.5 lb. Height 5 ft 3.75 in. Temperature 98°F. Heart rate 84. Blood pressure 110/62.

Skin: No rash or suspicious lesions. Numerous nevi and three lipomas; one on the left forearm, one on the upper arm, and one on the back. All soft, mobile, and nontender.

Eyes: Funduscopic exam grossly normal. Extraocular movements intact.

ENT: Oropharynx and mucous membranes show no inflammation or suspicious lesions. TMs, canals, and pinnae appear normal.

Neck: No palpable lymphadenopathy. Thyroid normal to inspection and palpation. No JVD. Carotid pulses are 2+. No bruits heard.

Heart: Heart sounds are normal. Regular rate and rhythm without murmur, gallop, or rub.

Lungs: Clear to auscultation and percussion.

Abdomen: Soft, nontender, bowel sounds present. No organomegaly or masses. No bruits heard.

Extremities: No cyanosis. No significant edema.

Neuro: Cranial nerves and gross motor and sensory exams performed. No focal deficits noted.

Vascular: DP and PT pulses palpated easily.

ASSESSMENT:

1. This is a 36-year-old woman essentially healthy with a past medical history of gestational diabetes, and I discussed the implications of being at an increased risk for diabetes in the future because of this history. I did recommend she have a fasting glucose and A1c at least once every other year. We discussed keeping her weight down and remaining active as a preventative.

2. History of borderline iron deficiency. Recheck hematocrit and ferritin level.

3. Preventative health. Tetanus today and lipid profile. Recommended to continue routine follow-ups with her gynecologist and return to see me for next preventative visit approximately every 2 years. The patient will be seen sooner if there are new concerns or abnormalities on testing or if the patient has recurrence of any respiratory symptoms.

Procedure code(s): _____
Diagnosis code(s): _____

Scenario 10-35

OPERATIVE REPORT

PREOPERATIVE DIAGNOSIS: Probable cancer right upper lobe with mediastinal involvement.

POSTOPERATIVE DIAGNOSIS: Probable squamous cell carcinoma right upper lobe with mediastinal involvement.

PROCEDURE:

1. Bronchoscopy with washing and brushing and forceps biopsy from right upper lobe and right mainstem.

2. Mediastinoscopy and biopsy of R-2 lymph node, with frozen section confirming cancer.

DESCRIPTION OF PROCEDURE: Under adequate general endotracheal anesthesia, a bronchoscopy was performed. The carina was marginally blunted. The left side was intact. On entering the right side, there was an obvious large tumor growing from the upper lobe, totally occluding it and extending onto the mainstem and up the lateral tracheal wall. Multiple biopsies were obtained from here with the forceps brush and with washings. The middle lobe and lower lobe were patent. However, the process did extend to the trachea. The scope was removed.

The patient was next positioned, prepared, and draped in the usual manner for a cervical mediastinoscopy. A transverse incision was made in the neck just above the suprasternal notch and deepened in the midline until the trachea was encountered. A finger was advanced along the anterior surface of the trachea and the mass was readily palpable, hard and firm, and right along the side of the trachea in the R-2 position. A large scope was advanced to this location and multiple biopsies were obtained from what appeared to be a sqamous type cancer. Frozen section confirmed malignancy, most likely a squamous cell carcinoma. Mediastinal involvement was significant. A check was made for hemostasis and found to be satisfactory. The scope was removed. The wound was closed in layers using interrupted Vicryl on the deeper tissue, closing the skin with running 5-0 nylon. She tolerated the procedure well.

Procedure code(s): _____
Diagnosis code(s): _____

Scenario 10-36

OPERATIVE REPORT

PREPROCEDURE DIAGNOSIS: Interstitial lung disease.

POSTPROCEDURE DIAGNOSIS: Interstitial lung disease (awaiting pathology report).

PROCEDURE: Left open lung biopsy.

DESCRIPTION OF PROCEDURE: Under adequate general endotracheal anesthesia, a double-lumen tube in place, the patient was positioned, prepared, and draped in the usual manner for left inframammary limited incision and an open lung biopsy. The incision was deepened, the intercostal space was encountered, and the intercostal musculature was opened in the middle. The lung was collapsed using a double-lumen tube and the lung looked abnormal, sort of micronodular in both lobes. A small section was taken from the upper lobe and a small section from the lower lobe using a GIA stapling device. Both of these specimens were sent for permanent pathology. A single chest tube was put through a separate stab incision and directed posteriorly and superiorly. The intercostal muscle was closed with interrupted 2-0 Vicryl, the chest wall muscle with running 2-0 Vicryl, the subcutaneous tissue with 2-0 Vicryl, and the skin with subcuticular stitch. Blood loss was less than 5 cc. She tolerated the procedure well.

Procedure code(s): _____

Diagnosis code(s): _____

Scenario 10-37

RADIOLOGY REPORT

Component Radiology Report:

Reason for Study

HISTORY: RT ankle twisted, ankle pain, and swelling.

Results Right ankle 3 views.

INDICATION: Injury.

FINDINGS: There is small avulsion fracture from the tip of the lateral malleolus. No other osseous injury. There is surrounding soft tissue swelling. Ankle mortise is preserved. Talar dome is normal. There is a small inferior calcaneal spur.

IMPRESSION:

1. Avulsion fracture tip of the lateral malleolus
2. A small inferior calcaneal spur

Procedure code(s): _____

Diagnosis code(s): _____

Scenario 10-38

RADIOLOGY REPORT

CT—Maxillofacial w/o Contrast

HISTORY: CT Sinuses Chronic Sinusitis.

Component Radiology Report:

Results CT of the paranasal sinuses.

There is a moderate amount of mucous seen in the left sphenoid sinus. Minor mucosal thickening is seen in the right sphenoid sinus. There is thickening of the mucous seen in both ostial meatal complexes leading to obstruction. The frontal sinuses are well aerated. There is a moderate amount of mucus seen within both ethmoid air cells. The maxillary sinuses are well aerated.

Conclusion minor inflammatory changes.

Procedure code(s): _____

Diagnosis code(s): _____

Scenario 10-39

OPERATIVE REPORT

INDICATION FOR THE PROCEDURE: Left upper lobe lung collapse.

The consent could not be obtained from the family because they could not be reached, and the procedure needed to be done on an urgent basis because of persistent hypoxemia despite mechanical ventilation and 100% oxygen.

PROCEDURE: The bronchoscope was passed via the 7.5 oral endotracheal tube. Bronchoscope was advanced into the level of the trachea, which was normal. Bronchoscope was then passed to the level of the main carina, which was also normal. The bronchoscope was then passed into the right lung, and all airways were inspected and found to be normal. Bronchoscope was then withdrawn and passed into the left main-stem bronchus, which was clear. The left lower lobe bronchus and segmental bronchi were also clear. However, the left upper lobe was occluded with a large mucus plug. This was removed with suctioning and using a saline lavage. A brush was inserted and protected brush specimen was obtained for culture. The left upper lobe was then lavaged with approximately 100 ml of normal saline with 60 ml of return. Following this, the bronchoscope was removed. The patient tolerated the procedure well. The postprocedure chest x-ray was ordered.

IMPRESSION: Left upper lobe collapse secondary to large mucus plug, now removed bronchoscopically. The patient tolerated the procedure very well. There were no complications noted.

Procedure code(s): _____

Diagnosis code(s): _____

Scenario 10-40

OFFICE NOTE

Karen is a 27-year-old patient who is here for comprehensive physical. She said that she has pain during intercourse, which has been going on for actually a couple of months. She said that when she examines herself, she feels that she has a lump around her cervix area. No drainage. No pelvic discharge. She gets pressure only during sex. She does not feel it otherwise. She has been with the same partner for more than one and a half years. No pelvic discharge. No dysuria. No fever. No chills. No abdominal pain. No other concerns or complaints.

Past medical history is significant for:

1. Anxiety

2. Depression

3. Migraine headache

4. The patient had numbness of her left upper and lower extremities, seen by neurologist. Recent workup was negative.

Past surgical history is benign.

ALLERGIES: No known drug allergies.

MEDICATIONS: She is on Lexapro 10 mg p.o. q.d. She is on birth control pill and Klonopin 0.25 mg as needed for panic episodes.

SOCIAL HISTORY: The patient lives with her parents. She has one boyfriend for almost two years. Uses a condom. She works at Electronic Modality Corporation. No smoking. No alcohol.

FAMILY HISTORY: Father is deceased from heart attack in his 50s. Mother is healthy. No history of diabetes mellitus. History of breast cancer in paternal grandmother in her late 50s. No colon or ovarian cancer in the family.

HEALTH MAINTENANCE: The patient is up-to-date with tetanus shot. Declined flu shot. Has had normal Pap smears in the past. Did a Pap smear today.

REVIEW OF SYSTEMS: Weight has been stable. Appetite is good. Sleep is okay. No change in vision. No hearing loss. No tinnitus. No vertigo. No syncope. No sore throat. No cold, cough, dyspnea, chest pain, angina, palpitation, edema, or claudication. No abdominal pain or bleeding. No nausea, vomiting, constipation, or diarrhea. No frequency or urgency. No incontinence. No arthralgia or myalgia.

PHYSICAL EXAMINATION: The patient is a pleasant lady, not in any distress. Blood pressure is 112/62. Pulse rate of 88. Temperature is 98.6° Fahrenheit.

HEENT: Pupils are equal and reactive to light. Extraocular muscles are intact. Ear canals are normal. Oropharynx is clear. Neck: Supple. No JVD. No carotid bruit.

Lungs: Good air entry. No rales or rhonchi.

CVS: S1 and S2. Regular rate and rhythm. No murmur heard.

Breasts: No discrete masses. No nipple retraction or discharge. No axillary lymph node. Abdomen is soft and nontender. Bowel sounds present.

Pelvic: External genitalia, normal female. Vagina, no lesions. Cervix visualized. Positive cystic lesion around the cervix present. Cervical culture sent off. Pap smear obtained. Nontender on examination. No cervical wall motion tenderness.

ASSESSMENT AND PLAN:

1. Positive cystic lesion on the cervix, pain during intercourse. Cervical cultures sent off. Pap smear obtained. We will make an appointment for her to see GYN; put in a referral for that. Advised Amy to call me if she does not have an appointment.

2. Health maintenance: Advised self-breast examination.

3. Up-to-date with tetanus shot. We will check a fasting sugar and cholesterol level. Advised skin care and seatbelt safety.

Procedure code(s): _____

Diagnosis code(s): _____

Glossary

abstracting   Reviewing medical records and identifying the appropriate diagnoses and procedures to be coded.

advanced life support (ALS)   Invoked when cardiac arrest has been established and includes basic life support (BLS) as well as defibrillation and the administration of medications. Oxygen is administered and endotracheal intubation may be attempted to secure the airway. *See also* basic life support (BLS).

ambulatory surgical center (ASC) groupings   Code groupings used to assign CPT and HCPCS codes with similar clinical services and resource costs for payment.

anesthesia conversion factor   The dollar value of each unit of anesthesia.

anesthesia modifiers   Modifiers used to reflect circumstances or conditions that change or modify the environment in which the anesthesia is provided.

assessment   The section in the medical record that contains the diagnostic statement and that may include the physician rationale for the diagnosis or additional findings.

base unit value (B)   The numerical value assigned to each anesthesia service.

basic life support   A specific level of prehospital medical care that involves establishing the ABCs of emergency care: airway, breathing, and circulation.

body areas   One of the recognized methods in *CPT* for purposes of describing and measuring the level of examinations for evaluation and management services (e.g., neck, abdomen).

bundled services   Services that are considered part of another reportable service and cannot be reported separately.

category   An organizational unit used in the *CPT* manual to identify code ranges by body system.

Centers for Medicare and Medicaid Services   The administrative agency in the federal Department of Health and Human Services for Medicare and Medicaid, formerly known as Healthcare Financing Administration (HCFA).

charge slip   The form completed by the physician that indicates the diagnoses and services provided to a patient. *See also* encounter form, superbill.

chief complaint (CC)   The main reason the patient has sought care, as identified by the patient.

Clinical Laboratory Improvement Act (CLIA)   A federal law that established quality standards, which must be followed by all clinical laboratory testing to ensure the accuracy, reliability, and timeliness of patient test results, regardless of where the test is performed.

code range   A series of codes in CPT listed in the index to be investigated prior to assigning an exact code.

colon The symbol used (:) in Tabular List of the *ICD-9* manual to indicate that an incomplete term is followed by one or more modifiers.

computerized tomography A procedure by which selected planes of tissue are pinpointed through computer enhancement by which images may be reconstructed by analysis of variance in absorption of the tissue.

conversion factor (CF) The dollar multiplier that converts a relative value unit into a dollar amount.

Correct Code Initiative (CCI) edits Edits developed by Healthcare Financing Administration (HCFA), now known as CMS, to encourage the correct and accurate use of CPT codes.

diagnostic procedure A procedure performed to determine the illness or injury experienced by a patient.

diagnostic radiology (imaging) A procedure in which radioactive substances are used to create images and determine a patient's illness or extent of injury.

diagnostic ultrasound A procedure using sound waves to determine the density of the outline of tissue in determining a patient's illness or injury.

durable medical equipment (DME) Equipment that can withstand repeated use, primarily used for a medical purpose, that is used in the patient's home, and that would not be used in the absence of illness or injury.

encounter form A form used by providers for the sole purpose of billing to indicate the diagnoses and services rendered to a patient at the time of a visit or when a procedure is performed. *See also* charge slip, superbill.

established patient Someone who has been seen by a physician of the same specialty in the same medical practice within the past three years.

evaluation and management (E&M) A category of CPT that represents patient office visits, hospital visits, nursing facility visits, consultations, and other visit types used by most providers to describe the level and type of evaluation performed regardless of the physician's specialty.

excludes The term used in the Tabular List of ICD-9 to direct the coder to another location in the codebook for the accurate assignment of a diagnosis code.

Federal Register The legal newspaper published every business day by the federal government.

follow-up care Care provided to a patient for the same reason after initial care was provided for the same illness or condition.

global period (days) A period that includes all services related to a procedure during a period of time (e.g., 10 days or 90 days).

global services Services rendered during a global period and not separately reportable.

HCPCS modifiers Modifiers used to provide more specific information related to Level I or Level II HCPCS codes.

history of present illness (HPI) The patient's description of the illness or injury for which he or she is seeking care.

impression A term used to identify the patient's diagnosis and physician rationale for it, as well as any additional findings. *See also* assessment.

includes Statements used in the Tabular List of ICD-9 that further define, clarify, or provide an example for the use of that particular code.

Index to Diseases An alphabetical listing of the main terms or conditions in the *ICD-9* manual.

inpatient (Inpt) Service performed when the patient is admitted to the hospital for treatment with the expectation that he or she will remain in the hospital for a period of 24 hours or more.

Level II codes   HCPCS codes used to report common medical services and supplies not included in CPT. *Also known as* national codes.

Level II modifiers   Another name for HCPCS modifiers.

level of service   A description that reflects the amount of work involved in providing health care to patients.

magnetic resonance imaging (MRI)   A procedure that uses nonionizing radiation to view the body in the cross-sectional view.

main terms   Terms used to locate an accurate diagnostic code. They are printed in boldface type in the *ICD-9* manual and followed by the code number.

medical decision making   The complexity of establishing a diagnosis and/or selecting a management option as measured by the number of diagnoses or management options, amount and/or complexity of data to be reviewed, and the risk of complications and/or morbidity or mortality.

mandatory multiple coding   Term used to reference instances in diagnostic coding when more than one code must be reported to accurately report a condition.

medical necessity   A diagnosis or condition that justifies the need for performing a procedure or providing a level of service.

moderate conscious sedation   A decreased level of consciousness in which the patient is not completely asleep.

modifiers   Two-digit codes (numeric, alphabetic, or alphanumeric) appended to a CPT or HCPCS code indicating that a procedure or service has been altered in some manner.

modifying terms   Terms that appear in parentheses after the diagnosis in the *ICD-9* manual and that may appear in a provider's diagnostic statement and would be appropriate for use with the code.

moderate (conscious) sedation   An altered level of consciousness that allows the patient to continue to respond to verbal and physical commands as well as maintain an airway.

national codes   *See* Level II codes.

National Coverage Determination (NCD)   The rules developed by CMS that specify the clinical circumstances under which a service or procedure is covered and correctly coded.

NEC (not elsewhere classified)   A notation that identifies a code that should be assigned when information needed to assign a more specific code is not available in the *ICD-9* manual. This is when a physician's documentation is specific but there is no specific code in the *ICD-9* manual.

nerve block   An injection of local anesthetic onto or near nerves. Nerve blocks are used to help control pain, but also offer diagnostic benefits by helping to identify specific nerves as pain generators.

new patient   A patient who has not received professional services from a physician or any other physician of the same specialty and same group in the past 3 years.

NOS (not otherwise specified)   Indicates that the code is unspecified. This is when the physician does not have the specific or detailed information in order to code the diagnosis to the highest level of specificity.

not elsewhere classified   *See* NEC (not elsewhere classified)

not otherwise specified   *See* NOS (not otherwise specified)

nuclear medicine   The branch of medicine and medical imaging that uses radionuclides or radioactive pharmaceuticals in diagnosing or treating disease.

Office of Inspector General (OIG) A subagency of the Department of Health and Human Services that focuses on the prevention of waste, fraud, and abuse in the Medicare system.

operative notes Reports dictated by the performing surgeon describing the procedure(s) performed on a patient and the diagnoses affecting that patient.

organ systems Categories of body parts organized into systems according to function and used as one of the methods of measuring the level of exam for an evaluation and management service (e.g., cardiovascular, digestive, and respiratory).

outpatient (Outpt) The service performed when a patient is treated in a setting for less than 24 hours, such as a provider's office, emergency room, ASC, clinic, same-day surgery or when the patient is admitted solely for the purpose of observation and is released after a short stay.

Outpatient Prospective Payment System (OPPS) A payment system whereby ambulatory payment classifications (APCs) are used to calculate reimbursement. This payment system was implemented by Medicare for the payment of hospital-based outpatient claims.

parentheses The symbols—()—used in the Tabular List of the *ICD-9* manual to enclose supplementary words that may be used in a patient note and that will not affect the code choice.

personal, family, and social history (PFSH) The past medical history of the patient, their family members and any habits such as smoking, alcohol consumption, exercise, etc. that contribute to the patient's wellbeing.

physical exam The physician's examination of the patient and formation of objective information about the patient's complaint(s) and/or problem(s).

physical status modifiers Modifiers used with anesthesia codes to indicate the patient's condition at the time of anesthesia administration, which can affect the outcome.

plan The physician's determination of what should be done for the patient's care (e.g., prescription, therapy, follow-up care, and the like).

place of service (POS) The location where the patient received care.

professional component The physician's interpretation and report of radiological, cardiovascular, therapeutic, and diagnostic services.

qualifying circumstances A five-digit CPT code used to describe situations or conditions that make the administration of anesthesia more difficult than usual.

radiation oncology Medical treatment utilizing radiation to destroy tumors.

range of motion (ROM) The measurement, in degrees, of joint flexibility from the starting point to the end of a movement.

relative value guide A publication of ASA that contains codes for anesthesia services that are in the *CPT* manual as well as an additional 23 codes that are not in the manual. Also included are several codes that have different components of the service than that listed in the *CPT* manual.

relative value modifiers The modifying units used in anesthesiology coding (e.g., physical status and qualifying circumstances).

review of systems (ROS) An inventory of body systems obtained from the patient through a series of questions, or the signs and symptoms the patient either is currently experiencing or has experienced, that is prepared to assist in the proper evaluation of the current illness.

section guidelines Guidelines, located at the beginning of each section of the *CPT* manual, that define terms and explain the assignment of the codes in that section.

See An ICD-9 coding convention that directs the coder to a more specific term under which the code can be found.

See also A notation that refers the coder to the ICD-9 index entry that may provide additional information to assign the code.

See condition A notation that refers the coder directly to the Tabular List category (three-digit code) for code assignment.

separate procedure A parenthetical note indicating a procedure that is an integral part of another procedure or service. This procedure can be reported when it is performed independently or if it is unrelated to or distinct from another procedure or service performed at the same time.

signs and symptoms Report of the current condition when the physician is unable to establish a definitive diagnosis based on patient description and provider's observation.

skilled nursing facility A nursing home that provides skilled medical care provided by trained individuals for a limited period of time.

skilled nursing facility prospective payment system (SNFPPS) A payment mechanism by which case mix and wage adjustments are applied to standardized federal per diem rates. This is then adjusted for case mix and geographical location.

slanted brackets Used in the Index to Diseases of ICD-9 to list secondary codes that are a manifestation of other conditions.

square brackets Used in the Tabular List of ICD-9 to enclose synonyms, alternate wording, or explanatory phrases.

subsection notes Additional information on the correct use of CPT codes within a particular section of a chapter.

superbill Another term used for the form used by the provider to indicate diagnoses and services rendered to a patient. *See also* charge slip, encounter form.

Surgery section guidelines Instructions at the beginning of the Surgery chapter in CPT that assist the coder in assigning accurate procedural codes.

symbols Symbols, located throughout the *CPT* manual, that highlight significant changes or special rules.

Tabular List The section of the *ICD-9* manual that arranges the codes in numerical order by body system and supplementary classifications.

technical component A report that describes the services of the technologist, as well as the use of the equipment, film, room, and other supplies.

temporary national codes Codes that allow for the establishment of a procedure code without waiting until the next January CPT update. They meet the short time-frame operational needs of a particular payer.

therapeutic surgical procedure A surgical procedure performed to provide relief or treatment of a condition.

third-party payers (TPP) Insurance companies that are responsible for paying a provider for medical services received by their members.

type of service (TOS) The kind of health care services provided to patients (e.g., surgery, laboratory, radiology, and the like).

Index

Note: Code names are indicated by italics